Phonotactics of Czech

European University Studies

Europäische Hochschulschriften

Publications Universitaires Européennes

Series XVI   Slavonic Languages and Literatures

Reihe XVI   Slawische Sprachen und Literaturen

Série XVI   Langue et littératures slaves

Volume/Band   **81**

Aleš Bičan

Phonotactics of Czech

Bibliographic Information published by the Deutsche Nationalbibliothek
The Deutsche Nationalbibliothek lists this publication in the Deutsche Nationalbibliografie;
detailed bibliographic data is available in the internet at http://dnb.d-nb.de.

ISSN 0721-3441
ISBN 978-3-631-63136-2 (Print)
E-ISBN 978-3-653-03482-0 (E-Book)
DOI 10.3726/978-3-653-03482-0

© Peter Lang GmbH
Internationaler Verlag der Wissenschaften
Frankfurt am Main 2013
All rights reserved.
PL Academic Research is an Imprint of Peter Lang GmbH.
Peter Lang – Frankfurt am Main · Bern · Bruxelles · New York ·Oxford · Warszawa · Wien

www.peterlang.de

TABLE OF CONTENTS

Appendices

SYMBOLS AND ABBREVIATIONS

/.../	phonological representation
[...]	phonetic (allophonic) representation
→	is interpreted as, corresponds to
/T/, /F/, /S/ etc.	archi-phonemes
'C'	peripheral (non-nuclear) phoneme
'C$_n$'	a certain number of peripheral phonemes
'V'	nuclear phoneme
'V$_R$'	nuclear semiconsonant
'O'	occlusive
'F'	fricative
'N'	nasal (also archi-position 'N')
'R'	sonant
'L'	labial
'P'	palatal
'A'	alveolar
'K'	velar
'I'	isolated phoneme, i.e. not specified as to the place of articulation (also archi-position 'I')

symbols for places and manners of articulation can be combined, so for example 'F$_P$' is a palatal fricative

'e1', 'pre1', 'i3' etc.	positions
'E2', 'E3' etc.	archi-positions
pos	position class (e.g. *pos* 'e1')
×	is opposed to
∀	all phonemes of a particular class
∈	includes, contains
~	complement, except for
{...}	a set/class of items
∩	intersection of classes
DU	distributional unit
AF	Axiomatic Functionalism
PerP	peripheral phoneme
PhF	phonological form
SSJČ	*Slovník spisovného jazyka českého*

PSJČ	*Příruční slovník jazyka českého*
NLA	*Novočeský lexikální archive*
ASCS	*Akademický slovník cizích slov*
VSČ	*Výslovnost spisovné češtiny*
imp., imper.	imperative
sg.	singular
pl.	plural
gen.	genitive
dat.	dative
loc.	locative
instr.	instrumental

PREFACE

This book is a revised version of my PhD thesis of the same title submitted at the Masaryk University, Czech Republic, in August 2011. After the successful defense in January 2012 I decided to publish it, but first I wanted to revise the text a little. I had some valuble feedback from my colleagues and from the reviewer's reports which I wanted to reflect, but what had seemed to be an easy and quick task at the beginning became a thorough revision in the end. Not that I was dissatisfied with the analysis or thought it was wrong; I only felt that some portions could be rewritten to be more comprehensible or expanded to be more comprehensive. A large part of the thesis was rewritten eventually, although most changes were just a matter of rephrasing or expansion (including the addition of more phoneme combinations discoved since then). Chapter 2 which outlines the theory and methodology behind my analysis is new, but it contains sections already existing in the thesis. The original chapter on the phonematics of Czech was split into two chapters, *Phonematics of Czech* and *Neutralization* the second of which was expanded with a discussion of the proper domain of neutralization of voicing in Czech and with a note on so-called incomplete neutralization. Chapter 5 newly considers the problem of the non-syllabic prepositions *s*, *z*, *v* and *k* which are problematic for a phonotactic analysis of Czech. The issue will still have to be considered in more detail. Finally, the last chapter which justifies our analysis in confrontation with the only other detailed phonotactic analysis of Czech by Henry Kučera is also new. It also mentions the way my analysis could be used for calculating potential phonemes combinations. Although this was already part of the original thesis, the discussion is supplemented with a list of potential candidates of such combinations reproduced in the third appendix. Besides these and other expansions, the only major revision of the original work can be found in the analysis of so-called minor-type phonotagms. I had assumed that these units could end only in one non-nuclear phoneme, but this had to be corrected in light of the data I had overlooked.

At this occasion I would like to express my gratitude to Marie Krčmová who was the supervisor of the original thesis. She gave me freedom to do it my way, but was always willing to read and comment on what I had written. I would also like to thank Partice Pognan, Jan Volín and Barry Heselwood who wrote reviewer's reports on the thesis. The suggestions the latter two made in the reports were very valuable for the revision of the text. Jan Volín suggested that I should also consider the non-syllabic prepositions, and Barry Heselwood, whose report was very detailed, suggested that I should reconsider the issue of the minor-type phonotagms. I am also very grateful to Paul Rastall who, at request by Tomáš Hoskovec, the chair of the examination committee, wrote a comprehensive review of my thesis which was eventually published as Rastall (2012). His suggestions and advices led to considerable improvements of the presentation of my analysis. As a pupil of the late Jan W. F. Mulder, the originator of Axiomatic Functionalism upon which this work is based, Paul Rastall also made valuable comments on chapter 2 where the theory is outlined. However, all errors and other shortcomings of this book are my own only.

My thanks go also to Helena Karlíková who as the coordinator of the project *Výzkumné centrum vývoje staré a střední češtiny (od praslovanských kořenů po současný stav)* [Center for the Research of Old Czech and Middle Czech (its development from the Proto-Slavonic roots to the present day)] suggested I should publish my thesis. The project has kindfully provided me with a publication subvention. Special thanks go to Renato Müller for scripting the computer program used to handle the freight-yard scheme algorithm referred to in the last chapter.

The last but not least I want to thank Lenka who encouraged and supported me when I was struggling with the revision. I am happy that in the meantime she agreed to become my wife.

Chapter One: INTRODUCTION

1.1 Goal

This book presents a phonotactic analysis of Czech. Czech is a language, a West Slavic one. Languages, in contrast to other systems of means of communication such as traffic lights or gestures, combine and order (i.e. arrange in a certain order) their means. It makes them highly effective and economic. Humans wanting to express an innumerable number of thoughts must cope with the inevitable fact that their lives and brain capacities are limited. Rather than expressing each message with a new and distinct means, it is more advantageous to have a limited stock of basic means which could be infinitely combined to produce new means for expressing novel messages. Of course, the ability to combine is not specific to languages only (and perhaps not even to human communication) because many other communication systems such as the Morse code make use of it, too. Still, languages are specific in taking advantage of *dual ordered combinability*. Each communication system has means for expressing some message or for conveying some meaning, and these means have an outward form or shape. In comparison to the other communication systems, languages combine and order both the meaning-expressing means and the formal means.

If one wants to understand how Czech (or any other language) functions as communication system, it is necessary to explain how its meaning-expressing and formal means are combined and arranged in combinations. Our goal is account for the combinability and the arrangement of formal means used by speakers of Czech. This area of research traditionally falls under the rubric of phonotactics which is a branch of linguistics that uses certain models to explain and to account for the mentioned characteristic property of languages. These models and other explanatory notions are formulated within some theoretical framework, and the one used in this work is based on the approach worked up by Jan Mulder and Sándor Hervey and known as Axiomatic Functionalism. The choice of such a framework is partly a result of an opinion shared with Mulder and Hervey and many others that science, the science of language included, should be an enterprise that enriches our knowledge by means of testable explanations and predictions about certain things. The testability implies the absence of speculation, which unfortunately diminishes the explanatory power of many current approaches to linguistics because they are purposely speculative. Although

speculations may enrich our knowledge, too, testability is superior in areas where it is an alternative to speculation. A synchronic description of a living language which our book wants to offer is one of such areas.

Axiomatic Functionalism is not the only non-speculative approach. Its adoption has also resulted from the conviction that it is capable to fulfill the goal of the linguistic science, that is, to explain how communication is achieved by languages, and that the explanation and the description it allows for are better than those offered by other approaches. The property of being better is hard to measure, but if we agree that consistency (both internal and with data), exhaustiveness and simplicity are evaluation criteria of a good theory and a good description (an idea to be elaborated in §2.1), then the selection of Axiomatic Functionalism can be justified also from this respect. Its originators formulated it with these criteria in mind.

In particular, Axiomatic Functionalism is capable of coping effectively with the problem of the distribution and combinations of phonemes. In 1968 Mulder introduced a model he called *distributional unit* (= DU) the purpose of which was to account for how formal means are combined and arranged in Peking Chinese (Mulder 1968). Enabling a novel approach to phonotactics and a more efficient description of these phenomena, it has since been applied to various languages such as Quechua (Howkins 1972), Yulu (Gabjanda 1976), English (El-Shakfeh 1987), Sudanese Arabic (Dickins 2007), French or Russian (Rastall 1993). Although it may appear similar to models later used by other approaches, for example syllable templates, it is not preordained to apply to bundles of sounds known as syllables, even though the syllable is traditionally viewed as the most effective domain of distribution. The combinability of formal means may be more complex in some languages; by acknowledging this, Axiomatic Functionalism has become more effective in explaining phonotactics. The fundamental idea of the DU is simple—it is a set of positions which can be occupied or empty—, but the exact shape of the DU derives from the combinability of formal means in the language under description. And its purpose is always the same: to provide means for explaining the way formal semiotic entities are combined and arranged in the most exhaustive and comprehensive way.

Although utterances are in their essence continuous non-discrete chunks of sounds, it makes reason to interpret them as sequences of phonemes. Within such sequences each phoneme stands in a position of the DU. Whereas phoneme sequences are in principle unlimited, the number of positions and the number of phonemes standing in them are finite. By setting up these positions and their memberships, it is possible to explain regularities of the occurrence and the combinability of formal communicational means. The recourse to positions is not new in linguistics, but the axiomatic-functionalist approach is specific in two respects. First, positions may be empty, but an empty position is not a mere nothingness; it is a simple way to explain why some formal means may be omitted from utterances with the result being still an admissible structure in the given language. Second, Axiomatic Functionalism recognizes that the syntagmatic difference between positions, which express distributional and combinatory properties of phonemes, may become irrelevant just as it recognizes that the paradigmatic difference between distinctive features, which express oppositional properties of phonemes, may be become irrelevant. The paradigmatic irrelevancy is sometimes recognized in phonological theories under the name of neutralization, but the syntagmatic irrelevancy has rather been neglected. Axiomatic Functionalism provides ways to account for both types of irrelevancy, which results in a more detailed and less redundant description of the use and the combinability of formal means in communication.

1.2 Organization

We present here only the results of our analysis of Czech. Even though it may seem to be done in successive steps, the sequence is only a matter of presentation. A phonological description rises (and falls) in its entirety, and it is only for practical reasons that some areas are dealt with before others. In the course of our analysis we will establish for Czech the inventory of 33 phonemes and the DU of nine positions along which the phonemes are distributed. We will explain under what circumstances particular phonemes occur in those positions, how they combine with one another and what function they fulfill within such combinations. In combinations some phonemes must be obligatorily present, while others are optional. The former will be called *nuclear phonemes*, and the latter *peripheral phonemes* (traditionally called *vowels* and *consonants*, but we will make a finer classification of phonemes in Czech). In particular, our work will provide a comprehensive description of the occurrence and the combinability of nuclear and peripheral phonemes, both with each other and within their own class. The combinability of peripheral phonemes is especially rich in Czech. They form more than 500 distinct combinations within a DU, and many other combinations are possible across two DUs. The latter combinations are not dealt with here, but the DU will be established so as to have such a structure that the combinability of phonemes within larger complexes is derivable from and conditioned by the combinability of phonemes within a single DU.

The distribution of phonemes in Czech has already been described by Kučera (1961) upon the syllable. We offer an alternative analysis, but much more importantly, we provide a more detailed account of this topic. Combinations of the Czech phonemes have also been described, but again besides being an alternative account, our work provides a more comprehensive treatise. Moreover, it deals with questions not addressed before such as whether the occurrence of some phonemes or their combinations before the nucleus of the DU constraints the occurrence of phonemes or their combinations after the nucleus. Another topic that has been insufficiently dealt with for Czech is the question of potentially possible combinations, that is, the question of recognizing phoneme combinations which are not actually attested, but which could function as potential forms of meaning-expressing means in Czech. The DU is as a device upon which this potentiality can be formalized and expressed.

The book is organized as follows. The rest of this introductory chapter briefly introduces the Czech language mentioning sources and data of our analysis. It is concluded with an outline of other works on the phonotactics of this language. Chapters 2, 3, 4 and 5 provide a necessary preamble to the main topic of this work. Chapter 2 *Outline of the Theory* lays out the theoretical and methodological background. In chapter 3 *Phonematics of Czech* we discuss the inventory of phonemes, and chapter 4 *Neutralization* then considers under what circumstances differences between the phonemes are valid and when they are not. The next chapter called *Prolegomena to the Phonotactic Analysis* deals with several issues relevant to the phonotactic analysis such as the analysis of phonological forms into sequences of DUs. It also explains why forms built of several phonotagms are not analyzed here because they belong to para-phonotactics where they must be considered together with features like accent, and how the occurrence of so-called non-syllabic prepositions will be dealt with.

Chapters 6 and 7 discuss the DU. The former explains the motivation behind this notion and its role as a domain of distribution of phonemes, while the latter applies it to Czech. We establish a unit of nine positions, determine what phonemes occur in them, and consider under which circumstances the differences between these positions become irrelevant. The next chapter called *Phonotagms* continues in the application and explication of the DU. Phonotagms are instances of the DU where every position of the DU is either occupied by a phoneme or empty. Two types of phonotagms are recognized: major-type phonotagms and minor-type phonotagms. The latter will be introduced as a special but limited group of phoneme combinations which may accompany major-type phonotagms.

Chapters 9, 10, 11 and 12 deal with the occurrence of phonemes within the positions of the DU. A position can be viewed as a sum of distributional and combinatory potentials of phonemes which are unique for each position. Sets of phonemes occurring in a given position are introduced in chapter 9 *Position Classes* where the idea of collocational restrictions is also explained. These are statements expressing limitations of phoneme occurrences. Chapter 10 *Distribu-*

tion in the Nuclear Context discusses distributional and combinatory properties of nuclear phonemes, that is, of vowels and of /r/ and /l/. The ability of the latter to function as nuclear entities is reviewed here, too. Chapter 11 *Distribution in the Pre-nuclear Context* and chapter 12 *Distribution in the Post-nuclear Context* examine properties of peripheral phonemes before and after the nucleus.

The topic of chapters 13, 14, 15 and 16 is combinations of phonemes in Czech. The first one called *Properties of Pre-nuclear and Post-nuclear Combinations* discusses the length, phonematic constituency, reducibility and resolvability of combinations of peripheral phonemes. They are inventoried and classified to subtypes in the next two chapters (chapter 14 *Pre-nuclear Combinations* and chapter 15 *Post-nuclear Combinations*). Finally, chapter 16 considers the ability of the nuclear phonemes to combine with the non-nuclear ones and the ability of the pre-nuclear phonemes to co-occur with the post-nuclear ones.

The last chapter (17) concludes this work. Instead of summarizing it, the chapter compares our analysis with the only phonotactic analysis of Czech worked up by Henry Kučera (1961). Kučera's analysis has its weak as well as strong points, and we show that the weaknesses overweight the strengths. However, the strengths can be taken advantage of, and we present an alternative analysis of Czech phonotagms inspired by Kučera's approach. Besides that, the final chapter shows how the DU can be used for predicting possibilities of the Czech phonotactics by means of so-called freight-yard schemes.

The book is supplemented with several appendices. Appendix A summarizes collocational restrictions introduced during the analysis. Appendix B provides a complete listing of pre-nuclear and post-nuclear combinations found in Modern Standard Czech. Appendix C provides a list of potential pre-nuclear and post-nuclear combinations. Finally, appendix D illustrates the distribution of nuclear phonemes, supplementing chapter 10.

1.3 Modern Standard Czech

Modern Czech is a West Slavic language spoken by the majority of inhabitants of the Czech Republic at the beginning of the 21st century and during the 20th century. By Standard Czech we mean a variety of Modern Czech which has been officially codified and which has a special status among all forms of Czech. In the local tradition the variety is known as *spisovná čeština*,[1] but we prefer the term *Standard Czech* without making any distinctions between them. Therefore, we describe one particular variety of Modern Czech, not Modern Czech as a

---

1   Although the term means "literary Czech", it is not confined to literature or even to written texts. It has a spoken form, too.

whole. Although such a description is possible in principle, it makes sense to view the language as a conglomeration of varieties with several intermixed systems. Standard Czech is one of such systems, one which is to a great extent clearly delimited by the codification. But this does not mean that Standard Czech is a closed set of linguistic items. In the course of time it may be enriched by new items or lose others. Still, it is relatively stable. Its pronunciation, grammar and vocabulary are well described in various handbooks, grammar books and dictionaries. Standard Czech serves as the norm for the other varieties of Czech, and it is in fact what a layman equates with *the* Czech language, in its purest form, even though it is not the variety normally used in everyday parlance.[2] The other varieties are judged against Standard Czech. The description of its phonotactics can serve as a point of reference for similar descriptions of the other varieties.

Once various varieties of Czech are recognized, they can be treated as separate communication systems differing from each other. The phonology of Standard Czech will not be the same as that of a non-standard variety. The latter may contain a different phoneme inventory as well as a different phonotactics. For example, Standard Czech does not allow word-final combinations of a fricative and /ř/, but such a combination exists in non-standard Czech: cf. *otevř* which is a non-standard variant of *otevři* "open (imper. sg.)". We will not also find there word-final combinations in which the velar occlusive is preceded by another occlusive, though again such combinations are encountered in non-standard Czech: cf. *nedotk'* which is a non-standard variant of *nedotkl* "he did not touch".

The pronunciation of Standard Czech has been codified and described in the official handbook *Výslovnost spisovné češtiny I* ("Pronunciation of literary Czech I" = VSČ, 2nd edition 1967) and its second volume *Výslovnost spisovné češtiny* (= Romportl et al. 1978).[3] It has later been outlined also in Hůrková (1995), Palková (1997), Krčmová (2008) and Zeman (2008). Several detailed phonetic descriptions of this variety exist as well, the most comprehensive and the most recent ones being Hála (1962) and Palková (*op. cit.*).

---

2   The language situation in the Czech Republic can be described as a diglossia between Standard Czech used in official situations (both in the spoken and written form) and so-called Common Czech ("obecná čeština") used in unofficial situations (cf. Bermel 2010). Common Czech derives from the dialect in and around the country's political and cultural center, Prague, and is mixed, mostly in Moravia, with other dialects. Standard Czech was modeled in the 19th century on the basis of older Czech literature. The codifiers ignored, for example, some sound changes which took place as early as 15th century and which are reflected in Common Czech. See Kučera (1961: 14 and references therein).

3   The book has the same title like the 1967 one except for the number I. Romportl et al. (1978) focuses on pronunciation of foreign words only.

Phonetic and orthoepic descriptions of Standard Czech are not by themselves sufficient if we aim to account for its phonotactics. Phonotactic units occur within phonological forms of meaningful units, hence if we want to describe the phonotactic structure of Czech, we must have in the first place a database of these meaningful units. We will focus on the phonotactic structure of words as the minimum syntactic entities. Most words are listed in dictionaries of Standard Czech the most important of which are *Slovník spisovného jazyka českého* ("Dictionary of the literary Czech language", 1960–1971, = SSJČ), and more recent *Slovník spisovné češtiny* ("Dictionary of literary Czech", 3rd edition 2008, = SSČ). The most comprehensive dictionary is *Příruční slovník jazyka českého* ("Concise dictionary of the Czech language", 1935–1957, = PSJČ), but it does not contain just words recognized as standard, but also words which are archaic or which have been created *ad hoc* by literary writers. If a word, and hence a certain phonotactic property, occurs only in PSJČ, it is explicitly acknowledged because there may be some disputes as to whether it belongs to the standard variety and whether the phonotactic peculiarity is a feature of this variety.

PSJČ and SSJČ have been digitalized and made available online (see the references at the end of this book) under the auspices of the Institute of the Czech Language of the Academy of Sciences of the Czech Republic.[4] The institute also maintains an online glossary of PSJČ, SSJČ, SSČ and other dictionaries of Czech as well as two unpublished lexical databases, *Heslář lexikálního standardu* ("Glossary of the lexical standard"), and *Heslář novočeského lexikálního archivu* ("Glossary of the New Czech lexical archive", = NLA). The second is particularly important because it provides a huge collection of words excerpted from literary texts. Some of them, and consequently some phoneme combinations, are attested only there. They are usually hapaxes legomena or markedly dialectal or archaic words, and although they are sometimes mentioned in our analysis, they are not the primary source of our data.

Besides the dictionaries and databases of the "normal" Czech vocabulary, we have also examined Czech place names and proper names because they contain phoneme combinations not attested elsewhere. By assumption, official names are part of Standard Czech and provide another piece of evidence of its potentials. For example, the word-final combination /jř/ is not found in the "normal" vocabulary, but is found in proper names, namely in the surname *Kejř*. Similarly, the word-initial combination /břv/ is attested only in the place names *Břve* and *Břvany*. It is always made clear when some phonotactic property is found exclusively in such words. Finally, it should be mentioned that no systematic

---

4   The Institute is the official workplace to look after the Czech language. It is also the publisher of some of the mentioned pronunciation handbooks and of grammar books.

analysis of onomatopoeic expressions has been attempted. Their phonotactic structure is sometimes deviant in comparison with the structure of "normal" vocabulary. These include expressions such as *bzz, kšc, pf* or *pšt*. Though they belong to Czech, it is better to view them as an auxiliary semiotic system with its own phonotactic rules.

Dictionaries and databases generally list words in their uninflected form. Yet many phoneme combinations are exclusive to inflected forms (such as /jSK/ in *vojsk*, gen. pl. of *vojsko*). Thus, we have also taken heed of rules of inflection and derivation; they are sufficiently described in various reference books such as *Česká mluvnice* ("Czech grammar", 6th edition, = Havránek – Jedlička 1986), *Mluvnice češtiny* ("Grammar of Czech", particularly the second volume, 1986, abbreviated MČ2), *Příruční mluvnice češtiny* ("Concise grammar of Czech", 2nd edition 1996, = PMČ), and *Mluvnice současné češtiny 1* ("Grammar of contemporary Czech 1", 2010, = MSČ). Another valuable resource is *Internetová jazyková příručka* ("Internet language reference book") available online and again maintained by the Institute of the Czech Language of the Academy of Sciences of the Czech Republic. We have also used *Český národní korpus* ("Czech National Corpus"), the synchronic base SYN, but this source does not contain only texts from Standard Czech and should be treated with caution.

1.4 Previous phonotactic descriptions of Czech

This work is not the first or the only phonotactic description of Modern Czech. Probably the earliest comprehensive treatise on phoneme combinations in Modern (or pre-Modern) Czech is Hattala (1870) which discusses word-initial consonantal combinations sorted into several classes. Some of the combinations mentioned are dubious or occurring in words probably no longer current in the Czech of Hattala's time, and some are missing (such as /vj/ in *věk* which is not a consonantal combination for him). Other descriptions of phoneme combinations stemmed from attempts to create shorthand for Czech. Summarizing these attempts, Trnka (1937, in particular pp. 31–41) discusses several combinatory restrictions on phonemes, and the ratio of occurrences of consonants with vowels and with other consonants; he also provides lists of attested consonantal combinations in a single morpheme and across morphological boundaries.

Phoneme combinations are discussed in some early articles by Mathesius (see below), but a properly phonological analysis of word-initial and word-final consonantal combinations was published as late as 1972 by Novotná (1972). Though her primary focus was spoken Standard Czech, and although she excludes combinations occurring in allegedly foreign-origin words, her work was at that time the most comprehensive description of this kind taking into account as many as 308 word-initial and 20 word-final combinations. A partial list of consonantal combinations is also found in Trnka (1972, reprinted in Trnka 1982) together with the frequency of their occurrence in words of different syllable length (see also Mazlová 1946). The quantitative aspect of phoneme distribution is investigated in Kučera (1963) and Kučera – Monroe (1968) and that of phoneme combinations in Ludvíková – Kraus (1966), Ludvíková (1968, 1972a), and Těšitelová et al. (1985). The frequency of Czech sounds (not phonemes!) and their combinations based on the Czech National Corpus has been provided in Bartoň et al. (2009).[5] Recently, the probability of the occurrence of consonantal combinations at the beginning, at the end of and in the middle of words, stress units and prosodic phrases has been analyzed in Volín – Churaňová (2010). Combinability of Czech phonemes is also discussed in Mathesius (1929, 1931a, 1931b and 1931c), Vachek (1932; see also Vachek 1968), Trnka (1966), Novotná-Hůrková (1980), MČ1 (1986), and Grygarová-Rechzieglová (1993).

Phoneme combinability has also been described for various Slavic languages, Czech included. Sawicka (1974) is one such attempt including lists and a partial classification of word-initial and word-final consonantal combinations. Tolstaja (1968, 1974) also deals with consonantal combinations in Slavic languages examining their properties. According to Sawicka (2009), which is a general account of phoneme combinations in Slavic languages, combinations of vowels in Slavic languages are discussed in the PhD. thesis *Grupy samogłoskowe w językach słowiańskich* (Toruń, 2002; unavailable to us) by Anna Korytowska. Analyzing several languages, not only the Slavic ones, Appel (1957–8) provides a list of initial and final consonantal combinations in Czech, some of them hardly found in any Czech word. Properties of word-initial and word-final consonantal combinations derived from an analysis of 104 languages, Czech included, are discussed in Greenberg (1978).

Another line of phonotactic research, not necessarily exclusive to the previous one, has focused on the phonological structure of higher-level units such as syllables or words. Mathesius (1929) describes the constituency of words whose phonological forms are built of one, two, three or four phonemes. With the basic criterion being whether a phoneme is a vowel or a consonant, there are 20 structural types of words (e.g. 'V' for *a*, 'CV' for *to*, 'CVVC' for *neuč*, 'CCC' for *sklo* etc.). Vachek (1940) supplemented Mathesius' analysis by examining words built of five phonemes; 24 more structural types were added. The structure of more complex words is described in Trnka (1972), though with a primary em-

---

5   The work, however, presents only rough data without interpretation, and is methodologically very dubious. See also the next note.

phasis on consonantal combinations occurring in words of different syllable length. One can also get some impression of the phonological structure of Czech words from Bartoň et al. (2009) based on the analysis of the Czech National Corpus.[6] A brief phonotactic analysis of the Czech word including prefixes, roots and suffices is found in Čermák (2011: 23–7).

Probably the only analysis of the syllable in Modern Czech was carried out by Kučera (1961) who accounted for its structure in terms of a grid of several positions.[7] For each position, he lists phonemes occurring there and introduces a number of constraints on their combinability. The model reappears in a reduced and slightly modified form in Kučera – Monroe (1968). The syllable has also been analyzed from the quantitative perspective in Ludvíková (1972a, 1972b, 1976 and 1978) and in Těšitelová et al. (1985). Deme (1966) discusses the structure of the Czech and Slovak syllable with a consonantal nucleus. The structure of monosyllabic words in Slavic languages is dealt with in Lekomceva (1968) and also in Sawicka (1985). A recent treatise, though mostly summarizing older research, on the syllable in Slavic languages can be found in Kelih (2012).

Finally, the present writer has discusseed a number of issues in the phonotactics of Czech (see Bičan 2010, 2011a, 2011b, 2011c, 2011d, 2011e), but all of these works are now superseced by the present work.

---

6   The data presented there are, as noted by the authors, distorted by a fact that abbreviations have been included, too. For example, words of the structure 'CC' are said to belong among the 100 most common types. Czech has no such word, only abbreviations like *př.* for *příklad* "example".

7   His use of the term *position* differs to ours; see chapter 17.

Chapter Two: OUTLINE OF THE THEORY

d 19

If you want to plow up a field, you need a plow or at least a spade. You cannot plow it up without an appropriate tool. But even the tool is not enough: you also need to know how to use it. It is the same with languages. When describing a language, you need a tool, some linguistic theory with which the analysis could be achieved, but you also need to have a certain methodology specifying how such an analysis is to proceed. The simile with the field and the spade is not to suggest that when linguists describe a language, the result is the same as a plowed field, that is, the same substance, only rearranged. In linguistics the result is more similar to geometrical observations and calculations leading to a map of a country. And even then you need some tool, a theory. The purpose of this chapter is to provide a short characterization of the tool we have chosen for our analysis—the theory of Axiomatic Functionalism—, and of the methods and philosophical assumptions this approach follows, but since this book is not meant to be a theoretical work, only those aspects necessary and relevant to our analysis will be mentioned. Although some points and ideas sketched here are elaborated on in the following chapters, it will be useful for the reader to get aware of the basic tenets, distinctions and terminology. However, before laying out the theory, we will start a consideration of what a theory and a description are, and what criteria they should meet to be acceptable and useful.

2.1 Theory and description

This work is based on Axiomatic Functionalism (AF) which is a semiotic paradigm introduced by Jan Mulder and later developed by him mainly in association with Sándor Hervey and others (see in particular Mulder 1968, 1989, 1998, Mulder – Hervey 1972, 1980, Hervey 1979, 1996, Dickins 1998, Mulder – Rastall 2005 and Bičan – Rastall 2011). Its name refers to the fact that the approach continues in the tradition of European functionalism and that it builds its theory on several fundamental propositions ("axioms") which are interpreted in a series of accompanying definitions. Thus, the theory is explicitly stated and open to testing in terms of its internal consistency and to external applicability to descriptions of communicational phenomena. The approach has stemmed from the teachings of Ferdinand de Saussure and of the Prague School, especially of Ni-

kolai Trubetzkoy (cf. Trubetzkoy 1939). In many respects, particularly in phonology, it is indebted to theories of André Martinet (cf. Martinet 1956, 1991;
Akamatsu 1988, 1992), but it differs from his approach in being more formalized and in laying more emphasis on the syntagmatic aspect of phonological descriptions. The formalization, which is viewed as a tool not as a goal, is achieved by the application of set theory and by recognizing different types of relations holding between entities and sets of entities.

In thinking about linguistic theories, AF is very similar to Louis Hjelmslev's
Glossematics. Though in effect quite different, both pay great emphasis on an
explicitly stated theory with clearly defined terms and methods. AF shares Hjelmslev's (1961: 14, cf. Mulder 1996: 18) view that a theory "is in itself independent of any experience; [i]n itself, it says nothing at all about the possibility of its
application and relation to empirical data". This should not be understood as implying that the theory is wholly fictional; it means that AF does not claim that
theoretical concepts such as phonemes, words etc. exist in the empirical data
waiting only for our discovery. Instead, they are useful means by which we describe and understand how communication works. AF maintains that theoretical
notions have the same status in linguistics as, for example, the notion triangle in
geometry. The triangle is a notion of Euclidian geometry (which is also axiomatically built) allowing us to describe and understand the world we live in, but
it does not mean that "triangleness" exists in the real world.[1] Things can only be
described as (approximately) having the shape of a triangle just as speech events
can be described as conforming to properties of a phoneme. The same reality
could well be described by other means, by another theory. In this respect AF is
in agreement with Glossematics, but the way the particular theory is constructed
in these approaches, and the way it is applied to the empirical data are different.

Speaking still in philosophical terms, AF has been much influenced by the
philosophy of science of Karl Popper (as expressed in his *Logic of Scientific
Discovery* and *Conjectures and Refutations*). It has adopted his falsificationism
and agrees that the main criterion of scientific validity for empirical theories or
conjectures, like descriptions, is a potential for refutation. However, unlike Popper, AF stresses that it is important to distinguish between a theory and a description (see Mulder – Hervey 1980: 15–28, Mulder 1996) because they represent two different sets of statements. A theory contains axioms, definitions and
theorems, but these cannot be proven or disproven, but must be accepted on the
grounds of their consistency, deductive inference and appropriateness. It is a description that contains statements falsifiable in confrontation with the empirical
data.

---

1   In fact, it cannot, because our world is curved, not flat as Euclidian space.

A theory is an axiomatically and deductively built set of notions and models whose purpose is to provide a means for producing descriptions of desired phenomena. Although it could in principle have various forms, it is shaped by the desire to be an appropriate tool for description. As already pointed out, the presence and the choice of some conceptual framework is inevitable, and it is erroneous to think that there can be a theory-free description just it is impossible to plow up a field without any tool, even if it were your own hands. Scientists choose theories for various reasons, but the choice is not always objective, i.e. totally independent of the subject who does the choosing. In fact, it is mostly subjective. We may justify our choice by appealing to certain allegedly objective criteria, but the validity of the criteria is dependent on whether people agree upon them. Others must be convinced that the criteria we present for selecting a particular theory are acceptable and appropriate. Here we get again to philosophy of science and in general to the way how theories are evaluated.

Mulder (in Mulder – Hervey 1980: 1–28; see also Mulder 1989: 51–65 and Hervey 1996) has proposed the three criteria for the evaluation of theories and descriptions: (i) CONSISTENCY, (ii) ADEQUACY, and (iii) SIMPLICITY. A theory is primarily evaluated in terms of deductive-logical consistency, and can only be indirectly tested in light of its adequacy. It is adequate if it is able to engender meaningful accounts of some phenomena which meet the mentioned criteria, that is, descriptions which are consistent, adequate, and simple. In other words, a theory must be internally consistent and must serve as an appropriate tool for accounting for the selected phenomena. It is also a virtue of a theory if it is simple, but one can have a relatively complicated theory provided that it allows for simple descriptions.

A description is an act of applying a theory to a particular range of phenomena in order to produce an account of it. It is not a mere mechanistic statement of some facts, of what things are like in a language. A description provides an analysis and explanation of some phenomena, and as Rastall (2012) points out, it could be called a kind of a theory of language if it were not for the fact that the term *theory* is used for other purposes in AF, i.e. it should not be assumed that "description" has here exactly the same meaning as, for example, in American structuralism of Leonard Bloomfield and his followers. A description contains a set of statements about entities, relations and models which are "projected" onto the phenomena. The statements have the form of hypothesis and are tested against data. AF agrees in this respect with Karl Popper and maintains that a hypothesis must be formulated in such terms, so that its refutation is, at least in principle, possible; therefore, AF rejects the idea that hypotheses can be positively proven—they can only be corroborated by withstanding refutation. Statements about phenomena which cannot even in principle be refuted (or even proven) are wholly speculative, and though speculation has its justification elsewhere, it is rejected in AF in favor of falsifiability.[2] For that reason, the present work does not make recourse to any form of explanation based on allegedly universal properties of languages. Statements like "no language has x" or "all languages have y" are not only theory-dependent but also in principle irrefutable. They can be partly confirmed by showing that no *known* language has x or that all *known* languages have y, but the ultimate proof is not available because we will hardly ever know every language of the past, the present and the future. However, this does not mean that the selected theoretical framework does not allow for description and comparison of more languages. It does, but one must realize that a comparison can only be done on the basis of one theory or at least on the basis of equivalent theories because descriptive statements are only meaningful within a given theoretical framework.

Apart from the falsifiability, descriptions are evaluated with the same criteria as theories: They should be consistent, adequate and simple. The consistency must be achieved both internally and externally. The first means that a description does not contain statements contradicting each other. The second means that a description is consistent with the selected theory on which it is based. It must not be an arbitrary mixture of statements and *ad hoc* solutions proposed to reach a desired goal at any cost. Unfortunately, one often comes across descriptions which operate with notions without defining them, rather assuming their universal validity. Such accounts, though seemingly plausible and appealing, are of little value because their vagueness makes them devoid of any meaning. Aware of these dangers, Mulder and Hervey have always, like Hjelmslev, insisted on precisely and explicitly formulated definitions of notions they employ. For that reason they have worked up the *Postulates for Axiomatic Functionalism* (the latest version in Mulder – Hervey 2009) which lay out the fundamental assumptions of the approach, the axioms, which are interpreted by a network of accompanying definitions of all theoretical notions of the theory. They are used for testing the external consistency of any description based on the theory of AF, the present one included.

Besides consistency it is also required of descriptions that they be adequate and simple.[3] Whereas consistency can be easily tested, adequacy and simplicity may rather be relative terms. A description is judged adequate if it provides an

---

2   To be precise, AF rejects speculation where it can be replaced by a better scientific method. It does not reject speculation as such because there are areas (such as historical linguistics) where it is probably the only method available.

3   It is reminiscent of Hjelmslev's *empirical principle*: "The description shall be free of contradiction (self-consistent), exhaustive, and as simple as possible" (1961: 11).

exhaustive, detailed and materially adequate account of a selected field of phenomena. The selection does not contradict the idea of exhaustiveness. We must always select what we will be describing. A single linguist cannot account for everything, but should exhaustively and in detail account for what he has selected. The selected area should be as broad as possible, but it will always be limited and circumscribed, e.g. by the fact that we describe Czech, not English, or by the fact that we focus on certain aspects of communication ignoring, for example, means of expression and appeal (i.e. what Trubetzkoy 1939 called *Lautstilistik* or phonostylistics). Once the selection is made, the goal of a description is to account for all relevant phenomena in as much detail as possible, and this also includes *potential* phenomena. A description is thus capable of making reasonable predictions about potential phenomena using normal processes of logical deduction; in this sense it is both descriptive and generative; it has an explanatory and predictive power. This is reflected in our analysis: besides accounting for the existing combinations of phonemes in Czech, we will also determine what possible but unattested combinations are in this language.

If descriptions are to have any usefulness, they should agree with the observed data, with actual facts. This is what it is meant by material adequacy mentioned in the previous paragraph. It is the most important mark of a good description. The exhaustiveness and the richness of detail cannot always be ensured because there is always a possibility that some important facts have been overlooked. However, it is imperative that the descriptions always fit the known facts, for otherwise they are wholly virtual. Phonological descriptions should thus be, as much as possible, consistent with phonetic descriptions. The total agreement is not necessarily required because phonology views speech phenomena differently from phonetics (and there may be even be concurrent phonetic accounts of the same thing), but phonological descriptive statements must not totally ignore phonetic facts. In AF the description is not the physical transmission of speech, but an account of how it serves as communicational mediation. The more a phonological description agrees with the phonetic description, the more materially adequate it is, and consequently, when choosing between two equally consistent, exhaustive, detailed and simple descriptions, we decide for the one which agrees more with the phonetic facts. This gives the description a fully empirical and realistic nature (cf. Mulder – Hervey 1980: 12–3). A word of caution should be said, though: The facts must be not confused with our intuitions about the facts, that is, with what language users know or think to know about their languages. As Martinet (1977: 7) points out, "[f]unctionalists retain direct observation as the normal approach to linguistic facts provided it is carried out within an axiomatically stated framework and reject the judgment of native speakers as the final criterion of linguistic validity". Still, if two descriptive accounts are judged to be equally realistic, we may appeal, as the last resort, to the intuition and choose the one agreeing more with intuitions of speakers. Such a description may be regarded as more materially adequate, but what we know or what we think to know cannot be given precedence to what we can prove or confirm, e.g. with experimental evidence in the case of phonetics. Speakers' judgments are influenced by various factors such as education or knowledge and may conflict with the evidence.

One would also expect descriptions to be simple. They should contain as few redundant elements as possible. If something can be accounted for by tools already at our disposal, it is usually expedient to introduce new ones unless it brings about the increase in adequacy of the description. For example, in Czech the affricates [ts] and [tʃ] could be interpreted as two single phonemes /c/ and /č/, but they could also be interpreted as combinations of two phonemes already established in the description.[4] However, sometimes it makes sense to sacrifice some simplicity in order to make a description more adequate. This is the case of English [h] and [ŋ]: being in complementary distribution and opposed to the same forms, they could be interpreted as allophones of one phoneme, but even though such an analysis would be simpler by assuming fewer phonemes in the phonematic system, it is more adequate to treat them as allophones of two different phonemes. Or we can afford to have some parts of our description less simple and gain more simplicity and adequacy elsewhere. Thus, in contrast to the affricates, Czech [ɪ] and [j] will be interpreted as realizations of two separate phonemes rather than as nuclear and non-nuclear realizations of one phoneme, even though the latter solution is theoretically possible. Having two phonemes /i/ and /j/ surely enlarges the phoneme inventory of Czech, but allows for a simpler phonotactic description. Hence, simplicity should not be sought in descriptions just for the sake of it—it must always be backed up with adequacy, and the two-phoneme analysis provides more of it. In general, the degree of adequacy and simplicity and the balance between them are always a matter of judgment and skills of the describer (cf. Dickins 1998: 42–6).

2.2 Language as a system of systems

Language will be defined here as a type of semiotic system, that is, as a special system of conventions used for communication (see Mulder – Hervey 1980: 73–87). AF thus views speech phenomena by means of systems. The system is not something to be found in the speech phenomena, which are like any events very complex, ephemeral and somewhat chaotic, or in the cognitive processes of the

---

4   Namely as /Ts/ and /Tš/, respectively. We will return to this in more detail in chapter 3.

human brain, which are directly unapproachable, so any claims about such processes are speculative at best. Instead, the theory holds that the speech phenomena can be *understood* by means of systems. A system is a set of entities and relations between them, and the entities and relations are constructs with reference to the observables. Every element of a semiotic system is a part of it because it has some role or function there, which means that those aspects of communication which do not have any function are left outside the scope of the theory and description.

The conventions used for communication can be viewed as two kinds of entities. We can treat them either as entities with a form (i.e. a certain physical manifestation) and an information-value (i.e. what is exchanged via communication) or as pure forms with which some information is or can be associated. The former will be called SIGNA and the latter FIGURAE. Figurae are usually forms of existing signa, i.e. one aspect of it, but they may also be forms not associated with any actual signum, and with a potential to acquire such a function. The recognition of the latter category is especially important in open-ended semiotic systems such as languages where signa with new forms come into existence by borrowing or other creative processes. This happened to the form [smog] in English. Until the signum *smog* was coined, it was just a potential figura, some form without any meaning. It is a task of phonological description to determine and explain which forms are potential figurae of the given semiotic system.

There being two types of semiotic entities, any semiotic system contains two subsystems: a system of signa and a system of figurae. Both subsystems may be simple, or complex if they allow for combinations of entities. So while in simple systems it holds that *ab* is the same as *a* + *b*, in complex systems, *ab* is something other than *a* + *b*, that is, *ab* is not just a sum of *a* and *b*, but is a separate unit (a subsystem) consisting of *a* and *b* and *the relation* between *a* and *b*. AF recognizes two basic types of relations to hold between semiotic entities: SYMMETRICAL (or unordered) and ASYMMETRICAL (or ordered). The relation between *a* and *b* is symmetrical or unordered if the relation of *a* to *b* is functionally equivalent to the relation of *b* to *a*, but if the relation of *a* to *b* is different from that of *b* to *a*, that is, if *ab* is something other than *ba*, then we speak about asymmetrical or ordered relations.[5]

The distinction between simple and complex systems on the one hand and the distinction between complex unordered and complex ordered systems on the other permits us to recognize various semiotic systems of several degrees of elaborateness, from the least elaborate ones with just simple systems of signa

---

5   To illustrate the idea in algebra, the relation "plus" is symmetrical because $3 + 1 = 1 + 3$, but the relation "minus" is asymmetrical because $3 - 1 \neq 1 - 3$.

and figurae, to the most elaborate ones containing not only simple systems of
signa and figurae but also complex unordered and complex ordered systems of
signa and figurae. This scale helps us explain and understood differences between communication systems such as traffic lights and so-called proper languages. The former belong to the least elaborate semiotic systems having only
simple figurae (different colors) and simple signa (a single color with a single
meaning), whereas what we casually designate Czech, English, French, Georgian, Hawaiian etc. can be described as the most elaborate and complex semiotic
systems, allowing for both simple and complex ordered and unordered figurae
and signa. Let us make clear that this does not mean that Czech possesses simple, complex unordered and complex ordered systems of signa and figurae, but
that the speech phenomena encompassed under the term Czech can be described
as sets of signa and figurae which form simple, complex unordered and complex
ordered systems.

   Within a system which allows for combinations of entities, two types of
such entities are recognized: minimum or basic entities, which are not further
analyzable into components at a given level of analysis, and maximum or complex entities, which are combinations of basic entities. Both in complex systems
of figurae and complex systems of signa, there are then logically four distinct
entities: on the one hand, A) basic entities of unordered systems and B) unordered combinations of such basic entities, and on the other hand, C) basic entities of ordered systems and D) ordered combinations of such basic entities. In
order to make the theory of semiotic systems as integrated as possible, AF operates with the idea of interlock by recognizing that one subsystem provides the
basic entities of another subsystem. It interlocks the unordered and the ordered
system by uniting B with C, that is, by saying that unordered combinations of
basic entities are at the same time the basic entities of ordered combinations. This
creates a hierarchy of complexity within semiotic systems of figurae and signa:
from simple, further unanalyzable figurae or signa through unordered combinations of simple figurae or signa to ordered combinations of unordered combinations of figurae and signa. The system of figurae and the system of signa are
also interlocked by the former providing the forms of the entities of the latter.

   Although AF is formulated so as to provide means for describing all semiotic systems (cf. Hervey 1982, chapter 7), it pays most attention to the most
elaborate ones, that is, to proper languages. The terminology used for various
types of entities within complex semiotic systems is given in figure I for figurae
and in figure II for signa. The basic, unanalyzable figurae are called DISTINCTIVE
FEATURES (= A; see the previous paragraph) and unordered combinations of distinctive features are PHONEMES (= B). The phoneme is the complex entity at the
level of unordered combinations, and this level has been called PHONEMATICS.

Unordered		Ordered		Para-tactic	
Basic entity	*Distinctive feature* (A)	Basic entity	*Phoneme* (C)	Basic entities	*Phonotagm* (E)
					Para-phon. f.
Complex entity	*Phoneme* (B)	Complex entity	*Phonotagm* (D)	Complex entity	*Para-phono-tactic entity*
PHONEMATICS		PHONOTACTICS		PARA-PHONOTACTICS	

FIGURE I: Complex systems of figurae in proper languages

Unordered		Ordered		Para-tactic	
Basic entity	*Moneme* (A)	Basic entity	*Plereme* (C)	Basic entities	*Syntagm* (E)
					Para-synt. f.
Complex entity	*Plereme* (B)	Complex entity	*Syntagm* (D)	Complex entity	*Para-syntactic entity*
MORPHOLOGY		SYNTAX		PARA-SYNTAX	

FIGURE II: Complex systems of signa in proper languages

Its purpose is to analyze phonemes into constituent distinctive features. By virtue of interlocking, the phoneme is at the same time the basic entity (= C) of ordered combinations of figurae. The latter are called PHONOTAGMS (= D). Phonotagms are complex entities at the level called PHONOTACTICS whose purpose is the analysis of phonotagms into constituent phonemes.

Similarly, the basic, unalyzable signa are MONEMES (= A), and unordered combinations of monemes are PLEREMES (= B). The plereme is the complex entity at the level of unordered combinations of signa. This level is called MORPHOLOGY, and its main goal is to analyze pleremes into constituent monemes. Once again by virtue of interlocking, the plereme functions as the basic entity (= C) of ordered combinations of signa, and such ordered combinations of pleremes are called SYNTAGMS (= D). The level which deals with the analysis of syntagms into constituent pleremes is called SYNTAX.

At this point it should be noted that *moneme* does not necessarily denote the same thing as the traditional term *morpheme*. Different theoretical foundations and definitions of these terms may yield dissimilar descriptions. In the present approach the moneme is always a signum, i.e. has a form and an information-value, whereas elsewhere the morpheme may be a purely formal entity.[6] Simi-

---

6   For this reason and the reasons of consistency, the English word *cranberry* is analyzed as consisting of a single moneme, though other approaches may recognize two morphemes there, *cran* and *berry*. See Mulder – Hervey (1980: 122ff.).

larly, pleremes are not necessarily the same as what is usually called *words*. Since the plereme is the minimum syntactic entity, the English possessive *'s* (as in *King of England's horse*) is best interpreted as a plereme, though other approaches would be reluctant to call it a word (cf. Mulder 1989: 301–4). What is more, as a type of signum, the plereme is a class of allomorphs, that is, of formal variants with the same meaning. For example, English *is* and *are* are allomorphs of one plereme BE, but the common practice is to regard them as two words. We will follow this practice and use the term *word* for allomorphs of pleremes. The word, as an allomorph of a plereme, is thus a minimum syntactic entity.

Returning to the classification of semiotic systems, let us consider the difference between English ['ɪmpɔːrt] and [ɪm'pɔːrt]. It can be accounted for either by postulating four different phonemes /ɪ₁/ (realized as stressed [ɪ]), /ɪ₂/ (realized as unstressed [ɪ]), /ɔ₁/ (realized as stressed [ɔ]) and /ɔ₂/ (realized as unstressed [ɔ]) or by postulating just two different phonemes /ɪ/ and /o/ and explaining the stress difference elsewhere. Similarly, the difference between Peking Chinese [ma˥] "mother" × [ma˩] "hemp" × [ma˧˩] "horse" × [ma˩˥]] "scold" could be interpreted in terms of four distinct phonemes just as the difference between Czech [dal] "he gave" × [daːl] "further" is explained in terms of phonemes. In principle, accounting for the mentioned differences at the level of phonemes is not *a priori* ruled out, but it is arguably a less simple solution. It is not only because we would have to operate with more phonemes, but also because we would have to introduce a distributional restriction saying that /ɪ₁/ cannot co-occur with /ɔ₁/.[7] Similarly, the difference between Czech [jɛ doma↘] "he is at home" and [jɛ doma↗] "is he at home?" could be accounted for either by postulating two pleremes *doma₁* (realized as [doma↘]) and *doma₂* (realized as [doma↗]) or by recognizing only one plereme *doma* and explaining the difference in intonation elsewhere. Again, although the first analysis is not in principle impossible, it would be less simple than the second one because the inventory of pleremes would be much greater in it.

To cope with analytical problems like these, AF operates with two additional systems of figurae and signa belonging to a para-tactic level: PARA-PHONOTACTIC FEATURES and PARA-SYNTACTIC FEATURES. They are mostly meant to account for phenomena such as stress, boundaries, tones or intonations. The complex entities at the para-tactic levels are PARA-PHONOTACTIC ENTITIES and PARA-SYNTACTIC ENTITIES. They are unions of a base and para-tactic features both of which are the basic entities or components here. Accordingly, PARA-PHONOTACTICS deals with para-phonotactic entities and their analysis into bases and para-phonotactic features, and PARA-SYNTAX with para-syntactic entities and their analysis into

---

7   Because only one syllable can bear the primary stress within an English word.

bases and para-syntactic features. The para-tactic levels are integrated with the other levels again by the interlock: the base of para-phonotactic entities is provided by phonotactics (phonotagms or their groups), and the base of para-syntactic entities is provided by syntax (syntagms or their groups).

Besides monemes, pleremes, syntagms, para-syntactic features and para-syntactic entities, the theory recognizes a special category of signum: SENTENCE. However, the sentence is not understood as another type of the signum in the hierarchy of complexity, but rather as a signum which is a self-contained vehicle for conveying messages. To put it otherwise, the theory holds that every signum which corresponds to a complete utterance is a realization of a sentence (cf. Rastall 1991). Such a view does not require sentences to be understood as syntactic entities of higher complexity. In some semiotic systems the sentence may coincide with a syntagm, but in proper languages it is usually a para-syntactic entity. In general, something is a sentence if it contains features that make it a self-contained vehicle for conveying some message (on messages, see Rastall 2000: 113). These sentence-forming features are most commonly features of intonation (interpreted as para-syntactic features), but they also may be discrete units such as *ka* marking questions in Japanese or *ma* with the same function in Chinese (Mulder 1989: 368ff.). Therefore, the necessary condition for sentences to be well-formed is not that they contain a predicate ("verb phrase") and a subject ("noun phrase"), but that they contain sentence-forming features making them self-contained vehicles for communication. The defining feature of sentences is their capacity to be models directly applying to entire speech events, or to say it in Hervey's (1978: 38) words, "[e]very spatio-emporally concrete speech-event is, in its entirety, a realization of at least one 'sentence'". An event transcribed as [strom] is a realization of a sentence in Czech if it is accompanied by appropriate intonation, and if it conveys a certain message (like "to je strom [it is a tree]" as opposed to "je to strom? [is it a tree]"). In this case the base of the sentence corresponds to a single plereme.[8] The purpose of the sentence is to account for all relevant aspects of speech phenomena, and therefore the linguistic analysis must begin with sentences because all other analytical levels, phonological, grammatical as well as semantic or pragmatic deal only with particular aspects of sentences (Hervey 1990).

The sub-theories of phonematics, phonotactics and para-phonotactics belong to PHONOLOGY, and the sub-theories of morphology, syntax, para-syntax and sentential level to GRAMMAR. As the present work is a phonological analysis, from now on we will focus mostly on the phonological part of the theory.

---

8   See Gardner – Hervey (1983), Gardner (1985) or Hervey (1990) for more on the AF view of sentences.

2.3 Phonological analysis

Since one of the goals of a good theory is to provide means for engendering materially adequate descriptions of speech phenomena (see §2.1), the concepts used in this work are motivated by this goal. Speaking only about phonological concepts, we can say that in descriptions phonemes capture the ways speech sounds are employed in the functioning of a language as a means of communication, and distinctive features capture articulatory and acoustic properties of speech sounds. Similarly, the chief purpose of para-phonotactic features is to account for the ways suprasegmental phonetic features are used in communication. Finally, the phonotagm reflects the fact that speech is organized in chunks of sounds with special features and patterning, that is, syllables. Neither of these phonological terms is, nevertheless, identical with the mentioned phonetic notions, and there does not even have to be one-to-one correspondence between them (as will be shown for example in §3.3 in the case of Czech affricates and in §6.6 in the case of phonotagms). Phonological notions such as distinctive features, phonemes, phonotagms or para-phonotactic features are models or projections of selected aspects of speech phenomena. There is an isomorphism or a correspondence between them. It can be compared to a map which is a projection of the real country, not the country itself. As just as a map captures, with various symbols, curves or colors, only selected relevant properties of some country, so does a linguistic description capture, with various notions, only selected and relevant properties of speech phenomena.

Although some of the terms mentioned here are normally used in linguistics, it should be obvious that they have acquired a purely deductive definition in the preceding section and may not overlap with the same terms used in other approaches. It concerns in particular the term *distinctive feature*. Though employed in various phonological theories, our conception of distinctive features has little to do with binaristic and universalist distinctive feature theories such as the one envisioned by Jakobson (e.g. in Jakobson – Halle 1956) or by Chomsky – Halle (1968) and their followers. The distinctive features of the Czech phonemes proposed in the next chapter are not chosen from a pre-established set of universal distinctive features, and there is no need for them to be binary (cf. also Akamatsu 1992: 35ff.). Under the present theoretical framework, distinctive features are phonological analytical properties of phonemes which correspond to, but are not identical with phonetic (i.e. articulatory and/or acoustic) properties of sounds. They are functional entities and their function is distinctive.[9] If something is dis-

---

9   Moreover, they are not necessarily identical with phonetic properties of sounds. So, if
     phonemes are described as containing the distinctive feature palatal, it does not mean

tinctive, it must distinguish one thing from another, and so a feature can be regarded as distinctive if and only if it distinguishes the phoneme it is part of from another one. For example, in Czech the phoneme /p/ is a bundle of distinctive features 'labial voiceless occlusive'. It is voiceless because it is not voiced (i.e. it is not /b/), it is labial because it is not alveolar, palatal, or velar (i.e. not /t/ or /d/, /t'/ or /d'/, /k/ or /g/), and it is occlusive because it is not fricative or nasal (i.e. not /f/ or /v/, /m/). The ways phonemes are analyzed into distinctive features is unique for every language, as each language embodies a different set of oppositions between phonemes and hence also different distinctive features. Now, unlike /p/ or /b/, the labial /m/ is neither voiceless nor voiced in Czech because the features voiceless and voiced do not distinguish anything in the case of the nasals, and cannot be distinctive for them. The phoneme /m/ is therefore 'labial nasal' in this language.

The phoneme may be viewed as the central concept of phonology. Since it is the entity which interlocks phonematics with phonotactics (see figure I above), it acquires two types of identity: paradigmatic and syntagmatic. From the paradigmatic perspective, which is the domain of phonematics, the phoneme is a self-contained unordered bundle of distinctive features. The distinctive features may be viewed as "expression" of the phoneme's distinctive function. The distinctive function is equal to the sum of oppositions a phoneme, via its allophones, partakes in. The oppositions determine the paradigmatic identity of a phoneme. From the syntagmatic perspective, which is the domain of phonotactics, the phoneme is the basic or minimum phonotactic entity; it is the smallest phonological entity capable of entering into ordering relations.

Phonemes are grouped into self-contained phonotactic entities. Unless a language has one-phoneme words like Czech *a*, phonotagms correspond to combinations of phonemes. Every phoneme has a phonotactic function within combinations. The phonemes upon which the others are dependent for their function as well as for their occurrence can be conveniently called VOWELS, while the dependent phonemes can be called CONSONANTS. In some languages such as Czech there is another phoneme class which could be called SEMICONSONANTS (or semivowels). These phonemes are capable of acquiring both the role of vowels and consonants. At the phonetic level, vowels usually correspond to vocoids, consonants to non-syllabic contoids and semiconsonants/semivowels to syllabic contoids or approximants and/or their corresponding vocoids (e.g. [j] and [ɪ] in English). The concrete state of affairs depends on the function of speech sounds in a particular language. As the terms *vowel, consonant* and *semiconsonant* have

---

they are all necessarily realized as palatal sounds. Distinctive features, just like phonemes, are *phonological*, not phonetic entities.

a purely phonological meaning here, we will use *vocoid* and *contoid* (after Pike 1947) for phonetically defined categories of sounds. We leave upon a phonetic theory how they are precisely defined.

The traditional method by which the paradigmatic identity of phonemes is set is known as the commutation test (cf. Akamatsu 1988 and 1992 with references). In phonology, commutation is a choice between phonological entities (or between the presence and absence of a phonological entity) in functional opposition in a given context (Mulder – Hervey 2009). The test calculates the distinctive function of particular phonetic entities in specific contexts, that is, the set of oppositions in which those phonetic entities partake (Mulder 1968: 127–8). Two phonetic forms in complementary distribution can be regarded as allophones of one phoneme if they have the non-different distinctive function, not necessarily because they are phonetically similar. For example, in Czech, [ŋ] and [n], which are in complementary distribution, are interpreted as allophones of one phoneme because they have the same distinctive function, that is, because both partake in the same oppositions (i.e. [ŋ] is opposed to [ɲ] and [m] just as [n] is opposed to [ɲ] and [m]). In functional phonology the criterion of phonetic similarity is only used for judging the material adequacy of a hypothesis that two sounds are allophones, but not as the reason why they are interpreted like this.

Phonemes are established on the basis of commutation. A semiotic entity must be commutable with at least one other entity or with its absence. Where there is no commutation, there is no function. The definition of commutation implies an oppositional relation between some entities in a certain context, and the context is here of crucial importance. A relation taking place in one context need not necessarily obtain in another. The absence of an opposition in a certain context is handled with two concepts: NEUTRALIZATION and DEFECTIVE DISTRIBUTION; they will be discussed in detail in chapter 4. For the time being, suffice to say that defective distribution means regular non-occurrence of a singular entity in a certain context, whereas neutralization refers to regular non-operability of an opposition in a certain context.

As a concept, neutralization has been operated with in many linguistic approaches and been variously defined (cf. Davidsen-Nielsen 1978, Akamatsu 1988, Silverman 2012). The notable difference between these and the present approach is the fact that functional phonology holds that the concept of neutralization necessarily implies another concept: ARCHI-PHONEME. Although the concept is much misunderstood, it is a logical possibility of the theory. It is an entity resulting from neutralization and occurring in the phonotactic context which has triggered the neutralization. It is formally defined as the intersection of sets of distinctive features qua sets characterizing two or more phonemes in the other contexts. Being an intersection, an archi-phoneme is logically included in the phonemes from which it has resulted and is functionally equivalent (but not identical!) to them. It means that an archi-phoneme is "a phoneme in a sub-system which, when projected into the over-all system, is represented there by two or more phonemes" (Mulder 1968: 114). The logic is simple. If there is an oppositional relation between two or more distinctive features characterizing certain phonemes in one context (context A), but the relation cannot be postulated in another context (context B) because the characterization is redundant there, the entity occurring in context B cannot be equated with any of the phonemes of context A. It is where the archi-phoneme is introduced.

Let us now move to the syntagmatic or phonotactic identity of phonemes. Phonotactic description rests on an assumption that it is possible to set up a determinate model of distribution upon which the occurrence and combinability of phonemes are describable in their entirety, so that all of their distributional and combinatory properties in larger structures are derivable from this model. In the present approach the model is called DISTRIBUTIONAL UNIT (= DU) defined as a bundle of positions. Within every self-contained combination of phonemes, each phoneme is assumed to occupy a position of the DU. A position is an expression of distributional and combinatory potentials of a certain class of phonemes, and the membership of a phoneme in a given position is what determines its syntagmatic identity. In every position of a DU a phoneme can stand or the position may be empty. A particular configuration of occupied and empty positions is a PHONOTAGM. A phonotagm is a self-contained phonotactic entity, and the rules of distribution and combination within it are derivable from the DU. To put it otherwise, a phonotagm is such a combination of phonemes which fits to the DU (the DU being, so to speak, a blueprint of all phonotagms). Thus, groups of phonotagms do not properly belong to phonotactics because distributional and combinatory properties of phonemes within such groups are derivable from and reducible to properties holding for singular phonotagms. However, groups of phonotagms as a whole may have some unique properties. In the first place they are characterized by features tying them into a particular group and distinguishing such a group from another. For example, the phonotagms /o/ and /na/ can, in Czech, be gathered into two groupings /o/ and /na/ (cf. the words *o* and *na*) or to one group /ona/ (cf. *ona*). Therefore, there are additional features involved that determine the grouping, and also the order of the grouped entities (see below). These features do not belong to phonotactics, but to another phonological compartment, to para-phonotactics. As already pointed out in the previous section, the purpose of para-phonotactics is to account for analytical properties that cannot be simply or adequately accounted for elsewhere.

Entities at the level of para-phonotactics consist of the BASE and PARA-PHO-NOTACTIC FEATURES. The former functions as the carrier of the para-phonotactic features, so to speak. We can recognize simple and complex para-phonotactic entities according to the nature of their bases. The simple para-phonotactic entity contains the base corresponding either to a single phonotagm or to a group of phonotagms plus accompanying para-phonotactic features, whereas the base of a complex para-phonotactic entity corresponds of several other para-phonotactic entities upon which additional para-phonotactic entities are attached. An example of a complex para-phonotactic entity is the phonological form of the Czech sentence *Pes ležel pod oknem* "the dog lay under the window". In itself, it is a para-phonotactic entity with a base and accompanying para-phonotactic features corresponding to intonation. The entity is complex because the base of the utterance is analyzable into several smaller para-phonotactic entities, that is, to accent groups corresponding to *pes*, *ležel* and *pod oknem*. The bases of *pes* and *ležel* correspond to simple phonotactic entities consisting, respectively, of a single phonotagm (i.e. /peS/) and of a group of two phonotagms (i.e. /le/ + /žel/).

More important than the bases are features attached to them, namely the para-phonotactic features. These are analytical phonological properties which accompany, but do not determine, the identity of the respective base. There are two types of such features according to the function they fulfill: DISTINCTIVE PARA-PHONOTACTIC FEATURES and CONTRASTIVE PARA-PHONOTACTIC FEATURES. Within these we can differentiate between several types on the basis of their realization or particular function. Distinctive para-phonotactic features are features in a relation of direct opposition with one or more para-phonotactic features. The two most common features of this kind are tones in tone languages such as Peking Chinese and phonological forms of intonations. Other examples are features determining the placement of accentual prominence in languages with a free stress (cf. English (*an*) *import* × (*to*) *import*), and features determining the sequence of phonotagms in bases (cf. Czech /masa/ *masa* "mass" × /sama/ *sama* "alone"). In the theory of AF, para-phonotactics is thus not necessarily the same as prosody or suprasegmental level in other approaches.

The function of contrastive para-phonotactic features is groupment over and above a phonotactic or para-phonotactic groupment. A phonotactic groupment is a group of two phonotagms, and a para-phonotactic groupment is a group of two or more para-phonotactic entities. If the base is simple, the function is trivial because the base has already its unity by being simple, but if the base is constituted by several entities, the function of contrastive para-phonotactic features is to gather them into one unit. In some languages two kinds of contrastive para-phonotactic features can be distinguished: ACCENT and DIAEREME. The function of both is to gather entities into higher-level groups (i.e. entities of the base into para-phonotactic entities), but diaereme may be employed as a means to account for the fact that a para-phonotactic entity is realized in such a way that its boundaries can be firmly set. Accordingly, some languages may have two types of para-phonotactic entities with contrastive para-phonotactic features: ACCENT GROUPS and DIAEREME GROUPS. Accent groups usually correspond, at the phonetic level, to stress units, and diaereme accounts for certain features marking boundaries between forms (such as the presence of a glottal stop at the beginning of Czech words). We will return to these notions in §5.2.

2.4 Signum theory

A full phonological description of a natural language usually contains a phonematic, a phonotactic as a well as a para-phonotactic part. The analysis is complemented with a description of allophony containing statements of realizations of phonological entities by means of their allophones. Allophony belongs to the separate component of the theory, so-called SIGNUM THEORY, which specifies the ontological nature of semiotic entities. From the perspective of signum theory, distinctive features, phonemes, phonotagms, para-phonotactic features and para-phonotactic entities are merely different types of figura, i.e. of semiotic entities with only a form. As every figura must have a certain physical manifestation, allophony puts figurae in relation with their physical substance. At the same time, signum theory specifies the relation between figura and signa.[10] The correspondence between signum theory and theory of semiotic systems (also called systemology) is sketched in figure III (on the next page).

As already mentioned, a SIGNUM is a semiotic entity with a form and an information-value. The relation between the form and the information-value is unmotivated, i.e. is not causal or given by nature, but it may or may not be fixed. If it is wholly fixed by conventions, we speak about SIGNS, and if it is only partially fixed or not fixed at all, we speak about SYMBOLS. To the latter belong so-called nonce words and proper names. The information-value of nonce words such as *slithy* or *chortle* used in Lewis Carroll's poem *Jabberwocky* from the book *Through the Looking-Glass* is wholly dependent on a separate definition, i.e. someone has to specifically decide what their meanings are. The information-value of proper names such as *John, Theresa* or *London* is also dependent on a separate definition because it must be specified who exactly the bearer of the particular name is. However, this time, some fixed conventions play a part because it is quite unlikely that the name *Theresa* will be borne by a male.

The distinction between signs and symbols is useful because the forms of the latter may be different from those of the former, for example, due to the fact

---

10 For more on signum theory, see Mulder – Hervey 1972, Hervey 1982: 184ff., Mulder 1989: 151ff.

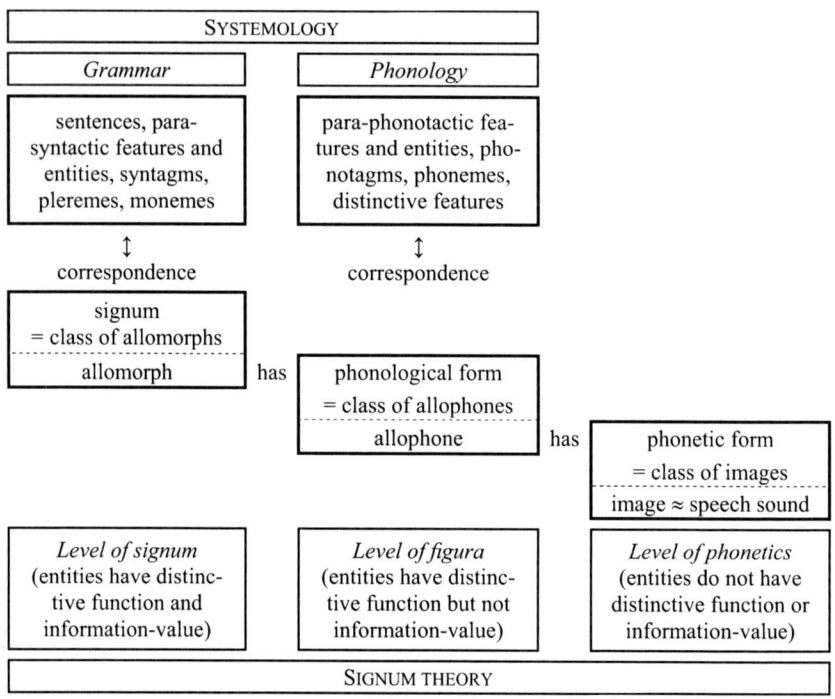

FIGURE III: Signum theory and its relation to systemology

that proper names contain remnants of earlier stages of the development a language or of the fact that they are often borrowed from other languages. It is particularly obvious in Czech because proper names contain here combinations of phonemes not attested elsewhere (e.g. /Kf/ in the place name *Kfely* or /rSK/ in the place name *Kursk*). We have found it reasonable to separate phonological forms of signs (i.e. of "normal" vocabulary) from those of symbols. As the latter have proven to contain phoneme combinations not found in the former, we will always make clear whether we speak about symbols or signs.

A signum is a conjunction of an EXPRESSION and a CONTENT. They are not two parts of a signum in the sense that a signum would be divisible into them, but they are rather two aspects or two ways of looking at the same thing or, as de Saussure ([1916] 1972: 157) puts it, like a recto and a verso of a sheet of paper. An expression is the converse of a content and a content the converse of an expression. They imply one another, and they are implied by the signum itself. These mutual implications allow us to speak about signa as if they were just their expressions because their contents are automatically implied. If viewed from the perspective of its expression, a signum is a self-contained class of allo-morphs with the same distinctive (i.e. not communicationally different) function. Strictly speaking, both a signum and an allomorph have the status of a signum; the difference between them is the difference between a set (= signum) and a member of the set (= allomorph). An ALLOMORPH of a signum is a phonological form (accounting for its formal aspect) which has a particular distinctive function in grammar (setting its identity) and which also has, by having the status of sig-num, an information-value. The grammatically distinctive function (given by the set of oppositions in which an allomorph partakes) is not the same as the infor-mation-value because synonyms have the same information-value (meaning) but different distinctive functions (otherwise they would be the same signa).

A PHONOLOGICAL FORM (PhF) is a self-contained class of allophones with the same distinctive function in phonology. Both a PhF and an allophone have the status of figura, i.e. of a semiotic entity with only a form; the difference be-tween them lies again in the difference between a set (= PhF) and a member of the set (= allophone). An ALLOPHONE is a phonetic form with a particular dis-tinctive function in phonology. In phonology the distinctive function equals to the set of oppositions between semiotic entities with only the formal nature, while in grammar it equals to the set of oppositions between semiotic entities with both form and information-value.

A PHONETIC FORM as a notion belongs to phonetics rather than to the signum theory proper. It covers simple as well as complex entities such as sounds and their combinations or their components ("sound gestures") or so-called proso-dic/suprasegmental features, i.e. changes in pitch, intensity or length of a sound. In short, a phonetic form is any entity or feature phonetics operates with. A pho-netic form represents a generalization of some phonetic facts: it is a class of im-pressionistically similar images. An image is finally a model for a single speech event occurring at a given time and place. Simply said, an image stands for a certain speech event, and a phonetic form is a generalization of these events. If a phonetic form happens to have a distinctive function by being distinctively op-posed to another phonetic form, it acquires the status of an allophone in a given language. Allophones with the same distinctive function belong under one PhF, and since a PhF is a cover term of various types of figurae, i.e. distinctive fea-tures, phonemes, phonotagms, para-phonotactic features and entities, it follows that each of these can be understood as a class of allophones. Consequently, the allophony of each of them could be stated. Usually, however, we only speak of allophones of phonemes, and this will be our practice in the next chapter where we discuss the phonemes of Czech.

Chapter Three: PHONEMATICS OF CZECH

This chapter discusses the inventory of phonemes in Czech, meant to be an alternative to the existing phonological analyses (Kučera 1961, Vachek 1968, Horálek in MČ1). Attention will only be paid here to issues where our analysis differs markedly from others. This concerns in particular the treatment of the affricates and diphthongs as well as neutralization of opposition between phonemes. The latter will be dealt with in the next chapter. We also provide a statement of allophony of the Czech phonemes, but the specifics of the phoneme realization are not discussed here. For detailed phonetic descriptions of the Czech sounds, the readers are directed to Hála (1962), Palková (1997) or Krčmová (2008).

3.1 Consonants

Consonants are phonemes that occur in non-nuclear positions of the DU only, which means they are never nuclei of phonotagms. Their occurrence and function are dependent on the occurrence and function of the nuclear entities. Figure I shows the decomposition of the Czech consonants into distinctive features and visualizes their mutual proportional oppositional relations. In addition, the figure lists allophones of the particular phonemes.

The backbone of the consonantal system is formed by two proportional oppositions dividing the phonemes into two separate series: *labial* × *alveolar* ×

	Labial		Alveolar		Palatal		Velar	
	v'less	*v'ed*	*v'less*	*v'ed*	*v'less*	*v'ed*	*v'less*	*v'ed*
Occlusive	/p/ [p]	/b/ [b]	/t/ [t] [c]	/d/ [d] [ɟ]	/t'/ [c]	/d'/ [ɟ]	/k/ [k]	/g/ [g]
Fricative	/f/ [f]	/v/ [v]	/s/ [s]	/z/ [z]	/š/ [ʃ]	/ž/ [ʒ]	/x/ [x]	/h/ [ɦ]
Nasal	/m/ [m] [ɱ]		/n/ [n] [ɲ] [ŋ]		/ň/ [ɲ]			

Outside the proportional system: /j/ [j] and /ř/ [r̝] [r̝̊]

FIGURE I: Consonants of Czech in the context of relevance and their allophones

palatal × *velar* on the one hand, and *occlusive* × *fricative* × *nasal* on the other.
The first will be referred to as MANNER OF ARTICULATION, and the second as
PLACE OF ARTICULATION, but it should be remembered that these are just convenient terms—it is the sounds the phonemes are realized with which are articu-
lated, not the phonemes themselves. Finally, there is a proportional opposition
voiceless × *voiced* which is not applicable to nasals. It will be referred to as
VOICING. Outside the proportional system stand /j/ and /ř/ (see below).

The phonemes /p/, /b/, /f/, /v/, /m/ are all grouped together as LABIALS, even
though /p/, /b/ and /m/ are bilabial in realization (oral stops [p], [b] and nasal
stop [m], respectively), whereas /f/, /v/ are realized as labio-dental fricatives [f],
[v],[1] respectively. The place of articulation is interconnected with the manner of
articulation here, and hence there is no need to postulate separate distinctive features bilabial for /p/, /b/, /m/ and labio-dental for /f/, /v/. The distinctive feature
labial is sufficient for them and it corresponds to the fact that all are characterized by the activity of lips. The labial nasal /m/ is also realized as labio-dental
nasal stop [ɱ] before /f/ and /v/ (in e.g. *tramvaj* or *nymfa*).

The phonemes /s/ and /z/ are grouped together with /t/, /d/, /n/ under ALVEO-
LARS. The first two are realized as alveolar sibilants [s], [z], respectively; /t/, /d/
are realized as alveolar oral stops [t], [d], respectively, and /n/ as alveolar nasal
stop [n]. Before /ň/, the phonemes /t/, /d/ may also—there is free variation—be
realized as palatal stops [c], [ɟ] in words like *matně* and *hodně*; similarly, /n/
may be realized before /ť/ or /ď/ as palatal nasal stop [ɲ] in words like *konte* and
blonďák (cf. VSČ: 61–2).[2] The phonemes /š/ and /ž/ are grouped together with
/ť/, /ď/ and /ň/ under PALATALS; they are realized, respectively, as post-alveolar
sibilants [ʃ], [ʒ], and oral palatal stops [c], [ɟ] and nasal palatal stop [ɲ].[3] The relation between /t/, /d/ and /s/, /z/ is the same as (i.e. is proportional to) the relation between /ť/, /ď/ and /š/, /ž/ as well as that between /p/, /b/ and /f/, /v/, and
between /k/, /g/ and /x/, /h/.

The phonemes /k/, /g/, /x/, /h/ are all interpreted as VELARS. In realization
they are characterized by articulation in the back of the mouth or the throat. The
phonemes /k/ and /g/ are realized as velar oral stops [k], [g], respectively, and /x/
is realized as voiceless velar fricative [x]. On the other hand, /h/ is realized as
voiced laryngeal fricative [ɦ]. Despite this realizational discrepancy, /h/ functions in the system as the voiced counterpart of /x/. The opposition /x/ × /h/ is
proportional to all other voicing oppositions and is liable to neutralization (see
the next chapter). The phonetic counter-domain of this neutralization is assimila-

---

1   The sound [v] has some peculiar phonetic properties; see p. 50.
2   The palatal realizations are more common according to Novotná (1962).
3   See Machač – Skarnitzl (2004) for a recent phonetic analysis of the Czech palatal stops.

Siμιτιc of X?

tion of voicing; in such processes [ɦ] is changed/assimilated to [x]—see the following examples, particularly the fourth one (the capital letters are archi-phonemes).

(1) [xata] *chata* "cottage" × [xat] *chat* "cottage (gen. pl.)" → /xata/ × /xaT/
     [brada] *brada* "chin" × [brat] *brad* "chin (gen. pl.)" → /brada/ × /braT/
     [soxa] *socha* "statue" × [sox] *soch* "statue (gen. pl.)" → /soxa/ × /soX/
     [noɦa] *noha* "leg" × [nox] *noh* "leg (gen. pl.)" → /noha/ × /noX/

Viewed from another perspective, /p/, /b/, /t/, /d/, /t'/, /d'/, /k/, /g/ are all interpreted as OCCLUSIVES; /f/, /v/, /s/, /z/, /š/, /ž/, /x/, /h/ as FRICATIVES; and /m/, /n/, /ň/ as NASALS. All occlusives are realized as oral stops, all fricatives as (oral) fricatives, and all nasals as nasal stops. Occlusives and fricatives are further distinguished as to being either VOICELESS (/p/, /t/, /t'/, /k/, /f/, /s/, /š/, /x/) or VOICED (/b/, /d/, /d'/, /g/, /v/, /z/, /ž/, /h/). The nasals /m/, /n/, /ň/ are indifferent to this distinction, even though they are in realization always voiced. A phoneme cannot be distinctively (phonologically) voiced unless it is opposed to its voiceless counterpart and *vice versa*.

Besides the occlusives, fricatives and nasals, there are two other consonants: /ř/ and /j/. For reasons of simplicity and consistency, they have not been incorporated in the main system of proportions and are analyzed as being characterized by one distinctive feature only. The features could just be called ř-ness and j-ness. The phoneme /ř/ is realized as a post-alveolar fricative vibrant, either as voiced [r̝] or as voiceless [r̝̊]. The voiced variant occurs word-initially before a vocoid, between two vocoids, and in the vicinity of a voiced contoid unless there is a voiceless contoid next to it (cf. *Petřvald*, a place name realized as [pɛtr̝̊valt]). The voiceless variant occurs before and after a voiceless sound and/or word-finally before a pause (in e.g. *keř* [kɛr̝̊] or *tři* [tr̝̊i]). The sounds are very unique in the world's languages, and there may be no other language but Czech where they would be realizations of a separate phoneme, not just facultative realizations of other phonemes.[4]

The phoneme /j/ is realized as voiced palatal approximant [j] in all instances of its occurrence. We will use the term SONANT for a class of phonemes which includes /j/, /ř/ and /r/, /l/ (for which see §3.4 below). In other words, sonants are those phonemes which are not vowels and which are not occlusives, fricatives or nasals.

---

4   See Chlumský (1911), Isačenko (1965), Hála 1962 (264–8), Romportl (1973: 84–104) or Pavlík (2009) for a discussion of phonetic properties of this sound.

3.2 Interpretation of the affricates

Traditional analyses of Czech usually operate with two other consonantal phonemes: /c/ and /č/, realized, respectively, as voiceless alveolar affricate [ʦ] and voiceless post-alveolar affricate [ʧ]. In fact, two other affricates should be included, namely their voiced counterparts: [ʣ] and [ʤ]. However, the latter (and in particular [ʣ]) are not usually viewed as separate phonemes. Either they are dismissed as occurring in words of foreign or onomatopoeic origin (cf. *džus* [ʤus] "juice" and the interjection *dzin* [ʣɪn]) or as assimilatory variants of [ʦ] and [ʧ] (cf. *lecjak* [lɛʦjak] "in various ways" × *leckde* [lɛʣgdɛ] "in various places", and [lɛːʧɪt] *léčit* "to treat" × *léčba* [lɛːʤba] "(medical) treatment"). Yet, since the words like *džus* or *džungle* "jungle" and words like *dzinkat* (SSJČ) are undoubtedly part of the Czech lexicon, these sounds should be considered, too.

The affricates will be interpreted here as corresponding to combinations of two phonemes: [ʦ] to /Ts/, [ʧ] to /Tš/, [ʣ] /Tz/ and [ʤ] /Tž/[5] where the archiphoneme /T/ corresponds to the stop phase of the affricates. Such an analysis is possible because the decision that something corresponds to one phoneme or two does not depend on whether it is one sound or two sounds, but on whether the analysis is justifiable by the chosen theory, whether it is not in contradiction with other facts in the language and whether it is an appropriate solution.

As regards the theoretical side, there is no obstacle: If [ʦ] is to correspond to two phonemes /Ts/, it must be demonstrated that the two alleged phonemes are indeed in agreement with the definition of the phoneme, particularly with the fact that the phoneme is the minimum phonological entity capable of entering into ordering relations. This is shown by finding out whether the relation between the alleged phonemes can be different.[6] Usually, it suffices to demonstrate the reversed sequence of the alleged phonemes corresponds to some phonetic entity. In that case the phonemes indeed stand in ordering relations because the relation between them is asymmetrical. Although the whole problem of whether a sound corresponds to one phoneme or two is more complicated than presented here and has been much discussed in the phonological literature, the details are not important.[7] It is important that in Czech such reversed sequences are found (see also figures II and III below), namely /St/ corresponding to [st] in e.g. *stát*,

---

5   In neutralization contexts they correspond to /TS/ and /TŠ/. This is the case of *leckde* and *léčba*: /leTSKde/ and /lēTŠba/ in our notation. See the next chapter.

6   Relations between distinctive features can never be shown to be different, and that is why phonemes are *unordered* bundles of distinctive features.

7   See e.g. Mulder (1968: 28–30), Hervey (1972: 355–9), Martinet (1965: 109–23) and Trubetzkoy (1939: 50–9) and references in these works. In Bičan (2008a) we discussed the problem in relation to Czech.

/Sd/ corresponding to [zd] in *zdát*, /Št/ corresponding to [ʃt] in *štáb* and /Šd/ corresponding to [ʒd] in *ždáti* (SSJČ).[8]

The examples show that the proposed two-phoneme analysis of the affricates is theoretically justified, but it remains to demonstrate that it is a solution simpler and more adequate than the traditional one. The simplicity can be instantly proven: If the affricates were interpreted as single phonemes, the Czech phoneme inventory would have additional members. So, instead of positing four additional phonemes for [ts], [ʧ], [ʣ], [ʤ], we account for them with combinations of phonemes already established in the system, namely with /Ts/, /Tš/, /Tz/, /Tž/. However, by itself, the simplicity may not be decisive; the appropriateness of such an analysis must also be demonstrated.

To begin with, let us review why most analysts of Czech prefer interpreting the affricates [ts] and [ʧ] as separate phonemes /c/ and /č/ (for the sake of simplicity, we will refer only to these affricates, but the arguments apply to the other two as well). The reasons are summarized in Novotná-Hůrková (1980) and Palková (1997: 240–1). First, phonetic arguments are offered. The affricates behave like single sounds, albeit with two phases, but the two phases cannot be separated by explosion. This is unlike real combinations /ts/, /tš/ where the stop and constrictive (fricative) phases are clearly distinguished. However, phonetic criteria need not be necessarily decisive in a phonological analysis. The fact that the affricates [ts] and [ʧ] have similar characteristics like single sounds does not mean that they must correspond to single phonemes. There is no a priori correlation "one sound = one phoneme" because phonemes are entities of a quite different ontological nature than sounds, that is to say, a phoneme in functional phonology is not a generalized family of sounds but an abstract model accounting for certain speech phenomena. A combination of two phonemes /ts/ (i.e. /Ts/) may be a model for a single speech sound [ts] if the model is appropriate and can be applied to the given speech event.

More importantly, the affricates [ts], [ʧ] are confrontable with genuine combinations of sounds [t.s], [t.ʃ]. This suggests that [ts], [ʧ] cannot correspond to /Ts/, /Tš/ because we would fail to account for a communicational difference between [ts], [ʧ] and [t.s], [t.ʃ]. Let us have a closer look at the examples mentioned in connection with this problem:[9]

(2) (a) [klatsku] *klacku* (dat. sg. of *klacek* "stick") × [klat.sku] *Kladsku* (loc. sg. of *Kladsko*, place name)

8   Just like in the case of /Ts/, /Tz/, /Tš/ and /Tž/, there is a contextual neutralization here. This is of no consequence for our analysis.
9   The examples were taken from Kučera (1961: 32), Vachek (1968: 71) and Palková (1997: 240).

[poʧiːt] *počít* "to conceive" × [pot.ʃiːt] *podšít* "to underline"
[ɦrʧiː] *hrči* (3ʳᵈ person sg. of *hrčet* "to rumble") × [ɦr̩t.ʃiː] *hrdší* (comparative of *hrdý* "proud")

(b) [praːʦɛ] *práce* "work" × [praːt.sɛ] *prát se* "to fight"
[vjɛʦɛm] *věcem* (dat. pl. of *věc* "thing") × [vjɛt.sɛm] *vjet sem* "to go in"
[raːʦɛ] *ráce* "race" × [raːt.sɛ] *rád se* "(he) likes to"

These pairs might be strong evidence that the affricates [ʦ], [ʧ] are functionally different from the combinations [t.s], [t.ʃ]. However, they must be carefully examined before any conclusion is reached. First of all, the difference between the forms under (2a) is somewhat artificial or rather potential. Although the words *Kladsku*, *hrdší* etc. can be pronounced with a stop + fricative sequence, the research has shown that the pronunciation with the affricate [ʦ], [ʧ] is much commoner (Novotná 1962, Novotná-Hůrková 1974); both pronunciations are recognized as orthoepic (VSČ: 56, Palková 1997: 334, Zeman 2008: 112), the pronunciation with [t.s], [t.ʃ] occurring only in careful speech, and apparently when a speaker wants to indicate a morphological boundary (cf. *hrdý* "proud" × *hrdší* "prouder"). Thus, the words mentioned under (2a) are homophonous under normal circumstances.

As regards the examples under (2b), the stop–fricative sequences occur here across word boundaries, such pronunciation being required by the orthoepy of Czech for *prát se, vjet sem, rád se* and similar examples. Although they are often pronounced with affricates, thus being indistinguishable from *práce, věcem* and *ráce*, this pronunciation is not considered as correct in Standard Czech. The stop–fricative pronunciation must be kept, so that the grammatical boundary between the particular words is not obliterated. Consequently, there is indeed a functional difference between [ʦ] and [t.s], and between [ʧ] and [t.ʃ] which must be accounted for, but it need not be by introducing separate phonemes /c/ and /č/.

Looking at examples (2) again, we see that they have one important feature in common: the stop–fricative pronunciation is used to highlight boundaries between forms, irrespective of whether they are boundaries between monemes as in (2a) or between words as in (2b). It makes sense to view the pronunciation as an instance of so-called boundary signals (*Grenzsignale*; Trubetzkoy 1939), that is, as a feature marking boundaries between forms. In the present theoretical framework this situation is accounted for by means of the notion *diaereme*, roughly corresponding to what others have called *(dis)juncture* (see §5.2). The diaereme (transcribed as '#') will be a phonological representation of phonetically salient boundaries between forms. Consequently, the opposition between [ʦ], [ʧ] and [t.s], [t.ʃ] does not obtain within one and the same unit, but across two units, because [t.s] and [t.ʃ] occur only across syllable boundaries. It is ir-

/Sp/ [sp]	/Sb/ [zb]	/St/ [st]	/Sd/ [zd]	/Sk/ [sk]	/Sg/ [zg]
spát	sbor	stát	zdar	skot	zgalvanizovat
/Ps/ [ps]	/Pz/ [bz]	?	?	/Ks/ [ks]	not found
psát	bzučet			xylofon	
/Šp/ [ʃp]	/Šb/ [ʒb]	/Št/ [ʃt]	/Šd/ [ʒd]	/Šk/ [ʃk]	not found
špatný	žbublati	štáb	ždáti	škola	
/Pš/ [pʃ]	/Pž/ [bʒ]	?	?	/Kš/ [kʃ]	not found
pšenice	bžunda			kšandy	

FIGURE II: Combinations of occlusives and fricatives at the beginning of a phonotagm

not found	/ST/ [st]	/SK/ [sk]	not found	/ŠT/ [ʃt]	not found
	past	vosk		mošt	
/PS/ [ps]	?	/KS/ [ks]	/PŠ/ [pʃ]	?	/KŠ/ [kʃ]
zips		koks	Hybš		jakžtakž

FIGURE III: Combinations of occlusives and fricatives at the end of a phonotagm

relevant whether the boundary coincides with a word boundary in *prát se* or with a moneme boundary in *hrdší* as long as the boundary is phonetically salient and relevant for communication. Accordingly, the forms under (2b) are interpreted in (3). It is to be remembered that the examples (2a) are distinguished only in very careful speech and if necessary, they will be analyzed similarly.

(3) [praːtsɛ] *práce* × [praːt.sɛ] *prát se* → /#prāTse#/ × /#prāT#se#/
     [vjɛtsɛm] *věcem* × [vjɛt.sɛm] *vjet sem* → /#vjeTsem#/ × /#vjeT#sem#/
     [raːtsɛ] *ráce* × [raːt.sɛ] *rád se* → /#rāTse#/ × /#rāT#se#/

One of the advantages of this analysis is such that the rule for expressing the merge of *práce* with *prát se* becomes quite simple in contrast with a similar rule formulated in analyses operating with the separate phonemes /c/ and /č/. For us, /#prāTse#/ *práce* and /#prāT#se#/ *prát se* coincide when the medial diaereme is deleted (i.e. /T#s/ becomes /Ts/), which happens when the boundary is neglected. The alternative analyses have to explain why two phonemes /t/ and /s/ change and merge to the phoneme /c/ if they stand next to each other.

Another advantage is gained at the phonotactic level, which is of particular importance for the present work.[10] The combinability of phonemes at the begin-

---

10 Admittedly, once the affricates are analyzed as two-phoneme combinations, we get unusual combinations /TTs/, /TTš/, /TSTs/ and /TŠTš/ across phonotagm boundaries as in [vjɛt.tsɛm] *vědcem* → /vjeTTsem/, [raːt.tsɛ] *rádce* → /rāTTse/, [rats.tsɪ] *racci* → /raTSTsi/, and [kʃɛtʃ.tʃiː] *křečí* → /křeTŠTši/. As far as we can see, this is the only disadvantage of our analysis.

	Front		Central	Back	
	high	*mid*		*high*	*mid*
Short	/i/ [ɪ]	/e/ [ɛ]	/a/ [a]	/u/ [u]	/o/ [o]
Long	/ī/ [iː]	/ē/ [ɛː]	/ā/ [aː]	/ū/ [uː]	/ō/ [oː]
Diphthongal	/ĕ/ [ɛu̯]		/ä/ [au̯]	/ö/ [ou̯]	

FIGURE IV: Vowels of Czech with their allophones

ning of a phonotagm becomes more transparent once /Ts/, /Tš/ and /Tz/, /Tž/ are accepted as combinations of an occlusive and an alveolar or a palatal fricative. They parallel other combinations of the same type. See figure II where the question marks can be replaced by /Ts/, /Tš/, /Tz/ and /Tž/, respectively.

The situation is similar in the post-nuclear context in which the combinations /TS/, /TŠ/ have the same constituency as /PS/, /PŠ/ and /KS/, /KŠ/. See figure III where the question marks can be replaced with /TS/ and /TŠ/, respectively. And there are in addition two post-nuclear three-consonant combinations /PST/ and /KST/ (in *zábst* and *text*). If the affricate in [pɛːʦ.t] *péct* is analyzed as /TS/, the resulting combination /TST/ parallels the structure of /PST/ and /KST/. Thus, if the affricates are analyzed as two-phoneme combinations, these combinations follow patterns attested for other pre-nuclear and post-nuclear combinations, which in turn simplifies the overall phonotactic analysis. If we analyzed the affricates as separate phonemes /c/ and /č/, we would have to set a restriction on the occurrence of /t/ and /d/ (better: on their archi-phoneme /T/); we would have to say that at the beginning and at the end of a phonotagm they cannot be followed by /s/, /z/ (or /S/) and by /š/, /ž/ (or /Š/), though the other occlusives are capable of this.

3.3 Vowels

Vowels are phonemes that occur in nuclear position of the DU only; they are not dependent on the occurrence or the function of any other phonemes. Their inventory is given in figure IV.

The Czech vowel system is traditionally sorted into high (/i/, /u/), mid (/e/, /o/) and low (/a/) vowels. The high and mid ones are distinguished as to being either front (/i/, /e/) or back (/u/, /o/), while /a/ is central. Furthermore, a distinction between short and long is made for all vowels, though sometimes the phonemic status is denied for /ō/ due to its prevalent occurrence in PhFs of words of foreign origin. However, the existence of minimal pairs such as [loʒɛ] *lože* "bed" × [loːʒɛ] *lóže* "lodge" proves the phonological value of [oː] (i.e. /ō/) as opposed to [o] (i.e. /o/).

Our analysis of the vocalic system is not in fact much dissimilar to the traditional one. The crucial difference lies in the interpretation of diphthongs [au̯], [ɛu̯] and [ou̯].[11] We take them as single phonemes, not as combinations of two as is usual in phonological analyses of Czech (Kučera 1961, Vachek 1968).[12] From the historical perspective, the diphthong [ou̯] is a "native" sound in Czech, whereas [au̯] and [ɛu̯] were introduced with the adoption of foreign words. The latter two do not occur in many words, but should still be regarded as part of the sound system of Czech. The diphthong [au̯] is attested, for example, in *auto* "car", which is one of the most used words, and, moreover, there is no other word for car in this language. The diphthong [ɛu̯] occurs, for example, in *euro*, which is a fairly common word, too.

The problem of the Czech diphthongs has been discussed in the phonological literature (see the discussion and references in Palková 1997: 196–8). Standpoints were various just as were the arguments for and against the monophonemic evaluation. However, it must be again emphasized that whether something is a phoneme or not should be decided on the grounds of the definition of the phoneme in the theory adopted for the description. Whether [ou̯] is a "native" sound and [au̯] and [ɛu̯] are of foreign origin is irrelevant as long as all are used in the contemporary Czech vocabulary. Similarly, phonic properties of the diphthongs need not necessitate their monophonemic or biphonemic analysis. For one thing, phoneticians are not in agreement whether diphthongs are single sounds in which the position of the tongue and/or the shape of the lips change or whether they are sequences of two sounds one of which is syllabic and the other non-syllabic. In fact, as the decision may be rather arbitrary, it cannot have any bearing on their phonological interpretation. Again, the whole point is to ascertain which of the available analyses is theoretically justifiable, and which of them allows for a simpler and more adequate analysis.

In the descriptions where the Czech diphthongs are treated as two phonemes, the latter are usually viewed as combinations of /a/, /e/, /o/ with /u/, that is, the [u̯] part is identified with the phoneme /u/ elsewhere realized as [u] (e.g. in [sut] *sud* "barrel" as opposed to [sou̯t] *soud* "judgment"). We do not hold this view because it is not in agreement with the definition of the phoneme. If [au̯], [ɛu̯]

---

11 See Studenovský – Trpák (2004) and Studenovský (2008, 2010) for recent phonetic analyses of the Czech diphthongs.
12 Some other linguists, e.g. Horálek in MČ1: 128, 131, view the Czech diphthongs as single phonemes.

and [ou̯] were to correspond to two-phoneme combinations /au/, /eu/ and /ou/, we must be able to show each element in these combinations is indeed a phoneme. Phonemes, being minimum syntagmatic entities, should be functionally orderable, but the alleged phoneme /u/ in /au/, /eu/ and /ou/ does not have this capacity because it cannot enter in any other relation with /a/, /e/ and /o/ within a single distributional domain. If /u/ occurs, it stands either on its own or accompanied by a contoid, in which case it is realized as [u], or it is preceded by /a/, /e/, /o/, in which case its realization is [u̯]. Thus, /u/ realized as [u̯] is always preceded by /a/, /e/ or /o/. In a single distributional domain their sequence cannot be reversed as was possible in the case of the affricates. By distributional domain we mean the phonotagm as the self-contained phonotactic entity. This is important because the reverse combinations /ua/, /ue/ and /uo/, realized as [u.a], [u.ɛ] and [u.o], are found in Czech but not within one phonotagm—they occur across two phonotagms. However, these sequences are opposed to genuine combinations of /a/, /e/, /o/ and /u/, i.e. to /au/, /eu/ and /ou/, which also occur across two phonotagms. See the following examples:

(4) [du.alɪta] *dualita* × [na.ut͡ʃ] *nauč* (as opposed to [ʔau̯t] *aut*)
    [du.ɛl] *duel* × [nɛ.umɲɛt] *neumět* (as opposed to [ʔɛu̯ro] *euro*)
    [vaku.ovi:] *vakuový* × [do.ut͡ʃ] *douč* (as opposed to [dou̯ʃɛk] *doušek*)

The examples show that two facts must be accounted for: 1) that [au̯], [ɛu̯], [ou̯] are opposed to [a.u], [ɛ.u], [o.u], and 2) that the latter are opposed to [u.a], [u.ɛ], [u.o]. If the diphthongs are to be interpreted as combinations of two phonemes /au/, /eu/ and /ou/, then the oppositions must be interpreted by viewing the syllable boundary in [a.u], [ɛ.u], [o.u] as a realization of some phonological feature (e.g. of a diaereme). It is reasonable to do the same in the case of [u.a], [u.ɛ], [u.o]. But it means that /ua/, /ue/ and /uo/, which correspond to [u.a], [u.ɛ] and [u.o], occur in another distributional domain than /au/, /eu/ and /ou/, which correspond to the diphthongs [au̯], [ɛu̯] and [ou̯]. The sequences /ua/, /ue/, /uo/ cannot thus be a proof that the ordering of the phonemes within the diphthongs is functional.

    The diphthongs can be compared to similar combinations [aj], [ɛj], [ɪj], [oj], [uj] which can be analyzed as single phonemes because the order of the segments is functional. If we assume that they correspond to /aj/, /ej/, /ij/, /oj/, /uj/, we can immediately show these are genuine combinations because we find, within one distributional domain, their permutations /ja/, /je/, /ji/, /jo/, /ju/. Furthermore, we can find, again within a single distributional domain, the same combinations with long vowels: /āj/, /īj/, /ōj/, /ūj/ and /jā/, /jī/, /jō/, /jū/.[13] In con-

---

13   The combinations /ēj/, /jē/ are very rare; see §16.1.

trast, if the diphthongs were analyzed as combinations of two phonemes, such combinations would only exist for short vowels. The only exception is /āu/ found in *náušnice*, but it corresponds to two syllables, not to one like the diphthongs. Therefore, the most appropriate solution is to analyze [au̯], [ɛu̯], [ou̯] as realizations of single phonemes and not of combinations of two phonemes. They will be transcribed here with a dieresis as /ë/, /ä/ and /ö/ rather than /eu/, /au/ and /ou/ to be distinguished from the true combinations of phonemes /eu/, /au/, /ou/. Cf. /pöTšeK/, [pou̯ʧɛk] *pouček* "little puck" and /pouTšeK/, [po.uʧɛk] *pouček* "theorem (gen. pl.)".

Once the diphthongs are accepted as realizations of single phonemes, we can see there are three types of vocalic quality: [ɪ], [ɛ], [a], [u], [o] × [iː], [ɛː], [aː], [uː], [oː] × [ɛu̯], [au̯], [ou̯].[14] To account for these differences, we posit a proportional opposition *short × long × diphthongal*, and interpret the vowels as SHORT /i/, /e/, /a/, /u/, /o/, LONG /ī/, /ē/, /ā/, /ū/, /ō/, and DIPHTHONGAL /ë/, /ä/, /ö/. The difference between the particular vowels within these sets is accounted for by two proportional oppositions: *front × central × back* on the one hand, and *high ×* MID on the other. The former accounts for the difference between FRONT /i/, /e/, /ī/, /ē/, /ë/, CENTRAL /a/, /ā/, /ä/, and BACK /u/, /o/, /ū/, /ō/, /ö/. The difference between /i/, /ī/ and /e/, /ē/, and that between /u/, /ū/ and /o/, /ō/ is accounted for by the second proportional opposition: /i/, /ī/, /u/, /ū/ are HIGH, and /e/, /ē/, /o/, /ō/ are MID. This distinction is not relevant for the diphthongal and central vowels.

3.4 Semiconsonants

Semiconsonants are phonemes that can stand both in nuclear position and non-nuclear position. Their occurrence is dependent on the presence of at least one other phoneme. Czech has two such phonemes, /r/ and /l/.[15] Realized as voiced alveolar vibrant [r], /r/ is characterized by one distinctive feature 'vibrant'.[16] The second, /l/, is also characterized by only one distinctive feature 'lateral' and is realized as voiced alveolar lateral approximant [l]. Both phonemes are analyzed with a single distinctive feature because these features are capable of distin-

---

14   The IPA symbols do not do justice to the realizations of the Czech vowels because they are neither open nor close but rather neutral to this phonetic distinction. It is only long [iː] that is more close than short [ɪ] (see Podlipský et al. 2009, Skarnitzl 2012). Both are high front unrounded vocoids. The vocoids [u], [uː] are high back and rounded. The vocoids [ɛ], [ɛː] are mid front unrounded, and [o], [o] are mid back rounded. The vocoids [a], [aː] are unrounded low central. See also Šimáčková et al. (2012).

15   Their nuclearity will be discussed in detail in §10.2.

16   It is interesting to note that /r/ is often realized as a flap (Machač 2009), and /l/ is often velarized (Volín 2002). Cf. also Machač – Skarnitzl (2009).

	Non-syllabic		Syllabic
Within a word in the vicinity of a vocoid	[ra:no] *ráno* [lɛs] *les*	Within a word between two contoids	[sr̩na] *srna* [vl̩k] *vlk*
At the beginning of a word, before a contoid	[rtuc] *rtut'* [lpjɛt] *lpět*	At the end of a word after a contoid	[vi:tr̩] *vítr* [nɛsl̩] *nesl*

FIGURE V: Occurrence of non-syllabic and syllabic realizations of /r/, /l/

guishing them from other phonemes, there being no need to postulate any additional distinctive features. The semiconsonant /l/ is the only Czech phoneme realized as a lateral contoid, and the distinctive feature *lateral* thus expresses its special status.

As regards /r/, it is true that it is not the only phoneme in Czech realized as a vibrant contoid; /ř/ is another one differing from /r/ in being realized with audible friction. However, from the phonotactic perspective, /ř/ is a consonant because it functions only as a peripheral entity, whereas /r/ has been interpreted as a semiconsonant for its ability to function both as a peripheral entity (as in /rum/ *rum* with nuclear /u/) and as a nuclear entity (as in /trn/ *trn* with nuclear /r/). Even though it might be desirable to express the relation between /r/ and /ř/ in terms of distinctive features as Šefčík (2004) does, for example by interpreting /r/ as an alveolar vibrant and /ř/ as a palatal vibrant, such an analysis is problematic exactly because the phonemes do not have the same phonotactic function. They are mutually opposable in non-nuclear contexts (cf. /raS/ *ras* × /řaS/ *řas*), but not in the nuclear context, as only /r/ occurs there. It would in fact mean that the opposition /r/ × /ř/ is neutralized there, and we would have to introduce an archi-phoneme for the nuclear vibrant. In the end such an analysis seems to be less simple than the one we have adopted.

Two types of realizations of /r/ and /l/ have been recognized in Czech: a syllabic and non-syllabic one. They are traditionally said to be non-syllabic when occurring within a word in the vicinity of a vocoid and at the beginning of a word before a contoid, and syllabic when occurring within a word between two contoids and at the end of a word after a contoid (Frinta 1909: 107, 115). Examples are given in figure V. However, there have been disputes as to whether the variants really differ in their sound characteristics. According to some authors, there is no relevant and obvious articulatory or acoustic difference, and the impression of syllabicity is determined by the context in which they occur (Hůrková – Hlaváč 1981, Palková 1997: 232–3). Be that as it may, from the phonological perspective, this issue is of little importance. As will be showed in §10.2, conditions under which /r/ and /l/ function as nuclear entities are clearly definable irrespective of their realization.

Finally, let us note that the phoneme /m/ is not treated here as a semiconsonant, even though it may be realized as syllabic [m̩] in the words *sedm*, *osm*, their derivates and in a handful of place names such as *Rožmberk*. All of these words are alternatively pronounced with [um], i.e. [sɛdum] instead of [sɛdm̩], [ʔosum] instead of [ʔosm̩] and [roʒumbɛrk] instead of [roʒm̩bɛrk]. The syllabic pronunciation of /m/ is thus best regarded to be accidental. Likewise, an occasional occurrence of syllabic [n̩] instead of [ɛn] in names like *Trautenberk* is viewed as accidental.

Chapter Four: NEUTRALIZATION

4.1 Neutralization as a way to account for distributional limitations

The inventory of phonemes presented in the previous chapter has been arrived at on the basis of the commutation test which examines mutual commutability of phonetic forms. Commutations take place in a specific context. If in some context a phonetic form is commutable with at least one other phonetic form, both of them have a distinctive function and are allophones of two separate phonological entities in that context. They can be mutually commutable in another context, but it may happen that there is some context where either or both of them do not occur. This non-occurrence might be simply accidental if there is no reason to suppose that they could not occur there. For example, although English [tʰ] and [d̥]¹ are commutable before [ɪp] (cf. *tip* and *dip*), only [tʰ] occurs before [ɛɪp] (cf. *tape*). The absence of [d̥] in this context must be accidental because there does not seem to be any reason why the form [d̥ɛɪp] could not be a realization of a potential word in English. Yet in other situations there will be good reasons for assuming that a certain non-occurrence is not random and that a sound is disallowed from appearing in some context. This may be said about English [h] and its absence in the word-initial context.

The distinction between the accidental and regular non-occurrence is not so straightforward and calls for further explanation. The question pertains to all semiotic entities, not just phonological ones. We will return to it in §5.4 because it is especially crucial in the case of combinations of phonemes. For the time being, some non-occurrence will be regarded as regular if and only if it is possible to state precisely what conditions it, and if the conditions apply to more than one situation, i.e. if it is not a matter of singular instances. In all other cases the non-occurrence will be regarded as accidental. Hence, the non-occurrence of [h] at the end of English words is regular because it applies to all words, but the non-occurrence of [d̥] before [ɛɪp] is accidental, as it applies to one specific context.

Obviously, linguistics should be mostly interested in explaining regularities than accidence. In phonology the regular non-occurrence of entities is usually accounted for with two notions, NEUTRALIZATION and DEFECTIVE DISTRIBUTION.

---

1 As is well known, the English so-called voiced stops are actually devoiced syllable-initially.

Even though these notions are used in many phonological theories, functional phonology clearly separates them. Neutralization refers to the situation when a certain communicative oppositional difference which is valid in some context is not valid for *any* member of the opposition in another context. In the case of defective distribution, the difference is valid for some, but not all members of the opposition.

Operated with in many linguistic approaches, neutralization has been variously defined (cf. Davidsen-Nielsen 1978, Akamatsu 1988, Silverman 2012), but the idea was originally developed in the Prague School, mostly by Trubetzkoy (1939) who connected it with another concept, the archi-phoneme.[2] Although some functionalists have abandoned the latter concept, the followers of Martinet and Mulder hold that the two notions are mutually interconnected and implied. Neutralization accounts for situations when a communicative difference existing between phonetic forms X and Y in a context a does not obtain in a context b. It may be that one of the forms does not regularly occur in the context b or it may even happen that none of them occur in that context b in which case there is another phonetic entity Z occurring in the context b but not in the context a. The first situation applies to Czech [p] and [b]. Both are found word-initially, but only [p] occurs word-finally before a pause. An example of the second situation comes from English where [pʰ] and [b̥] are found word-initially, but they do not occur word-medially after [s] where instead we find [p].

Let us put it otherwise. If the difference between the phonetic forms X and Y is expressed by some opposition O_1 in the context a (e.g. by the opposition of voicing in the case of Czech [p] × [b]), we cannot operate with this opposition in the context b if there is no difference between X and Y. Consequently, it is logical that whatever occurs in the context b, it cannot be identified with either X or Y. If it were identified, say, with X, we would claim that although there is no difference between X and Y in the context b, it is X, but not Y, that occurs there. This is absurd because if there is no difference, the forms cannot be distinguished. What is more, the X would obviously have another function in communication than it has in the context a where it is confronted with Y. Hence, what matters is whether there is a choice or a possibility of comparison between alternatives. The actual quality of the occurring phonetic form is irrelevant. It is like in the comparison of people's height. A person *1* can be said to be taller than a person *2* if they can be compared, but if the person *1* cannot be confronted with the person *2*, we cannot claim that he is taller or shorter. The person still has some physical height, but the values 'taller' and 'shorter' cannot be ascribed to

---

2   Neutralization is in fact a general term for the suspension of some opposition. In principle, it may apply to any opposition, not just to that between phonemes.

him unless there is someone else to compare.[3] It is the same with phonological distinctions such as distinctive features. The latter are confused with concrete physical properties, even though they are rather comparative values.

To avoid these dangers and at the same time to stress that the function rather than the substance of speech phenomena is essential in communication, functional phonology has introduced the ARCHI-PHONEME. The phonetic form which occurs in the context of neutralization of some opposition is not interpreted as an allophone of any of the members of the opposition (irrespective of whether it is pronounced alike), but as an allophone of a different phonological entity because it has another communicative function. The archi-phoneme is the entity resulting from neutralization of a phonematic opposition. Although it is ontologically an entity of a different status than phonemes found in contexts where the opposition is valid, it is still related and connected to them. It is because the archi-phoneme is a type of phoneme and as such it is a bundle of distinctive features. The distinctive features the archi-phoneme contains are equal to features common to the phonemes participating in the neutralized opposition. In other words, the archi-phoneme does not contain those distinctive features by which the phonemes in question are mutually distinguished, simply because the distinction is not functional; it contains only those features by which the phonemes are distinguished from others in a given context.

Archi-phonemes are established on the basis on the commutation test. The basic condition is that in certain contexts (contexts of relevance) there is some difference which is completely irrelevant in other contexts (contexts of neutralization). The difference must obtain between two or more phonemes, and the phonemes must have at least one distinctive feature in common. Otherwise the intersection between them would be an empty set, but an archi-phoneme must contain at least one distinctive feature expressing its distinctive function. It must be opposed to at least one other phoneme or archi-phoneme (cf. Mulder 1968: 112–3, 198, Mulder 1989: 238).

In contrast, defective distribution designates situations when the occurrence of some entity, usually a phoneme, is limited in a certain context. In a way, neutralization is a special type of defective distribution because all terms of some opposition are limited from occurring in some context. However, we will speak about defective distribution only in situations when the occurrence of some, but not all terms of some opposition is limited. For example, /ŋ/ has defective distribution in English because it does not occur word-initially; however, the other

---

3   Unfortunately, this simple logic is often misunderstood in many phonological theories where neutralization is in effect the same as defective distribution, even though they are terminologically (but not conceptually) distinguished.

nasals /m/ and /n/ occur there, so the difference between various places of articulation is not totally suspended for nasals there. To be more precise, the term *defective distribution* will cover those regular non-occurrences which cannot be interpreted as instances of neutralization. This is important because if it is not possible to explain a certain distributional limitation as neutralization, it will be interpreted as defective distribution. Some problematic cases are discussed in the last section of this chapter. The next section, however, considers in detail one obvious instance of neutralization in Czech.

4.2 Neutralization of voicing

This section reviews the way how two basic actions of the vocal folds are utilized in Czech. The commutation test has revealed that there is a functional difference in the phonetic voicing of obstruents in the following contexts:

(1) CONTEXTS WHERE THE VOICING DIFFERENCE IS FUNCTIONAL
(a) At the beginning of a word before a sonorant or [r̝]/[r̝̊] followed by a sono-
     rant:[4] [tɛn] *ten* × [dɛn] *den*, [prak] *prak* × [brak] *brak*, [tr̝̊i] *tři* × *dři* [dr̩].
(b) Between two sonorants or [r̩]: [kosa] *kosa* × [koza] *koza*, [pr̩sɲiː] *prsní* ×
     [pr̩zɲiː] *przní*, [nutniː] *nutný* × [nudniː] *nudný*, [fronta] *fronta* × [fronda]
     fronda.
(c) Before [v]: [xvost] *chvost* × [ɦvost] *hvozd*.

If a phonetically voiceless obstruent is replaced with its phonetically voiced counterpart (or the other way round) in any of these contexts, it will bring about the change in the identity (meaning) of the word. To account for this, we have introduced the distinctive features 'voiceless' and 'voiced'. The former is a value pertaining to all phonemes which are realized by voiceless sounds and which are replaceable by voiced counterparts, namely it pertains to to /p/, /f/, /t/, /s/, /t'/, /š/, /k/ and /x/. The distinctive feature 'voiced' pertains to all phonemes realized by voiced sounds and replaceable by their voiceless counterparts, namely to /b/, /v/, /d/, /z/, /d'/, /ž/, /g/ and /h/.

None of the contexts under (1) involves the end of words because the difference between the two actions of the vocal folds does not have a distinctive function there.[5] The voicing of the word-final obstruents is completely predictable,

---

4   If [r̩] or [r̝̊] is not followed by a sonorant, that is, if they are followed by an obstruent, the
     voicing opposition is not valid; see below under the context (3e). Let us also note that for
     the sake of simplicity, [r̩] and [r̝̊] are treated as if they were just one sound.
5   More correctly: at the end of a word when the end is specially signaled by phonic means
     such as a pause. See §4.3.

i.e. always the same under particular conditions, and the predictability is summarized as follows:

(2) THE WORD-FINAL OBSTRUENT IS PHONETICALLY
(a) Voiceless if the word is terminated by a pause: *let* "flight" × *led* "ice", both
[lɛt]; *kos* "blackbird" × *koz* "goat (gen. pl.)", both [kos]; *mák* "poppy" ×
mág "magician", both [maːk].
(b) Voiceless if the word is followed by another word which begins with a
voiceless sound (including [r̥]):[6] *mák přijde* "the poppy will come" × *mág
přijde* "the magician will come", both [maːk p̥r̥ɪjdɛ].
(c) Voiceless if there is no pause and if the next word begins with a sonorant or
with [v]: *let může* "the flight can" × *led může* "the ice can", both [lɛt͜ muːʒɛ];
plot visí "the fence hangs" × *plod visí* "the fruit hangs", both [plot͜ vɪsiː].
(d) Voiced if there is no pause and the next word begins with a voiced obstruent or with [r]: *let bude* "the flight will be" × *led bude* "the ice will be", both
[lɛd͜ budɛ]; *mák řidne* "the poppy becomes thin", pronounced [maːg͜ r̝iːdnɛ] ×
mág řekl "the magician said", pronounced [maːg͜ r̝ɛkl].

This predictability is interpreted here as NEUTRALIZATION OF VOICING. It means
that the voicing opposition which is valid in the contexts under (1) is not relevant for communication in the contexts under (2). It is suspended or neutralized.
The other oppositions are not affected, so that there is a communicative difference between various manners of articulations (cf. [lɛt] *let* × [lɛs] *les* × [lɛn] *len*)
and various places of articulation (cf. [lɛp] *lep* × [lɛt] *let* × [lɛc] *leť* × [lɛk] *lek*).
The voicing opposition holds for the pairs /p/ × /b/, /f/ × /v/, /t/ × /d/, /s/ × /z/, /t'/
× /d'/, /š/ × /ž/, /k/ × /g/, and /x/ × /h/, where the first phonemes are phonologically voiceless, and the second are phonologically voiced. But since the phonetic
voicing is completely predicable at the end of words, it cannot be functionally
relevant there. For that reason, the final obstruents in the words cannot be allophones of any of these phonemes and are instead interpreted as allophones of
archi-phonemes resulting from neutralization of voicing.
    The system of these archi-phonemes is given in figure I together with their
allophones. The capital letters are ar traditional way to transcribe archi-phonemes; they show the relationship between an archi-phoneme and the phonemes
from it has arisen. For example, /P/ has resulted from neutralization of the opposition /p/ × /b/. The archi-phonemes are realized like the phonemes to which
they are related, but their phonetic voicing is predictable from the given context.
The archi-phoneme /P/ is realized as bilabial stop like /p/ and /b/.

---

6   The voiceless [r̥] occurs at the beginning of a stress unit only if followed by a voiceless
    obstruent, cf. [r̥ka] *řka*.

	Labial	Alveolar	Palatal	Velar
Occlusive	/P/ [p] [b]	/T/ [t] [d]	/Ť/ [c] [ɟ]	/K/ [k] [g]
Fricative	/F/ [f] [v]	/S/ [s] [z]	/Š/ [ʃ] [ʒ]	/X/ [x] [ɦ]
Nasal	/m/ [m] [ɱ]	/n/ [n] [ɲ] [ŋ]	/ň/ [ɲ]	
Outside the proportional system: /j/ [j] and /ř/ [r̝], [r̝̊]				

FIGURE I: Consonants of Czech in the context of neutralization of voicing with their allophones

The archi-phonemes in figure I are phonologically neither voiceless nor voiced. This is not to be confused with the fact that they are realized either as phonetically voiceless or phonetically voiced obstruents. One thing is their physical properties, and another their phonological values.[7] The terms *voiceless* and *voiced* merely describe two actions of the vocal folds, whereas the distinctive features voiceless and voiced refer to the fact that phonetic forms produced without the vibration of the vocal folds can be replaced with phonetic forms produced with the vibration, so that the replacement brings about the change in meaning. For the sake of convenience, they will be called VOICING ARCHI-PHONEMES. The phonological contexts of neutralization of voicing are summarized under (3) and discussed in the following paragraphs.

(3)   CONTEXTS OF NEUTRALIZATION OF VOICING
(a)   The end of a phonotagm provided that the phonotagm is the last of the diaereme group.
(b)   Before any voiceless or any voiced consonant (the latter with the exception of /v/).
(c)   Before any voicing archi-phoneme.
(d)   Before /ř/ if the latter is followed by a voiceless or a voiced consonant with the exception of /v/.
(e)   Before /ř/ if the latter is the last consonant of the diaereme group.

Phonotagm-final context

The first context is the one we have been until now referring to in somewhat informal terms. It is the end of the PhF of a word provided that the end is phonetically signaled. We explain in §4.3 why such a stipulation is necessary. The phonological interpretation of some of the forms mentioned under (2) follows:

---

7   Recall the simile with the height in §4.1.

(4) [lɛt] *let* → /leT/   [let] *led* → /leT/
     [kos] *kos* → /koS/   [kos] *koz* → /koS/
     [maːk] *mák* → /māK/   [maːk] *mág* → /māK/

Before voiceless and voiced consonants

The second context is the one before a voiceless consonant or before a voiced consonant with the exception of /v/. Viewed from the phonetic perspective, in Czech (like in many other languages) it holds that only a voiceless obstruent can stand next to a voiceless obstruent, and only a voiced obstruent can stand next to a voiced obstruent (i.e. combinations like [sp] or [zb] exist, but not [sb] or [zp]).

There are several ways to interpret this in phonology. In the present theoretical framework it is appropriate to make use of the notions *neutralization* and *archi-phoneme* (in fact, they were introduced to cope with situations like this). It only remains to be determined which of the obstruents in the group corresponds to an archi-phoneme. It is obvious that the first obstruent agrees in voicing with the second, and the second agrees with the first, but both cannot be interpreted as archi-phonemes. So, to take the example of [sp] × [zb], we can declare [s] and [z] to be realizations of the phonemes /s/ and /z/, while the voicing of the following [p] and [b] is predictable from the context, that is, the latter are realizations of archi-phonemes. The alternative is to say that [p] and [b] are realizations of the phonemes /p/ and /b/, while the voicing of the preceding [s] and [z] is predictable from the context, i.e. the latter are realizations of archi-phonemes. There is nothing in the theory forcing us to prefer either solution, but having considered the adequacy and simplicity of both of them, the second solution is the best candidate. Consequently, the groups [sp] and [zb] are interpreted as /Sp/ and /Sb/, respectively. In realization, the voicing of the archi-phoneme agrees with the voicing of the next consonant: in /Sp/ the /S/ is realized as voiceless like /p/, and in /Sb/ it is realized voiced like /b/. The chosen solution is in accord with the fact that most of assimilatory processes are regressive (anticipatory) in Czech: When an obstruent is combined with another, the voicing of the first is assimilated to the voicing of the second, as illustrated by the examples under (5). This takes place both in derivation of words (= (5a)) and in juxtaposition of words (= (5b)), that is, when two words stand next to each other.

(5) (a) [ʒaːba] *žába* "frog" × [ʒapka] *žabka* "little frog" → /žāba/ × /žaPka/
          [prosiː] *prosí* "(he) pleads" × [prozba] *prosba* "plea" → /prosī/ × /proSba/
     (b) [lɛt] *let* "flight" × [lɛd̯bɪl] *let byl* "the flight was" → /leT/ × /leT bil/
          [ɦat] *had* "snake" × [ɦat̯sɪtʃɛl] *had syčel* "the snake hissed" → /haT/ × /haT siTšel/

There is one important exception to what has just been said: Neutralization of voicing does not take place before /v/ within one diaereme group, and the opposition between voiceless and voiced consonants is relevant there. In this respect, /v/ behaves like the nasals /m/, /n/, /ň/, the sonants /r/, /l/, /j/ and /ř/ (the last with two exceptions mentioned immediately):

(6) [sval] *sval* × [zval] *zval* → /sval/ × /zval/
     [smɲɛna] *směna* × [zmɲɛna] *změna* → /sMňena/ × /zMňena/
     [tli:] *tlí* × [dli:] *dlí* → /tlī/ × /dlī/
     [pjɛt] *pět* × [bjɛt] *běd* → /pjeT/ × /bjeT/
     [tr̥ɪ] *tři* × [dr̥ɪ] *dři* → /tři/ × /dři/

However, while /r/, /l/, /j/ and /ř/ have been interpreted as being phonologically neither voiceless nor voiced, /v/ is characterized as a voiced labial fricative, i.e. the voiced counterpart of /f/ with which it forms a pair proportional to pairs like /h/ × /x/, /z/ × /s/. Thus, /v/ is the only phonologically voiced consonant before which the voicing opposition is valid.

The reasons for this peculiarity seem to be partly diachronic, partly perhaps due to the phonetic nature of [v] by which the phoneme /v/ is realized. The sound [v] is usually described as "voiced labio-dental fricative", but its friction is acoustically very small compared to the other fricative contoids (see Volín – Skarnitzl 2005, 2006a and 2006b for details).[8] From the historical point of view, this peculiarity is usually explained by assuming that the v-sound was originally labial-velar approximant [w] (Frinta 1916, Romportl 1973: 105–17). In that case it was a sound with similar characteristics like [r], [l] and [j], before which both voiceless and voiced sounds can stand. Be that as it may, in Modern Czech the origin of the sound is blurred because [v] loses, in morphological processes, its voicing at the end of a word and before a voiceless sound, behaving like any other voiced obstruent. Compare the following with the examples under (5a):

(7) (a) [ɦlava] *hlava* "head" × [ɦlaf] *hlav* "head (gen. pl.)" → /hlava/ × /hlaF/
          [sli:va] *slíva* "plum" × [sli:fka] *slívka* "little plum" → /slīva/ × /slīFka/
     (b) [koza] *koza* "goat" × [kos] *koz* "goat (gen. pl.)" → /koza/ × /koS/
          [brada] *brada* "chin" × [brat] *brad* "chin (gen. pl.)" → /brada/ × /braT/

We find most appropriate the analysis treating the pair /f/ × /v/ as proportional to the other voicing pairs. The opposition [ɦlava] × [ɦlaf] can then be handled in

---

8 Czech is not the only language where [v] does not trigger neutralization of voicing. In Russian (Padgett 2002), Hungarian and Slovak (Bárkányi – Kiss 2010) it behaves similarly.

the same way as that between [koza] × [kos]. However, it must be remembered that /v/ is exceptional because it undergoes neutralization of voicing like the other voiced consonants, but does not trigger it like the nasals and the sonants.

Before voicing archi-phonemes

The third context of neutralization is the one before any voicing archi-phoneme. From the phonetic perspective, it is a consequence of the fact that combinations of obstruents are either voiceless or voiced in Czech (with the exception of [v]). They need not be only of two but also of three or four obstruents. Neutralization of voicing is therefore transitive; it applies whenever occlusives and fricatives stand next to each other, irrespective of whether it is at the beginning or at the end of a PhF of a word or within it:

(8) [fskvjɛt] *vzkvět* → /FSkvjeT/
     [zaːpst] *zábst* → /zāPST/
     [xɛpskiː] *chebský* → /xePSkī/

Before /ř/ + occlusive or fricative

The fourth context is the context '_řC$_1$' where 'C$_1$' is either phonologically a voiceless or a voiced occlusive or fricative. As presently explained, in case 'C$_1$' is /v/, there is no neutralization, i.e. /v/ is again an exception. Let us look at the following examples:

(9) (a) [xr̝taːn] *chřtán* → /Xřtān/
          [kr̝cɪnɪ] *křtiny* → /Křťini/
          [tr̝pɪt] *třpyt* → /TřpiT/
          [dɛpr̝skiː] *debřský* (derived from the place name *Debř*) → /dePřSkī/
     (b) [fir̝bɛt] *hřbet* → /XřbeT/
          [ʔotɛvr̝ɦuba] *otevřhuba* (SSJČ) → /oteFřhuba/

The examples show that at the phonetic level the ř-sound devoices in the vicinity of a voiceless obstruent, irrespective of whether the latter precedes or follows it (hence *tři* = [tr̝ɪ], *věřte* = [vjɛr̝tɛ]). Thus, if such an obstruent stands both before and after the ř-sound, all of them, i.e. the obstruents and the ř-sound, must be voiceless as shown in (9a). And if one of the obstruents is voiced, then the other obstruent and the ř-sound are voiced as well (with one exception) as shown by (9b). The ř-sound behaves here as if it were phonetically an obstruent—recall that in groups the obstruents are either all voiceless or all voiced (with the exception of [v]). Phonologically, there is no reason not to treat this fact in the same way as we treated the groups of obstruents (see above), i.e. to say that there is neutralization of voicing before /ř/ followed by a voiceless or a voiced occlusive or a voiced fricative.

In this context one can also witness the exceptional behavior of /v/: if /ř/ precedes /v/, the voicing opposition is valid before the /ř/. Again, /v/ acts here as if it were a sonant. The following examples exemplify this. Although we do not have a minimal pair here, they show that both voiceless and voiced obstruents stand before the ř-sound which precedes [v] or a nasal, and therefore the voicing opposition is valid before /v/ and the nasal phonemes.[9]

(10) (a) [br̩vɛ] *Břve* (place name) → /břve/
          [pɛtr̩valt] *Petřvald* (place name) → /petřvalT/
     (b) [fir̩mɲɛt] *hřmět* → /hřMňeT/
          [fir̩mot] *hřmot* → /hřmoT/
          [tr̩mɛn] *třmen* → /třmen/

Before phonotagm-final /ř/

The last context also involves /ř/, namely the situation when it occurs at the end of a diaereme group. The opposition voiceless × voiced is canceled before such /ř/. It is a consequence of the fact that if the ř-sound occurs at the end of a word terminated by a pause, it devoices to [r̥]. The devoicing also takes place if the word is followed by another word with an initial voiceless obstruent or with a sonorant. If it is followed by one beginning with a voiced obstruent, there is no devoicing. The ř-sound behaves again as if it were phonetically an obstruent.[10] The following examples demonstrate it:

(11) (a) [fioɟɪt] *hodit* "to throw" × [fioc] *hoď* "throw! (sg.)"
          [mi:rɪt] *mířit* "to aim" × [mɪr̥] *miř* "aim! (sg.)"
     (b) [fioc‿tam] *hoď tam* "throw there! (sg.)"
          [mɪr̥‿tam] *miř tam* "aim there! (sg.)"
     (c) [fioc‿ɲɛkam] *hoď někam* "throw somewhere! (sg.)"
          [mɪr̥‿ɲɛkam] *miř někam* "aim somewhere! (sg.)"
     (c) [fioɟ‿dalɛko] *hoď daleko* "throw far! (sg.)"
          [mɪr‿dalɛko] *miř daleko* "aim far! (sg.)"

The final ř-sound also devoices when combined with an obstruent which can either precede or follow it. If it is preceded by an obstruent, the voicing of the lat-

---

9   Again, the ř-sound devoices if it is preceded by a voiceless obstruent.
10 Compare it with the behavior of final obstruents described in (2) above.

ter agrees with that of the ř-sound.[11] It means that the voicing of the obstruent is again contextually predictable and non-functional. The non-functionality is interpreted by neutralization of voicing:

(12) (a)   [pɛpř] *pepř* → /pePř/
          [ʔuvɲɪtř̩] *uvnitř* → /uvňiTř/
          [mokr̩] *mokř* (SSJČ) → /moKř/

     (b)   [pɛpř̩ muːʒɛ] *pepř může* → /pePř může/
          [ʔuvɲɪtř̩ mɲɛsta] *uvnitř města* → /uvňiTř MňeSta/
          [mokr̩ mɲɛla] *mokř měla* → /moKř Mňela/

     (c)   [pɛbr̩ doʃɛl] *pepř došel* → /pePř došel/
          [ʔuvɲɪdr̩ domu] *uvnitř domu* → /uvňiTř domu/
          [mogr̩ bɪla] *mokř byla* → /moKř bila/

4.3 Diaereme group as the domain of neutralization of voicing

Having discussed the contexts where neutralization of voicing takes place in Czech, we would now like to clarify why we have made reference to the diaereme group. Although the neutralization is traditionally said to take place at the end of a word, it is only true when the end is specifically signaled by phonic means. The boundary-signaling phonic means will be interpreted as manifestations of diaereme, and the phenomena falling in between two consecutive boundaries will be said to belong to one diaereme group. The signalization may take various forms such as a pause, a glottal stop, a specific realization of a sound or an intonation contour. If a word boundary is not signaled in any phonologically relevant way, the word is part of a larger diaereme group.

In Czech, diaereme groups often coincide with accent groups whose phonetic counter-domains are stress units.[12] The latter may be larger than a single word because certain words adjoin the neighboring words to form a stress unit with them. Among such words belong so-called primary prepositions.[13] We will be particularly interested in those terminated by an obstruent, namely with *pod* "under", *nad* "above", *od* "from", *ob* "every other" (e.g. *ob den* "every other

---

11   In Standard Czech the obstruent can only be a stop. In non-standard varieties it can also be a fricative, cf. [ʔotɛfř̩] *otevř*, imp. sg. of *otevřít*, equivalent to Standard Czech *otevři*.

12   As will be explained in §5.2, it is necessary to distinguish between diaereme and accent groups in Czech because the syntagm *s okem* corresponds to two diaereme groups but to one accent group. The boundary signal is here a glottal stop in between *s* and *o*.

13   Czech has also so-called secondary prepositions such as *skrz* "through" which originated from "normal" words (e.g. from adverbs) and which do not show any special behavior.

day"), *přes* "through", *před* "before", *bez* "without". If they are pronounced in isolation, the obstruent is voiceless like any other final obstruent. For example, pronounced as [pot] and [bɛs], respectively, the prepositions *pod* and *bez* are homophonous with the nouns *pot* "sweat" and *bez* "elderberry". However, in other situations the behavior of the primary prepositions is different from that of the nouns like *pot* and *bez*.

If the prepositions are followed by another word, they take over the stress and form a stress unit with that word.[14] Examples are under (13). Note that there is no pause or any other boundary signal in between the preposition and the word. To put it otherwise, the syntagms are pronounced as if they were single words, and so, for example, *od bytu* "from the flat" is homophonous with the word *odbytu* "sales (gen. sg.)".

(13) NOUNS

    ['kluka] *kluka*

      "boy (gen. sg.)"

    ['stolɛm] *stolem*

      "table (inst. sg.)"

    ['firadɛm] *hradem*

      "castle (inst. sg.)"

    ['bɪtu] *bytu*

      "flat (gen. sg.)"

PREPOSITIONAL SYNTAGMS

    ['bɛskluka] *bez kluka*

      "without a boy"

    ['potstolɛm] *pod stolem*

      "under a table"

    ['nadfiradɛm] *nad hradem*

      "over a castle"

    ['ʔodbɪtu] *od bytu*

      "from a flat"

In contrast to the prepositions, there is no shift in the stress when the nouns such as *pot* "sweat" and *bez* "elderberry" are followed by another word; the latter always retain their stress:

(14) [bɛs'kluka] *bez kluka* "a boy's elderberry"

    [pod'ɟiːfkɪ] *pot dívky* "a girl's sweat"

    [paːd'firadu] *pád hradu* "the fall of a castle"

    [fxod'bɪtu] *vchod bytu* "an entrance of a flat"

The examples such as those under (14) are a little problematic, though. There is no agreement as to whether the mentioned syntagms correspond to two stress units or just to one; both opinions are found in the literature (see e.g. Daneš 1957: 22–3, Hála 1962: 316, Ondráčková 1967, Palková 2004b). If it were just one stress unit, the consequence would be that the placement of stress is distinc-

---

14   An exception to this rule is the situation when the following word is too long (e.g. *pod velikánským stolem* "under the huge table") or marked with an emphatic stress or if it is not directly dependent on the preposition (e.g. *pod velmi velkým stolem* "under the very (= *velmi*) big table") in which case the word usually retains its stress.

tive in Czech because the syntagms *bez kluka* "without the boy" and *bez kluka* "the boy's elderberry", both of which being one stress unit, would only be distinguished by the placement of stress. However, it remains yet to be seen whether examples like these are really pronounced dissimilarly. The placement of stress follows the rules prescribed for the pronunciation of Czech, but it is not certain whether Czechs would really distinguish the pairs. Be that as it may, we will assume that the rules have an empirical basis and that the syntagms are pronounced differently. Moreover, we will assume that the syntagms such as those under (14) correspond to two stress units.

The second peculiarity of the obstruent-final primary prepositions as opposed to the nouns of similar constituency concerns the final obstruent when it is followed by a word beginning with a sonorant or with [v]. As we have just said, primary prepositions form a stress unit with the following word, and so the final obstruent of the preposition lies inside a stress unit. On the other hand, in the case of the nouns like *pot* "sweat" or *bez* "elderberry", we assume that the obstruent lies at the end of a stress unit because the following word belongs to a separate stress unit. Now, the descriptions of Czech suggest that there is a difference in the voicing of the obstruents in these two situations. To be more specific, we can get pairs like these:

(15) ONE STRESS UNIT

['podmuʒı] *pod muži*
"under men"

['bɛzlɛŋkı] *bez Lenky*
"without Lenka"

['nadvodou̯] *nad vodou*
"above water"

['bezalɛnı] *bez Aleny*
"without Alena"

TWO STRESS UNITS

[pot'muʒɛ] *pot muže*
"sweat of a man"

[bɛs'lɛŋkı] *bez Lenky*
"Lenka's elderberry"

[raːt'vodu] *rád vodu*
"(he) likes water"

[bɛs'alɛnı] *bez Aleny*
"Alena's elderberry"[15]

As we see, the obstruents in the primary prepositions do not lose voicing, whereas those of the nouns do. In the latter situation the obstruents occur before the onset of stress which functions as a boundary signal. The syntagms corresponding to two stress units are interpreted as two diaereme (and accent) groups, while the prepositional syntagms consisting of one stress unit are interpreted as one diaereme (and accent) group, since no boundary signal is involved in them. The prepositional syntagms are pronounced as if they were single words, and they

---

15 An alternative pronunciation of *Alena* is, in both cases, with an initial glottal stop. The pair differs then only in the placement of stress: ['bɛsʔalɛnı] "without Alena" × [bɛs'ʔalɛnı] "Alena's elderberry".

have the same phonological properties as single words, which gets us finally to the point of this discussion: Neutralization of voicing is not operative at the end of a word if the word is part of a diaereme group and if its boundary is not specifically marked, because the preposition-final voiced obstruents are opposed to the voiceless obstruents:

(16) [ˈpodmuʒɪ] *pod muži* × [ˈrotmɪstr̩] *rotmistr*
     [ˈbɛzlɛŋkɪ] *bez Lenky* × [ˈʧɛslɛ] *česle*
     [ˈnadvodou̯] *nad vodou* × [ˈʒatva] *žatva*

In short, there is no neutralization of voicing if the prepositions occur before an unstressed word with an initial nasal stop, [j], [r], [l], [v] or a vocoid. Elsewhere the neutralization obtains irrespective of whether there is a boundary signal or not. In particular, it concerns words with an initial obstruent (including the glottal stop) or with an initial [r̩]. If the obstruent is voiceless (or a glottal stop), the preceding final obstruent is voiceless as well; if the obstruent is voiced, it is voiced, too. Finally, the final obstruent is voiced before the initial [r̩]:

(17) [ˈbɛskluka] *bez kluka*   [bɛsˈkluka] *bez kluka*
     "without a boy"   "a boy's elderberry"
     [ˈbɛsʔalɛnɪ] *bez Aleny*   [bɛsˈʔalɛnɪ] *bez Aleny*
     "without Alena"   "Alena's elderberry"
     [ˈpodʒɛnɪ] *pod ženy*   [podˈʒɛnɪ] *pot ženy*
     "under women"   "a woman's sweat"
     [ˈnadr̩ɛkou̯] *nad řekou*   [prou̯dˈr̩ɛkɪ] *proud řeky*
     "over a river"   "the current of a river"

The fact that neutralization of voicing does not take place is also confirmed by the behavior of the so-called non-syllabic prepositions *k* "to", *v* "in", *s* "with", *z* "from" and *s* "from some surface down".[16] Normally, they follow the rules of assimilation when standing before an obstruent—see the examples under (18). In this respect they behave like any other word-final obstruents and are thus subject to neutralization of voicing.

(18) [ˈktomu] *k tomu* "to it"   [ˈftɛpu] *v tepu* "in the pulse"
     [ˈgdomu] *k domu* "to the house" [ˈvdɛpu] *v depu* "in the depot"
     [ˈscɛlɛm] *s tělem* "with the body" [ˈspaːrɪ] *z páry* "from the steam"
     [ˈzɟɛlɛm] *s dělem* "with the canon" [ˈzbaːrɪ] *z Bára* "from Bára"

---

16   We will return to them in §5.3 and §5.4.

When followed by a word beginning with a sonorant or with [v], they are not assimilated in Standard Czech (cf. VSČ: 53–4, Zeman 2008: 99). This becomes clear after we examine their distribution and pronunciation:

(19) (a) *k* "to" (+ dat.)
['kjabloɲɪ] *k jabloni* "to the apple tree"
['kvjɛʒɪ] *k věži* "to the tower"
(b) *v* "in" (+ loc.)
['vjabloɲɪ] *v jabloni* "in the apple tree"
(c) *s* "with" (+ instr.)
['sjabloɲiː] or ['zjabloɲiː] *s jabloní* "with the apple tree"
['svjɛʒiː] or ['zvjɛʒiː] *s věží* "with the tower"
['sɲiːm] *s ním* "with him"
['snaːmɪ] *s námi* "with us"
['svaːmɪ] *s vámi* "with you"[17]
(d) *z* "from" (+ gen.)
['zjabloɲɛ] *z jabloně* "from the apple tree"
['zvjɛʒɛ] *z věže* "from the tower"
['znaʃiː] *z naší (jabloně)* "from our (apple tree)"
['zvaʃiː] *z vaší (jabloně)* "from your (apple tree)"
(e) *s* "from some surface down" (+ gen.)
['sjabloɲɛ] *s jabloně* "from the apple tree down"
['svjɛʒɛ] *s věže* "from the tower down"
['snaʃiː] *s naší (jabloně)* "from our (apple tree) down"
['svaʃiː] *s vaší (jabloně)* "from your (apple tree) down"

The pair ['kjabloɲɪ] *k jabloni* and ['vjabloɲɪ] *v jabloni* shows that there can be both a voiceless and voiced obstruent before a word beginning with a sonorant other than a vocoid. The other examples under (19) support this conclusion, but the situation is complicated because of two facts: First, the preposition *s* has two pronunciations, [s] and [z], and if pronounced as [z], it is homophonous with the preposition *z*. Second, although in genitive the preposition *z* "from" is opposed to *s* "from some surface down", the semantic difference between them is very subtle, and the prepositions are distinguished probably only in higher (or archaic) styles of Standard Czech.[18] Still, the point is that the prepositions *k*, *s*, *z*

17 It is quite interesting that the preposition *s* "with" can be and is pronounced only as [s] when connected with *ním* "him", *námi* "us" and *vámi* "you". In all other situations there is a free variation between [s] and [z].
18 Hypothetically, we could have a pair like *je z naší jabloně* "it is from our apple tree" in the sense "it is made out of our apple tree" and *je s naší jabloně* "it is from our apple

and *v* do not undergo assimilation of voicing before a sonorant and are thus not subject to neutralization of voicing. The prepositions form one diaereme group with the following word and the boundary between them is not specially signaled, which is confirmed by the fact that *s věží* "with the tower" is homophonous with *svěží* "fresh".

To sum it up, the opposition between voiceless and voiced consonants is neutralized at the end of PhF of a word provided that the form coincides with the end of a diaereme group, but it is not neutralized at the end of PhF of a word provided that the word is not at the end of a diaereme group.

4.4 Incomplete neutralization of voicing

Concluding the discussion of neutralization of voicing in Czech, we must note that the traditional view that the opposition between voiceless and voiced consonants is canceled in Czech has recently been challenged. Examining the length of the vocoid [a] in nonsense words *tapka* and *tabka* pronounced by Czechs, Podlipský (2009: 49ff.) has found out that the vocoid tends to be slightly longer in the second word, even though the words should be homophonous (i.e. pronounced as [tapka]) under the traditional view because only voiceless obstruents can occur before a voiceless obstruent like [k] (see above). A difference in the vocoid length has also been found for the pair of the actually attested Czech words *kapky* and *babky* believed to be realized as [kapkɪ] and [bapkɪ], respectively: the vocoid [a] in *babky* has revealed to be longer than in *kapky*. The assumption is that since *kapky* "drops" is derived from *kapat* "to drop" with underlying /p/ and *babky* "old women" from *bába* "old woman" with underlying /b/, the difference between these phonemes is only partially neutralized because the preceding vocoid [a] is longer before [p] in *babky* arisen from /b/ than before [p] in *kapky* arisen from /p/.

This phenomenon is not peculiar to Czech and has been described for several languages such as Catalan, German, Polish, Dutch or Russian. In the literature it has become known as *incomplete neutralization* (for a most recent overview, see Shrager 2012). However, the issue still need to be investigated further because although some differences have been found for Czech, Podlipský himself (*op. cit.*: 54) admits it is a tentative conclusion.[19] What is more, even if the

---

tree" in the sense "it is fallen down from our apple tree". However, the latter idea can also be expressed with the *z* preposition which is more general and not restricted to the downward movement.

19 To the best of our knowledge, no other study has so far tried to prove or disprove Podlipský's findings (cf. Skarnitzl 2011: 135–8).

pronunciations differed, it remains to be seen whether the difference is perceived and evaluated as significant by listeners. This, in fact, has not been positively shown for the other languages said to display this phenomenon, that is, the voicing opposition is indeed sometimes completely neutralized there. As Podlipský (*op. cit.*: 62) concludes for Czech, "a vowel needs to last slightly longer when followed by a voiced coda to be perceived as long than it does when followed by voiceless coda (the provisions being that not all individuals in this study followed this pattern, and that the coda obstruent had to be phonetically voiced, not only phonologically voiced [that is, as in *babka* where, in Podlipský's view, the underlying /b/ is realized as [p] – *ab*] or word-finally devoiced on the surface)". Thus, until further evidence is available, we will assume that the voicing opposition is indeed completely neutralized in Czech in all the contexts previously described.

4.5 Neutralization of place of articulation of nasals

There is one other distributional limitation which can be accounted for by neutralization. It concerns the nasals. In most contexts there is a functional difference between various places of articulation as the examples under (20) show:

(20) WORD-INITIALLY   BEFORE [k]
    [m] [matratsɛ] *matrace*   [mamka] *mamka*
    [n] [naːdraʒiː] *nádraží*   *not found*
    [ɲ] [ɲadra] *ňadra*   [baɲka] *baňka*
    [ŋ] *not found*   [baŋka] *banka*

Thus, there is an opposition between [m], [n] and [ɲ] before a vocoid, and an opposition between [m], [n] and [ŋ] before velars. Due to the same distinctive function, the sounds [n] and [ŋ] are interpreted as allophones of one phoneme, the alveolar nasal /n/, and [m] as an allophone of the labial nasal /m/, and [ɲ] of the palatal nasal /ň/. However, this opposition is not functionally relevant in one particular context because it is not possible to choose there between various places of articulations. The context in question is the beginning of a syllable before a contoid where only bilabial nasal [m] occurs out of all other nasals. See the following examples:

(21) [mʃɛ] *mše* → /Mše/   [vmlaːcɪt] *vmlátit* → /vMlāťiT/
    [mstniː] *mstný* → /MStnī/   [mdliː] *mdlý* → /Mdlī/
    [smlou̯va] *smlouva* → /sMlöva/   [mɲɛna] *měna* → /Mňena/
    [smrt] *smrt* → /sMrT/   [tmɲɛ] *tmě* → /tMňe/

Since [m] is not opposed to any nasal in the mentioned context, it cannot be a realization of the phoneme /m/ because the latter is functionally *labial*, that is, a nasal for which the feature labial is relevant for communication. To account for this distributional limitation, we propose to interpret the [m] as a realization of the archi-phoneme resulting from neutralization of the opposition /m/ × /n/ × /ň/. As the phonological representation in (21) suggests, we will transcribe it as /M/. The archi-phoneme is characterized by one distinctive feature, nasal, which is common to the phonemes /m/, /n/, /ň/ and by which they are distinguished from other, non-nasal phonemes.

The mentioned neutralization raises one important question. Originally, we assumed that the same neutralization takes place in yet another context, namely at the beginning of a phonotagm after /ř/ because the occurrence of nasals is also limited there. The reason for this conclusion was the fact that it is again only [m] found after [r] in Standard Czech as the following examples show:[20]

(22) [fi̯rmot] *hřmot*
      [tr̥mɛn] *třmen*

Although it seems reasonable to analyze this limitation also as an instance of neutralization of the opposition /m/ × /n/ × /ň/, we realized eventually that it was not consistent with how we interpreted similar cases of the limited occurrence of sounds. The most conspicuous example is the non-occurrence of fricatives and nasals in the vicinity of [ř] at the end of a syllable. Here, only stops are found:

(23) (a)   [pɛpř̥] *pepř*
             [ʔuvɲɪtř̥] *uvnitř*
             [mokr̥] *mokř* (SSJČ)
      (b)   [buř̥t] *buřt*
             [pɪř̥k] *Pyřk* (proper name)[21]

We already mentioned examples (23a) under (12) and analyzed the stops as re-alizations of the archi-phonemes /P/, /T/ and /K/. However, in light of the fact that the archi-phonemes are not opposed here to fricatives or nasals, it may be argued that it is actually the opposition between various manners of articulation that is suspended. Elsewhere, there is a functional difference between oral stops [p], [t], [c], [k], fricatives [f], [s], [ʃ], [x], and nasal stops [m], [n], [ɲ] (cf. e.g.

---

20 Except for derivates of these words, there is no other example of the occurrence or the ř-sound before a nasal in Standard Czech. NLA and Kott I mention the word *křmen*, but it is hardly used in Modern Czech. Let us also note that in non-standard (dialectal) Czech, other nasals are possible after [r], cf. [rnoṷcɪ] *řnouti* (NLA) and [ɱavi:] *řňavý* (NLA).

21 [ř̥p] has not been found. [c] does not occur in the vicinity of [ř̥] at the end of a syllable.

[lɛp] *lep* × [lɛf] *lev* × [lɛm] *lem*), but this difference is not utilized syllable-finally in the vicinity of [r̝]. Thus, the stops in the examples under (23) should rather be interpreted as archi-phonemes (let us mark them /P̲/, /T̲/ and /K̲/) resulting from neutralization of the oppositions /p/ × /b/ × /f/ × /v/ × /m/, /t/ × /d/ × /s/ × /z/ × /n/, and /k/ × /g/ × /x/ × /h/.

However, situations similar to this are found elsewhere, too. Having examined the constituency of Czech words, we will find out that the occurrence of many sounds is limited in certain contexts. One other limitation concerns again the ř-sound. At the beginning of a syllable it can be followed by no other fricative than [v]:

(24) [r̝vaːt] *řvát*
    [br̝vɛ] *Břve* (place name)

As shown above, the place of articulation of nasals seems not to be functional in this context, and it appears that even the place of articulation of fricatives is not functional, for only [v] occurs there. In contrast, the place of articulation of stops is distinctive in this situation: cf. [fi̯rbɛt] *hřbet* or [kr̝tu] *křtu*. Still, the occurrence of fricatives is limited, which may induce us to interpret it as neutralization and to introduce another archi-phoneme /F̲/ as its result.

The occurrence of fricatives is not only limited after the ř-sound, though. Once again only [v] occurs syllable-initially after velar fricative [x] and laryngeal fricative [ɦ] as the examples under (25) show. This limitation could also be interpreted as neutralization the result of which is the archi-phoneme /F̲/ realized as [v].

(25) [xviːlɛ] *chvíle*
    [ɦvost] *hvozd*

More examples of similar limited occurrence of phonetic forms can be found. In the end it seems that all oppositions postulated for the Czech consonantal system get neutralized under certain circumstances. These neutralizations necessarily require the introduction of additional archi-phonemes whose appearance would be limited to specific contexts. The analysis gets quite complicated. It may be argued that the loss of simplicity is compensated by a more precise analysis, but the appropriateness of such an analysis should also be considered. The limitations under question could perhaps be accounted for by other means.

If we examine the conditions under which neutralization of voicing and phonotagm-initial neutralization of /m/ × /n/ × /ɲ/ take place with the conditions for the other tentative neutralizations, we will realize that they are not the same. Neutralization of voicing takes place at end of a diaereme group irrespective of what phonemes occur in that particular place. It is also operative before all voiceless consonants and, with the exception of /v/, before all voiced consonants. It thus affects *all* phoneme pairs participating in the voicing opposition. Similarly, neutralization of /m/ × /n/ × /ň/ takes place before any consonant and any semiconsonant, although only nasals are affected this time. Yet, the conditions under which it takes place are very general: it is before *any* consonant and *any* semiconsonant. On the contrary, if we assume that the same neutralization takes place before /ř/, it is obvious that the conditions pertain to only one phoneme. The same is true for the tentative neutralization of the manner of articulation proposed in connection with examples (23), and also the tentative neutralization suggested in connection with examples (24): in both cases the conditions would again pertain only to /ř/. Admittedly, the latter tentative neutralization would also affect fricatives (see examples (22)), but not occlusives. To put it otherwise, if we claimed that the communication difference between various places of articulation is suspended before /ř/, it would have to be specified that in the case of occlusives the difference is maintained.

Similar problems would have to be coped with in other tentative neutralizations, but none of them is as general as the neutralization of voicing and the phonotagm-initial neutralization of nasals. It seems more appropriate not to pursue such a solution and to interpret the discussed limitations as instances of defective distribution. In effect, we will account for the problem in more general terms because neutralization is just a special type of defective distribution. For example, the fricatives and the nasals will be said to have defective distribution because they cannot co-occur with /ř/ phonotagm-finally. Similarly, the fricatives /f/, /s/, /z/, /š/, /ž/, /x/ and /h/ will be said to have defective distribution because they cannot occur after a velar fricative. All such limitations will be accounted for with special collocational restrictions (see §9.2 on this notion).

Chapter Five: PROLEGOMENA TO THE PHONOTACTIC ANALYSIS

5.1 Self-contained phonotactic entities

Phonotactics may be understood as a system of phonotactic entities or, which amounts to the same, as a system of syntagmatic entities in a phonological system (Mulder – Hervey 2009).[1] When applied in description, phonotactics is an analytic account of such a system. A syntagmatic entity is an entity capable of functional ordering or an entity with constituents commutable with orderable entities. In effect, there are two kinds of phonotactic entity, the minimum and maximum one. The minimum phonotactic entity is a PHONEME. Phonemes are capable of functional ordering and are the smallest phonological entities with this capacity because their constituents, i.e. distinctive features, are not functionally orderable. The bundle of distinctive features 'labial nasal' is equal to the bundle 'nasal labial' (i.e. to the phoneme /m/ in Czech), but the bundle of phonemes /lem/ is not equal to the bundle /mel/ (cf. the words *lem* × *mel*). The maximal phonotactic entity is a PHONOTACTIC CONSTRUCTION. It is a self-contained combination of phonemes which are its immediate as well as ultimate constituents. The phonotactics describes both types of entity. On the one hand, it accounts for the structure and constituency of phonotactic constructions (i.e. it determines of which phonemes or phoneme types phonotactic constructions are built), and on the other, it accounts for the distribution and combinations of phonemes within such constructions (i.e. it determines the limits of actual occurrences and mutual combinability of phonemes).

By DISTRIBUTION of a phoneme is meant the set of its occurrences within phonotactic constructions in a given language (Mulder – Hervey *op. cit.*). Basically, two types of occurrence are distinguished. First, an entity (a phoneme) can occur in a certain place within a selected frame of reference (e.g. in nuclear position or at the beginning of a phonotagm). Second, it can occur in the presence of some other entity (e.g. after /t/ or before /a/). In short, phonemes not only occur in a certain context, they also combine with each other. A COMBINATION OF PHONEMES (or a phoneme combination) will be defined as any complex of two or

---

1   On the theory of phonotactics in general, see e.g. Sigurd (1968) and Goldsmith (2011) with references.

more phonemes. Only combinations which are self-contained are phonotactic constructions.

Something is self-contained if it represents all relative dependencies of all of its constituents or of all of its members, i.e. of phonemes in the case of phoneme combinations (Mulder 1989: 84–7). A phonotactic construction is a complete, autonomous and well-formed combination of phonemes which does not require, at a given level of analysis, anything else. At another level of analysis it may require other features, but as a phonotactic entity it is self-sufficient. The other level is here the level of para-phonotactics because phonotactic entities are usually accompanied by para-phonotactic features (such as accent) to form para-phonotactic entities (such as accent groups). PhFs of directly attested sentences usually correspond to para-phonotactic entities, and since sentences are autonomous signa, it follows that the phonotactic bases of sentences are self-contained.

The self-containedness of a combination is not the same as its well-formedness. Although a self-contained combination is necessarily well-formed, a well-formed combination need not be self-contained. The pre-nuclear combination /Tb/ is well-formed in Czech (but not in English, for instance), but it is not self-contained because it is not an autonomous phonotactic entity. By definition, consonants are dependent on some other entity whose presence they require. In Czech this entity is either a vowel or a semiconsonant. However, this dependency is not represented in the combination in question. On the other hand, the combination /TbāT/ (cf. *dbát*) is well-formed and self-contained in Czech because all dependencies of its constituents, i.e. of /T/, /b/, /ā/ and /T/, are represented there: the consonants /T/ and /b/ are dependent on the vowel /a/, and so is the final /T/; the complex as a whole does not, at the level of phonotactics, require anything else.

In the next chapter it will argued that self-contained entities are describable upon the DU defined as a self-contained bundle of positions. Every phoneme of a phonotactic construction is assumed to occupy a certain position. A DU is an underlying network of these positions. An instance of a DU where all of its positions are occupied by a phoneme or left empty is a PHONOTAGM. From the perspective of its constituency, a phonotagm may be either a single phoneme or a phonotactic construction. In the first case all but one positions of the DU are empty. Czech is such a language where the PhF of the word *a* "and" corresponds to a single phoneme /a/ which is at the same time a phonotagm. French is another example (cf. /o/ = *eau* "water"). But if a phonotagm corresponds to a phonotactic construction, then at least two positions are occupied by phonemes. This is the most common situation. In some languages it is the normal situation: according to Gabjanda (1976), PhFs of words in San Martín Quechua are always built of at least two phonemes. Now, since a phonotagm may contain only one phoneme, the terms *phonotagm* and *phonotactic construction* are not synonymous. Both are, however, self-contained phonotactic entities.

The phonotagm is the most complex entity in phonotactics. However, PhFs of words usually contain more phonotagms. Thus, there can be groups of phonotagms, but such groups are not separate phonotactic entities. First of all, if a PhF of a word can be analyzed into two phonotagms, it follows that phonotactic properties holding for the two phonotagms must also hold for the whole form; otherwise, the phonotagms would not be self-contained. Furthermore, groups of phonotagms do not occur by themselves, but are generally accompanied by other phonological features.

Let us take a look at the Czech word *ona*. Its PhF can be analyzed into two phonotagms /o/ and /na/. However, this group of two phonotagms is something other than /o/ and /na/.[2] There is a functional difference between *ona* "she" on the one hand and *o* "about" and *na* "upon" on the other. In both cases we have the same phonotagms /o/ and /na/, but their groupment is not the same. The features determining the groupment are therefore important here. As already explained in §2.3, the description of such features is relegated to another level of analysis, namely to para-phonotactics.

5.2 Accent and diaereme

Every linguistic analysis should start with sentences, since the sentence is the model of any complete utterance, and we naturally want to begin our investigation with such utterances. Sentences are signa and their allomorphs have PhFs. PhFs of Czech sentences are para-phonotactic entities analyzable into a group of phonotagms accompanied by para-phonotactic features. Suprasegmental features such as a melody contour or intensity are always involved in sentence utterances, and para-phonotactics accounts for their phonological functions. The function of the para-phonotactic features is distinctive if one such feature is commutable with another, or contrastive if their purpose is to group entities into higher-order structures. In Czech, PhFs of sentence intonations are distinctive para-phonotactic entities, but we will not be interested in these. Much more important are contrastive para-phonotactic features. In §2.3 we mentioned two types of them: accent and diaereme. Para-phonotactic entities involving accent have been called accent groups, and those involving diaereme have been called diaereme groups. We will demonstrate in this section the usefulness of these concepts in the analysis of Czech.

---

2   The group must here be understood as a set. The point is that a set containing two members *x* and *y* is something else than two sets, one containing *x* and the other containing *y*.

Accent groups are phonological models of certain aspects of articulatory and acoustic properties relevant for communication and usually associated with stress units. The latter are purely phonic entities defined as sequences of syllables with specific articulatory and acoustic properties; usually one of these syllables is marked with some phonic prominence known as stress. The exact phonetic nature and characteristics of a stress unit are specific to particular languages as well as the way stress is used in communication. Differently realized stresses may have the same phonological function, and similarly realized stresses may have distinct phonological functions. It is one of the reasons why accent as a sum of functional properties will be distinguished from stress as a sum of physical properties.

The phonetic nature and the phonological function of stress in Czech have for a long time been a subject of research and controversy. Although the language is traditionally described as having a stress fixed on the first syllable, it has not been possible to find any stable phonetic properties of this first syllable that would make it different from the other syllables. The initial syllable may have some specific phonic properties, but they are not always realized. Stress units are in Czech rather marked by internal cohesion given by a certain melodic contour, and it is this cohesion that distinguishes one stress unit from another. The stressedness of the first syllable is then derived from this cohesion (see Palková 2012 for an overview).

The phonetic cohesion of Czech stress units has been investigated, for example, on the pairs of syntagms reproduced under (1). The research (Palková – Volín 2003, Palková 2004a) has shown that the pairs are phonetically different and that the hearers can tell them apart. In the examples the small vertical lines indicate the assumed onset of stress units. The onset can be realized in various ways, and it is interesting that it may even be realized by a melodic downfall (cf. Duběda 2005: 142).

(1) [ˈsvjɛtloˈvɲiːmajiː] *světlo vnímají*   [ˈsvjɛtlovɲiːˈmajiː] *světlo v ní mají*
     "they perceive light"   "they have light in it"
     [ˈprocɪˈvɲɛjʃiːm] *proti vnějším*   [ˈprocɪvɲɛjʃiːm] *protivnějším*
     "against internal"   "more bothering"
     [ˈjɛʃcɛjɛˈtɛlɛ] *ještě je tele*   [ˈjɛʃcɛˈjɛtɛlɛ] *ještě jetele*
     "it is still a calf"   "more shamrock"
     [ˈʔokolovraːtɛk] *o kolovrátek*   [ˈʔokoloˈvraːtɛk] *okolo vrátek*
     "for a spinning-wheel"   "around the turnstile"

The syntagms such as *světlo vnímají* and *světlo v ní mají* are distinguished by a melodic contour which organizes the utterances in a certain but distinct way.

Phonology must account for this difference, as it is relevant for communication, and the most appropriate way is to do it is by means of para-phonotactic features. The utterances will be said to correspond to the same string of phonemes, since they consist of the same speech sounds, but the phonemes are grouped to different units by means of para-phonotactic features called for convenience accent. This interpretation is in agreement with the function of the melodic contour in examples such as (1). In Czech, accent groups are therefore para-phonotactic entities realized by sequences of syllables with particular suprasegmental/prosodic properties. They are analyzable into bases corresponding to phonotagms (i.e. bundles of phonemes) and para-phonotactic features of accent which gather the phonotagms to particular groups. Accent corresponds here to the sum of properties uniting syllables into one stress unit.

Examples under (1) are analyzed as follows. The underlining indicates extensions of the accent groups.

(2) /svjetlo vňīmajī/   /svjetlovňī majī/
     /proťi vňejšīm/   /proťivňejšīm/
     /ješťeje tele/   /ješťe jetele/
     /okolovrāteK/   /okolo vrāteK/

Although the melodic contour helps determine boundaries between the individual accent groups, it need not signal sharp boundaries precisely as the contour is simply continuous. Sharp boundaries may be signaled by other means. Pauses, unless they are accidental interruptions of speech, are the most obvious signals of boundaries. Quite often, too, phonemes across boundaries of a unit are realized in a markedly different way than those inside the unit. This fact has been known from many languages, for instance, from English where there is a difference between pairs like *a name* × *an aim*, *see them eat* × *see the meat* etc.[3] In Czech, boundary-initial vowels may be realized with a glottal stop or with a period of irregular or breathy phonation.[4] The utterances given below under (3a–e) differ only in the presence of a glottal stop or its equivalents. The latter are usually said to occur word-initially before a vocoid, but as examples (3f–k) prove, they occur also across what might be grammatically described as a moneme boundary, namely before a prefix attached to the base with an initial vocoid. However, in these cases the use of the glottal stop is optional (VSČ: 34–40, Ze-

---

3   See Jones (1931, 1956), Lehiste (1960) and Hoard (1966). Malmberg (1964) mentions
    similar examples from other languages.
4   Non-modal phonation in Czech has been investigated by Skarnitzl (2004). — The glottal
    stop in Czech was also investigated by Lehiste (1965). See also Romportl (1984) who
    discusses the function and distribution of the Czech glottal stop.

man 2008: 74–6), and according to Novotná-Hůrková (1974) it is not even much common.[5]

(3) (a) ['sʔok] *z ok* "from eyes" × ['sok] *sok* "rival"
    (b) ['sʔuxɛm] *s uchem* "with the ear" × ['suxɛm] *suchem* "dryness (ins. sg.)"
    (c) ['kʔosaːm] *k osám* "to the axes" × ['kosaːm] *kosám* "scythe (dat. pl.)"
    (d) ['fʔaktɛx] *v aktech* "in acta" × ['faktɛx] *faktech* "fact (loc. pl.)"
    (e) ['potʔokɛm] *pod okem* "under the eye" × ['potokɛm] *potokem* "through a rivulet"
    (f) ['nɛjʔobliːbɛːɲɛjʃiː] *nejoblíbenější* "most likeable"
    (g) ['bɛsʔotkladɲɛ] *bezodkladně* "without delay"
    (h) ['poʔuʒɪl] *použil* "he used"
    (i) ['naʔopak] *naopak* "the other way round"
    (j) ['naʔutʃɪt] *naučit* "to learn someone"
    (k) ['nɛʔuːstupɲiː] *neústupní* "insistent (pl.)"

Let us start with the forms ['potʔokɛm] *pod okem* "under the eye" and ['potokɛm] "through a rivulet". Both constitute one stress unit characterized by a particular melodic contour, but the former contains a glottal stop, whereas the latter does not. It would be possible to analyze this sound as a realization of a new phoneme /ʔ/, and to say that the words differ in their phonematic constituency. However, the adequacy of such an analysis is doubtful because, as pointed out, there are forms in which the presence of the glottal stop is optional. The word *nejoblíbenější* is one of them: it can be pronounced as ['nɛjʔobliːbɛːɲɛjʃiː] or as ['nɛjobliːbɛːɲɛjʃiː]. The same holds for *použil, naopak, naučit* or *neústupní*. The syntagm *pod oknem* can also be pronounced without the glottal stop as ['podokɛm] (note that obstruents devoice before a glottal stop), but in that case its pronunciation would not be distinguished from that of a hypothetical word *podokem*.

This brings us to the function of the glottal stop in Czech: Czechs use it to indicate that what they pronounce are two words (or monemes), not one. It is most obvious in the pronunciation of syntagms such as *z ok, s uchem, k osám* and *v aktech*, that is, of syntagms involving the prepositions *z* "from", *s* "with",

---

5 Novotná-Hůrková (*op. cit.*: 118) has made one interesting observation: if occurring between two vocoids as in *použil, naopak, naučit* or *neústupní*, the glottal stop is less common provided that the two vocoids are articulatorily and acoustically close as in *použil* and *naopak*. To put it otherwise, she suggests that it is more probable that the glottal stop will be used in words like *naučit* and *neústupný* than in the words like *použil* and *naopak*. See also Volín (2012) on the frequency of the use of the glottal stop. It is less common in normal, not prepared (i.e. not read) speech.

k "to" and *v* "in". If these prepositions precede words beginning with a vowel, the pronunciation of the glottal stop is prescribed for them, so that they are not pronounced like *sok, suchem, kosám* and *faktech* (see VSČ: 39, Zeman 2008: 74). The function of the glottal stop is thus to indicate the boundary between forms. It is obvious that it is a function of groupment: the glottal stop marks where one form ends and the other begins. It is therefore most adequate to interpret it as a realization of contrastive para-phonotactic features. But these features cannot be the features of accent if the latter is to correlate with stress units and melodic contours. As mentioned, the pairs like [ˈpotʔokɛm] *pod okem* × [ˈpotokɛm] *potokem* are both single stress units with comparable melodic contours. To explain the functional difference between them, we introduce diaereme as a type of contrastive para-phonotactic features corresponding to phonetic properties marking boundaries between forms. The diaereme is realized here by a glottal stop (or by irregular phonation or glottalization). The most conspicuous realization of diaereme is of course a pause, but pauses are seldom used in connected speech.[6]

The para-phonotactic entity characterized by boundary-signaling features is a diaereme group. The stress unit [ˈpotʔokɛm] *pod okem* corresponds to two diaereme groups constituting one accent group, but the form [ˈpotokɛm] *potokem* corresponds to just one diaereme group. In the latter the diaereme group coincides with an accent group because the melodic contour and the onset of stress already mark its boundaries. Transcribing diaereme by a double cross, we can express the difference between the pairs like this: /#poT#okem#/ × /#potokem#/. The former is a complex para-phonotactic entity, namely an accent group whose base is two diaereme groups /#poT#/ and /#okem#/. The para-phonotactic analysis of all of the utterances mentioned under (3) will then be as follows:

(4) (a) [ˈsʔok] *z ok* × [ˈsok] *sok* → /#S#oK#/ × /#soK#/
(b) [ˈsʔuxɛm] *s uchem* × [ˈsuxɛm] *suchem* → /#S#uxem#/ × /#suxem#/
(c) [ˈkʔosaːm] *k osám* × [ˈkosaːm] *kosám* → /#K#osám#/ × /#kosám#/
(d) [ˈfʔaktɛx] *v aktech* × [ˈfaktɛx] *faktech* → /#F#aKteX#/ × /#faKteX#/
(e) [ˈpotʔokɛm] *pod okem* × [ˈpotokɛm] *potokem* → /#poT#okem#/ × /#potokem#/
(f) [ˈnɛjʔobliːbɛːɲɛjʃiː] *nejoblíbenější* → /#nej#oblíbeňejšī#/
(g) [ˈbɛsʔotkladɲɛ] *bezodkladně* → /#beS#oTkladňe#/
(h) [ˈpoʔuʒɪl] *použil* → /#po#užil#/
(i) [ˈnaʔopak] *naopak* → /#na#opaK#/

---

6   Naturally, we means deliberately produced pauses, not pauses such as those which are necessarily part of the articulation of stops.

(j)   [ˈnaʔuʧɪt] *naučit* → /#na#utšiT#/
(k)   [ˈnɛʔuːstupɲiː] *neústupní* → /#ne#ūStupňī#/

We can now see why the para-phonotactic level is important for the phonotactic analysis: If the syntagm *pod okem* is realized with a glottal stop, it will not have the same phonotactic structure as the syntagm *potokem*, even though both are realized with three phonic syllables. The former contains two distinct phonotactic bases /poT/ and /okem/, whereas the latter only one, i.e. /potokem/. The bases will further be analyzed from the phonotactic perspective, but it is obvious that para-phonotactic features conditions such an analysis.

5.3 Analysis of the non-syllabic prepositions

Some of the examples presented above under (3) or (4) involve non-syllabic prepositions obligatorily separated from the following words by a glottal stop. We will now examine further the occurrence of these prepositions because their treatment has significant consequences for the phonotactic analysis. First of all, however, a few words need to be said about the mode of analysis.

Every analysis begins with sentences as self-contained vehicles for conveying information. A sentence is a subject of a grammatical analysis. Besides para-syntactic features, a Czech sentence usually contains a syntagm which is analyzed into smaller syntagms and ultimately into pleremes (i.e. words), which are the minimum syntactic entities. But being a signum, a sentence (that is, its particular allomorph) has a PhF which is a subject of a phonological analysis. The PhF of Czech sentences correspond to para-phonotactic entities analyzable into smaller para-phonotactic entities (such as accent groups) which are ultimately analyzed into phonotagms or groups of phonotagms. Now, what we should realize is that grammatical constituents of a sentence need not agree with its phonological constituents.

For example, the grammatical analysis will recognize that the Czech sentence *Lezu na horu.* "I climb the mountain." consists, besides the intonation, of three words *lezu, na* and *horu,* but the phonological analysis will recognize that it consists, besides the PhF of the intonation, of only two units, namely of accent groups /#lezu#/ and /#nahoru#/. These units have some specific phonological (and phonetic) properties which allow us to treat them as phonological constituents in the phonological analysis. The mentioned sentence is homophonous with *Lezu nahoru.* "I climb upward". It has a different grammatical constituency (it consists of only two words), but its phonological organization is the same as that of *Lezu na horu.,* i.e. it also contains two accent groups /#lezu#/ and /#nahoru#/. If, however, the grammatical structure of these sentences was taken into account, the phonological analyses would not be the same. We would recognize that *Lezu na nohu.* contains three words each of which has a PhF, namely /lezu/, /na/ and /horu/. The para-phonotactic features could now be ignored because they would be dealt with in the phonological analysis of sentential para-syntatic features (intonation). The second sentence *Lezu nahoru.* would then be analyzed into two words whose PhFs are /lezu/ and /nahoru/.

Although both approaches are justifiable, it is obvious they yield dissimilar phonological analyzes in the end. The differences are not quite significant for the mentioned sentences, but if a sentence contains a non-syllabic preposition, the two modes of analysis will result in wholly distinct accounts. The non-syllabic prepositions *v* "in", *k* "to", *s* "with" and *z* "from" were already mentioned in §4.3 in connection with neutralization of voicing. They adjoin the following word, namely its first syllable, and may or may not undergo neutralization of voicing. The prepositions have vocalized, i.e. syllabic variants (allomorphs) *ve, ke, se* and *ze,* respectively. Their distribution has not been sufficiently described yet (see Trávníček 1951: 53–9, Kučera 1984, Dickins 1998, Holdeman 2000),[7] and there are probably only three situations summarized under (5) in which one of the variants is obligatorily used. There seems to be a free variance between them elsewhere, although the choice or the probability of either may be conditioned by various means such as the rhythmical structure of the whole sentence, the phonemic constituency of the following word or perhaps even the age or the education of the speaker.

(5)   OBLIGATORY OCCURRENCE OF THE ALLOMORPHS OF V, K, S, Z
(a)   The non-vocalized variants *v, k, s, z* always occur before a vowel-initial word.
(b)   The non-vocalized variants *v, k, s, z* always occur before a word beginning with a single PerP which is not of the same place and manner of articulation, that is, *v* does not occur before a word with an initial /f/ or /v/ etc.
(c)   The vocalized variants *ve, ke, se, ze* always occur before a word beginning with a PerP of the same manner and place of articulation irrespective of the number of PerPs the word begins with (i.e. *ve* always before a word-initial /f/, /v/ or /F/ etc.).

Two facts are important for our discussion: first, except for the situation (5c), the non-syllabic prepositions may occur probably before any word of any constituency, and second, they may be probably always replaced there with their vocal-

---

7   See also the entry in Internet Language Reference Book, <http://prirucka.ujc.cas.cz/?id=770&dotaz=vokalizace> (accessed 3 March 2013).

ized variants except for the situations (5a) and (5b). To put it otherwise, we are dealing with three types of occurrence of the non-syllabic prepositions:

(6) (a) Before words with an initial vowel; the occurrence is obligatory.
     (b) Before words with an initial single PerP (except for the case described under (5b)); the occurrence is obligatory.
     (c) Before words with an initial combination of PerPs; the occurrence is optional (except for the case described under (5c)).

The first occurrence was already touched upon in the previous section. It is the situation when the word-initial vowel is obligatorily realized with a glottal stop as in *z ok* ['sʔok], *s uchem* ['sʔuxɛm], *k osám* ['kʔosaːm] or *v aktech* ['fʔaktɛx] (see (3) above). Viewing the glottal stop as a boundary signal and as a realization of diaereme, we have interpreted the syntagms as two diaereme groups within a single accent group, which makes them different from the PhFs of *sok* ['sok], *suchem* ['suxɛm], *kosám* ['kosaːm] and *faktech* ['faktɛx] interpreted as single diaereme groups (see under (4a–d) above). The consequence of this analysis is such that we have to recognize the diaereme groups /#S#/, /#K#/ and /#F#/ which are self-contained para-phonotactic entities; their bases are formed by a single voicing archi-phoneme: /S/ for both *s* and *z*, /K/ for *k* and /F/ for *v*.[8]

A question now suggests itself: what is the status of these archi-phonemes in phonotactics, that is, can the archi-phonemes /S/, /K/, /F/ be interpreted as self-contained phonotactic entities (phonotagms)? They surely can, but the resultant analysis will become unnecessarily complicated. It is rather a matter of accidence that these and no other archi-phonemes function as self-contained phonotactic entities. It could be hardly claimed that the sounds [s], [z], [k] and [f] the archi-phonemes are realized with are phonetically or phonologically preordained to function as non-syllabic prepositions, and Czech could well have other non-syllabic prepositions realized, for example, as [p], [ʃ] or [x]. Much more problematic is nevertheless the dilemma we will have when analyzing a form like /oK/ *ok* "eye (gen. pl.)". We will have found out that both /o/ and /K/ can function as self-contained phonotactic entities—we assume that about /K/, and /o/ is the base of the word *o* "about". Now, since /ona/ *ona* "she" is analyzed into /o/ and /na/ because both are self-contained phonotactic entities (cf. *o* "about" and *na* "on"), we are in a position to analyze /oK/ into two self-contained entities /o/ and /K/ for the very same reasons. Nevertheless, we would not like to pursue such an analysis because the word *ok* is realized as a single syllable. Although

---

8 That there is neutralization of voicing is proven by the fact that the voicing of the prepositions is always predictable from the context: the prepositions are realized as voiceless before the glottal stop.

our phonotactic analysis is not dependent on the syllabic structure (a point to be explained in §6.6), the agreement with phonetic facts is a significant aspect of the justification of the analysis. Thus, we would view /oK/ as a single phonotagm, but then we would have to determine which phoneme functions there as its nucleus. Since both /o/ and /K/ can, by assumption, acquire this function, the choice of one of them will be arbitrary. The choice of /o/ as the nucleus is more reasonable, but that means that /K/ is a non-nuclear entity. Analogically, the same analysis will hold for every occurrence of /K/ (as well as /S/ and /F/) in conjunction of phonemes we called vowels. Consequently, the only situation in which /K/ (and the same holds for /S/ and /F/) would function as the nucleus of phonotagms is in the base of the diaereme group /#K#/.

From the overall perspective, it seems more appropriate to choose an alternative approach in which problems of this kind can be avoided and which, we believe, is simpler and more adequate. The base of the diaereme groups /#S#/, /#K#/ and /#F#/ will not be interpreted as self-contained phonotactic entities. Instead, it will be proposed that a genuine phonotagm in Czech may only contain a phoneme we called a vowel or, under special circumstances, a semiconsonant /r/ or /l/. Therefore, /S/, /K/ and /F/ are not self-contained phonotactic entities and are not well-formed at the phonotactic level. Still, they can and do function as bases of well-formed and self-contained para-phonotactic entities. Following Gardner – Hervey (1983) who encountered a similar problem in the syntax of English, we propose calling such bases A-PHONOTACTIC BASES.[9] A-phonotactic bases are bases of para-phonotactic entities which are built of phonotactic entities (i.e. phonemes) but which do not have the status of phonotagms and are not self-contained phonotactic entities. Accordingly, such bases are removed from the domain of phonotactics.

Let us now return to the occurrence of non-syllabic prepositions. At the beginning of this section two modes of analysis were outlined: one which takes heed of the syntactic analysis of a sentence, and one which does not. When the non-syllabic prepositions occur before a vowel-initial word, both modes will give the same analysis—the prepositions will be singled out—, but in the other situations the resultant analyses will be dissimilar. We will start with the situation when the prepositions occur before a single PerP; as said, this occurrence is obligatory except for the homorganic word-initial PerPs.

The combinations we get from the occurrence of non-syllabic prepositions before a word beginning with one PerP are for a large part identical to those

---

9   In Bičan (2008b) we viewed them as phonotagms with empty nuclei. However, as Barry Heselwood (personal communication) pointed out, the nucleus cannot by definition be empty. We correct our analysis here.

found at the beginning of words, for example /kr/ in *k roku* "to the year" and /kr/ in *kroku* "step (gen. sg.)", /svj/ in *s věže* "from the tower down" and /svj/ in *svěže* "freshly". However, there are several unique combinations:

(7) /Kp/ in *k poslechu* (cf. /Kb/ in *kbelík*)
     /Kz/ in *k zemi* (cf. /Ks/ in *xylofon*)
     /Kď/ in *k dívce* (cf. /Kť/ in the place name *Ktiš*)
     /Kž/ in *k životu* (cf. /Kš/ in *kšilt*)
     /Kx/ in *k chalupě*
     /Kh/ in *k houslím*

As we see, /Kp/, /Kz/, /Kď/ and /Kž/ have at least a parallel in the word-initial combinations where their voicing counterparts are attested. Their non-occurrence at the beginning of a word can therefore be viewed as a matter of accidence. On the other hand, the combinations /Kx/ and /Kh/ do not have any comparable parallel in PhFs of single words. Both are combinations of two velars. No word begins with such a combination, although it can begin with a combination of two labials, two alveolars or two palatals: cf. /Fp/ in *vpálit*, /Fb/ in *vbalit*, /Ts/ in *cena*, /Tz/ in *dzinkat*, /Šť/ in *štěstí* and /Šď/ in *ždímat*. Examining further the constituency of combinations found at the beginning and at the end of words, we will find out that no such combination contains two instances of a velar irrespective of whether they would stand next to each other or would be separated by another PerP. In contrast, such combinations may contain two instances of a labial (cf. /FSpj/ in *vzpěrač*), of an alveolar (cf. /Tkn/ in *tknout*) or of a palatal (cf. /ŠTkň/ in *štkni*).

It is obvious that if Czech sentences are analyzed without regard to their syntactic structure, then the combinations /Kx/ and /Kh/ are possible at the beginning of a phonotagm because the PhF of the accent group /#Kxalupje#/ begins with such a combination. However, if the analysis is conducted with regard to the syntactic structure, that is, if *k chalupě* is said to consist of two PhFs /K/ and /xalupje/, then /Kx/ would never be found at the beginning of a phonotagm. Since the same applies also to /Kh/, it means that combinations of two velars are not possible phonotagm-initially. And such combinations are not even possible phonotagm-finally. But this conclusion can only be reached if the syntactic structure is considered.

The last context where the non-syllabic prepositions occur is before a word with an initial combination of PerPs. It seems that they are freely replaceable with their vocalized variants *ve*, *ke*, *se* and *ze* here. Again, the resultant combinations are of two types: First, we get combinations also attested word-initially (e.g. /Str/ in *s traktorem*, cf. /Str/ in *strach*); they are not interesting for us now.

The second type is more important because these are combinations which are not found word-initially. Here are some examples:

(8) (a) /SKt/ in *s kterým* (also *se kterým*)
          /SXřb/ in *z hřbetu* (also *ze hřbetu*)
          /kjm/ in *k jménu* (also *ke jménu*)
     (b) /KPŠtr/ in *k pštrosovi* (also *ke pštrosovi*)
          /vMdl/ in *v mdlobách* (also *ve mdlobách*)
          /KTkl/ in *k tklivému* (also *ke tklivému*)
     (c) /zrt/ in *z rtů* (also *ze rtů*)
          /vlž/ in *v lžíci* (also *ve lžíci*)

All of these examples have a variant with a vocalized preposition. It is usually asserted that the vocalized prepositions are used in case a difficult combination would arise, but it is not specified what a difficult combination is. The combinations under (8b) could be labeled as such, yet the native speakers may not have problems with them, and the non-vocalized variants are more common for these particular syntagms than the vocalized ones *ke pštrosovi*, *ve mdlobách* and *ke tklivému*. For (8a) and (8c), however, the vocalized variants are commoner.[10] Finally, the combinations under (8c) are unique because there may be some doubt whether the /r/ and /l/ are nuclear in them; we will return to this problem in §10.2.

The combinations such as these are not found word-initially, and their constituency does not usually have a parallel there. For instance, if /K/ stands before an occlusive like /t/ in *který*, it is always the first phoneme of the phonotagm, that is, it is never preceded by another PerP. In this respect, /SKt/ in *s kterým* is exceptional. Similarly, /j/ is never found between two PerPs at the beginning of a word, which makes /kjm/ in *k jménu* exceptional, too. Likewise, no word begins with a combination of three occlusives, and /KTkl/ in *k tklivému* is thus quite unusual. Now, it is obvious that when Czech sentences are analyzed with regard to their syntactic structure, such combinations will not be found word-initially, which gives us a reason to view them as impossible due to their unattested and usual constituency. If the syntactic structure is disregarded, they must be accounted for as a structural possibility, even though all of the unusual combinations may be avoided by using the vocalized variants.

There are therefore two ways how the non-syllabic prepositions can be approached, and in general, two ways how PhFs of sentences are to be analyzed. The first disregards the syntactic structure and divides their PhFs into para-pho-

---

10 Checked against the Czech National Corpus and Google.com (the situation as of 3 March 2013). We must realize that the examples were taken from written texts, and the situation may be quite different in spoken communication.

notactic constituents the bases of which are then analyzed in phonotactics. The second takes heed of the sentential syntactic structure; it divides sentences into pleremes (words) whose PhFs are then investigated in phonotactics. From the methodological point of view, the first approach is nevertheless preferable because the phonological analysis is not dependent on grammar or distorted with it. Yet in the case of Czech the second approach seems to be more appropriate. Starting with words as syntactic constituents, we can account for regularities and limitations of phoneme combinations within them, and then point out differences in combinations arising from the occurrence of non-syllabic prepositions. In particular, we will be able to state and explain the following points:

(9) (a) Since some combinations are also found word-initially, certain prepositional syntagms are potentially confusable with single words (for example, *Co s ní?* "What [to do] with her?" is homophonous with *Co sní?* "What will he/she eat?").

  (b) Since other combinations are not found word-initially, it may be a reason why they are quite often avoided by employing vocalized prepositions instead (for example, this may explain why *ke jménu* is more common than *k jménu*).

  (c) The occurrence of a sequence of phonemes not found word-initially may be viewed as a signal of a boundary between grammatical units (for example, the occurrence of /Kx/ may suggest that there is a grammatical boundary between the velars).

These are some advantages of the word-based approach, and it is the one we have chosen in our phonotactic analysis. This choice, however, requires that the PhFs of the non-syllabic prepositions *s, z, v* and *k* are treated as a separate category, namely, as a-phonotactic bases because they cannot be viewed as self-contained phonotactic entities for reasons explained above in connection with *v aktech × faktech*.

5.4 Accidental gaps vs. structural restrictions

Phonotactics analyzes the syntagmactic aspect of PhFs. Following Hervey (1978), we will distinguish between three types of such forms.

The first type is DIRECTLY ATTESTED PHONOLOGICAL FORMS. These are PhFs of allomorphs of signa, and are thus directly attested in the data, so to speak. They form the basis for our analysis. To be precise, directly attested PhFs are only the forms of sentences because sentences are self-contained vehicles for communication, and every speech event corresponds to a sentence. All other forms are indirectly attested. However, since words can function as bases of sentences and since words are recorded in dictionaries of Standard Czech, we will also regard their PhFs to be directly attested.

Secondly, there are INDIRECTLY ATTESTED PHONOLOGICAL FORMS. These are functional components of directly attested PhFs. Allomorphs are seldom phonologically simple—they are generally complexes of several phonological entities. For example, the PhF /#perñīK#/ of Czech *perník* is analyzable into the phonotagms /per/ and /ñīK/ and the respective para-phonotactic features (accent and diaereme). The phonotagm /per/ is analyzable into the components (phonemes) /p/, /e/ and /r/; these phonemes are ultimately analyzable into bundles of distinctive features, for example /p/ into voiceless labial occlusive. All of these are merely analytical components of the directly attested PhF /#perñīK#/, and are consequently only indirectly attested by its courtesy.

Finally, the third type is POTENTIAL PHONOLOGICAL FORMS. These forms are neither directly attested as PhFs of allomorphs nor indirectly attested as their analytical components. Nevertheless, they are still regarded to be phonologically well-formed in a particular language. They are established by implication, by a method of extrapolation, which is "calculation from known terms of a series of other terms which lie outside the range of known terms" (Hervey 1978: 41, fn. 4). To put it otherwise, it is calculation of potential PhFs from the set of directly and indirectly attested PhFs. Potential PhFs are those which are well-formed, and which, should there ever be such a need, could function as forms of signa or of their analytical components. A phonological theory, if it is to be an adequate tool for the explanation of the functioning of language, must take into its account even such forms. It would be wrong to adopt a strictly corpus-based approach and assume that only the forms attested in our data are possible. A language is an open-ended system which can acquire new words with previously unattested form, for example by coinage or borrowing. At the same time, however, it is wrong to assume that anything is really possible in a language, that is, any combination of phonemes could function as a PhF of some signum (e.g. /mjhtgbsj/ in English or Czech).

In short, we must admit that besides directly and indirectly attested PhFs there are forms which are not directly or indirectly attested, but which are still possible, and forms which are also not attested, but which are impossible. The former are accidentally missing, i.e. they are accidental gaps in the structure, whereas the latter are regularly missing, i.e. their occurrence is restricted by the structure. Now, is it possible to draw a line between these two cases? Can we determine what the potential PhFs are? Let us express the problem in more general terms: If some entity (or a combination of entities) is found to occur under conditions *a*, but is not found to occur under conditions *b*, is it possible to ascertain whether the non-occurrence is a consequence of the conditions *b* or whether it is independent of them? If the non-occurrence is dependent on the conditions, we can say that the semiotic system in question is so shaped that it regularly prevents the entity from occurring under certain conditions. But if the non-occurrence is independent of the conditions, it is from the perspective of the semiotic system purely accidental that the entity does not occur there. It may be that the data are incomplete or that the semiotic system does not make use of all of its potentials. The point is whether these two theoretical possibilities can be clearly and precisely differentiated by some criteria.

The mentioned problem is not relevant to phonology only, but to linguistics (or semiotics) in general, but it will be considered here only in reference to combinations of phonemes. Many linguists take for granted the distinction between regular and accidental non-occurrence of phoneme combinations, but few of them have really considered whether the categories can be set apart and how. The problem was especially discussed in Fischer-Jørgensen (1952), Saporta – Olson (1958), Spang-Hanssen (1958 and 1959), Scholes (1966), Vestergaard (1967), Mulder (1968), Hervey (1978) or Algeo (1978). For example, Fischer-Jørgensen (1952: 33), in agreement with Spang-Hanssen (1958 and 1959, chapter 1), argues that "it is theoretically impossible to fix a non-arbitrary borderline between law and accident. Laws may be stated as deviations from accidental distributions; and there are many degrees of deviation". While there is some reason in their arguments, we think it is not only possible but above all desirable to have criteria by which some non-occurring combinations could be declared well-formed (i.e. actually or potentially possible) and others ill-formed (i.e. impossible). Moreover, we are convinced that the issue can be solved internally within the semiotic system itself, and not externally in reference to intuitions of speakers. Therefore, we will not exploit the idea of, for example, Scholes (1966) according to whom there are several degrees of well-formedness and of acceptability of a potential PhF.

To begin with, we propose a simple criterion of well-formedness based on the idea that a hypothesis is corroborated as long as it is not refuted:

(10) CRITERION OF WELL-FORMEDNESS
    A combination of phonemes is well-formed (i.e. possible) as long as it does not violate any structural rule otherwise valid elsewhere in the description.

The criterion does not, however, solve our problem because it just says that accidental is what cannot be considered systematic. This is in fact the opposite of Fischer-Jørgensen's (1952) and Spang-Hanssen's views according to which systematic is "what cannot reasonably be considered accidental" (see Spang-Hanssen

1959: 26–5). However, we find it simpler and more reasonable to assume that any unattested combination is possible in a given language as long as it cannot be demonstrated that it disagrees with some regular pattern of the language expressible by a structural rule. The criterion can also be applied to directly attested combinations of phonemes: If there is some pattern in certain combinations and if this pattern is not followed in some other combination, it is a reason either to reject the pattern as not regular or the combination as alien to the system in question. The latter option refers to the fact that spontaneous everyday speech often contains mispronounced words or onomatopoeia or elements from other languages.

The criterion of well-formedness under (10) makes recourse to a structural rule, so the next step is the definition of what a structural rule is. One useful definition was proposed by Vogt (1954: 31). We adopt it here adding two necessary conditions:

(11) DEFINITION OF STRUCTURAL RULE

A structural rule is a statement concerning the distribution of entities in which at least one of the terms brought into relation by the statement is a class of entities or features.

Necessary conditions: The class must be clearly and unambiguously defined. The statement must hold without exceptions.

The motivation behind this definition is obvious: as Mulder (1968: 198) noted "[n]o theory should include statements which are not simpler or more general than the corresponding statements of fact". Any descriptive statement, if it is to be a structural rule, must generalize. A statement like "/f/ does not occur before /ř/ in Czech" cannot be a structural rule because it does not generalize anything; it just says that some combination is not found. On the contrary, a statement like "the semiconsonants /r/ and /l/ do not occur before /ř/ in Czech" can be a structural rule because it is a generalization—it concerns a well-defined class of phonemes. One may object that if the statement "/f/ does not occur before /ř/ in Czech" is not a structural rule because it does not concern a class of phonemes, then the structural rule must be a statement like "/f/ and /g/ do not occur before /ř/ in Czech" because here a class of phonemes is involved. However, this class is not unambiguously defined. There is no property the two phonemes have in common, i.e. something that would differentiate them from the other phonemes.[11] On the other hand, the class of /r/ and /l/ is unambiguously defined be-

---

11   That these phonemes are sometimes regarded as marginal phonemes or phonemes of foreign origin is a pseudo-property. There is no way of proving it synchronically.

cause these are all and the only members of the class of semiconsonants, and the rule applies to both of them.

The class of features referred to in a structural rule must be clearly delimited, for otherwise the rule will be vague. The rule has always the form of hypothesis, and a hypothesis must be clearly formulated to allow for potential refutation. Of course, it need not be refuted, but the possibility of refutation should not be ruled out beforehand. The rule saying that semiconsonants cannot be combined with /ř/ within a phonotagm is refutable by the existence of a phonotagm in which such a combination is found. It might be that we have overlooked a word where it is attested or that one day there will be a Czech word with such a combination, but until then the generalization holds. Moreover, we will accept only those rules which hold without exceptions. The idea of exceptions is tricky because it could be claimed that any generalization holds except for those cases when it does not. This can make any hypothesis irrefutable: once a refuting counterexample is found, it is relegated to the exceptions, and the hypothesis will stand on unrefuted.

The definition of a structural rule provides a criterion for telling apart whether something is systematically or accidentally missing. If no structural rule can be established other than an ad hoc statement about the non-occurrence in question, it is accidental (cf. Mulder 1968: 233). As already noted, it is possible we have missed some important generalization for which a structural rule could be formulated, but until it is formulated, the non-occurrence is as accidental. Thus, the combinations /fř/ and /gř/ are regarded to be well-formed in Czech, even though they are not attested.

5.5 On "syllabification"

An analysis of the phonotactic aspect of PhF deals with the constituency of all self-contained phonotactic entities and begins with directly attested PhFs. They can be para-phonotactically complex, but we will be interested only in those corresponding to simple para-phonotactic entities. It is because complex para-phonotactic entities are ultimately analyzable into simple para-phonotactic entities. The bases of the latter correspond either to single phonotagms or to conglomerations of two or more phonotagms. A PhF of a word is then either MONO-PHONOTAGMIC if its phonotactic base consists of a single phonotagm, or POLY-PHONOTAGMIC if its base consists of two or more phonotagms (cf. El-Shakfeh 1987: 95).[12]

---

12   As we argued in §5.3, some bases can also be a-phonotactic, but their analysis does not fall under the topic of this section.

For deciding whether the phonotactic base is poly-phonotagmic or mono-phonotagmic the following criterion is proposed:

(12) CRITERION OF POLY-PHONOTAGMICITY
The base of a PhF of a word is poly-phonotagmic if it can be analyzed (divided) into two or more phonotagms.

Since a phonotagm is a self-contained phonotactic entity, it follows that a PhF 'α' can be divided into two phonotagms 'βγ' if and only if both 'β' and 'γ' are self-contained phonotactic entities. A phonotactic base is self-contained if it is either directly attested as a phonotactic base or if it does not violate any structural rule valid for directly attested phonotactic entities (see the previous section). The first case is illustrated by /jelen/ which is the PhF of *jelen*, and the second case by /klavīr/, the PhF of *klavír* (for the sake of simplicity, we ignore para-phonotactic features here).

Initially, we assume that /jelen/ is a single phonotagm, but this hypothesis is rejected because it can be divided into smaller phonotagms, namely to /je/ attested as the PhF of *je* and /len/ attested as the PhF of *len*. Alternatively, it can be divided into /jel/ attested in *jel* and /len/ attested in *len* (with functional amalgamation; see below). In either case it has been demonstrated that /jelen/ is poly-phonotagmic because it equals to the sum of two phonotagms.

The form /klavīr/ is also initially assumed to be a single phonotagm. We attempt to refute this hypothesis by dividing it into possible phonotagms. One option is /kla/ and /vīr/ of which the latter is attested as the PhF of *vír*, but the reminder /kla/ is not attested. Can it be a potential phonotagm in Czech? As argued in the previous section, a phoneme combination is regarded as possible as long as it does not violate some structural rule. However, no such structural rule can be proposed here, and so there is no ground for rejecting it as a potential phonotagm. The validity of /kla/ is further strengthened by the attested phonotagms /kli/, /klu/ or /Skla/ (cf. *kly*, *klu* and *skla*). Consequently, /klavīr/ is poly-phonotagmic because it can be analyzed into the sum of two phonotagms.

Contrary to the mentioned examples, forms like /jel/ or /kla/ cannot be further divided into smaller phonotagms. Although /jel/ can be analyzed into /je/ directly attested in *je* and to /l/ which is not directly attested, the latter cannot be a well-formed phonotactic entity. There is no directly attested phonotagm which would be built only of /l/. When this phoneme occurs in a phonotagm, it is always accompanied by at least one other phoneme (cf. /ūl/ *úl* or /plŠ/ *plž*). It holds that a semiconsonant (i.e. /l/ as well as /r/) must either be accompanied by a vowel (in which case it is non-nuclear), or preceded by at least one consonant (in which case it is nuclear; see §10.2). If these facts are adopted as structural rules, the analysis of /jel/ into two phonotagms /je/ and /l/ must be rejected.

Although the criterion given under (12) is a reasonable one, it must be supplemented by another one. Let us explain it on the example of the form /hra/ *hra*. When deciding whether this form is poly-phonotagmic, we may conclude that it is because it can be analyzed into /hr/ and /a/. Both of these are directly attested, cf. *hr* in *být hr* and *a*. This kind of analysis will, nevertheless, be rejected on the grounds of material adequacy which has been accepted as a criterion for evaluating good descriptions (see §2.1). Although the phonotagm is not the same entity as the syllable and they need not overlap (see the discussion in §6.6), it makes sense to prefer those analyses where the number of phonotagms agrees with the number of syllables, provided that such an analysis is otherwise consistent with the theory and the rest of the description. In the case of /hra/ there are two equally consistent analyses: one which views it as a single phonotagm, and one which divides it into /hr/ and /a/. The second analysis will be turned down for its assumption that a form realized by one phonotagm (i.e. /hra/) is to be divided into forms realized by two syllables (i.e. /hr/ and /a/). In other words, we will assume that a phonotagm in Czech is never realized by something less than a syllable. Accordingly, the criterion (12) will be supplemented with the following one:

(13) CRITERION OF MATERIAL ADEQUACY
    If several analyses are possible, the most materially adequate one (the one agreeing more with the facts) will be preferred.

The mentioned criteria help us decide whether a PhF contains two or more phonotagms, but they do not tell us how it is actually analyzed into the individual phonotagms. Returning to /jelen/, two concurrent analyses were possible. Which of them is to be preferred, if any preference is given at all? This question is a general analytic problem. In phonotactic descriptions which use the syllable as the unit of reference, it is known as the problem of syllabification. A lot of literature has been devoted to it, but we do not want to deal with or solve all problems connected with it.[13] Suffice to say that the main goal of syllabification can be summed up as follows (cf. Kahn 1976: 35–9): Given a PhF consisting of a certain string of phonemes, syllabification is to divide the string into several well-formed sub-strings (i.e. syllables), so that every phoneme of the string belongs to some sub-string, and no two phonemes belong to two or more substrings. Though it seems clear and obvious, achieving this has not always proven so easy. If a PhF is to be divided into phonotagms, there must be criteria for set-

---

13   See e.g. Pulgram (1970), Clements (1990), Blevins (1995) or Goldsmith (2011).

ting boundaries between the sub-strings. Various strategies have been offered, but it is generally agreed that the output of syllabification should only be well-formed sub-strings. And since sub-strings attested at the beginning or at the end of forms are by assumption well-formed, a criterion sometimes called the Kuryłowicz condition is explicitly or implicitly used (see Bell 1976: 255); here it is rendered to our terminology:[14]

(14) THE KURYŁOWICZ CONDITION
    If an inter-nuclear sequence of PerPs is analyzable into permissible word-initial and word-final combinations, then the phonotagm boundary does not fall between non-permissible combinations.

The condition says in fact nothing else than what has been our practice so far. The analysis of an inter-nuclear combination which produces combinations of phonemes which are directly attested should be preferred over the analysis producing unattested combinations. Since the combinations found at the beginning and at the end of a PhF are well-formed, the inter-nuclear combinations should be divided into such combinations. If we analyze a PhF like /riPka/ *rybka*, the only thinkable division is the one into /riP/ and /ka/. If it were /riPk/ + /a/ or /ri/ + /Pka/, we would get a non-attested combination of consonants in both cases—final or initial /Pk/. Since neither /Pg/ is attested, it is reasonable to have a rule stating that a velar occlusive cannot be preceded by a labial occlusive within a phonotagm. This generalization is valid for all directly attested phonotagms. For that reason, /Pka/ or /piPk/ will be rejected as possible phonotagms in Czech. On the other hand, the analysis of /riPka/ to /riP/ and /ka/ does not violate any thinkable distributional rule, and it is the analysis to be chosen.

In some situations, however, the Kuryłowicz condition falls short. One example is the analysis of /oteFřte/, the PhF of *otevřte* (imp. pl. of *otevřít*). Intuitively, we would say that it is analyzed into three phonotagms because it contains three phonemes functioning elsewhere as nuclear phonemes (i.e. /o/, /e/, /e/). But however /oteFřte/ is treated, we get non-attested combinations: /ote–Fřte/, /oteF–řte/, /oteFř–te/ or /oteFřt–e/.[15] The last two divisions are at once rejected because /Fř/ and /Fřt/ are unparalleled final combinations: /ř/ is attested to precede only occlusives at the end of directly attested phonotagms. So we are left with /ote–Fřte/ and /oteF–řte/, but neither /Fřt/ nor /řt/ is an attested initial combination. Yet it is not possible to postulate any rule other than an ad hoc statement which would declare them impossible. Such a rule would not more-

---

14 After Kuryłowicz (1948) who was the first to exploit it systematically, though, as he notes, the idea was known for a long time.
15 We are only interested here in the analysis of the combination /Fřt/.

over be appropriate because there are similar combinations attested: /Xřt/ in *chřtán* and /řk/ in *řka*. Consequently, it may be assumed that /Fřte/ or /řte/ are potential phonotagms in Czech, and hence /oteFřte/ is analyzable into three phonotagms. Nevertheless, for some potentially poly-phonotagmic forms, for example /loďmi/ *loďmi* (instr. pl. of *loď*), a similar analysis would not be possible. We will return to this in §8.2 as they require a special discussion.

The Kuryłowicz condition is also of no help in situations when there are several analyses possible, which could have already been noticed in the case of /oteFřte/, but it also concerns simpler forms such as /jelen/ which can be analyzed in two ways. The first analysis divides it into /jel/ and /en/, and the second into /je/ and /len/, both being in accord with the Kuryłowicz condition. There are no combinations of PerPs here, but the point is whether either /jel/ or /je/ is a permissible word-final phonotagm, and whether either /len/ or /en/ is a permissible word-initial phonotagm. All of them are permissible due their direct attestation (cf. *je, jel, len* and *en* (the name of the letter *n*), respectively). The medial /l/ could thus belong to both phonotagms, and if it is to be assigned to one or to the other, the choice between the two mentioned divisions must be conditioned by criteria other than the Kuryłowicz condition.

Linguists have approached this problem variously (see the discussion in Bell 1976). Many would choose the division /je–len/ instead of /jel–en/ because the former analysis yields a so-called open syllable /je/ instead of a closed syllable /jel/.[16] In our theoretical framework it can be rephrased to the principle that phonotagms with no final PerP are preferred to those with such a phoneme. In the case of syllables the argument is supported by asserting that open syllables are more common than the closed ones in the world's languages (Pulgram 1970: 66ff.). Some (e.g. Jakobson – Halle 1956, Malmberg 1967, Clements – Keyser 1983) even claim that open syllables exist in *all* languages, but this is a pure speculation. Not only does it depend on how the syllable is defined and on how words are syllabified, such statements are actually unfalsifiable because we will never know anything about languages which disappeared in the past (cf. also the discussion in Hyman 2011). Other linguists have not gone so far to assume the universal validity of open syllables, and as an alternative they have proposed that the preferable division is the one whose output is syllables (or phonotagms for us) with a structure statistically more common in a given language (e.g. O'Connor – Trim 1953). This method was, for example, applied to Czech by Kučera (1961: 81ff.). According to this idea, the PhF /jelen/ should be divided

---

16 Of similar purport is a principle employed in many phonological theories known as
    Maximal Syllable Onset Principle (see e.g. Selkirk 1982). Cf. also Pulgram's (1970: 47,
    66ff.) Principle of Maximal Open Syllabicity.

into /je/ and /len/ because phonotagm types 'CV' and 'CVC' are claimed to be more common than types 'CVC' and 'VC' in this language.

It is obvious that what decides where the border falls are criteria other than distributional. But what should also be obvious is the fact that the /l/ in /jelen/ can belong to *both* phonotagms because it can occur at the end of the first as well as at the beginning of the second (cf. *jel* and *len*). Whether /je–len/ or /jel–en/ is eventually chosen on the basis of some additional criterion is another matter. Distributionally, both divisions are possible, which suggests another solution. To reflect that the medial /l/ is distributionally ambiguous, the form /jelen/ will be analyzed into /jel/ and /len/, that is, into phonotagms both of which contain /l/. From the perspective of distribution, it is immaterial whether /jelen/ is divided into /je–len/ or /jel–en/, as either is possible. Hence, just as a wall between two rooms belongs to both rooms, so does the /l/ belong to both phonotagms. In phonotactic analyses employing the notion *syllable*, such a situation is known as *ambisyllabicity* (Hockett 1955, Kahn 1976). Although linguists are not agreed as to whether this notion is to be allowed in phonological descriptions at all (see e.g. Jensen 2000), there is some reason in the idea. One should remember that the foremost goal of a phonotactic analysis is to describe the structure of phonotagms. We know that /je/, /jel/, /len/ and even /en/ are possible phonotagms in Czech because all are attested as PhFs of words. Thus, no matter how /jelen/ is analyzed, we will not get a structure previously unattested. To put it otherwise, the form /jelen/ can in fact be ignored in a phonotactic analysis of Czech because it will not provide any new piece of information. We already know that /l/ occurs at the beginning of a phonotagm as well as at the end of it. Following Mulder (1968: 178ff.), we will call the situation when a phoneme belongs to two phonotagms FUNCTIONAL AMALGAMATION.

In general, every single inter-nuclear phoneme is functionally amalgamated in Czech because every PerP can occur both at the beginning and at the end of a phonotagm. Accordingly, the PhFs /lano/ *lano*, /jaro/ *jaro*, /řijen/ *řijen* contain phonotagms /lan/ and /no/, /jar/ and /ro/, and /řij/ and /jen/, respectively. In the case of inter-nuclear occlusives and fricatives, there is functional amalgamation between the occlusive or the fricative and its archi-phoneme. For example, the form /kňiha/ *kniha* is analyzed into /kňiX/ and /ha/ with functional amalgamation between /X/ and /h/. As the opposition between voiceless and voiced occlusives and fricatives is neutralized at the end of phonotagms, it holds that if an occlusive or a fricative appears in such a context, it is always in the form of an archi-phoneme which represents both phonemes of the voicing pair.

Inter-nuclear combinations may or may not be amalgamated. It depends on whether they are allowed both at the beginning and at the end of a phonotagm. For instance, in the already mentioned form /riPka/ there is not functional amal-

gamation because /Pk/ cannot occur at the beginning or at the end of a phono-tagm. On the other hand, /Sk/ in /miSka/ *miska* is functionally amalgamated because the combination /Sk/ occurs at the beginning of a phonotagm (cf. /Skāla/ *skála*) as well as at its end (cf. /voSK/ *vosk* where /K/ represents /k/).

To sum it up: a PhF is poly-phonotagmic if it can be analyzed into two or more well-formed phonotagms. A phonotagm is well-formed if it does not violate any structural rule. The well-formedness is judged against attested PhFs of words, hence the analysis of PhFs into individual phonotagms is governed by the condition that only those phonotagms possible at the beginning and at the end of PhFs of words are allowed. In case a phoneme or a phoneme combination can be assigned to both of two neighboring phonotagms, they are declared to be functionally amalgamated. We have not, as is commonly done in works on syllabification, sought for criteria for the decision whether an inter-nuclear phoneme should be unequivocally assigned to the first or to the second phonotagm because this is not relevant for our analysis. What is important is whether it *can* belong to either or both. We do not deny that at some later stage of the analysis such auxiliary criteria may be used, but they are not important at this point.

Chapter Six: DISTRIBUTIONAL UNIT: THEORETICAL BACKGROUND

6.1 Distributional unit as a domain of distribution

If a linguist wants to describe the distribution of some linguistic items, he has to do it in reference to a certain distributional domain upon which this could be related (as already pointed out by Trubetzkoy 1939: 224). Without wishing to provide a detailed overview here, we content ourselves with saying that, in order to account for the distribution of phonemes, linguists have employed several such domains like a morpheme (e.g. Trubetzkoy 1939, Uhlenbeck 1950), a word (e.g. Mathesius 1929, Vachek 1940, Martinet 1956), or a so-called contour (Garvin 1948)[1] and perhaps even others. Still, most linguists seem to agree that the most economical phonological distributional domain is the syllable (e.g. Pike 1947, Fischer-Jørgensen 1952, O'Connor – Trim 1953, Haugen 1956b, Selkirk 1982, Zec 2007 and others). However, this idea has occasionally been challenged by linguists who have pointed to inadequacies of the syllable-based phonotactics (Bell 1976, Stediade 1999 and in particular Blevins 2003). The major argument is that in some languages phonological sequencing generalizations cannot be adequately accounted for upon the frame of a single syllable. Blevins (*op. cit.*) mentions a number of such languages. A good example is provided by Australian languages. According to Dixon (1980: 159), words are typically at least disyllabic there, and have either the structure '$C_1VC_2C_3V(C_4)$' or '$C_1VC_5V(C_4)$'. He further specifies (*ibid.*):

> It is not thus possible, for an Australian language, to give a structure $C_1V(C_2)$ for syllables, and then to describe a word as a sequence of these syllables. The possibilities at C_3 may be similar to those at C_1, but they never coincide; similar remarks apply to C_2 and C_4. And the occasional occurrence at C_5 of phonemes that are found in no other position further discredits a monosyllabic model.

Thus, the domain of phoneme distribution must be more complex than one syllable here. Other languages such as Japanese, Italian or even English (though for

---

1   Cf. Sigurd (1965: 14–6; 1968). Garvin's contour is a unit containing one stress; it may consist of one, two or even more words in Kutenai, an isolated language spoken in Canada (see also Haugen 1956a who uses the syllable for the description of this language).

other reasons) may require a distributional domain other than the syllable. Another language where the syllable seems to fail altogether is Gokana of a Niger-Congo branch (Hyman 2011).[2]

Mulder (1968) was one of the few to realize the limits of syllable-based phonotactics. Although he did not deny the usefulness of the syllable, he proposed a more general model of distribution called *distributional unit*. Its definition runs as follows (adapted from Mulder – Hervey 2009):

(1)   DISTRIBUTIONAL UNIT (DU) is a self-contained bundle of positions in phonotactics, where positions are divisions within a phonotactic construction, such that in every such division an entity, as an immediate constituent of that construction, can stand and alternate (i.e. commute) with other entities, or with Ø (i.e. be left out).

The DU is meant to be a model for the phonotactic aspect of languages which can be applied to any language. In many languages it may be coextensive with the syllable as traditionally understood, but others (such as Japanese or Australian languages) require DUs of larger complexity since, as suggested above, the distribution and combinations of phonemes cannot be exhaustively accounted for in the domain of a single syllable. The DU is a general model of the distribution of phonemes. It is constructed in such as way so as to ensure that phonotactic descriptions are relatively simple, adequate to the data and maximally exhaustive. The positions are set up for each language individually, and their quantity and function will differ. Phonemes in every language display unique distributional and combinatory potentials, and in some other ones the description of their distribution may necessitate the introduction of several types of DU (we will return to this in §6.5 and §8.2).

6.2 Positions

The notion *position* is crucial for understanding what a DU is. It may be viewed as a slot that can be occupied by a phoneme, one at a time, or that can be empty, depending on a situation. No single instance of a phoneme can occur in more than one position at a time, even though several instances of one phoneme can occur in more positions like in Czech /jej/ *jej* where /j/ occurs in a pre-nuclear

---

2   Accordingly to Hyman (*op. cit.*), the syllable is hardly used in Gokana in any way. To use his terminology, it is not a domain of distributional constraints on phonemes, of phonological, morphological or allomorphic rules, of prosodies or of prosodic grouping. Though Gokana has certainly phonic syllables, phonologically there is very little need to operate with such a unit.

and post-nuclear position. However, these are two instances of the same phoneme in different positions, not one phoneme in two positions. It is like a person who can only sit on one chair, not on two, even though he may sit on several chairs at different times.

We have said that positions may also be empty; this situation will be expressed by the symbol 'Ø'. However, the zero is here not an entity of any kind, but it is what Haas (1957)[3] has called *operation of omission*: a position is empty if a phoneme occurring there in a certain phonotactic construction can be omitted, so that the result is still a self-contained construction. For instance, the position in which the final /T/ occurs in /jeT/, the PhF of Czech *jet*, can be empty because its omission produces /je/ which is also self-contained (cf. the word *je*). But the same cannot be said about /e/ because its omission produces /jT/ which is not self-contained or well-formed in Czech. Returning to our chair simile, we could say that even though a person may sit upon a chair, it happens that the chair is sometimes empty, but it is a chair nonetheless. In phonology it is convenient to regard the functional omission of a phoneme from a position as it were occupied by Ø (cf. Mulder 1968: 126–7). A position is empty if it is not occupied by a phoneme, but it holds that every position which happens to be empty in a certain situation must be occupied by at least one phoneme under other circumstances. There must be a choice between the presence of a phoneme and its absence. Positions which are always empty are prohibited because they would hardly have any purpose.

The idea of empty positions has one important consequence: once the DU is set up in terms of the positions it consists of, the number of positions remains constant. What changes is THE WAY POSITIONS ARE OCCUPIED BY PHONEMES OR LEFT EMPTY. It is this particular aspect of Mulder's conception of position, and ultimately his idea of the DU, that makes it different to the way other linguists use this notion.[4] The term *position* has been widely used in phonology (see e.g. Trubetzkoy 1939, Fischer-Jørgensen 1952, Haugen 1956b or Kučera 1961), though seldom specifically defined. In general, it stands for a certain relative placement of a phoneme, mostly with regard to the beginning of a syllable or a word or to the core of a syllable. Hence, for example, Czech /v/ in /vaS/ *vaz* and /k/ in /kaS/ *kaz* are said to occur in the first position of a syllable, i.e. in the same position. This is not how positions will be understood here (see also the discus-

---

3 Incidentally, Haas may not agree with our use of empty positions, explicitly rejecting them (*op. cit.*: 48), but then, his understanding of positions differs to ours.

4 Among the few linguists who also operate with empty positions is Fudge (1969): "[English] *sixths* [is represented] as /s.i.kSθS/, where the symbol . indicates the selection of zero" (p. 269).

sion in §17.3). Although we do not deny that /v/ and /k/ are the very first phonemes in the forms given, the subsequent analysis will have shown that they do
not occur in one and the same position. Due to the existence of forms like
/kvaS/, they must occur in different positions because it is not possible that they
occur in the same position in /kvaS/. The forms /kaS/ and /vaS/ differ from each
other in the way particular positions of the DU are filled with a phoneme or left
empty. Strictly speaking, the phonotactic representation of the words *kaz* and
vaz is /ØØkØØaØSØ/ and /ØØØvØaØSØ/, respectively. The zeros are for practical reasons usually omitted, but they are indicators that the given positions can
be occupied by phonemes under other circumstances; cf. /FSkØØaØSØ/ *vzkaz*,
for example, where the first two zeros of /ØØkØØaØSØ/ *kaz* are replaced by /F/
and /S/. In /kaS/ the /k/ occurs in the third position of the DU, while the first position is empty. It is therefore more correct to say that the /k/ occurs in the first
position that is occupied by a phoneme.

The purpose of the DU is to account for the structure of phonotactic entities.
It is assumed that every phoneme is assignable to at least one position of the
DU, and that the number of the positions is finite. The DU is then an underlying
model behind all phonotactic constructions in a given language, and its positions
are expressions of distributional and combinatory properties of particular phonemes. However, it is not a mere taxonomic tool without any wider application,
as it may seem at the first sight. It is a common and wrong belief that structural-
ist models are not capable of explaining anything, merely describing it. The DU
formalizes phonotactic descriptions, presents them in a clear and systematic
way, and besides that, it functions as a formal device for predicting ("generat-
ing" or still better, for calculating) well-formed but unattested phonotactic constructions. To put it otherwise, the model also accounts for *potential* phonotactic
constructions which are not actually attested, but which are nevertheless well-
formed in the sense they could function as fully-fledged PhFs (or their parts) of
words if ever there be such a need. Linguists are widely agreed that a phonological theory should consider the question why some combinations of phonemes are permitted and others not (see e.g. Fischer-Jørgensen 1952, Vogt 1954,
Hooper 1972, Selkirk 1982, Goldsmith 2011), but, as mentioned in §5.4, only a
handful of them have provided a detailed procedure for answering this. Under
the present approach the DU offers a key to such an answer: since it captures the
phonotactic structure of all attested phonotactic constructions of a given language, it follows that those unattested phonotactic constructions which do not
conform to it cannot be considered as well-formed. An example is a confrontation of two constructions /tvje/ and /pvje/, both unattested in Czech. The first of
them is well-formed, but the second is not, even though both are of similar constituency. As becomes clear in the next chapter, /p/ and /v/ are mutually exclu-

sive, and do not combine with one another. The structure of the DU is such that its output can be /tvje/, but never /pvje/, which makes the latter ill-formed. The DU thus offers a principled basis for distinguishing accidental gaps from non-accidental gaps (cf. Chomsky 1964: 31). This said, it should be obvious that functionalist models cannot be accused of lacking predictive power, and are thus on a par with the other, mainstream linguistic approaches.

In order for it to be applicable at all, the DU must comprise at least two positions, but there is no restriction on their maximal number; it depends on a particular language how many positions will be necessary. One-position DU would be useless because all items would occur in that position, and no distributional properties could be derived from it. In fact, it would be the same as saying that the semiotic system under description does not allow for any ordered combinations of figurae, i.e. does not have any phonotactics, but all natural languages allow such combinations (cf. §2.2).

Even though two is the logical minimum number of positions, languages with such a DU are probably very rare. It is because fewer positions imply that the number of distinct combinations of phonemes found in the language is quite small. Since there is usually a certain degree of isomorphism between phonological vowels and phonetic vocoids and phonological consonants and phonetic contoids, we may suppose, without making any definite statement, that languages where syllables always consist of a vocoid accompanied with an optional contoid will be describable with the DU consisting of only two positions, one for the phoneme realized as the vocoid, the other for the phoneme realized as the optional contoid. Languages where a vocoid is always followed by a contoid without being preceded by one appear to be very rare. Arrernte, an Aboriginal language of Australia, is claimed to be one, but this conclusion is dependent on certain assumptions (Breen – Pensalfini 1999, Tabain – Breen – Butcher 2004).[5]

More common are said to be languages containing only syllables formed by a vocoid preceded by an optional contoid. Blevins (1995) mentions two of them: Hua, a Papuan language, and Cayuvava, a Bolivian language. Provided that the vocoid corresponds to the phoneme occurring in one position and the optional contoid to the phoneme occurring in another position, these languages could have DUs with just two positions. In Hua, syllables allegedly contain either a vocoid or a vocoid preceded by one contoid; however, if one inspects the original source Blevins used (i.e. Haiman 1980), it will be obvious that the situation

---

5   Phonetically ("on the surface"), Arrernte does not only have only 'vc' syllables because
     it has words beginning with a contoid and ending in a vocoid. The analysts argue that
     there are good reasons to interpret the final vocoids as non-phonological, and to say that
     all contoid-beginning words actually begin with the vowel /e/.

Positions	Pre-nuclear	Nuclear	Post-nuclear
Position classes	p k ʔ h l m n w Ø	i e a u o ī ē ā ū ō	i e o u Ø
Phonotagms	Ø	i	Ø
	Ø	ā	i
	m	a	Ø
	p	i	u
	m	ā	e

FIGURE I: Distributional unit in Hawaiian; an initial hypothesis

is a little more complicated because other syllable types are also possible (cf. also Zec 2007: 169, 192). Problematic is also Cayuvava; again, the inspection of the original source (i.e. Key 1961) will reveal that it contains also syllables formed by a vocoid preceded by two contoids in which case two positions would rather be necessary.

Yet another candidate of a language where the DU with just two positions would be sufficient is a Senari dialect of Senufo, a branch of Niger-Congo languages.[6] According to the analysis by Mills (1984), the Senufo syllable is formed either by a single vocoid, a syllabic contoid, a vocoid preceded by a contoid or a vocoid preceded by a contoid with a secondary release. Provided that one position of the DU corresponds to the vocoid or the syllabic contoid, and the other position to the antecedent contoid (with or without a secondary release), this language could have a DU with merely two positions. More research is necessary, though.

Languages whose phonotactics could be described with just three positions will not probably be very common, too. Rotokas, a Papuan language often cited as possessing the smallest phoneme inventory, may have a DU of no more than three positions because the only attested syllables are of the structure 'v', 'vv', 'cv' and 'cvv' (Firchow – Firchow 1969). The 'vv' and 'cvv' syllables correspond to long vocoid and diphthongs; more research is needed for deciding whether they should be interpreted as combinations of two phonemes or of single phonemes. The latter being the case, the Rotokas DU would probably have only two positions.

Another example may be Hawaiian with the syllable structure similar to Rotokas and also having diphthongs; in this language the DU appears to have three positions as shown in figure I (based on Schütz 1981). The figure shows the positions of the DU, the classes of phonemes capable of occupying the individual

6   Commonly cited in the literature, mentioned e.g. in Clements – Keyser (1983: 29) without a source.

positions (so-called *position classes*), and several examples of phonotagms in which all positions are either filled with a phoneme or left empty.

In general, however, more than three positions are required for describing the phonotactics of the world's languages, simply because many languages allow consonantal combinations before or after a vowel. Peking Chinese (Mulder 1968) and Thai (Mulder 1987) have four positions. San Martín Quechua, a language spoken in Peru, has been analyzed by Howkins (1972) to have four positions. Sudanese Arabic has five positions (according to Dickins 2007), and so does Yulu (Gabjanda 1976).[7] The DU in Russian has eight and in French nine (Rastall 1993). As we will show, Czech can be analyzed with nine positions. The main DU in English has ten positions (according to El-Shakfeh 1987). More complex DUs may still occur, e.g. in Georgian which is known to have a very rich and complex structure of pre-nuclear and post-nuclear combinations (see Vogt 1958, Butskhrikidze 2002).

In many (if not most) languages the phonotactics is more complicated because some phonemes may have peculiar distribution. These peculiarities can be handled with the notion *archi-position*. It is best to explicate it in conjunction with specific examples, and we will return to it in the next chapter.

6.3 Functional dependency: nuclear and peripheral entities

Although phonotactic constructions are made of phonemes, they are not just sets of phonemes. They are complexes of phonemes between which certain relations hold. Such constructional relations are called *tactic relations* (because phonemes are phono*tactic* entities). Several types are recognized, but the most important one for phonology is the RELATION OF SUBORDINATION. It is an asymmetrical relation between two entities such that one entity is functionally dependent on another, which means that it is dependent on the other for the role it fulfills in a phonotactic construction. The dependent entity is sub-ordinate to the governing one which is, consequently, declared to be the NUCLEAR ENTITY of the construction while the dependent one is given the status of a PERIPHERAL ENTITY (Mulder – Hervey 2009). Since all phonemes are assumed to occupy some position, nuclei stand in NUCLEAR POSITION, and peripheral entities in PERIPHERAL POSITIONS. There is only one nuclear position within the DU.

Peripheral positions are gathered around the nucleus as planets gather around the sun (or like peels of an onion, Mulder 1989: 293); the DU is a centripetal model. However, as speech occurs in space and time, positions are arranged in a certain sequence. This logical necessity should not be misunderstood as implying that the linear sequencing is necessarily functional; it is only a fact that cannot be ignored in phonology. Accordingly, there may be two kinds of peripheral positions: those occurring before the nucleus (i.e. PRE-NUCLEAR) and those after it (i.e. POST-NUCLEAR).[8] But a language need not have both types. Though not necessarily identical, there are usually strong correlations between the DU and syllables (see §6.6), and so it is likely that the absence of either type of peripheral positions will be encountered in languages with no syllable onset or in those with no syllable coda. As Cayuvava, mentioned earlier, has only open syllables, it is likely that the DU would not have any post-nuclear positions there. However, it does not mean that all coda-less languages, which are in fact commonly cited to occur (cf. Hyman 2008: 103, note 13), would have DUs without post-nuclear positions. Many (e.g. Rotokas or Hawaiian, see above) contain long vocoids or diphthongs, and if these are interpreted as combinations of two phonemes, they would have a post-nuclear position. But Cayuvava has only open syllables and no complex syllable cores. As regards onset-less languages, they are extremely rare, if known at all. Arrernte mentioned above is claimed to be one. It all depends on the phonological interpretation of the data. In short, languages need not have both types of peripheral positions, but it appears that pre-nuclear positions are more often occurring than post-nuclear ones.

Now, phonemes which always function as nuclei of phonotactic constructions can be called VOWELS, and those always functioning as peripheral entities can be called CONSONANTS. The terms are convenient but somewhat misleading because they designate here two basic distributional phonological classes, whereas the common practice is to use them for two basic types of speech sounds. The reader will recall that we use *vocoids* and *contoids* for the latter to avoid the confusion. It is true that vowels are often phonemes realized as vocoids, but there may be languages where vowels could be realized as contoids (e.g. in languages where [r] occurs only in the syllable core). Yet another class of phonemes can be set up from the distributional point of view: phonemes which function both as nuclear entities and peripheral entities. Such phonemes appear to be common in the world's languages (cf. Bell 1978), and they can be called SEMIVOWELS or SEMICONSONANTS.[9] Again, it should be remembered that

8   They have also been called *explosive* and *implosive* (by Mulder 1968; after de Saussure ([1916] 1972: 79ff.).

9   From the phonological perspective, there is no difference between the terms, though semivowels may be used for phonemes with more affinity to vocoids, and semiconsonants for phonemes with more affinity to contoids (see Mulder 1989: 226ff.).

these are phonological terms, not names of speech sounds; semivowels/semiconsonants can be realized both as vocoids and contoids, for example in English, where [ɪ] and [j] are interpreted as allophones of the semivowel /i/ (Mulder – Hurren 1968). Czech is also a language where this category is justified because syllabic and non-syllabic [r] and [l] are interpreted here as allophones of the semiconsonants /r/ and /l/, respectively (see §3.5 and §10.2).

The conceptual difference between vowels, consonants and semiconsonants on the one hand and vocoids and contoids on the other is important for another reason: Although all languages probably have contoids and vocoids, there are some where either the distributional phonological category of consonants or that of vowels is redundant. For instance, in Tashlhiyt Berber (a language spoken in Morocco; Dell – Elmedlaoui 2002), every contoid can be a syllable core as well as a syllable margin.[10] If we assume that this fact is interpreted by saying that every peripheral entity can also function as a nuclear entity, then this language would only have a class of vowels (i.e. phonemes realized as syllabic vocoids) and a class of semiconsonants (i.e. phonemes realized as syllabic and non-syllabic contoids). The term *consonant* would be redundant for it, as no phoneme would function there only as a peripheral entity. Similarly, Sudanese Arabic, as analyzed by Dickins (2007), has only consonants and semiconsonants because every nuclear entity functions there as a peripheral entity. It is a consequence of the fact that vocoids and their corresponding glides have been interpreted as allophones of one phoneme. And if the same analysis is advanced for Tashlhiyt Berber, for which there is some justification, we would have to conclude that this language has only semiconsonants. In other words, every phoneme would function there both as a nuclear entity and a peripheral entity. Of course, this is always depends on the final analysis of the data, but the point is that vowels and consonants need not coincide with vocoids and contoids.

6.4 Occurrence dependency

There is one important point about peripheral entities: besides being functionally dependent, they are occurrence-dependent on the nuclear entities, which means that the latter condition the occurrence of the former. To put it simply, peripheral entities cannot occur without the nuclear, governing entities. The presence of the governing entity is compulsory, it being the identity element of a phonotactic construction. The occurrence dependency is A NECESSARY CRITERION for

---

10   Bella Coola, a Salishan language spoken in Canada, is also often cited as a language where every contoid can be syllabic, though alternative analyses have been proposed (Bagemihl 1991).

determining whether an entity is peripheral or not. It would be logically absurd to maintain the contrary, i.e. that there are entities which are not dependent on the occurrence of other entities, but which are still dependent on them for their function in the phonotactic construction. However, even though the occurrence dependency is a necessary criterion, it is not a sufficient one. Peripheral entities are always dependent on the occurrence of nuclear ones, but it does not imply the latter are necessarily occurrence independent (Mulder 1989: 288–93). Despite being functionally superior, so to speak, a nuclear entity may still require the presence of another entity to assert its function. Accordingly, there are two types of sub-ordination, that is, of functional dependency:

The first one can be called *sub-ordination with unilateral occurrence dependency*. It refers to a situation when a peripheral, subordinate entity *a* is dependent on the occurrence of a nuclear, governing entity *b*, but *b* is not at the same time dependent on the occurrence of *a* (Mulder – Hervey 2009). So whereas *a* requires the presence of *b*, *b* does not require the same of *a*, simply because *b* can occur without *a*. In a word, the *a* can be omitted from the phonotactic construction, so that the result will still be a valid construction. This type of sub-ordination holds, for example, between vowels and consonants in Czech. Consonants must always be accompanied by vowels, but vowels need not be accompanied by consonants. The latter are omissible with the resulting phonotactic construction still being well-formed (cf. /ta/, the form of *ta*, as opposed to /a/, the form of *a*). However, the opposite does not hold: if a vowel is omitted, the result is not a well-formed construction (cf. /ta/ *ta* as opposed to /t/ which is not well-formed, i.e. it is not a PhF of any Czech word).

The second type of sub-ordination can be called *sub-ordination with bilateral occurrence dependency*. It refers to a situation when a peripheral, subordinate entity *a* is dependent on the occurrence of a nuclear, governing entity *b*, and *b* is at the same time dependent on the occurrence of *a* (Mulder – Hervey *op. cit.*). In effect, neither of them can be left out, though they can be replaced by other phonemes. This is a case of nuclear /r/ and /l/ in Czech. Although they can function as nuclei, they require the presence of at least one consonant, so that a given phonotactic construction is well-formed. It is because /r/ and /l/, unlike vowels (cf. /a/ *a* above), cannot form self-contained phonotactic entities by themselves, and must be preceded by at least one consonant. For example, in /hr/ *hr* (from *být hr* "to be rash") neither /h/ nor /r/ can be omitted because neither /h/ nor /r/ are well-formed PhFs. We will discuss the nuclearity and occurrence dependency of /r/ and /l/ in §10.2 in more detail.

6.5 Minor distributional unit

It has been said that the purpose of the DU is to serve as a tool upon which the phonotactic phenomena can be described in their entirety. The assumption is that it is possible to set up one definite network of positions which accounts for all distributional and combinatory properties of phonemes in a given language. However, it seems that this task is too complicated (or perhaps even impossible) for some languages because the ways phonemes combine there is very complex. As Mulder noted himself on several occasions (e.g. in 1998: 146–7), it may sometimes be necessary to introduce several types of DU to account for the complexity. Some languages may have phonotactic phenomena, usually marginal, which are better to be described upon a special type of structure rather than including everything into one overall model. Mulder (1987: 41ff. and 1989: 268–71) has suggested such an analysis for Japanese poly-syllabic words mentioning the term *semi-distributional unit* as a structure accounting for dependent syllables in poly-syllabic words such as *nippon*.[11] A similar idea has been suggested by Rastall (1993: 83) who speaks about a minor distributional unit in his analysis of Russian.

Within the framework of AF, the fullest treatment of the idea of there being several DUs is provided by El-Shakfeh (1987). In his analysis of the phonotactics of English, he introduced a distinction between major-type and minor-type phonotagms. The former are basic, independent phonotagms corresponding to autonomous stressed syllables with unreduced vocalic elements, whereas the latter account for unstressed syllables prone to reduction of their vocalic elements to schwas. As is well known, an English unstressed syllable cannot occur without the accompaniment of a stressed one, whereas the latter can. It is problematic to view them as corresponding to separate phonotagms, since phonotagms are by definition self-contained (i.e. autonomous) entities. Thus, for example, the PhF of English *comforters* (realized with two unstressed syllables) could not be an instance of three phonotagms, but attests a single phonotagm / krNFrtrz/ (the nucleus underlined).[12] However, as Heselwood (2007: 165) has correctly pointed out, it is in principle possible that in English a stressed syllable could be followed by any number of unstressed syllables. This means that phonotagms in this language would have an open-ended structure, i.e. we would never be able

---

11 The second syllable in this word is dependent on the first because of the gemination: the first phoneme of the second syllable is the same at the last phoneme of the first syllable. In essence, the situation is similar to the one cited for the Australian languages in §6.1 above. — On the term *semi-distributional unit*, see also Mulder (1968: 58).

12 This example is actually taken from Hervey (1978). Hervey was the supervisor of El-Shakfeh's thesis, and no doubt some inspiration was found in his paper.

to determine their finite structure. This observation diminishes the usefulness of the notion distributional unit because if phonotagms have a potentially infinite structure, then they cannot be described upon a finite set of positions. The exact structure of the DU could never be properly set, and so it cannot serve as a descriptive tool.

The idea of minor-type phonotagms offers a solution. If the unstressed syllables are, for the convenience of description, treated as if they corresponded to independent and self-contained phonotagms, then their structure could be described in a similar vein as that of the stressed syllables, and a special type of DU (i.e. a special network of positions) may be set up for them. This unit may have its own nuclear position. In the end, however, it must be recognized that this minor DU is dependent on the main DU, in particular on its nuclear position which functions as the *nucleus nucleorum* of the DU as a whole. An example may be /nrreitr/ (a PhF of *narrator*) where the underlined parts are minor-type phonotagms with /r/ being twice their nuclei. The phoneme /e/ occurs in the nucleus nucleorum of the whole construction.

It follows from El-Shakfeh's idea of minor-type phonotagms as well as from Mulder's semi-distributional unit or from Rastall's minor distributional unit that it is necessary to recognize several degrees of nuclearity in phonotactics and hence several levels of phonotactic analysis. Constituents recognized at every analytical level will be self-contained from the perspective of that level. This has already been recognized for syntax where the notion *position* (in a grammatical sense) is also employed (Mulder 1989: 278). We can illustrate it on the Czech sentence meaning "a black cat lied on the table" whose base is the predicative-based syntagm *černá kočka ležela na stole*. At the first level of analysis it is divided into three immediate constituents which are the nominal syntagm *černá kočka*, the verbal syntagm *ležela* and the nominal syntagm *na stole*. At the second level each of these is further analyzed into its constituents, e.g. *černá kočka* into *černá* and *kočka*. In the syntagm *černá kočka ležela na stole*, the nominal syntagm *černá kočka* is dependent on the rest, whereas the rest is not because *ležela na stole* "she lied on the table" is a well-formed predicative-based syntagm. But within the range of the phenomena we call nominal syntagms, the construction *černá kočka* is self-contained, and so is the prepositional syntagm *na stole*. It is of course possible to analyze the syntam *černá kočka ležela na stole* as one structure, but the multilevel analysis offers greater delicacy and simplicity.

In phonotactics the possibility of having several analytical levels has hardly been explicitly recognized in AF. It is usually assumed that phonotagms are analyzed into phonemes which are their immediate and at the same time ultimate constituents. But if the multilevel analysis is adopted for phonotactics, too, we can effectively deal with problems similar to that of unstressed syllables in English. Phonotactic bases of English words can then be, at the first level, analyzed into two types of immediate constituents, one being a major-type phonotagm which can occur on its own, and the other being a minor-type phonotagm which can be absent but which, if present, must accompany the major-type phonotagm. Following El-Shakfeh (1987: 513), we will define minor-type phonotagms as the entirety of phenomena which do not fall within the range of major-type phonotagms, i.e. which cannot occur on their own. Minor-type and major-type phonotagms are, at the second level, analyzed into the ultimate phonotactic constituents, phonemes. At that second level the minor-type phonotagms are viewed as self-contained combinations, and it is at the level where the major-type phonotagms are excluded. Still, it must be acknowledged that they are, from the overall perspective, dependent on the major-type ones, since they are always accompanied by the latter. Major-type phonotagms may occur without minor-type phonotagms.

The notion minor-type phonotagm will be particularly useful in chapter 8 where we argue for such a category in Czech. We will assume that the PhF /ŠkrābnöT/ is first analyzed into the minor-type phonotagm /Škrāb/ and the major-type phonotagm /nöT/, and then both are analyzed into particular phonemes. To distinguish the DU upon which major-type phonotagms are described from the DU upon which minor-type phonotagms are described, the latter will be called a MINOR DISTRIBUTIONAL UNIT.

6.6 Phonotagms and syllables

The DU is a network of positions mutually connected via phonotactic relations between their members. A position is a slot occupied either by a phoneme from a certain paradigmatic class or left empty. A particular instance of a DU where all positions are either occupied or empty is a PHONOTAGM. Phonotagms attested in a language differ from each other in the way positions of the underlying DU are filled. The DU may then be compared to syllable templates with which some linguists operate (e.g. Selkirk 1982), and phonotagms to concrete phoneme sequences. Although our approach is different, the basic idea is the same: the structure of phoneme sequences (i.e. phonotagms), whose number is in principle infinite, can be described upon one underlying template (i.e. the DU).

However, the term *syllable* will not be used in any phonological sense in this work. In the first place, phoneme distribution may be more intricate in some languages, so that the syllable is not able to accommodate all these intricacies. What is more, to speak about syllables may be rather misleading because the term has become overused in linguistic literature (cf. Bell – Hooper 1978): it stands for a great many things, and the dissimilar conceptions get confused with each other (see Hála 1956, 1961, Awedyk 1975, van der Hulst – Ritter 1999, Meynadier 2001, Duanmu 2008, Goldsmith 2011, Cairns – Raimy 2011, Bosch 2011, Szigetvári 2011, Côté 2012 for some overviews and discussions). Used by phoneticians and phonologists alike, it denotes anything from a certain "real" portion of utterance to a very abstract linguistic model (cf. e.g. Lowenstamm 1996). In order to avoid terminological confusion, we will stick to the term *phonotagm* as the name of a unit of phoneme distribution and to the term *distributional unit* as its underlying model ("template"). The syllable will be used here in a purely phonetic sense as a unit of physiological organization of speech. This is, however, far from being unproblematic; it is well-known that phoneticians have long struggled with how the (phonic) syllable is to be properly defined, if it can be defined at all (see Krakow 1999). It is not our intention to resolve it here, but we will assume that something like a phonic syllable does exist however phonetic theories define it (see also Cholin 2011 and Côté *op. cit.* for psycholinguistic evidence of the syllable).

Once the syllable is recognized as a phonetic entity and the phonotagm as a phonological entity, it is legitimate to ask what the relationship between them is. At the level of segments we can consider relationships between speech sounds and phonemes because the latter serve as models of the commuciationally relevant properties of sounds. Similarly, at a higher level, phonotagms may be viewed as being in essence models of communicationally relevant properties of syllables. But just as there need not be one-to-one correspondence between speech sounds and phonemes, neither should we expect it to exist between syllables and phonotagms. So although a phonotagm appears to be most commonly realized by a single syllable—at least in languages we know of—, this should not be understood as a universal rule (cf. also Pike 1947: 65, Fudge 1969: 254 in this respect). Accordingly, there are three possible relationships between phonotagms and syllables:

(2) (a) One phonotagm is realized by exactly one syllable.
     (b) One phonotagm is realized by a unit of greater complexity than one syllable.
     (c) One phonotagm is realized by a unit of lesser complexity than one syllable.

Out of these possibilities, the first one (2a) appears as the ideal. The number of phonotagms in a PhF of a signum agrees with the number of syllables of the phonetic form of this signum. It is probably the most common situation, though particular languages may exploit other options. Rotokas with its simple phonotactic structure seems to be one where it always holds. The same is probably true for Cayuvava (see the discussion and references in §6.2). And it is almost exclusively the relationship holding in Czech.[13] PhFs of Czech words consisting of just one phonotagm are realized by one syllable,[14] and in words built of two or more phonotagms the number of phonotagms is the same as that of syllables by which the forms are realized. For example, the word *náhrdelník* which is analyzable into four phonotagms /nāX/, /hrT/, /deĺ/, /lňīK/ is realized by four syllables [na:.hr̩.dɛl.ɲi:k]. To put it otherwise, in languages falling under (2a) every syllabic vocoid and contoid is a realization of a nuclear entiy of a phonotagm.

There are languages where not all vocalic phonic segments are realizations of nuclear phonemes. It is the case of British English for which the second relationships (2b) holds, though the first one is encountered, too (e.g. [naɪt] *night* corresponding to one phonotagm /nait/). In this language a phonotagm may be realized by a unit of greater complexity than one syllable because some schwas occurring in unstressed syllables are merely epenthetic elements fully predictable from the context; see the examples under (3) (taken from El-Shakfeh 1987: 378; cf. also Hervey 1978: 50–2, Fudge 1969: 269 and Heselwood 2007). Such syllables cannot correspond to separate phonotagms because a distinctive function would be ascribed to something not capable of distinguishing anything.

(3) [ri:dʒəntəl] (3 syllables) → /rIidŠntl/ (1 phonotagm) (cf. *regental*)
[fɔ:lʧənz] (2 syllables) → /forltŠnz/ (1 phonotagm) (cf. *falchions*)
[sɪmpəltənz] (3 syllables) → /siNplTnz/ (1 phonotagm) (cf. *simpletons*)
[bʌmblədəmz] (3 syllables) → /brNblTmz/ (1 phonotagm) (cf. *bumbledoms*)

Another interesting case is found in Piro, an Arawakan language spoken in Peru, which, according to Matteson (1965), has only syllables of the structure 'cv', 'ccv' and 'cccv'. However, what Matteson calls syllables rather corresponds to our phonotagms because every consonant which does not stand right before a vowel is realized here either as syllabic or with a short epenthetic vowel (*op. cit.*: 129–34, Lin 1997: 405–6), e.g. /šwamkalo/ [ʃˤwaṃkalo] "spider". As this is completely predictable, the consonants cannot constitute separate phonotagms, i.e. /šwamkalo/ consists of three phonotagms but of five phonic syllables.

Finally, as regards the last relationship (2c), i.e. a phonotagm realized by a unit of lesser complexity than one syllable, its possibility is above all dependent

---

13 With an exception of *stárl* which is distributionally a single phonotagm (/Stārl/) corresponding to two syllables (a point discussed in detail in §10.2).

14 However, it also depends on how the syllable is defined. If the Czech words *msta*, *rty* or *lhát* are disyllabic as some definitions of the syllable suggest, then the single phonotagms /MSta/, /rti/ and /lhāT/ are realized by two syllables. See again §10.2 on this problem.

on how the phonic syllable is defined. If it is declared, as is sometimes done, to be the smallest pronounceable unit of speech, it is obvious that a singular phonotagm could never be realized by something less than a syllable. It may even be argued that anything uttered by a human is a syllable, no matter what phonetic segments such an utterance contains, even interjections such as *pst*.[15] In that case the commonly held opinion that a syllable should contain a vocalic element is not valid. But this is not something specific to interjections only. Linguists have long been aware of languages with words pronounced without any vocoid or even without a voiced element. Two such languages are usually mentioned: the already referred-to Bella Coola and Tashlhiyt Berber. The latter has words like those given under (4) where voiceless obstruents function as syllable cores (examples from Ridouane 2008, syllable cores underlined).[16]

(4)   [f̱k] "give" (1 syllable)
      [tf̱.tḵ.tṣtt] "you strained it" (3 syllables)
      [tṣ.sḵ.ʃf̱.tṣtt] "you dried it" (4 syllables)

A priori, there is no reason to assume the notions distributional unit and phonotagm are not applicable to languages like Bella Coola or Tashlhiyt Berber, too. A rather preliminary analysis by the present writer has suggested that the DU in Tashlhiyt Berber consists of three positions, one pre-nuclear, one nuclear and one post-nuclear, though further research is still needed. The point is that phonotagms are in this language realized by utterances which lack any vocalic element, but which are still regarded as genuine syllables by its users. It suggests that, there being no limits on what sounds a syllable must contain, a single phonotagm is always realized by a syllable. A different situation may arise when phonotagms do not occur in isolation but as part of PhFs, for it is common that words are built of more than one phonotagm. It is then possible that these forms are realized by a sequence of syllables whose number is fewer than the number of the phonotagms. They may, so to speak, coalesce into one syllable. This happens in the case of underarticulation, i.e. when articulation of one syllable is neglected in rapid and careless speech as in Czech *vole* "dude, man (voc. sg.)", phonologically two phonotagms /vole/, which is often underarticulated, via [voɛ], to sound like monosyllabic [wɛ], instead of orthoepic [volɛ].

---

15   An idea rejected e.g. by Hála (1956: 54, 1961: 114–5). A detailed overview of opinions on this problem is found in Awedyk (*op. cit.*). Whether something is a syllable or not depends on the chosen theory, as aptly demonstrated by Hyman (2011).

16   The opinions on the exact nature of such words are not unitary. Coleman (2001) suggested they may contain epenthetic vocalic segments. However, Ridouane (*op. cit.*) presented strong evidence that they are completely devoid of vocoids or of any voiced segment.

To sum up, a phonotagm is always realized by at least one syllable, but it may be realized by more than one syllable because all non-functional, predictable features (e.g. certain schwas in unstressed syllables in English) are left at the level of phonetic realization without being accommodated in any way into the phonological representation of words.[17]

6.7 Constructing a distributional unit

The purpose of the DU is to be a model upon which occurrences and combinations of phonemes are described in a non-contradictory, non-redundant and non-deficient manner. It must contain no fewer positions than is necessary to account for all occurrences of phonemes, and, likewise, it must not contain extra positions to avoid redundancy. Mulder (1993 and 1996) has developed a methodology allowing analysts to consider and operate with only those elements that are essential for describing certain phenomena. In short, in a description one puts forth hypotheses about speech phenomena. These hypotheses must be in principle refutable, i.e. they must be testable against available data. The goal is to refute them. Should they remain unrefuted, they are corroborated becoming part of the description. If refuted, they are replaced by new hypotheses which are further tested. Refuted hypotheses are actually very important for showing what is not possible. On the other hand, corroborated hypotheses leave us with a doubt they could be refuted one day by relevant data. A linguistic analysis is not a straightforward procedure, but rather a series of conjectures and refutations.

Before illustrating in detail how a DU is arrived at, we would like to give a general outline of the way the analysis may be conducted. With every language being unique, the actual procedure will of course be unique for every language. Two points should be stressed. First, the heuristic methods presented here are just a convenient way of working in practice and not any sort of discovery procedures. The DU is not discovered in the data; we apply this theoretical model on the data with an aim to get a better understanding of them. Second, although we act here as if the phonotactic analysis of a language were independent of the phonematic one (as presented in chapters 3 and 4) and the other way round, it is certainly not true. The paradigmatic identity of phonemes is determined hand in hand with their syntagmatic identity. It is only for presentational purposes that the two are treated separately here.

---

17 It does not mean such features are ignored altogether; they are only dealt with, in a systematic manner, elsewhere, in a description of the allophony, which is, however, not at issue in this work.

When describing the phonotactics of a certain language, we may proceed in the following way: As there must be, for logical reasons, at least two positions within a DU, our initial hypothesis is such that it contains two positions, and that no more are necessary for the exhaustive description of all phoneme occurrences within phonotactic constructions in a given language. This hypothesis will be held until refuted. It will usually be very easily refuted, as it is rare that only two positions would do the job.[18] Once it is refuted, we launch a new hypothesis: that no more than three positions are necessary. If even this one is refuted, it is replaced with a new hypothesis. We proceed this way until arriving at a hypothesis about a certain number of positions we are not able to refute by relevant examples. This will usually result in our knowing how many positions are necessary, though we should still and always consider the adequacy of our findings. In practice, however, it is not necessary to go this long way round; as Mulder (1987: 36) has noted, there is a way to cut it short, but this shortcut has a rational background behind it.

To begin with, we should consider whether there is some ground for postulating the nuclear position which is a position where nuclear entities occur. Although it is theoretically possible to have a DU without the nuclear position, the need for such a unit appears to be quite rare. One must remember that nuclear entities are those upon which the others are functionally dependent and those which cannot be left out. So we should first try to find out whether a language under investigation has words whose PhFs are built of a single phoneme because these will usually be the nuclear entities. Czech or French has such words. Even if the language has no such words, the diagnostic test for nuclearity will still be the same: the presence of a nuclear entity is compulsory for a phonotactic construction to be well-formed and self-contained. Let us take English as an example. Vowels must always be accompanied by a consonant there; yet they may never be omitted from a phonotactic construction.[19] Naturally, the whole thing may sometimes be quite complicated, and we have to consider carefully the choice of nuclear entities and of the nuclear position. Some linguists have tried to establish vowels and consonants on distributional criteria but without any recourse to nuclearity. O'Connor – Trim (1953) suggested one method, and applied it successfully to English. But although the same method was applied to French by Arnold (1955–6), the same linguist eventually showed it fails on lan-

---

18 Rotokas or Cayuvava could be such languages; see above.

19 We simplify here a little bit because the classes of vowels and consonants are established only after the nuclear position has been set up, never before! Our point is that although there may be no English word with the form /a/, the phoneme /a/ is a nuclear entity because it and its communants cannot be left out (cf. /pat/ *pat* against /at/ *at* against illformed /pt/).

guages such as Greek and Polish (Arnold 1964). Greenberg (1962) proposed another and a more sophisticated method, but even this one fails in languages like Hottentot or Guaraní (Bell 1976). The bottom line is that it may be difficult for some languages, if possible at all, to define vowels and consonants as separate distributional classes of phonemes. However, the distribution of phonemes in such languages should be in principle describable even without these notions. The point is to set up a grid of positions functioning as slots where phonemes occur and commute with each other.

Should the nuclear position be introduced or not, the next step in analysis is determination of the set of phonemes capable of occurring in a certain position. The commutation test is the best procedure at this point. Once we have determined that /a/ is a nuclear entity in English /pat/ (see footnote 19), its commutants can be listed; they are /e/, /i/, /o/, /u/ and /r/ (cf. *pet, pit, pot, put* and *putt*, respectively). The occurrence of any of them is compulsory, but the same could not be said about /p/ and its commutants. Phonemes occurring in the nuclear position in these examples will be, for the time being, declared vowels; this will be later corrected because some are in fact semivowels (namely /r/) capable of occurring in non-nuclear positions, too.

As there must be at least two positions within a DU, it is obvious that if one is nuclear, the others are peripheral unless we introduce a minor DU, but even in that case there will be only one nucleus nucleorum (see §6.5). Due to the linearity of speech, there are two kinds of peripheral positions, pre-nuclear and post-nuclear, so the next step is evaluation of the possibility of setting up pre-nuclear and/or post-nuclear positions, and determination of their number. This can be easily determined—and this is the shortcut alluded to above—by considering the maximum number of PerPs capable of occurring in between the beginning of PhF of a word and the first nuclear entity, and the maximum number of PerPs capable of occurring in between the last nuclear entity and the end of PhF of a word. Since the assumption is that only one phoneme occurs in a position at a time, their number corresponds to the number of pre-nuclear and post-nuclear positions. By now we have gained a rough idea of the form of the DU. It may still be altered by further considerations and circumstances peculiar to a given language such as by the introduction of archi-positions and/or a minor DU.

With the positions of the DU set up, the next task is to map onto them attested phonotactic constructions. Our analysis will be based on the following two principles:

(5) (a) PRINCIPLE OF EXCLUSIVE MEMBERSHIP
A phoneme assigned to a certain position does not occupy any other position unless proven otherwise.

(b) PRINCIPLE OF MUTUAL COMMUTABILITY
Phonemes mutually commutable in equivalent contexts do not occupy
different positions unless proven otherwise.

The first principle assumes the following: Having assigned a phoneme /α/ to a
position 'β' in a construction *A*, we will hold that it occurs in the very same position in any other construction *B* it belongs to unless such an assumption is in
contradiction with other facts. This derives from the general principle of simplicity of descriptions: we should not introduce new elements (new statements,
features, entities, concepts etc.) into a description if it is not necessary. It is simpler to assume that a phoneme always occupies the same position than that it occupies several ones. However, hypotheses of this kind are often refuted. For instance, we cannot hold the hypothesis about the English phoneme /t/ due to the
existence of the two different constructions /tip/ and /pit/ (cf. *tip* and *pit*). The
phoneme must occur in at least two positions, one pre-nuclear and one post-
nuclear. But we can still assume that /t/ in /tip/, /t/ in /trip/ and /t/ in /Strip/ (cf.
trip and *strip*) occur in the same pre-nuclear position in which case this hypothesis will not be refuted.
      The second principle derives from the mutual commutability of phonemes in
functionally equivalent contexts. It will be assumed that if two or more phonemes are mutually commutable, they occupy the same position. It is because a
position is a slot where a phoneme occurs and commutes with other phonemes.
In a phonotactic construction a phoneme not only occurs in a certain position but
also in the presence of other phonemes. A certain other context is functionally
equivalent to it provided that it is identical to it or that it represents the same
(Mulder 1968: 119). For example, in a construction /na/ the phoneme /n/ occurs
in a pre-nuclear position and in the presence of /a/. In constructions /ma/ and /ta/
the phonemes /m/ and /t/ occur in functionally equivalent contexts because they
also occur in a pre-nuclear position and in the presence of /a/. The hypothesis
will thus be that the mutually commutable phonemes /n/, /m/ and /t/ occur in the
same position. However, we would at once like to make clear that by introducing this principle we do not want to suggest that all phonemes which are mutually commutable in equivalent contexts must always belong to the same position. Although our initial hypothesis may be that /n/, /m/ and /t/ occur in the
same pre-nuclear position in Czech due to their mutual commutability, it will
later prove that such a hypothesis cannot be maintained. The existence of the
form /tma/ (cf. *tma*) indicates that at least /t/ or /m/ occurs in two different positions. On the other hand, we will not be able to refute the hypothesis that /m/ and
/n/ do not occur in the same position. In this case the Principle of Mutual Commutability is the way to assign both to the same position.

Chapter Seven: DISTRIBUTIONAL UNIT: APPLICATION TO CZECH

In the previous chapter we outlined the theoretical and methodological background of the construction of the DU, and in this chapter we construct one for Modern Standard Czech. The analysis is presented here in several steps, but its actual course was not so straightforward; we offer here only the final analysis.

7.1 Nuclear position

Following the principles introduced at the end of the previous chapter, we must first consider whether it is possible to establish the nuclear position and to recognize the class of nuclear entities which would occur there (see §6.3 and §6.7 on the rationale behind this). The examples (1) prove there are. As these PhFs are built of one phoneme only, it is evident that /a/, /o/, /i/ and /u/ are not dependent on any other item, either for their phonotactic function or for their occurrence. Thus, they are nuclear entities occurring in the nuclear position.

(1) /a/ *a*, realized [ʔa][1]
    /o/ *o*, realized [ʔo]
    /i/ *i*, realized [ʔɪ]
    /u/ *u*, realized [ʔu]

Having assigned /a/, /o/, /i/, /u/ to the nuclear position, we will assume, by the Principle of Exclusive Membership (see §6.7), that they do not occupy any other position as long as this hypothesis withstands refutation. It has withstood, and it is adopted as a descriptive statement. Hence, in phonotagms like /na/ *na*, /on/ *on*, /sin/ *syn*, /kruX/ *kruh* and others, the phonemes /a/, /o/, /i/, /u/ are assumed to occupy the very same nuclear position. We will now determine which phonemes are commutable with them in functionally equivalent contexts. See the following examples:

(2) /paST/ *past* × /poST/ *post* × /pāST/ *pást* × /prST/ *prst* × /plST/ *plst* × /pīST/ *píst* × /pūST/ *půst*

---

1 The glottal stop is only a concomitant feature and a realization of diaereme (see §5.2).

/paS/ *pas* × /pāS/ *pás* × /peS/ *pes* × /puS/ *pus* × /pōS/ *póz* × /prS/ *prs*
/vaS/ *vaz* × /vāS/ *vás* × /veS/ *ves* × /viS/ *viz* × /vīS/ *víz* × /voS/ *vos* × /vūS/
vůz × /vöS/ *vous*
/ar/ *ar* × /ēr/ *ér* (gen. pl. of *éra*) × /ir/ *Ir* × /är/ *aur* × /ër/ *eur*

The phonemes commutable with /a/, /o/, /i/, /u/ in equivalent contexts are /e/, /ā/,
/ē/, /ō/, /ī/, /ū/, /ä/, /ë/, /ö/ and /r/, /l/. The latter two have been deliberately separated from the others because the subsequent analysis has revealed that they are
different from the rest. Our initial assumption is that all of the mentioned phonemes occur only in the nuclear position due to their commutability with /a/, /o/,
/i/, /u/, but this hypothesis must be reconsidered for /r/ and /l/ in light of the following examples:

(3) /praK/ *prak* × /parK/ *park*   /sni/ *sny* × /sin/ *syn*
     /kloT/ *klot* × /kolT/ *kolt*   /kru/ *kru* × /kur/ *kur*

Since only one phoneme may occupy a position at a time, the oppositions /ra/ ×
/ar/, /lo/ × /ol/, /ni/ × /in/ and /ru/ × /ur/ show that if /a/ and /o/ occur in the nuclear position, then /r/ and /l/ must occur in a non-nuclear position, or if, on the
contrary, /r/ and /l/ occur in the nuclear position in these examples, then /a/, /o/,
/i/ and /u/ occur elsewhere. In short, at least one of these phonemes occurs in a
non-nuclear position. Having considered all options, we will assign /r/ and /l/
both to the nuclear position and to a non-nuclear position, thereby keeping /a/,
/o/, /i/ and /u/ in the nuclear position only. This analysis is simpler than the alternative because it is then only /r/ and /l/ that have the capacity to occur in nuclear and non-nuclear position. Otherwise, we would to assume this for all of the
phonemes /i/, /e/, /a/, /o/, /u/, /ā/, /ē/, /ō/, /ī/, /ū/, /ä/, /ë/, /ö/ because similar examples like those under (3) exist for all of them. The proposed analysis is also
more materially adequate because it holds that all of the phonemes occurring
only in the nuclear position are realized by vocoids standing in the syllable core.
There is thus affinity between nuclei of phonotagms and cores of syllables at the
realizational level.

Consequently, on the basis of the commutations in (2) we arrive at the class
of vowels which includes /i/, /ī/, /e/, /ē/, /a/, /ā/, /o/, /ō/, /u/, /ū/, /ë/, /ä/, /ö/, and
the class of semiconsonants which includes /r/, /l/. The former are phonemes always functioning as nuclear entities and occurring only in the nuclear position.
The latter are phonemes functioning both as nuclear entities and as peripheral
entities and occurring in the nuclear position as well as in a non-nuclear position. By further commutations we have determined that the remaining phonemes
are consonants, namely /p/, /b/, /f/, /v/, /m/, /t/, /d/, /s/, /z/, /n/, /ť/, /ď/, /š/, /ž/, /ň/,
/k/, /g/, /x/, /h/, /ř/, /j/ (including their archi-phonemes). These phonemes always

function as peripheral entities; they occur in non-nuclear positions and require the presence of a nuclear entity. Now, since the semiconsonants function both as vowels and consonants, we will talk about NUCLEAR PHONEMES when dealing with vowels and semiconsonants in the nuclear function, and about PERIPHERAL PHONEMES (= PerP) when dealing with consonants and semiconsonants in the peripheral function.

7.2 Peripheral positions

Having established the nuclear position, we will move to the non-nuclear or peripheral positions. In Czech, PerPs can occur before and after a nuclear phoneme (cf. /lem/ *lem* × /mel/ *mel*). By physical necessity, phonemes (and hence the positions) are arranged in a linear sequence. Therefore, there are two domains of the distribution of peripheral entities in this language: the PRE-NUCLEAR CONTEXT and the POST-NUCLEAR CONTEXT. The former includes all positions postulated for phonemes capable of occurring before the nuclear entity; the latter all positions postulated for phonemes capable of occurring after it. The domain of the distribution of nuclear phonemes will be called the NUCLEAR CONTEXT; it includes the nuclear position and the nuclear archi-position (see below).

By examining combinations at the beginning of words before a nuclear phoneme and at their end after a nuclear phoneme, we can determine the maximum number of phonemes preceding and following it. See the examples (4).

(4)   /FSkvjeT/ *vzkvět*, realized [fskvjɛt]
      /vojSK/ *vojsk*, realized [vojsk]

As every phoneme occurs in just one position, we now have a rough idea about the constituency of the DU: it contains one nuclear position, and it must contain at least five pre-nuclear positions and at least three post-nuclear positions to accommodate all the phonemes in the examples under (4). This is still a hypothesis to be further tested, but so far it has withstood refutations in the sense that more positions than these nine are not necessary, and fewer are insufficient for the exhaustive description the distributional properties of the Czech phonemes. Some modifications will be necessary later, though. The initial hypothesis about the structure of the DU is schemed in figure I on the next page alongside with the way the initial and final parts of /FSkvjeT/ and /vojSK/ are assigned to the particular positions. There are two rows in the scheme of the DU and two types of labels. In both, 'n' stands for the nuclear position; the other markings are for peripheral positions. The more distant from the nucleus, the more peripheral a position is. In the first row the positive and negative numbers indicate the degree of

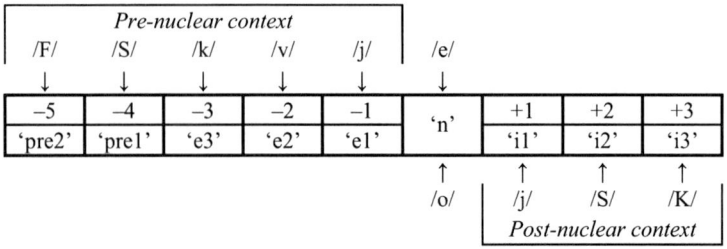

FIGURE I: Assignment of phonemes to positions of the pre-nuclear and post-nuclear context

peripherality of non-nuclear positions. Pre-nuclear positions '–1', '–2' and '–3' (along with their archi-positions) will be called EXPLOSIVE, and post-nuclear positions '+1', '+2' and '+3' (along with their archi-position) will be called IMPLOSIVE. Thus, in the second type of labeling the minus sign has been replaced by 'e' for positions '–1', '–2' and '–3', and the plus sign by 'i'. Pre-nuclear positions '–4' and '–5' have been relabeled to 'pre1' and 'pre2'. The prefix 'pre' stands here for PRE-EXPLOSIVE, and in our conception a pre-explosive position is such a pre-nuclear position which is only occupied by a phoneme provided that at least one of the explosive positions 'e1', 'e2', 'e3' or their archi-positions is occupied by a phoneme. Otherwise, pre-explosive positions are empty. They function as extensions to the explosive positions. We will return to this in chapter 11.

The question to be resolved now is how to assign phonemes to the individual positions. This is done through a series of hypotheses, their corroborations or refutations, and postulations of new ones. Some phonemes were already assigned to the nuclear position. As to the non-nuclear context, it is reasonable to base our further analysis on the forms where all positions are filled. For the pre-nuclear context, the best starting point is /FSkvjeT/. The same procedure will be applied to the post-nuclear context where we start with /vojSK/ or any other PhF ending in three PerPs. Let us note that although there are many examples of phonotagms where all three post-nuclear positions are filled with a phoneme, phonotagms where all five pre-nuclear positions are occupied are rare. Besides /FSkvjeT/, there is also /STkvjel/ *stkvěl*, an archaic variant of /Skvjel/ *skvěl*.

The five pre-nuclear phonemes of /FSkvjeT/ have been assigned to the five pre-nuclear positions, and we assume they always and only occur there as long as this is not proven untenable. The phoneme /j/ has been assigned to position 'e1', /v/ to position 'e2', /k/ to 'e3', /S/ to 'pre1', and /F/ to 'pre2'. By assumption, they occupy the very same positions also in PhFs like /kvjeT/, /vjeT/, /jeT/, /kveT/, /veT/, and /SkeT/ which are plotted onto the DU as shown in the A section of figure II. Even though not containing the same number of phonemes, the phonotagms are still mapped onto the same grid of positions. The remaining po-

'−5' 'pre2'	'−4' 'pre1'	'−3' 'e3'	'−2' 'e2'	'−1' 'e1'	'n'	Phonological form
/F/	/S/	/k/	/v/	/j/	/e/	/FSkvjeT/ *vzkvět*
Ø	Ø	/k/	/v/	/j/	/e/	/kvjeT/ *květ*
Ø	Ø	Ø	/v/	/j/	/e/	/vjeT/ *vjet*
Ø	Ø	Ø	Ø	/j/	/e/	/jeT/ *jet*
Ø	Ø	/k/	/v/	Ø	/e/	/kveT/ from *kvetoucí*
Ø	Ø	Ø	/v/	Ø	/e/	/veT/ *vet* (gen. pl. of *veto*)
Ø	/S/	/k/	Ø	Ø	/e/	/SkeT/ *sket* (gen. pl. of *sketa*)
Ø	Ø	/x/	/v/	/j/	/e/	/xvjeT/ *chvět*
Ø	Ø	/h/	/v/	/j/	/e/	/hvjeST/ *hvězd*
Ø	Ø	/d/	/v/	/j/	/e/	/dvje/ *dvě*
Ø	Ø	/s/	/v/	/j/	/e/	/svjeT/ *svět*
Ø	Ø	/z/	/v/	/j/	/e/	/zvjeT/ *zvěd*
Ø	Ø	/s/	/v/	/r/	/a/	/svraP/ *svrab*
Ø	Ø	/z/	/v/	/l/	/ā/	/zvlāŠŤ/ *zvlášť*
Ø	Ø	/s/	/v/	Ø	/ē/	/svēST/ *svést*
Ø	Ø	/z/	/v/	Ø	/ā/	/zvāT/ *zvát*
/F/	/S/	/d/	Ø	Ø	/ā/	/FSdāT/ *vzdát*
Ø	Ø	/t/	/v/	Ø	/ā/	/tvā/ *tvá*
/F/	/S/	/t/	Ø	Ø	/ā/	/FStāT/ *vstát*
Ø	/S/	/t/	Ø	/r/	/a/	/StraX/ *strach*

FIGURE II: Application of the Principles of Exclusive Membership and Mutual Commutability

sitions of the DU are empty. However, it should be remembered that a position may only be empty if and only if it is occupied by a phoneme under other circumstances, which figure II clearly proves. Now, having assigned /F/, /S/, /k/, /v/, /j/ to their positions, we find out which phonemes are commutable with them because, following the Principle of Exclusive Membership, we assume that their commutants occupy the same positions. For example, /h/, /x/, /d/, /s/ and /z/ can be assigned to the same position as /k/ due to their mutual commutability with it in forms like /xvjeT/, /hvjeST/, /dvje/, /svjeT/ and /zvjeT/. Taking the last two, we find out which phonemes are commutable in functionally equivalent contexts with /j/ (namely /r/, /l/ in /svraP/ and /zvlāŠŤ/), and so on. The way these forms are mapped onto the DU is illustrated in the B section of figure II.

We keep assigning phonemes to the positions in a similar manner. However, even if it looks straightforward, there may be—and usually are—situations requiring special treatment. One of them concerns /r/ and /l/. Due to the mutual commutability with /j/, they have been assigned to position 'e1'. Our initial hy-

'pre2'	'pre1'	'e3'	'e2'	'e1'	'n'	Phonological form
/r/	Ø	/z/	Ø	Ø	/i/	/rzi/ *rzi*
Ø	Ø	/z/	Ø	/r/	/ĩ/	/zrĩT/ *zrýt*
/l/	Ø	/z/	Ø	Ø	/e/	/lze/ *lze*
Ø	Ø	/z/	Ø	/l/	/e/	/zle/ *zle*

FIGURE III: Analysis of the difference between /rzi/ and /zrĩT/ and between /lze/ and /zle/

pothesis is that they always occur in this pre-nuclear position.[2] This assumption will have to be corrected once we come across PhFs like those given in (5a) below. If /r/ and /l/ occupy 'e1' here, where does /z/ occur? Previously, it has been assigned to 'e3' which, however, precedes 'e1', not follows it. The position following 'e1' is the nuclear position occupied by /i/ in /rzi/ and by /e/ in /lze/. Consequently, if /r/, /l/ occupy 'e1' in these forms, /z/ would have to remain unassigned, which is not possible. This proves that /r/, /l/ cannot occur in /rzi/ and /lze/ in position 'e1'.

(5) (a) /rzi/ *rzi* (gen. sg. of *rez*)   (b) /zrĩT/ *zrýt*
         /lze/ *lze*   /zle/ *zle*
    (c) /rvjete/ *rvĕte*   (d) /StraX/ *strach*
         /lStnĩ/ *lstný*   /zvlāŠŤ/ *zvlášť*

There are two possibilities how to interpret this: One is that our initial hypothesis about the occurrence of /r/, /l/ in pre-nuclear position 'e1' was wrong, and these phonemes occupy another position. The second is that they do indeed occupy this position, but are in addition capable of occurring in yet another. Further analysis and evidence of the forms given in (5b), and also of those in (5c) and (5d) will decide that the second alternative is to be preferred. Hence, /r/ and /l/ occupy *two* pre-nuclear positions, namely in 'e1' and 'pre2'. The final analysis is given in figure III. It reflects several facts: In the pre-nuclear context the phonemes /r/ and /l/ can be both preceded and followed by a PerP or a group of PerPs. If they are *preceded* by other PerPs, the phoneme which in turn follows them is always nuclear (cf. /StraX/ and /zvlāŠŤ/). On the other hand, if they are followed by a PerP in the pre-nuclear context, they are always the first phonemes of the phonotagm, i.e. they cannot be at the same time preceded and followed by a PerP. In fact, they are the very first phonemes of a word. In this case the resulting phonotagms are realized by so-called side syllables (see §10.2).

We have sketched the basics of how phonemes are assigned to particular pre-nuclear positions. There are still other problems to deal with, and we will do

---

2   As shown earlier, they also occur in the nuclear position, but this is irrelevant now.

'*n*'	'-1' 'i1'	'-2' 'i2'	'-3' 'i3'	*Phonological form*
/u/	/m/	/Š/	/T/	/kumŠT/ *kumšt*
/a/	/r/	/K/	/T/	/farKT/ from *infarkt*
/e/	/K/	/S/	/T/	/teKST/ *text*
/o/	/j/	/S/	/K/	/vojSK/ *vojsk*
/o/	/m/	/S/	/T/	/pomST/ *pomst*
/ā/	/P/	/S/	/T/	/zāPST/ *zábst*
/ē/	/T/	/S/	/T/	/pēTST/ *péct*
/i/	/n/	/T/	/S/	/prinTS/ *princ*
/u/	/l/	/T/	/S/	/sulTS/ *sulc*
/ā/	/T/	/S/	/P/	/zāTSP/ *zácp*

FIGURE IV: Phonotactic analysis of three-phoneme post-nuclear combinations

so in the next section. Once the way phonotagms are analyzed has been illustrated, the analysis of the post-nuclear context for which three positions have been postulated need not be discussed in any great detail. The assignment of phonemes into these positions is simpler because there are at least 19 post-nuclear combinations of three phonemes, and their mapping is very straightforward. Figure IV provides some examples.

7.3 Archi-positions

Phonemes are assigned to particular positions according to phonotactic properties they possess; a position is an expression of these properties. However, some phonemes may display unique phonotactic properties, and it will not be possible to assign them to any of the already established positions without violating the consistency of the description. Such cases can usually be accounted for by an ARCHI-POSITION (Mulder 1968). An archi-position is a product of the suspension of the syntagmatic difference between two or more positions. As positions in phonology are sequenced in a linear order, the suspension concerns only two or more immediately adjacent positions. If the position is an expression of certain phonotactic properties, then the archi-position is an expression of phonotactic properties common to two or more adjacent positions. It is in fact the syntagmatic equivalent of the archi-phoneme which is a product of the suspension of a paradigmatic difference between two or more phonemes.

The usefulness of archi-positions is best shown on the occurrence of the phonemes /t'/ and /d'/ in the pre-nuclear context. Their special distributional and combinatory properties are summarized as follows:

(6) PHONOTACTIC PROPERTIES OF /t'/, /d'/ IN THE PRE-NUCLEAR CONTEXT
(a) They can be preceded by one or two PerPs, but no more.
(b) They are always followed by a vowel, never by another consonant or a
     semiconsonant (i.e. never by a PerP).

Let us start with the assumption that /t'/ and /d'/ have been assigned to position
'e3' because of their commutability with the phonemes already assigned there,
namely with /t/ and /d/, cf. /TŠte/ *čte* × /TŠt'i/ *čti*, /FSdāT/ *vzdát (se)* × /FSd'el/
from *vzdělaný*.[3] This hypothesis will soon have to be abandoned, though. The
process of assignment of phonemes to particular positions is not a game whose
goal is merely to fill up all slots without any consequences. On the contrary: by
assigning a phoneme to a position we imply it shares phonotactic properties ascribed to the given position; they define the position in question. The following
are two fundamental phonotactic properties of position 'e3'; they are shared by
all phonemes belonging there:

(7) PHONOTACTIC PROPERTIES OF POSITION 'e3'
(a) A phoneme belonging to 'e3' can be preceded by up to two phonemes be-
     longing to positions 'pre1' and 'pre2', respectively.
(b) A phoneme belonging to 'e3' can be followed by up two phonemes belong-
     ing to positions 'e2' and 'e1', respectively.[4]

Let us now compare these with the two facts about /t'/ and /d'/ given under (6).
Whereas (6a) is compatible with (7a), there is a discrepancy between (6b) and
(7b): /t'/ and /d'/ can *never* be followed by any PerP in the pre-nuclear context—
on the contrary, they are always followed by a vowel. This is not compatible
with the phonotactic property (7b), and so /t'/ and /d'/ cannot be without contradiction assigned to position 'e3'. The initial hypothesis is refuted.
     We must launch a new hypothesis about the occurrence of /t'/ and /d'/. It is
obvious they do not occur in 'pre1' and 'pre2', since according to (6a) they can
be preceded by two PerPs, which is not possible for phonemes occurring in
'pre1' and 'pre2'. We are left with 'e2' and 'e1', but once again, the assignment
of the phonemes to either of them is thinkable only if /t'/ and /d'/ share the properties of these positions. Before long we will find out it cannot be 'e2'. Pho-

---

3   The front vowels /i/ and /e/ do not condition the choice of the preceding phoneme.
4   In general, a phoneme /α/ occurring in a position β can be preceded by and combined
     with one or more phonemes belonging to the position(s) preceding β (if they are any such
     positions). Similarly, a phoneme /α/ occurring in a position β can be followed by and
     combined with one or more phonemes belonging to the position(s) following β (if there
     are any such positions).

The overall distributional unit, pre-nuclear context

'pre2'	'prel'	'e3'	'e2'	'el'	'n'

A contextual distributional unit, pre-nuclear context

	'pre2'	'prel'	'e3∩e2∩el' / 'E3'	'n'	Phonological form
A	/T/	/Š/	/ť/	/i/	/TŠťi/ *čti*
	/F/	/S/	/ď/	/e/	/FSďel/ from *vzdělaný*

	'pre2'	'prel'	'e3∩e2' / 'E2'	'el'	'n'	Phonological form
B	∅	∅	/p/	/r/	/a/	/praX/ *prach*
	/T/	/Š/	/p/	/j/	/e/	/TŠpjeT/ *čpět*
	∅	∅	/b/	/ř/	/e/	/břeX/ *břeh*
	/F/	/S/	/b/	∅	/u/	/FSbuŤ/ *vzbuď*
	∅	∅	/f/	/ň/	/u/	/fňuK/ from *fňukat*
	∅	/S/	/f/	∅	/ö/	/SföK/ from *sfouknout*
	/K/	∅	/f/	∅	/e/	/Kfeli/ *Kfely*

FIGURE V: Phonotactic analysis of /ť/, /ď/, and of /p/, /b/, /f/ in the pre-nuclear context

nemes belonging there have the capacity of being followed by one phoneme from position 'el', which is again not the case for /ť/ and /ď/ because of (6b). The only option left is to assign them to 'el' which is the position immediately next to the nucleus. Although this is in accord with (6b), it violates (6a), as /ť/ and /ď/ can only be preceded by up to two PerPs, whereas phonemes occurring in 'el' can be preceded by to *five* PerPs (cf. /j/ in /FSkvjeT/). Moreover, there are two other significant factors. First, neutralization of voicing takes place before /ť/ and /ď/, which never happens before any phoneme belonging to 'el' (cf. /Sťīn/ *stín* × /sňīT/ *snít*). Second, all phonemes or combinations preceding /ť/ and /ď/ can be easily mapped onto positions 'prel' and 'pre2', and there is no reason not to assign them there in accord with the Principle of Exclusive Membership. The neutralization and the ability to be preceded by just two phonemes from 'prel' and 'pre2' is a thing that /ť/ and /ď/ share with phonemes belonging to position 'e3'. However, the ability to be always followed by a vowel is a thing shared with phonemes belonging to 'el'. They have the properties of 'e3' and 'el', yet they cannot belong to either (and not even to 'e2'). At the same time we cannot leave them unassigned to any pre-nuclear position. In order to find a way out, it is now the point where the concept archi-position comes in.

An archi-position, formally defined as the intersection of two or more positions, may be viewed as a position in a sub-system which represents two or more positions in the overall system (Mulder – Hervey 2009). By a sub-system is here meant a particular constellation of entities in a certain situation, here to the occurrence of /ť/ and /ď/ for which the difference between positions 'e3', 'e2' and 'el' (which were postulated to capture certain phonotactic properties) has been made redundant. The purpose of archi-positions is to account for the distribution of phonemes in certain contexts which have the distribution equivalent to two or more phonemes in other contexts. For /t'/ and /d'/, we posit an archi-position 'E1' which is the intersection of positions 'e3', 'e2' and 'e1' (formally: 'e3∩e2∩e1'). Equivalent to these three positions, it represents them in a given sub-system. Let us note that functional equivalency does not imply functional identity, and 'E3' is not identical to any of positions 'e3', 'e2' or 'e1'; it is only their representative. The way /t'/ and /d'/ are plotted onto the DU is schematized in the A section of figure V (see the preceding page).

Another pre-nuclear archi-position we find necessary to introduce is 'E2' accounting for the distribution of /p/, /b/, /f/. It is the product of the suspension of the difference between positions 'e3' and 'e2' (formally: 'e3∩e2'). These phonemes are preceded by up to two phonemes only—the phonemes that can be mapped onto positions 'pre1' and 'pre2'. Second, they are only followed by one phoneme which can be mapped onto position 'e1'; see the B section in figure V. From this follows that /p/, /b/, /f/ cannot be without contradiction assigned to positions 'e3' or 'e2', and the difference between them is suspended.

We will now move to the post-nuclear context for which three positions have been postulated on the basis of forms like /vojSK/, /pomST/ and others. Having analyzed further the distribution of phonemes in this context, we have come to a conclusion that one archi-position should be introduced here: archi-position 'I'. It is needed for dealing with the distribution of /m/, /n/, /ň/, /r/ and /l/ in forms like /jilm/ *jilm*, /hejn/ *hejn*, /Tšerň/ *čerň*, /xejr/ *chejr* (SSJČ) and /Ktejl/ from *koktejl*, respectively. Namely, we have to account for the post-nuclear combinations /lm/, /jn/, /rň/, /jr/ and /jl/. The first phonemes of these combinations are /l/, /j/ and /r/; they can be assigned to position 'i1'.[5] On the other hand, the second phonemes, /m/, /n/, /ň/, /r/ and /l/ cannot be without contradiction assigned to any of post-nuclear positions 'i2', and 'i3'. The reason is simple: in these particular combinations they cannot be further followed by another phoneme or even preceded by one. Our conclusion is that the difference between positions 'i2' and 'i3' is suspended resulting in archi-position 'I' (formally: 'i2∩i3'). The way the phonemes are mapped into this archi-position is given in figure VI. One point should be mentioned: archi-position 'I' is filled with a phoneme only if position 'i1' is not empty. It is because the phonemes /m/, /n/, /ň/, /r/ and /l/ normally occur in position 'i1' where they can be followed by one or two PerPs, but never preceded by any. On the other hand, when occurring in 'I', they are preceded by exactly one PerP, but never followed by any.

---

5   Where they have already been assigned in the previous analysis; see figure IV above.

The overall distributional unit, post-nuclear context

'n'	'i1'	'i2'	'i3'

A contextual distributional unit, post-nuclear context

'n'	'i1'	'i2∩i3' / 'I'	Phonological form
/i/	/l/	/m/	/jilm/ *jilm*
/e/	/j/	/n/	/hejn/ *hejn*
/e/	/r/	/ň/	/Tšerň/ *čerň*
/e/	/j/	/l/	/Ktejl/ from *koktejl*
/e/	/j/	/r/	/xejr/ *chejr*

FIGURE VI: Phonotactic analysis of /m/, /n/, /ň/, /l/ and /r/ in the post-nuclear context

The overall distributional unit

'pre2'	'pre1'	'e3'	'e2'	'e1'	'n'	'i1'	'i2'	'i3'

A contextual distributional unit

'pre2'	'pre1'	'e3'	'e2'	'e1∩n' / 'N'	'i1'	'i2'	'i3'	Phonol. form
Ø	Ø	/s/	/M/	/r/	/T/	Ø	Ø	/sMrT/ *smrt*
/T/	/Š/	/t/	/v/	/r/	/T/	Ø	Ø	/TŠtvrT/ *čtvrt*
/F/	/S/	/t/	Ø	/r/	/T/	/Š/	Ø	/FStrTŠ/ *vstrč*
Ø	Ø	/p/	/r/		Ø	/S/	/T/	/prST/ *prst*
Ø	Ø	/š/	/M/	/r/	/n/	/T/	/S/	/šMrnTS/ *šmrnc*

FIGURE VII: Phonotactic analysis of nuclear /r/ and /l/

The very last archi-position necessary is 'N'. It results from the suspension of the difference between pre-nuclear position 'e1' and nuclear position 'n' (formally: 'e1∩n'). It is a slot where /r/ and /l/ occur when functioning as nuclear entities of phonotagms. The archi-position has been introduced to account for the following properties of nuclear /r/, /l/. Consequently, nuclear /r/, /l/ are mapped onto the DU in the way given in figure VII.

(8)   PHONOTACTIC PROPERTIES OF NUCLEAR /r/, /l/

(a)   They cannot be preceded by any of the phonemes belonging to position 'e1', i.e. by /m/, /n/, /ň/, /r/, /l/, /j/ or /ř/.

(b)   They can be preceded by one, two, three or four phonemes all of which can be mapped onto positions 'e2', 'e3', 'pre1' and 'pre2'.

(c)   They can be followed by one, two or three phonemes belonging to positions 'i1', 'i2' or 'i3'.

In conclusion, one point ought to be mentioned. Although an archi-position is an effective concept by which the special distribution of some phonemes can be expressed, it is not always possible or desirable to employ it without making arbitrary decisions. Unmotivated decisions are to be avoided in an analysis, for otherwise we would loose control over it. For instance, /g/ (and it holds for /f/, too) has, due to historical reasons, rather limited distribution. It can be followed by one phoneme belonging either to 'e2' or to 'e1', and it can also be preceded by one phoneme belonging either to 'pre1' or to 'pre2'. If we were to introduce archi-positions to capture these facts, our choices would be arbitrary. As /g/ displays similar distributional properties like the other velars occurring in position 'e3', it makes reason to assign /g/ there as well.

7.4 Postscript

Originally,[6] we operated with four post-nuclear positions on the basis of the form /borŠTŠ/ *boršč* "borsch", but this analysis was eventually turned down, and the form /borŠTŠ/ excluded from our analysis. The decisive reason was the fact that it is the only example of a nuclear phoneme followed by four post-nuclear phonemes. On the other hand, there are at least 19 three-phoneme post-nuclear combinations. With the four post-nuclear positions, the phonotactic analysis of these combinations proved complicated and quite redundant because we had to either postulate several archi-positions or declare many positions empty. There being four post-nuclear positions, either one of the phonemes had to occur in an archi-position or one position had to be empty in a form like /vojSK/. The establishment of archi-positions complicated the analysis, and empty positions probably introduced a great degree of inconsistency. Once the form /borŠTŠ/ was removed from consideration, the whole analysis became neater.

Other reasons, though not decisive, support the exclusion. The phonotagm /borŠTŠ/ is a PhF of *boršč* introduced to Czech from Russian, and thus it may resemble the structure of Russian rather than that of Czech. It is also suggested by the fact that the combinations /rŠT/ and /ŠTŠ/, included in /rŠTŠ/, are not otherwise attested in Czech. The latter point is more important than the former because the origin of words is actually irrelevant for a synchronic analysis.

---

6   E.g. in Bičan (2011b).

Chapter Eight: PHONOTAGMS

8.1 Major-type phonotagms

The phonotagms dealt with so far function either by themselves as phonotactic bases of PhFs of words or as parts of such bases in the case of poly-phonotagmic PhFs (cf. §5.5); the latter are potentially capable of functioning by themselves as phonotactic bases. We will call such phonotactic entities MAJOR-TYPE PHONO-TAGMS to distinguish them from minor-type phonotagms which do not have this capacity. The latter are considered in the next section.

Major-type phonotagms are exhaustively describable upon the DU constructed in the preceding chapter. We will call it the MAIN DISTRIBUTIONAL UNIT. In its default form it consists of nine positions: five pre-nuclear, one nuclear and three post-nuclear ones. The syntagmatic difference between some of these positions becomes redundant in certain contexts; we have introduced four archi-positions to account for these suspensions. The DU with at least one archi-position is a contextual variant of the main DU. There are 9 such variants; see figure I. The row marked with '0' is the default variant. The rows marked with '1' are contextual variants with one archi-position. Number '2' designates variants with two archi-positions, and number '3' stands for the variant with three archi-positions. All attested major-type phonotagms in Czech can be mapped onto the default variant of the DU or on any of its contextual variants.

0	'pre2'	'pre1'	'e3'	'e2'	'e1'	'n'	'i1'	'i2'	'i3'
1a	'pre2'	'pre1'	'E1'			'n'	'i1'	'i2'	'i3'
1b	'pre2'	'pre1'	'E2'		'e1'	'n'	'i1'	'i2'	'i3'
1c	'pre2'	'pre1'	'e3'	'e2'	'e1'	'n'	'i1'	'I'	
1d	'pre2'	'pre1'	'e3'	'e2'	'N'		'i1'	'i2'	'i3'
2a	'pre2'	'pre1'	'E1'			'n'	'i1'	'I'	
2b	'pre2'	'pre1'	'E2'		'e1'	'n'	'i1'	'I'	
2c	'pre2'	'pre1'	'E2'		'N'		'i1'	'i2'	'i3'
2d	'pre2'	'pre1'	'e3'	'e2'	'N'		'i1'	'I'	
3	'pre2'	'pre1'	'E2'		'N'		'i1'	'I'	

FIGURE I: Main distributional unit and its contextual variants

	F0	*F1*	*F2*	*F3*
P0	'V'	'VC'	'VCC'	'VCCC'
P1	*'CV'*	*'CVC'*	*'CVCC'*	'CVCCC'
P2	*'CCV'*	*'CCVC'*	*'CCVCC'*	*'CCVCCC'*
P3	'CCCV'	*'CCCVC'*	*'CCCVCC'*	'CCCVCCC'
P4	'CCCCV'	*'CCCCVC'*	'CCCCVCC'	**'CCCCVCCC'**
P5	**'CCCCCV'**	'CCCCCVC'	**'CCCCCVCC'**	**'CCCCCVCCC'**

FIGURE II: Logically possible phonotagm types

Not all positions of the unit must always be occupied by a phoneme. In the default variant it is only the nuclear position that is compulsorily occupied; the others may be empty. The nuclear position must not be empty in any variant of the DU. In the variants involving one or more archi-positions, the archi-positions are always occupied. In the variants involving nuclear archi-position 'N', at least one of the explosive positions must be occupied because nuclear /r/ and /l/ are always preceded by at least one consonant (this condition will be discussed in detail in §10.2). Finally, archi-position 'I' can only be occupied by a phoneme if 'i1' is occupied by one, which derives from the fact that this archi-position has been introduced to account for the occurrence of post-nuclear phonemes after /j/, /r/, /l/ (which belong to 'i1').

All positions of the main DU (in any variant) can be occupied by a phoneme, and some of them can also be empty. Classes of phonemes capable of standing in the positions will be discussed in detail in the chapters to come. For the time being, we will not be interested in these particular phonemes, but rather in whether a position is occupied by a phoneme at all. To put it otherwise, we will examine phonotagms according to the number of positions filled with a phoneme, not according to which positions are actually filled. Since the phonotagm must contain the nuclear entity, the nuclear position ('n') or the nuclear archi-position ('N') is always occupied. The nuclear entity can be preceded by up to five PerPs or by none, and followed by up to three PerPs or by none. The combination of all these options results in a list of all logically possible major-type phonotagms in Czech. They are reproduced in figure II. In that table, 'F' stands for "followed by", 'P' for "preceded by", and the number indicates by how many PerPs a nuclear phoneme is followed or preceded. Note that 'V' stands for any nuclear phoneme, i.e. for vowels as well as nuclear /r/, /l/. In case a type is italicized, it is attested both for vowels and nuclear /r/ or /l/; otherwise it is found only for vowels. The bold face indicates that no example has been found for the respective type. Examples are given in figure III, but before getting to them, we must say a few words about the unattested phonotagm types.

The types we have found no example for are 'CCCCCV' (a nuclear phoneme preceded by five PerPs and followed by none), 'CCCCCVCC' (a nuclear phoneme preceded by five PerPs and followed by two), 'CCCCVCCC' (a nuclear phoneme preceded by four PerPs and followed by three) and 'CCCCCVCCC' (a nuclear phoneme preceded by five PerPs and followed by three). The question to be answered now is whether the absences are to be viewed as accidence or as a regular phenomenon. The first means that such phonotagms could exist and that it is only a matter of chance that they are not included in our data. The second means that it is a characteristic of Modern Standard Czech that it prohibits such phonotagms, and their absence is therefore conditioned.

The absence of type 'CCCCCV' is interpreted as being accidental, that is, we view such phonotagms as possible. The opposite would mean that when a nuclear phoneme is preceded by five PerPs, it must be obligatorily followed by one PerP (recall that 'CCCCCVC' is attested). However, we see no reason why Czech could not have phonotagms like /FSkvje/ if it has /FSkvjeT/. In contrast, the absence of types 'CCCCCVCCC', 'CCCCCVCC' and 'CCCCVCCC' will be interpreted as a regular phenomenon derivable from the following restriction:

(1)   No phonotagm can contain more than six non-vowels.

Non-vowels are phonemes which are not vowels, i.e. consonants and semiconsonants. The reason we speak about such phonemes becomes clear once we look at phonotagm types attested for the nuclear semiconsonants (i.e. the italicized one in figure II). In particular, we should notice that no example has been found for 'CCCCCVC', 'CCCCVCC' and 'CCCVCCC' for the nuclear semiconsonants. All of these types contain seven non-vowels, namely, six PerPs + a semiconsonant. All of these types are attested for vowels, though: /FSkvjeT/ *vzkvět*, /FSkvēST/ *vzkvést* and /StlöTST/ *stlouct*. Hence, if the phonotagm nucleus is a vowel, the phonotagm can contain six non-vowels, but if the nucleus is /r/ or /l/, it can only contain five other non-vowels.

Three other important distributional restrictions on nuclear /r/ and /l/ should be mentioned. First, types 'V', 'VC', 'VCC' and 'VCCC' are not possible for them because a nuclear semiconsonant must be preceded by at least one consonant if it is to be a nuclear entity. Moreover, they cannot be preceded by five PerPs, but this fact is already encoded in the DU—see figure I above for the variants involving archi-position 'N' (it is in fact one of the reasons we have introduced the archi-position). Finally, types 'CCCV' and 'CCCCV' are also not attested for nuclear /r/ and /l/. If these phonemes are not followed any PerP, the phonotagm in question is always the last one in a PhF of a word. Consequently, we conclude that if nuclear /r/ or /l/ occurs at the end of a PhF, it cannot be pre-

Phonotagm type	Example
'V'	/a/ *a*, /i/ *i*, /o/ *o*
'CV'	/ta/ *ta*, /se/ *se*, /hr/ *hr* (cf. *být hr*)
'CCV'	/Sto/ *sto*, /dvö/ *dvou*, /Str/ from *mistr*, /Sxl/ from *uschl*
'CCCV'	/MSda/ *mzda*, /Tkvī/ *tkví*, /Sklo/, /TStl/ from *octl*
'CCCCV'	/STkvī/ *stkví* (archaic form of *skví*), /lStnī/ *lstný*
'CCCCCV'	*not found but possible*
'VC'	/on/ *on*, /aŠ/ *až*, /ēr/ *ér*
'CVC'	/ten/ *ten*, /noS/ *nos*, /köT/ *kout*, /vrT/ *vrt*, /hlT/ *hlt*
'CCVC'	/sňīT/ *snít*, /SdāT/ *zdát*, /SprX/ *sprch*, /Splň/ *splň*
'CCCVC'	/StraX/ *strach*, /Xřtān/ *chřtán*, /Skvrn/ *skvrn*
'CCCCVC'	/FSplāT/ *vzplát*, /PStruX/ *pstruh*, /TŠtvrT/ *čtvrt*
'CCCCCVC'	/FSkvjeT/ *vzkvět*, /STkvjel/ *stkvěl*
'VCC'	/erP/ *erb*, /aKT/ *akt*, /uST/ *uzd*
'CVCC'	/pūST/ *půst*, /tanK/ *tank*, /prST/ *prst*, /plST/ *plst*
'CCVCC'	/zmāST/ *zmást*, /SporT/ *sport*, /sMrŠŤ/ *smršť*
'CCCVCC'	/FznēST/ *vznést*, /SkvoST/ *skvost*, /FStrTŠ/ *vstrč*
'CCCCVCC'	/FSkvēST/ *vzkvést*, /TStnoST/ *ctnost*, /FStřīTS/ *vstříc*
'CCCCCVCC'	*not found and not possible*
'VCCC'	/ūTST/ *úct*
'CVCCC'	/vojSK/ *vojsk*, /pomST/ *pomst*, /verST/ *verst*
'CCVCCC'	/StēTST/ *stéct*, /zřīTST/ *zříct*, /šMrnTS/ *šmrnc*
'CCCVCCC'	/SxlamST/ from *schlamstnout*, /StlöTST/ *stlouct*
'CCCCVCCC'	*not found and not possible*
'CCCCCVCCC'	*not found and not possible*

FIGURE III: Examples for the particular phonotagm types

ceded by three or more PerPs. Details will be provided in §10.2 where the nuclearity of these phonemes is discussed.

Let us now move to figure III with examples of the attested types. Again, the italicized ones are found both for vowels and nuclear /r/ or /l/. More examples can be found in appendix D. We have preferred phonotagms attested in mono-phonotagmic words. In case no such word has been found, examples of phonotagms from poly-phonotagmic words are given.

We have not examined the frequency of the occurrence of the particular types or of individual phonotagms (or combinations within them) because our primary and foremost interest is the description of the phonotagm structure. That is, our goal is only to determine whether a certain type is attested and/or possible, and whether some other type is not attested and/or impossible, not whether some types are more often occurring than others. The research of this kind has already been done for Czech by others, particularly by Ludvíková (1972a, 1972b, 1976, 1978; cf. also Těšitelová et al. 1985: 21–8).[1] However, this re-search was based on other theoretical and methodological foundations. The way PhFs of words are analyzed into smaller units (syllables in Ludvíková's case) is different from ours. She uses morphological criteria for this analysis. She would apparently analyze the word *prostát* "to spend standing" into *pro* and *stát* be-cause the former is a prefix. Here, a morphological fact is given preference. On the contrary, the word *prostat* "prostate (gen. pl.)" would be analyzed into *pros* and *tat* because there is no morphological boundary, and the analysis is gov-erned here by phonological criteria or, to be precise, by the statistical criteria ac-cording to which 'CVC' is a more common syllable type than 'CV' (Ludvíková 1972b, Těšitelová et al. 1985: 22–3; see also Kučera 1961: 81–3). However, apart from the length of /a/, these words are phonologically and phonetically identical, and should be treated alike. The analysis making recourse to morpho-logical boundaries is based on a false assumption that the extension of a moneme (morpheme) coincides with the extension of a syllable. It is hardly true cross-linguistically, let alone in Czech (cf. *jet* "to go", one moneme, one sylla-ble, but *sjet* "to go down", two monemes, one syllable). It is wrong and inconsis-tent to use the criterion of morphological boundaries only in cases where it fits our initial assumptions. Consequently, in our analysis both of the words contain the same phonotagm types, whereas in Ludvíková's analysis they differ in this respect. Having said this, it is obvious that the frequency of particular types must be different, too.

8.2 Minor-type phonotagms

Before explicating the notion *minor-type phonotagm*, we need to return the so-called Kuryłowicz condition introduced in §5.5 as a reasonable guideline for the analysis of poly-phonotagmic PhFs. We noted there that there were situations where the condition fell short. One example was the form /jelen/ *jelen* which could be, according to this condition, divided into /je–len/ as well as into /jel–en/. Phonemes capable of being assigned to two phonotagms (/l/ in this case) were said to be instances of functional amalgamation; distributionally, they be-

---

1   And recently also by Volín – Churaňová (2010) who have examined whether occurrences of peripheral combinations in phonological forms of words, stress units (presumably cor-responding to our accent groups) and prosodic phrases (presumably corresponding to phonological forms of sentences) are random in Czech texts. Their conclusion is that they "are not entirely random, although they do not depart substantially from hypothetical un-constrained distributions" (p. 61).

long to both phonotagms. There are still other situations when even this kind of analysis is not possible. Certain presumably poly-phonotagmic PhFs cannot be analyzed into smaller phonotagms because it would result in combinations of phonemes not permitted at the beginning or at the end of PhFs violating the Kuryłowicz condition. This problem is known from many languages (see Bell 1976 for an overview). One obvious conclusion is that the Kuryłowicz condition is not a reasonable criterion and should be abandoned, but this is not a good option. The whole problem is more general. A description of any phenomena should not make use of elements (hypotheses, models etc.) whose validity cannot be ascertained. In our particular case it means that our analysis should not allow for phonotagms whose structure is not attested and whose well-formedness is not supported by any evidence. If the analysis cannot be backed up with some reasonable support, it becomes wholly fictional.

Not wanting to abandon the Kuryłowicz condition, we must deal with the problem because we encounter it in Czech when faced with the analysis of the PhFs of the words such as *obvaz, odjet* or *škrábnout*. From all we know so far, /obvaS/, /odjeT/ and /ŠkrābnöT/ might be analyzed into two phonotagms because each of them contains two phonemes which function elsewhere as nuclear entities (i.e. /o/ and /a/, /o/ and /e/, and /ā/ and /ö/, respectively). It makes sense to assume that these PhFs contain two phonotagms, and the question is then only how to set the boundaries. The possible analyses are given under (2).[2] None of them is in accord with the Kuryłowicz condition, though.

(2) /obvas/ *obvaz*   /odjeT/ *odjet*   /ŠkrābnöT/ *škrábnout*
(a) /obv–aS/   /odj–eT/   /Škrābn–öT/
(b) /o–bvaS/   /o–djeT/   /Škrā–bnöT/
(c) /ob–vaS/   /od–jeT/   /Škrāb–nöT/

In the first analysis (2a) the combinations /bv/, /dj/ and /bn/ are assigned to the end of the first phonotagm, but none of them is found phonotagm-finally in directly attested forms. Moreover, there is no combination of a similar structure in the given context. A sonant never follows an occlusive, and the same is true of nasals; /dj/ and /bn/ would therefore be quite anomalous in the post-nuclear context. As regards /bv/, fricatives are found to be preceded by an occlusive (cf. /TS/ in *moc* or /TŠ/ in *meč*), but the fricative is never labial (or velar), i.e. it is always alveolar or palatal. This also makes the phonotagm-final combination /bv/ quite unusual. In short, the analysis under (3a) is problematic because it introduces unparalleled combinations.

---

2   Initially, we do not assume there is functional amalgamation.

The second analysis (3b) assigns /bv/, /dj/ and /bn/ to the second phonotagm, making them phonotagm-initial. Even in this case they are not attested in the given context, but they have at least some parallels in the attested combinations. In /bv/ the voiced labial fricative /v/ is preceded by an occlusive, and similar combinations are found phonotagm-initially: /tv/, /dv/, /kv/ and /gv/. However, in none of them the phoneme /v/ is preceded by a labial; in fact, it holds that a labial fricative is not preceded by another labial in the directly attested combinations irrespective of whether the former is /v/ or /f/. As regards /dj/, here the sonant /j/ is preceded by an occlusive, and similar combinations are found, too: /pj/, /bj/ and /kj/. Moreover, there are combinations where /j/ is preceded by a fricative (cf. /fj/, /vj/ /sj/, /zj/) and by a nasal (cf. /Mj/ in the surname *Mjachký*). One can notice at once that the preceding occlusive is no other than labial or velar. And if /j/ is preceded by a fricative, it can also be a labial, though combinations with an alveolar fricative are found, too. It is obvious that in the attested combinations, /j/ is not preceded by any other occlusive than labial or velar, and any other fricative than labial or alveolar.

Finally, let us we look at /bn/. This particular initial combination is not attested, but its voiced counterpart is: /pn/ in *pnout*; there is also another combination of a labial occlusive with a nasal: /pň/ in *pni* (imp. sg. of *pnout*). However, there is no combination in which a nasal is preceded by /b/. We may either regard this fact as an important characteristic of Modern Standard Czech, or view it as accidence. The combination /bn/ was probably found in Old Czech in the word *bnedovanie*.[3] It is also found in the old place names *Bnečice, Bniny* and *Bnišice* (all recorded in NLA), but none of these is any longer used. It is worth noting that *Bnečice* eventually changed to *Mlečice* (see Profous 1951: 104), which suggests that the combination *bn-* was somewhat peculiar. Be that as it may, the point is that there is no word in Modern Standard Czech beginning with /bn/, which means that there is no direct evidence that /bn/ is a possible phonotagm-initial combination.

To sum it up, the tentative initial combinations /bv/, /dj/ and /bn/ violate the following generalizations otherwise valid for the directly attested forms:

---

3   According to Nejedlý (2009), this word is dubious because it is found only in one source and its meaning is uncertain, and because it might even be a scriber's error "nebot' fonematická skupina *bn-* je v češtině v násloví nemožná [because the phonematic group *bn-* is impossible word-initially in Czech]" (p. 275). Note, however, that Nejedlý's reasoning is actually circular: *bn-* is impossible word-initially only if *bnedovanie* is an error. What he no doubt wanted to say is that it is probable that *bnedovanie* is an error because *bn-* is otherwise not attested. But even this need not be true, as the place names we cite immediately suggest.

(3) (a) In the pre-nuclear context a labial fricative is not preceded by another labial.

(b) In the pre-nuclear context, /j/ is not preceded by an occlusive other than labial or velar.

(c) In the pre-nuclear context a nasal is not preceded by /b/.

If the (2b) division into /o–bvaS/, /o–djeT/ and /Škrā–bnöT/ is accepted, these generalizations will not hold. The question is whether we should accept them and reject the analysis, or whether we should reject the generalizations and accept the division. Before deciding for one of these options, we need to discuss the third possible analysis, i.e. (2c).

The divisions into /ob–vaS/, /od–jeT/ and /Škrāb–nöT/ are probably the ones a native speaker would regard as appropriate, and the one sthat other analysts of Czech would prefer. They would not quite probably be viewed as problematic at all, even though they produce phonotagms ending in a voiced consonant, which is in conflict with the fact that neutralization of voicing takes place at the end of words. One might object that this is no problem because in Czech we find many phonotagms ending in a voiced occlusive, for example, /hod/ in /hodňī/ *hodní*. There is some misunderstanding involved, though. We do not know this before-hand—we can only decide that in our analysis! We are aware of no phonetic or phonological signal indicating that the form should be analyzed into /hod/ and /ňī/ instead of /ho/ and /dňī/.[4] The choice of the division is thus a matter of consistency and adequacy of the eventually selected analysis. In the case of /hodňī/ the analysis into /ho/ and /dňī/ is preferable because it produces no unusual phonotagm. However, no such choice is possible for /obvaS/ etc. because /bv/, /dj/ and /bn/ cannot be assigned in their entirety to one or the other phonotagm due to their non-attestedness in the pre-nuclear and post-nuclear context. What it means is that there is no direct evidence that a phonotagm can end in a voiced consonant.[5] That there is no neutralization of voicing in the mentioned forms is proven by the fact that both /b/ and /p/ occur before /v/ (cf. /kapverTskī/ *kapverdský*), that both /d/ and /t/ occur before /j/ (cf. /matjeS/ *matjes* (SSJČ)), and that both /b/ and /p/ occur before /n/ (cf. /napnöT/ *napnout*) in the contexts under question. It should be noted that it is not our recourse to neutralization which

---

4   The morphological boundary, often invoked as a criterion, is irrelevant. In *všední* (historically *vše+dní*) it is elsewhere, and so it is in *povodní* (from *povodeň+í* with syncope).

5   Out of the analysts of Czech, Kučera (1961) was at least aware of the problem. When listing phonemes capable of occurring at the end of the syllable, he included both voiceless and voiced obstruents noting that the difference between them is suspended in this context. He argued that "this [would] later simplify the procedure for dividing interludes into codas and onsets" (p. 80). It does not in fact solve the problem, though.

makes the phonotagms /ob/, /od/ and /Škrāb/ problematic, but the fact that if we analyze, for example, /obvaS/ to /ob/ and /vaS/, we assume the occurrence of /b/ in a context where it is not otherwise found, i.e. phonotagm-finally.

In short, whatever analysis we opt for, we will have to introduce a new descriptive statement. One option is to assume the phonotagm-final combinations /bv/, /dj/ and /bn/ whose constituency is not paralleled elsewhere. The second option is to assume the phonotagm-initial combinations /bv/, /dj/ and /bn/ which have counterparts but which violate the generalizations under (3). The third option is to assume that neutralization of voicing is not operative phonotagm-finally under certain circumstances. And the last option is of course to abandon the very assumption that the forms /obvaS/, /odjeT/ and /ŠkrābnöT/ contain two phonotagms. In either case we must consider consistency, adequacy as well as simplicity of the particular solution.

The last of the mentioned analyses is most problematic. If /ŠkrābnöT/ is a single phonotagm, then /ā/ must function here as a PerP because a phonotagm may contain only one nuclear entity, which is /ö/ here. Hence, what we have called vowels would actually be semiconsonants because they would function both as nuclear and peripheral entities. Secondly, if /ŠkrābnöT/ is a single phonotagm and /ö/ is a nuclear entity, then each of the six phonemes in the (by assumption) pre-nuclear combination /Škrābn/ must be assignable to a pre-nuclear position. The DU set up so far cannot account for such a combination, though. We might reject our initial hypothesis about the DU and replace it with a new one, but we leave this as the last resort. Rather than abandoning the whole analysis, it makes more sense to assume that the forms in question are indeed built of two phonotagms, but such an analysis bears some costs, as we have shown.

The (2a) analysis is rejected for reasons of simplicity and adequacy. We must therefore decide whether to choose the (2b) or the (2c) analysis, that is, whether we will allow for phonotagm-initial combinations otherwise not attested, or whether we will allow for the absence of neutralization of voicing phonotagm-finally. Judging all pros and cons, we have decided for the second solution. Even though the choice may be arbitrary, it is motivated by the fact that the (2c) analysis is more intuitively acceptable than the (2b) one, and that the only problem with the alleged phonotagms /ob/, /od/ and /Škrāb/ is that they end in a voiced consonant. Otherwise, their constituency is similar to that of the other phonotagms—compare in particular /oP/ *op* "ape", /ōT/ *ód* "ode (gen. pl.)" and /ŠkrāP/ *škráb* "a scratch" (SSJČ). The statements under (3) can thus be preserved as important generalizations the combinability of phonemes. The limitation mentioned under (3a) will be discussed in §13.3, and the one under (3a) in §11.2. Finally, we will return to the limitation under (3c) in §14.2 under DE2c.

Now, if /ob/, /od/ and /škrāb/ are recognized as a new type of phonotagms, our analysis must account for them, too. As noted, they differ from the phonotagms like /op/, /ōT/ and /škrāP/ in not undergoing neutralization of voicing of the final consonant. To distinguish these two types, we have called the latter major-type phonotagms, whereas the phonotagms with no final neutralization of voicing will be MINOR-TYPE PHONOTAGMS. Inspired by El-Shakfeh (1987: 513), we define minor-type phonotagms as the entirety of the phenomena which do not fall within the range of the main DU upon which major-type phonotagms are describable. Thus, in /škrābnöT/, /nöT/ is a major-type phonotagm in which /n/ occurs in 'el', /ö/ in 'n' and /T/ in 'il'. The rest, i.e. /škrāb/, which cannot be described upon the main DU, is a minor-type phonotagm.

Having defined minor-type phonotagms, our next task to show how they are identified. Let us recall the main problem of the forms like /obvaS/, /odjeT/ and /škrābnöT/. They apparently contain two phonotagms due to there being two nuclear phonemes in each of them, but the inter-nuclear combinations /bv/, /dj/ and /bn/ cannot be assigned in their entirety to either phonotagm. We have decided to split the combinations between a minor-type and major-type phonotagm. Accordingly, PhFs of words with combinations of this kind contain a minor-type phonotagm. To put it schematically, minor-type phonotagms occur in PhFs of words of the following pattern:

(4)   '$(C_n)V(C_n)C_1C_2(C_n)V(C_n)$'

'C_n' stands here for any number of PerPs with parentheses indicating they are optional; 'V' is a nuclear phoneme; and 'C_1C_2' is a combination of PerPs not permissible either at the beginning or at the end of a major-type phonotagm. In such forms, '$(C_n)V(C_n)C_1$' is a minor-type phonotagm and '$C_2(C_n)V(C_n)$' is a major-type phonotagm. In effect, 'C_1' can be either a voiceless or a voiced occlusive or fricative, and 'C_2' is a sonant. Having analyzed PhFs of Czech words, we conclude that the problematic 'C_1C_2' combinations are those listed in figure IV; none of them occurs at the beginning or at the end of a phonotagm. The bold face indicates the extension of minor-type phonotagms.

As regards the constituency of minor-type phonotagms, they must contain at least two phonemes. One is a phoneme functioning as the nuclear entity in major-type phonotagms. It is reasonable to assume that the same phonemes acquire this function in minor-type phonotagms, too. The second obligatorily present phoneme is of course the final voiceless or the voiced occlusive or the final voiceless or the voiced fricative—remember that their presence is the defining feature of such phonotagms. The nuclear phoneme can be preceded by no PerP or by one, two, three or four PerPs, as the following examples demonstrate:

'C₁C₂'	Occurring in
/pv/	/**kap**verTSkī/ *kapverdský*
/pm/	/**Sklep**miStr/ *sklepmistr*
/bm/	/**ob**mikaT/ *obmykat*, /**ob**meziT/ *obmezit*
/fm/	/**hof**miStr/ *hofmistr*, /**šēf**mexaniK/ *šéfmechanik*
/t'm/	/**hut'**miStr/ *hut'mistr*
/d'm/	/**lod'**mi/ *lod'mi*, /**hňed'**mi/ *hněd'mi*
/bn/	/**Škrāb**nöT/ *škrábnout*, /**drob**nī/ *drobný*
/bň/	/**Škrāb**ňi/ *škrábni*, /**drob**ňī/ *drobní*, /**neblb**ňi/ *neblbni*
/t'n/	/**rtut'**natī/ *rtut'natý*
/d'n/	/**Mňed'**natī/ *měd'natý*
/bM/	/**ob**Mňen/ *obměn*, /**ob**MňeKTšiT/ *obměkčit*
/kM/	/**šik**Mňc/ *šikmě*, /**tak**Mňeř/ *takměř*
/gM/	/**zēg**Mňe/ *zeugmě*
/xM/	/**drax**Mňe/ *drachmě*
/bv/	/**ob**vaS/ *obvaz*, /**ob**voT/ *obvod*
/fv/	/**šēf**vijednavaTŠ/ *šéfvyjednavač*
/tj/	/**mat**jeS/ *matjes*
/dj/	/**od**jeT/ *odjet*, /**pod**jatī/ *podjatý* (SSJČ)

FIGURE IV: Peripheral combinations across minor-type and major-type phonotagms

(5) /ob/ from /obmikaT/ *obmykat*
  /kap/ from /kapverTSkī/ *kapverdský*
  /rtut'/ from /rtut'natī/ *rtut'natý*
  /Škrāb/ from /ŠkrābnöT/ *škrábnout*
  /FŠkrāb/ from /FŠkrābnöT *vškrábnout* (SSJČ)

No example of a minor-type phonotagm beginning with five PerPs has been found, which is not surprising given that such combinations are rare even in the case of major-type phonotagms. The inventory of minor-type phonotagms is limited, but it can be safely concluded that the combinatorics of phonemes at their beginning is not different from that of phonemes at the beginning of major-type phonotagms. In fact, it is not expected to be because, as noted above, minor-type phonotagms differ from the major-type phonotagms mainly in the absence of the final neutralization of voicing. Therefore, we will assume that the distribution of phonemes in the pre-nuclear context as well as in the nuclear context is the same for major-type phonotagms and minor-type phonotagms.

On the other hand, the situation at the end of minor-type phonotagms is not so straightforward because we have not found many examples of such phonotagms ending in two PerPs, and any example of a minor-type phonotagm ending in three Perps. To find them, we have looked for words containing 'CC₁C₂' where 'C₁C₂' is one of the combinations from figure IV and 'C' is a Perp. Among the few we have found belong the following words:

(6) *Verbný* (surname) → /verb–nī/
     Korfmann (foreign surname) → /korf–man/
     Bergmann (foreign surname) → /berg–man/
     postjugoslávský "post-Yugoslavian" → /post–jugoslāFSkī/
     halfvolej (ASCS, from English *halfwolley*) → /half–volej/
     prst'mi (instr. pl. of *prst'*) → /prsť–mi/
     trest'mi (instr. pl. of *trest'*) → /tresť–mi/

Admittedly, the inclusion of some of these words into the inventory of Modern Standard Czech may be a matter of disagreement, but at least *Verbný*, *prst'mi* and *trest'mi* suggest that minor-type phonotagms can end in two PerPs.[6]

Putting these findings together, we conclude that pre-nuclear phonemes of minor-type phonotagms are distributed over the same grid of the five pre-nuclear positions postulated for the major-type phonotagms, and that the post-nuclear phonemes are distributed over two positions. The latter cannot be, logically, identical with any of the three post-nuclear positions of major-type phonotagms. We have thus arrived at the form of a special type of DU which will be called the MINOR DISTRIBUTIONAL UNIT. The phonotactic analysis of some minor-type phonotagms is given in figure V where the top row is the default variant of this unit. The difference between certain pre-nuclear positions becomes suspended in some situations giving rise to archi-positions like in the main DU.

In figure V the post-nuclear positions are marked as 'j1' and 'j2'. Considering what has found out about minor-type phonotagms, we conclude that 'j1' is occupied by /S/, /r/ or /l/, and 'j2' by /p/, /b/, /f/, /ť/, /ď/, /t/, /d/, /k/, /g/ or /x/. The membership of 'j1' is limited due to the few examples of minor-type phonotagms ending in two Perps. More phonemes could perhaps occur there (e.g. /j/ or /Š/), but until further evidence is available, we will not extend the membership. The position can also be empty. On the contrary, position 'j2' must always be non-empty. It is occupied by all 'C₁' phonemes from figure IV. The phonemes /f/ and /x/ are the only fricatives to occur there; their voiced counterparts /v/ and /h/ are not attested. The voiced labial fricative /v/ does not occur in the position because there is no inter-nuclear combination whose division would assign it there. For instance, unlike /pm/, /bm/ and /fm/, the inter-nuclear combination /vm/ as in /revma/ *revma* is attested at the beginning of phonotagms, cf.

---

6 Let us note that *trest'mi* has a variant *trestěmi* [trɛscɛmɪ] with the *-emi* suffix. No such variant is recorded for *prst'mi*.

'pre2'	'pre1'	'e3'	'e2'	'el'	'n'	'j1'	'j2'	Example
Ø	Ø	Ø	Ø	Ø	/o/	Ø	/b/	/ob/ *obmykat*
Ø	/Š/	/k/	Ø	/r/	/ā/	Ø	/b/	/Škrāb/ *škrábnout*
/F/	/Š/	/k/	Ø	/r/	/ā/	Ø	/b/	/FŠkrāb/ *vškrábnout*
/r/	Ø	/t/	Ø	Ø	/u/	Ø	/t'/	/rtut'/ *rtut'natý*
Ø	Ø	/d/	Ø	/r/	/o/	Ø	/b/	/drob/ *drobný*
Ø	Ø	Ø	/M/	/ň/	/e/	Ø	/ď/	/Mňeď/ *mědnatý*
Ø	Ø	/b/		/l/		Ø	/b/	/blb/ *blbnout*
Ø	Ø	/t/	Ø	/r/	/e/	/S/	/t'/	/treSt'/ *trest'mi*
Ø	Ø	/p/		/r/		/S/	/t'/	/prSt'/ *prst'mi*
Ø	Ø	/h/	Ø	Ø	/a/	/l/	/f/	/half/ *halfvolej*
Ø	Ø	Ø	/v/	Ø	/e/	/r/	/b/	/verb/ *Verbný*

FIGURE V: Phonotactic analysis of minor-type phonotagms

0	'pre2'	'pre1'	'e3'	'e2'	'el'	'n'	'j1'	'j2'
1a	'pre2'	'pre1'	'E1'			'n'	'j1'	'j2'
1b	'pre2'	'pre1'	'E2'		'el'	'n'	'j1'	'j2'
1c	'pre2'	'pre1'	'e3'	'e2'	'N'		'j1'	'j2'
2	'pre2'	'pre1'	'E2'		'N'		'j1'	'j2'

FIGURE VI: Minor distributional unit and its contextual variants

/vmīxaT/ *vmíchat*. As to /h/, it might occur in this position because we see no reason a combination /hMň/ could not be possible when /xMň/ is.

Like in the case of the main DU, we will speak about the default variant of the minor DU and its contextual variants; all of them are reproduced in figure VI. The occurrence of phonemes in the particular positions is subject to the same conditions as in the case of the main DU, which will be discussed in the chapters to come. Concluding our discussion, we must mention one important thing. Minor-type phonotagms occur at the beginning of a PhF as in /obvaS/, but they can also be further preceded by another major-type phonotagm (and possibly more of them) as in /objet'mi/ where the bold face indicates the extension of the minor-type phonotagm /bjet'/ which is here in between two major-type phonotagms /o(P)/ and /mi/, the latter being the one upon which it is dependent. Other examples are /neblbňi/ or /enigMňe/. In general, however, the occurrence of minor-type phonotagms is limited in PhFs of Czech words, constituting indeed only a minor subset of phonotactic phenomena.

Chapter Nine: POSITION CLASSES

9.1 Position classes

In chapter 7 we outlined how the notion *distributional unit* can be applied to Czech, and how we can arrive at the positions of the DU. Analyzing self-contained combinations of phonemes, we determine which positions or archi-positions these phonemes occupy, and by assigning them to the positions, we explain their occurrence. It is assumed, first, that a phoneme, once assigned to a position, always occurs there, and second, that phonemes with which it commutes also occur there. Although such assumptions may be later modified, they are good starting hypotheses. A phoneme initially assigned to one position may prove to belong in another position. Its distribution may also be more complex, and it will be assigned to more positions. Eventually, we will come to a certain finite set of phonemes ascribable to one position. This set will be called POSITION CLASS defined as a set of items which occur in the same position or archi-position, including Ø for empty positions (Mulder 1968: 118). It will be abbreviated as *pos*, so for example *pos* 'e2' stands for the position class of pre-nuclear position 'e2'.

Position classes for each position and archi-position of the main DU are summarized in figure I. In the following chapters we will provide arguments why particular phonemes occur in these positions and under what conditions. The first row of the scheme is the grid of the nine positions below each of which there is the respective position class. Cells stretching over two or more positions are position classes for archi-positions. Thus, /r/ and /l/ are given below 'e1' and 'n' because they belong to archi-position 'N', the latter being the product of suspension of the difference between these positions. If a position class includes Ø, the respective position need not be occupied by a phoneme.

'pre2'	'pre1'	'e3'	'e2'	'el'	'n'	'il'	'i2'	'i3'
P F K X	T	k g x h	v	r l			P T K	P T K
T S Š	S Š	t d s z	M	m n ň		j r l	S Š	S Š
M j r l	ř	š ž	Ø	j ř	i e a o u	P T K	F X	Ť
v t h (b)	Ø	Ø		r l	ī ē ā ō ū	m n ň	ř	Ø
Ø		p b f		Ø	ë ä ö	Ø	Ø	
		t' d'					m n ň r l	

FIGURE I: Main distributional unit and its position classes

'j1'	'j2'
S r l	p b f
Ø	t' d' t d
	k g x

FIGURE II: Post-nuclear section of the minor distributional unit and its position classes

Three sections (or contexts) are recognized within the DU: the nuclear one, the pre-nuclear one, and the post-nuclear one. The nuclear section includes position 'n' and archi-position 'N'. The occurrence of phonemes in these positions is dealt with in chapter 10. Since archi-position 'N' has arisen from cancelation of the difference between pre-nuclear position 'e1' and nuclear position 'n', it belongs partly to the nuclear and partly to the pre-nuclear section. The pre-nuclear section further includes positions 'pre2', 'pre1', 'e3', 'e2', 'e1' and archi-positions 'E2' and 'E3'. The occurrence of phonemes in these positions is discussed in chapter 11. Finally, the post-nuclear section includes positions 'i1', 'i2', 'i3' and archi-position 'I', and the occurrence of phonemes in these positions is the topic of chapter 12.

Figure I displays the main DU which underlies all major-type phonotagms. As argued in the preceding chapter, it is necessary to recognize minor-type phonotagms as another type of phonotactic entity, for which a minor DU was postulated. We assume that its pre-nuclear section is identical with that of the main DU and it consists of the same positions and archi-positions. However, since the minor DU accounts for a limited range of phonotactic phenomena, there is not enough evidence that the pre-nuclear positions of the minor DU can be occupied by all of the phonemes which occur there in the main DU. We can still assume that because the crucial difference between the main DU and the minor DU is in the post-nuclear section. The latter has only two positions there; they are reproduced in figure II.

Most phonemes of Czech occur in more than one position. The vowels occur only in the nuclear position. The consonants /š/, /ž/ also occur only in one position, namely in 'e3', although their archi-phoneme occurs in other positions, too. The remaining consonants occur in two or more positions, including the post-nuclear positions of the minor DU. The semiconsonants /r/, /l/ also occur in more positions. The occurrence of PerPs in particular peripheral positions is shown in figure III reproduced on the next page. Nuclear phonemes are not included, as the vowels occur only in position 'n', and the nuclear semiconsonants only in archi-position 'N'. Cells stretching horizontally over two or more positions stand for an archi-position; thus, /r/ occurs in post-nuclear archi-position 'I' which corresponds to the intersection of 'i2' and 'i3'. Cells stretching verti-

	'pre2'	'pre1'	'e3'	'e2'	'e1'	'i1'	'i2'	'i3'	'j1'	'j2'
/ř/		+			+	+				
/j/	+				+	+				
/r/	+				+	+	+		+	
/l/	+				+	+	+		+	
/m/					+	+	+			
/n/	+			+	+	+	+			
/ň/					+	+	+			
/x/	+		+				+			+
/h/			+							
/š/	+	+	+				+	+		
/ž/			+							
/s/	+	+	+				+	+	+	
/z/			+							
/t/	+	+	+			+	+	+		+
/d/			+							+
/k/	+		+			+	+	+		+
/g/			+							+
/p/	+			+		+	+	+		+
/b/				+						+
/f/	+			+			+			+
/v/				+						
/t'/				+				+		+
/d'/				+						+

FIGURE III: Occurrence of peripheral phonemes in peripheral positions

cally over two or more phonemes stand for archi-phonemes. For example, /S/ corresponding to the intersection of /s/ and /z/ occurs in 'pre1'; neither /s/ nor /z/ occurs there. The phonemes /t/, /h/, /v/ and /b/ occur in addition in 'pre2', which is not shown in the figure.

If some phonemes occur in more positions, an obvious question to ask is under what circumstances they occur there. Since a position is an expression of distributional and combinatory potentials of a phoneme (see the next section), phonemes are assigned to positions according to their properties. For example, /r/ occurs both in 'e1' and 'pre2'. In forms such as /trām/ *trám* it is obvious that it occurs in 'e1' because 'pre2' is the leftmost position and phonemes occurring there cannot be preceded by any other PerP. Similarly, in /rti/ *rty*, /r/ occurs in 'pre2' because 'e1' is the rightmost pre-nuclear position, and phonemes occurring there can only be followed by a vowel. However, in forms like /rām/ *rám*, we do not have any of these "hints" as to which position the /r/ could belong because its particular occurrence conforms to properties of both 'pre2' and 'e1'. In order to deal with situations like this, we introduce the PRINCIPLE OF LESSER PERIPHERALITY which is based on the centripetal nature of the DU, which means that positions more distant from the nuclear are more peripheral.

(1)   PRINCIPLE OF LESSER PERIPHERALITY
      In case PerPs can be assigned to several positions in a particular PhF, they
      are assigned to the least peripheral position.

9.2 Phonotactic properties and collocational restrictions

A phoneme is assigned to a position if and only if it has properties characterizing this position, that is, if its distribution is the same as the distribution of other phonemes belonging there. Such common characteristics will be called PHONOTACTIC PROPERTIES by which we mean distributional and combinatory capacities of a phoneme, i.e its occurrences in various positions of the DU, and its ability to combine with other phonemes from other positions.

Position classes are sets of phonemes which share certain phonotactic properties, and a position is an expression of these properties. Every position is defined by a unique set of phonotactic properties. For a phoneme to belong to a certain position, it is necessary that it have phonotactic properties which unambiguously determine its membership. For example, even though both /o/ and nuclear /r/ are preceded by up to four PerPs (cf. /PštroS/ *pštros* and /TŠtvrT/ *čtvrt*), and followed by up to three PerPs (cf. /vojSK/ *vojsk* and /šMrnTS/ *šmrnc*), they do not belong to the same positions because /r/ is not preceded by phonemes from *pos* 'e1' whereas /o/ is (cf. /noS/ *nos*). Therefore, there is a phonotactic property which /o/ has, but /r/ does not.

Some phonemes belong to more positions provided that they display phonotactic properties of more positions. The total sum of their phonotactic properties is equal to the sum of the properties of the individual positions. Thus, /j/ is a member of three position classes, *pos* 'e1', *pos* 'pre1' and *pos* 'i1' because it displays phonotactic properties of all of them. It stands right before a nuclear phoneme preceded by other PerPs (cf. /svjeT/ *svět*) or it stands before a PerP being the phoneme in the first phonotagm (cf. /jSte/ *jste*) or it stands right after a nuclear phoneme followed by other PerPs (cf. /vojSK/ *vojsk*). For each of these possibilities, there are other phonemes with the same properties (cf. /r/ in /svraP/ *svrab*, /rti/ *rty* and /verST/ *verst*, respectively).

A phoneme occurring in a position has in principle all phonotactic properties of the position in question. However, not each and every one phoneme must be actually attested to display each and every one phonotactic property. To put it simply: not all combinations of phonemes are always attested. The absence of some may be accidental if there is not enough evidence to declare it regular. As we argued in §5.4, regular non-occurrences pertain to some well-defined class of entities, but single non-occurrences are just accidental. For instance, all phonemes of *pos* 'e1' (i.e. /m/, /n/, /ň/, /j/, /ř/, /r/, /l/) have the ability to be preceded by two PerPs 'C₁C₂' where 'C₁' is from *pos* 'pre2' (i.e. /P/, /F/, /K/, /X/, /T/, /S/, /Š/, /M/, /j/, /r/, /l/, /v/, /t/, /h/, /b/) and 'C₂' from *pos* 'e2' (i.e. /v/, /M/). However, this particular property is only attested for /ň/, /j/ and /l/, cf. /vMň/ in *vměstnat*, /rvj/ in *rvěte* and /vMl/ in *vmlátit*. Yet, there is no reason to think the other phonemes do not have this property, too, that is, it can be safely assumed that /vMn/, /vMř/ or /vMr/ are potential pre-nuclear combinations in Czech. They are missing by accidence because it is not possible to discern some regularity behind their absence. On the contrary, the absence of the combination /vMm/ is not accidental because it is predictable from another fact. Although all phonemes from *pos* 'e1' have the capacity to be preceded by all phonemes from *pos* 'e2' (i.e. /v/, /M/), the combination /Mm/ is not found. The nasal /m/ is a labial, and if the combinability of labials is examined in the pre-nuclear context, we find out that no labial is attested to be preceded by /M/. This fact can be regularized by proposing that no labial is capable of being preceded by a nasal in the pre-nuclear context, and by failing to refute this hypothesis, we adopt it as a descriptive statement about the distribution of labials.

Statements like these, that is, unrefuted hypotheses about co-occurrences of certain classes of phonemes, will be called COLLOCATIONAL RESTRICTIONS (a term adopted from Fudge 1969; analyzing Czech, Kučera 1961 speaks about sequential constraints). They will be introduced in the course of the analysis, and eventually, for the sake of reference and clarity, numbered and summarized in appendix A. Some of the restrictions may be viewed as resulting from general phonetic restrictions or from the historical development of Czech. The mentioned impossibility of /Mm/ (i.e. of [mm]) can be explained by the fact that no Czech word begins with two identical contoids. Similarly, the impossibility of diphthongal vowels /ĕ/, /ä/, /ö/, which are realized as [ɛu̯], [au̯], [ou̯], to be followed by /j/ can be explained by saying that within single syllable two glides (i.e. [u̯]/[w] and [j]) cannot stand next to each other in Czech. Other restrictions cannot perhaps be readily explained. For example, it is hard to say why the nasals /m/, /n/, /ň/ cannot be preceded by /b/ if they can be by /p/ (cf. /pnöT/ *pnout* and /pňi/ *pni*).

At this point two important limitations on the occurrence of phonemes will be mentioned. First, no phonotagm can contain two identical phonemes standing next two each other, and second, no occlusive or fricative is found to be preceded by its voicing archi-phoneme within a single phonotagm. To put it bluntly, Czech does not allow geminates within a single phonotagm (remember that /Tt/ is realized as [tt] and /Td/ as [dd]). No such combinations have been found at the beginning and at the end of a word. They are found within words, for example in /TŠtvrTtōn/ *čtvrttón* or /oTdanī/ *oddaný*, but such combinations must be divided between two phonotagms exactly because there is no evidence they can occur at the beginning or at the end of a phonotagm. Accordingly, we propose the following two restrictions:[1]

(2) (a) Two identical phonemes cannot stand in close proximity.
     (b) A voiceless or a voiced consonant (i.e. an occlusive or a fricative) cannot stand in close proximity with a voicing archi-phoneme of the same place and manner of articulation.

If not said otherwise, all collocational restrictions introduced in this work apply to the phonotagm as a whole. Some may apply only to the pre-nuclear or to the post-nuclear context, but this fact is always made clear. All of them should be understood as being applicable to both major-type and minor-type phonotagms. Finally, all restrictions pertain exclusively to Czech, as we do not make any claims about other languages or all languages for that matter. Such claims are in fact highly speculative in their nature, and we have rejected speculation as a method.

---

1   The restrictions could be violated by the PhF of *dcera* provided that it is realized as [ttsɛra] (→ /TTsera/), but since much more common and stylistically neutral pronunciation of this word is [tsɛra] (→ /Tsera/), we do not considered it to be a valid refuting example. Another possible refutation may come from the imperative *přesvěd̓*. Since it is derived from *přesvěd̓it* with the PhF /přesvjeTTŠiT/, its PhF is expected to be /přesvjeTTŠ/. However, its pronunciation is probably always [přesvjeʧ], so its PhF will be /přesvjeTŠ/.

Chapter Ten: NUCLEAR DISTRIBUTION

For Czech, we have made a distinction between two types of nuclear phonemes, vowels and semiconsonants. The former are phonemes with the sole function of being identity elements of phonotagms on which the other phonemes are dependent for their occurrence and function. The latter are phonemes which, like vowels, function as identity elements in the sense that other phonemes are dependent on them for their occurrence and function, but they can also, like consonants, function as the dependent entities. This chapter discusses the distribution of these two classes in the nuclear context.

10.1 Position class 'n'

Position 'n' has been introduced to account for the occurrence of phonemes capable of being self-contained phonotactic entities on their own. The set of entities occurring in this position is given under (1); we have called these phonemes vowels. Position 'n' is never empty because the phoneme occurring there is the identity element of the phonotagm in question. Phonotactic properties of the position class are schematized in figure I, and examples provided in appendix D. However, as we presently show, the distribution of some of the phonemes is restricted in certain situations.

(1) *pos* 'n' ∈ {/i/, /e/, /a/, /o/, /u/, /ī/, /ē/, /ā/, /ō/, /ū/, /ĕ/, /ä/, /ö/}

In dealing with phonotactic properties of individual positions in this and the following chapters we will provide for every position class a list of phonotactic properties pertinent to it. In a phonotagm a phoneme may be preceded or followed by another phoneme. The former will be marked by 'P', and the latter by 'F'. In both cases the number of the preceding and following phonemes will be marked. When discussing the occurrence of PerPs in the next two chapters, we will specify the membership of these phonemes, but such a practice is not used for the nuclear phonemes because it would be quite cumbersome and extensive. There are a great many possibilities as to which positions the preceding and following phonemes may be distributed.

	F0	F1	F2	F3
P0	/e/ /ī, /ĕ/ /ā/ /ō/ /ū/ /ĕ/ /ä/ /ö/	/ī/ /ö/	/ī/ /ĕ/ /ā/ /ō/ /ĕ/ /ä/ /ö/	/i/ /e/ /a/ /o/ /u/ /ī/ /ĕ/ /ä/ /ō/ /ĕ/ /ä/ /ö/
P1	/ū/		/ō/ /ĕ/	(/i/) /ō/ /ū/ /ĕ/ /ä/ /ö/
P2	/ĕ/	/ĕ/ /ö/	/ō/ /ĕ/ /ä/	/i/ /e/ /a/ /o/ /u/ /ä/ /ō/ /ū/ /ĕ/ /ä/
P3	/ō/ /ĕ/ /ä/	/ō/ /ĕ/ /ä/	/ō/ /ĕ/ /ä/ /ö/	/i/ /e/ /o/ /u/ /ī/ /ä/ /ō/ /ū/ /ĕ/ /ä/
P4	/i/ /a/ /o/ /u/ /ō/ /ū/ /ĕ/ /ä/	/ō/ /ū/ /ĕ/ /ä/ /ö/	/i/ /e/ /a/ /u/ /ä/ /ō/ /ū/ /ĕ/ /ä/ /ö/	all
P5	all	/i/ /a/ /o/ /u/ /ī/ /ĕ/ /ā/ /ō/ /ū/ /ĕ/ /ä/ /ö/	all	all

FIGURE I: Phonotactic properties for *pos* 'n' and phonemes for which particular properties are not attested

Let us examine figure I. Each cell of the table corresponds to one phonotactic property. The figure lists phonemes for which a given phonotactic property is NOT attested. Some properties are not attested for all members of *pos* 'n'. Our task is to determine whether phonemes not found to have a certain property lack this property by accidence, or whether they are regularly incapable of having it.

The absence of property 'P5'/'F0' which corresponds to phonotagm type 'CCCCCV' was already mentioned in §8.1 where we concluded that it was accidental that no vowel was found to preceded by five PerPs while being followed by none. However, as is obvious from figure I, only the short vowels are found to be preceded by five PerPs. Accordingly, we propose the following collocational restriction:

(2)   A non-short vowel cannot be preceded by more than four PerPs.

Figure I also shows that no vowel is attested to display properties 'P4'/'F3', 'P5'/'F2' and 'P5'/'F3'. This fact was already regularized in §8.1 by a rule stating that no phonotagm can contain more than six non-vowels.

Besides these regular non-occurrences, there are also some which must be regarded simply as accidental. Yet we can see that there are tendencies to avoid certain combinations. First, not all vowels are attested to be preceded by a PerP (cf. property 'P0'). Second, there are not many phonotagms ending in three

Perps (cf. property 'F3'). Third, there are not many phonotagms beginning with four or five Perps (cf. properties 'P4' and 'P5'). The most defective distribution is shown by the diphthongal vowels (especially /ä/ and /ĕ/) and /ō/. Finally, it is apparent that vowels prefer phonotagms which begin with one or two Perps, and end in none or one or two Perps.

10.2 Nuclearity of /r/, /l/

Vowels are not the only nuclear entities in Czech. The phonemes /r/ and /l/ assume this function, too, but they function in addition as peripheral entities. It is natural to ask under what circumstances they fulfill these functions. Although the answer was already suggested in the preceding chapters, the issue has not been fully considered.

In §3.5 we referred to the phonetic research which had shown that there was probably no relevant articulatory and acoustic difference between the allophones of the nuclear /r/, /l/, and those of the non-nuclear /r/, /l/. It cannot therefore be claimed that /r/, /l/ are nuclear when realized as syllabic [r̩], [l̩], and non-nuclear when realized as non-syllabic [r], [l]. The decision whether /r/ and /l/ function as nuclear or non-nuclear phonemes is not dependent and does not follow from the fact that they are syllabic or non-syllabic. Nuclearity is not the same thing as syllabicity; the former is a phonological function, whereas the latter is a certain phonetic or perceptional property. Yet the notions are to some extent connected because nuclear phonemes are usually realized as syllabic sounds, and non-nuclear phonemes are usually realized as non-syllabic sounds.

Before reviewing of the nuclearity of /r/ and /l/, let us repeat what was said about this notion in §6.3. Phonemes are nuclear if (and because) they comply with the definition of a nuclear entity: it is the entity upon which other entities in self-contained combinations are dependent for their function. The function of the dependent, peripheral entities is derived from the function of the nuclear entity. The function an entity has is not something to be discovered, that is, the function is not inherent in a given phoneme (or its allophone). It is ascribed to phonemes on the basis of certain criteria. The necessary (but not sufficient) condition for a phoneme to be nuclear is that it cannot be omitted from the self-contained combination in question. When omitted, the result is not self-contained. By this we can test that in /Sto/ *sto* it is /o/ that is nuclear because once it is omitted, the result /St/ is not self-contained (because Czech does not words with such a form). To put it otherwise, those phonemes which can be omitted cannot be nuclear phonemes. The condition is, however, not sufficient because some non-nuclear phonemes cannot also be omitted from the construction. This situation is encountered in languages where phonotagms always consist of at least two phonemes. In such languages the decision as to which phonemes function as nuclear entities is governed by other criteria.

In chapter 7 we determined that the phonemes /i/, /e/, /a/, /o/, /u/, /ī/, /ē/, /ā/, /ō/, /ū/, /ë/, /ä/ and /ö/ functioned as nuclear entities. To be precise, if they occur, they have this function. They need not always occur because there are many PhFs of Czech words which do not contain any vowel (e.g. /TŠtvrT/ *čtvrt* or /plST/ *plst*). Such forms, by being directly attested, are self-contained like those with vowels. Examining the constituency of the vowel-less forms, we notice two things. First, they always contain at least two phonemes (whereas forms with a vowel may contain only the vowel; cf. /a/ *a*, /o/ *o*); second, one of these phonemes is always either /r/ or /l/. It is for this reason we have concluded that /r/ and /l/ function as nuclear entities. Nevertheless, we must also acknowledge that they cannot fulfill this role on their own but must be accompanied by at least one other phoneme. Accordingly, the following statement holds without exception in Czech:

(3)   If /r/ or /l/ appears in a PhF of a word, at least one other phoneme stands next to it.

The statement does not specify whether /r/ and /l/ are nuclear or not. It holds for them in general. If these phonemes function as peripheral entities, then they are by definition dependent on the occurrence of another phoneme.

If the neighboring phoneme is a vowel, /r/ and /l/ do not function as nuclear entities; the nuclear function is carried out by the vowel. It is a consequence of the fact that within such a combination the phoneme /r/ or /l/ is omissible, but the vowel is not. For example, in /ar/ the /r/ can be omitted and the result will still be a self-contained entity because /a/ is attested as the PhF of *a*; /r/ cannot thus be a nuclear entity. On the other hand, if /a/ is left out, the result is not a self-contained entity because /r/ is not directly attested as a form of any Czech signum. It may be objected that in the case /hra/ (cf. *hra*) the vowel can be omitted with the result being a self-contained entity (i.e. /hr/ attested in *hr*—see below). However, this assumes that /hra/ consists of two phonotagms, /hr/ and /a/, but such an analysis has been rejected on the grounds of material adequacy. See §5.5 for the argument. Consequently, the following statement holds:

(4)   If, within a PhF of a word, /r/ or /l/ stands next to a vowel, it is not nuclear.

Having said this, we must add at once that it does not follow from (4) that if /r/ and /l/ do not stand next to a vowel, they are nuclear. This is not true. To demonstrate it, we will discuss particular situations when /r/ and /l/ do not stand next to a vowel.

One such situation is when /r/ and /l/ are both preceded and followed by a consonant as in /prST/, /plST/, /vlK/ or /drn/. The reason they are nuclear here follows from the fact they are commutable with vowels; see the commutations under (5). This conclusion is based on the Principle of Mutual Commutability introduced in §6.7. In /paST/, /vaK/ and /den/, the vowels can be replaced only by other vowels or by /r/ or /l/; if they are replaced by any other phoneme, the result will not be a well-formed phonotagm (e.g. /pmST/, /vnK/, /dřn/).

(5) (a) /paST/ *past* × /pūST/ *půst* × /prST/ *prst* × /plST/ *plst*
    (b) /vaK/ *vak* × /vīK/ *vík* × /vlK/ *vlk*
    (c) /den/ *den* × /dun/ *dun* (gen. pl. of *duna*) × /drn/ *drn*

However, as shown below, this occurrence of /r/ and /l/ may not be without problems. One concerns the analysis of the forms such as /umrlTšī/ *umrlčí*, and another concerns the analysis of forms such as /zrdösiT/ *zrdousit*. Before getting to them, we will consider the other situation in which /r/ and /l/ are nuclear.

It is traditionally asserted that /r/ and /l/ also have the nuclear function (or are syllabic) when occurring after a consonant at the end of a word (see e.g. Frinta 1909: 107, 115, Kučera 1961: 72), namely in forms like these:

(6) (a) /vītr/ *vítr*, /obr/ *obr*, /hadr/ *hadr*, /miStr/ *mistr*
    (b) /hňetl/ *hnětl*, /mandl/ *mandl*, /māvl/ *mávl*, /roStl/ *rostl*

The nuclearity of /r/ and /l/ is not so straightforward in this case, though. The commutation test and the Principle of Mutual Commutability are of no help here because, for example, /r/ in /vītr/ can be replaced both by a vowel (cf. /vīte/ *víte*) and a PerP (cf. /vīTS/ *víc*, with contextual neutralization of voicing). It may be argued that there is a difference in these two commutations: /vīte/ contains two phonotagms whereas /vīTS/ only one. This is true, but it does not prove whether /vītr/ contains two phonotagms or one. For something to be a phonotagm it must be a self-contained phonotactic entity, which means it is not dependent on anything else at a given level of analysis. If /vītr/ is to be analyzed into two phonotagms one of which contains a nuclear /r/, it must be proven that the form can indeed be divided into them (see the discussion in §5.5). The possible analyses are /vī–tr/, /vīT–tr/ (with functional amalgamation of /T/ and /t/) and /vīt–r/. We reject the last at once because, as we have said, /r/ does not occur on its own. It is then irrelevant which of the remaining analyses is chosen because both assume the phonotagm /tr/. The point is now to determine whether /tr/ is a self-contained and self-contained phonotactic construction, as the analysis presumes.

Self-containedness is shown by direct attestation. Such a proof is not available here because there is no word with the form /tr/. But this does not necessarily mean that it is not self-contained. In fact, the situation is not uncommon. For example, the form /mele/ (cf. *mele* "he grinds") is analyzable into two phonotagms, /mel/ and /le/, even though the latter is not directly attested (/mel/ is, cf. *mel* ("grind! (sg.)"). The reason it is a self-contained phonotagm follows from the fact that /le/ does not violate any distributional restriction in Czech, that is, we assume it is self-contained (well-formed) by failing to prove the opposite. Now, is there, in the case of /tr/, a phonological rule it violates? In other words, is it appropriate to assume that phonotagms of the structure *consonant – semiconsonant* are not possible in Czech? A possible example of a directly attested phonotagm of this structure may be supplied by /hr/, the form of the word *hr*[1] which is part of the idiom *být hr* "to be rash, hasty". This word is, however, in origin an onomatopoeic expression, and its acceptance may be questionable. It creates precedence for admission of other onomatopoeic expressions, which might not be quite desirable because their phonotactic structure differs from the rest of the Czech vocabulary (cf. Fidler 2010). But if /hr/ is accepted after all, it can be used as the evidence that Czech allows phonotagms built only of a consonant followed by a semiconsonant. If it is rejected, no such evidence is available because we are not aware of any other word of this phonological structure.[2] In that case, we do not have any argument with which we could justify that /vītr/, but also /miStr/ and similar forms, can be divided into two phonotagms. Consequently, they would have to be regarded as mono-phonotagmic. Although it is possible to pursue this conclusion, we do not find it appropriate for two reasons. First, we do not think that /hr/ as the form of *hr* should really be rejected only because it is onomatopoeic in origin. The expression *být hr* has been fully lexicalized, and if nothing else, /hr/ suggests that phonotagms of the structure *consonant – semiconsonant* are possible in Czech. Second, the analysis of /vītr/ into two phonotagms is more materially adequate than the analysis which views it as a single phonotagm. The word *vítr* is disyllabic, and even though we do not operate with syllabicity, it is a virtue of a description if it agrees with the facts, in this case, if nuclearity agrees with syllabicity.

Having accepted /hr/ as a well-formed phonotagm, we will now look at a related problem. The property common to the forms given under (6) above is that

---

1   We could, at least hypothetically, also have *schl* as a variant of *schnul* "he was getting dry". However, such a form is apparently avoided and not used, even though its prefixed derivate *uschl* "he got dry" is found.

2   Apart from other onomatopoeic expressions such as *pr* used to make horses stop or *vr* used to express the snarl of a dog.

	2 syllables	1 syllable
Tyrl	19 (59.4 %)	12 (37.5 %)

	2 syllables	1 syllable
Karl	17 (53.1 %)	15 (46.9 %)

	3 syllables	2 syllables
zestárl	27 (84.4 %)	5 (15.6 %)

FIGURE II: Results of the test done by students

/r/ or /l/ occurs at the end of a PhF of a word and is not preceded by a vowel. If it were preceded by a vowel, it would of course not be nuclear (cf. /mīr/ *mír*, /vūl/ *vůl*). Let us now consider other examples in which /r/ or /l/ is final and is not preceded by a vowel:

(7) (a)   /Stārl/ *stárl* "he was getting old", /zeStārl/ *zestárl* "he got old"
     (b)   /tirl/ *Tyrl*, /karl/ *Karl* (both proper names)

The words are all interpreted as ending in /rl/ or, to put it otherwise, in a vocoid followed by [rl]. However, we have been suggested that at least for some people these words are different: While *stárl* is dissyllabic (and *zestárl* trisyllabic), *Tyrl* and *Karl* are monosyllabic. We have tried to confirm this by testing our first-year phonetics students. They were given a list of 37 Czech sentences in which one word was underlined, and their task was to write down how many syllables the underlined word contained. The words included *Tyrl*, *Karl* and *zestárl*, but also several other words such as *fonologie, křtiny, sestřenice, knihkupectví, do-hodl* to distract their attention, so that the students did not know the intention of the test. The test was filled in by 32 students, and its results are in figure II.[3]

The results confirm that the mentioned words are indeed perceived differ-ently.[4] The obvious question is whether it is because the final [rl] sequence is pronounced differently, which results in different perception, or because it is pronounced alike and the words are perceived differently due to other reasons. If their pronunciations differ, then it must be accounted for in phonology. How-ever, to the best of our knowledge, no phonetic study has been conducted to find

---

3   One student apparently did not understand his/her task and gave very strange numbers for the first 14 words, so *Tyrl* consisted of 21 syllables according to him/her. Let us also note that the only conclusion we draw from the test is that the words are perceived differ-ently. The tested sample of people was too small for any other conclusion.
4   According to the dictionary of rhymes, the word *stárl* and *Karl* both contain two sylla-bles (see Cvrček – Cvrčková 2011: 264). However, in the dictionary the number of sylla-bles was automatically counted, so such a result is expectable.

our whether these words are really pronounced differently, that is, whether the final [l] in *(ze)stárl* is articulatorily and/or acoustically distinct from the final [l] in *Karl* or *Tyrl*. Considering the fact that no significant difference has been found between syllabic and non-syllabic [r] and [l] in other contexts (see §3.5 for the references), it is reasonable to assume that the pronunciation is the same. Hence the reason they are not perceived alike must be in something else. It is quite likely that what induces some Czechs to view the names *Tyrl* and *Karl* as monosyllabic is their foreign origin, and that what enforces the disyllabic interpretation of *stárl* is the fact that it contains two monemes (morphemes), namely *stár* "old" and the verbal suffix *-l*. In either case, the difference cannot be phonological. If it were, it should, in the first place, have a back-up in the pronunciation for which there is no evidence, and secondly, the inevitable conclusion would be that Czech has two phonemes /l/: one syllabic in *stárl* and one non-syllabic in *Karl*. This conclusion seems to be unwarranted.

Having concluded that /rl/ in /Stārl/, /karl/ and /tirl/ is phononologically identical, we must treat it so in the phonotactic analysis. Our concern here is not whether the mentioned forms are realized as one or two syllables, but whether they can be analyzed into two phonotagms or whether they are single units. In essence, they are not different from the forms like /vītr/ or /hňetl/ mentioned under (6) above. If the latter contain two phonotagms, /vīT/ and /tr/, and /hňeT/ and /tl/ (both with functional amalgamation), can /Stārl/, /karl/ and /tirl/ be analyzed into two phonotagms, namely to /Stār/ and /rl/, /kar/ and /rl/, and /tir/ and /rl/? Can the mentioned forms contain the phonotagm /rl/? Having accepted /tr/ (as well as /tl/) as a potential phonotagm, we might accept /rl/, too. Nevertheless, there is a fundamental difference between /rl/ and /tr/ (or /tl/).

Let us recall why /tr/ was accepted as possible above. The directly attested form /hr/ has been taken as evidence that phonotagms of the structure *consonant – semiconsonant* are possible in Czech. The same argument cannot be used for the alleged phonotagm /rl/ because it does not have the mentioned structure. It is to be remembered that /r/ and /l/ have been given the status of semiconsonants because they function both as nuclear entities and peripheral entities, whereas a consonant is a phoneme which functions only as a peripheral entity. Phonologically, /r/ and /l/ are thus different from /t/, and so /rl/ does not have the same phonological structure as /tr/ or /hr/. Now, we do not have any evidence that phonotagms of the structure *semiconsonant – semiconsonant* are possible in Czech because no such form is attested. Of course, we could still assume that they are possible, but it is not appropriate to assume something which cannot be backed up with evidence.

Consequently, /Stārl/, /tirl/ and /karl/ will be treated as single phonotagms. This analysis must not be misunderstood, though. The fact they are interpreted as single phonotagms does not mean that they correspond to single syllables. We do not make any claim about this. What we actually say is that the combination /rl/ cannot, unlike /tr/, function as a self-contained phonotactic entity because its occurrence is dependent on the preceding vowel, namely on /ā/ in /Stārl/, /i/ in /tirl/ and /a/ in /karl/. In other words, if a combination of two semiconsonants occurs in a PhF of a Czech word, it is *always* preceded by at least one other phoneme. This statement holds without exception. In contrast, the mentioned dependency does not hold for combinations of the structure *consonant – semiconsonant* as the form /hr/ demonstrates.

/Stārl/, /tirl/ and /karl/ being single phonotagms, they all contain the post-nuclear combination /rl/ which is comparable to /lm/, /jn/, /řň/, /jr/, /jl/ (cf. *jilm, hejn, čerň, chejr, koktejl*). To begin with, /rl/ is not expandable[5] because no PerP can come before /r/ or after /l/, and this is also true for /lm/, /jn/, /rň/, /jr/, /jl/. To analyze the latter combinations, we proposed in §7.3 that the left phonemes occurred in position 'i', where they had been mapped in the previous analysis, and that the right phonemes, that is, /m/ of /lm/, /n/ of /jn/, /ň/ of /rň/, /r/ of /jr/, and /l/ of /jl/, occurred in archi-position 'I'. The same analysis can be applied to /rl/: the /r/ will be mapped onto position 'i1', where it does indeed occur, and the /l/ onto archi-position 'I' where it occurs, too (as we have just shown).

Before continuing, we will summarize conclusions of the preceding paragraphs in the following collocational restriction. It is not violated by /tr/ or by /hr/ where /t/ and /h/ are consonants, but it is violated by /rl/ because /r/ and /l/ are semiconsonants, not consonants.

(8)   A nuclear semiconsonant must be preceded by at least one consonant.

This restriction will help us in dealing with another occurrence of the combination /rl/. It is not found only at the end of a PhF of a word but also within it; see the following examples:

(9)   /umrlTse/ *umrlce*, /umrlTšī/ *umrlčí*, /Štamprlka/ *štamprlka*, /povrlŠtī/ *povr-lští*[6]

---

5   See §13.6 on expandability.
6   The word *umrlce* is gen. sg. of *umrlec* "dead man", and *umrlčí* is an adjective derived from it; both are listed in Czech dictionaries. *Štamprlka*, a diminutive of *štamprle* "jigger", is not mentioned in any dictionary, but can be found in the Czech National Corpus and through Google.com (as of 11 March 2013). Admittedly, it could be withdrawn as a non-standard word, but we mention it here because there are not many words illustrating the phenomenon under discussion. *Povrlští* is an adjective derived from the place name *Povrly*.

The forms are problematic for the traditional analysis of the syllabicity of /r/ and /l/ which asserts that they are syllabic between two consonants. The traditional analysis does not usually recognize semiconsonants as a separate class of phonemes distinct from consonants, classifying /r/ and /l/ as consonants. The consequence must then be that *both* /r/ and /l/ are syllabic in the mentioned forms because both occur between two consonants (i.e. in /umrlTse/, /r/ stands in between /m/ and /l/, and /l/ stands in between /r/ and /T/). Such a conclusion is, however, in contradiction with how the words *umrlce* and *umrlčí* are treated in verses like this one:[7]

(10) [tak takɛ: trɛst trɛst z nɛkonɛʧna]   *Tak také trest, trest z nekonečna,*
      [do xvi:lɛ zbalɛn sɛvr̥ɛ pjɛst]   *do chvíle zbalen, sevře pěst,*
      [ʔa ra:na stř̥elna: bodna: seʧna:]   *a rána střelná, bodná, sečná*
      [ʔumrlʧiː: rasu ʔumi: smɛ:st]   *umrlčí rasu umí smést...*

If we assume that the first and third line agree in the number of syllables (nine) and that the second and fourth line agree (which is confirmed by other verses in the poem), then *umrlčí* is trisyllabic. This has also been confirmed by the test mentioned above: out of 32 students, 26 (81.5 %) wrote that *umrlčí* contains 3 syllables (2 students wrote 2 syllables, and 1 student wrote 4 syllables). Another confirmation comes from Cvrček – Cvrčková (2011: 168) according to whom the word is also trisyllabic. However, the traditional descriptions predict that the word *umrlčí* contains four syllables, while it behaves and is perceived as trisyllabic. The same is true for *štamprlka* and *povrlští*: the traditional analysis predicts these words contain four syllables, while they are perceived as trisyllabic.[8]

Even if only one of the phonemes /r/ and /l/ is realized as syllabic in the mentioned words, we should still ask which one it is. Whether it can be resolved on phonetic or other grounds is far from certain. But let us leave the topic of syllabicity and consider the forms under (9) in light of the approach of this work. Despite the problems with the syllabicity, the forms are easy to analyze in our theoretical framework. It is here where the restriction (8) becomes relevant. It follows from it that it is the /r/ that is nuclear in the forms under question; it cannot be /l/ because the latter is not preceded by a consonant. Moreover, each of the forms can be divided into three phonotagms in the following manner:

---

7   Taken from the collection *Dokument* by Vladimír Holan, Prague, 1949, p. 15. The phonetic transcription is our own. Other examples of the use of these words in verse will be gained by looking in the database of PSJČ available online.

8   Cvrček – Cvrčková (2011) does not mention these words, but our test has confirmed it: out of 32 students, 31 (96.9 %) viewed *štamprlka* as trisyllabic, and 29 (90.6 %) viewed *povrlští* as trisyllabic.

(11) /umrlTšī/ → /um/ + /Mrl/ + /lTšī/
     /Štamprlka/ → /ŠtamP/ + /prl/ + /lka/
     /povrlŠtʾī/ → /poF/ + /vrl/ + /lŠtʾī/

In all cases we assume functional amalgamation because the phonemes in question can belong, as regards their distribution, to the pre-nuclear as well as to the
post-nuclear context.[9] The analysis produces the phonotagms /Mrl/, /prl/ and
/vrl/. They have no parallel in directly attested forms, but we see no reason to
declare them ill-formed. They do not violate the restriction (8) introduced above
or any other restriction on the occurrence of the particular phonemes. In all of
them the phoneme /r/ is nuclear and is followed by /l/ standing in a post-nuclear
position. The alternative analysis is to regard the /rl/ as part of the preceding
phonotagms, i.e. to assume that the forms contain the phonotagms /umrl/,
/Štamprl/ and /povrl/. Such an interpretation, though possible, would considerably complicate the whole phonotactic analysis, as we would have to account for
the post-nuclear combinations /mrl/, /mprl/ and /vrl/. In particular, /mprl/ would
be problematic because Czech does not otherwise allow post-nuclear combination of four phonemes. For this reason, this alternative analysis is rejected.

    We have said the necessary condition for /r/ and /l/ to be nuclear entities is
that they do not stand next to a vowel, but it has also been pointed out that it
does not follow from it that they function as nuclear entities if not standing next
to a vowel. One case in point has just been shown: in forms like /tirl/ the final /l/
is not nuclear. Another situation is when /r/ or /l/ occurs at the beginning of a
word followed by a consonant, for example as in /rti/ *rty*, /rdösiT/ *rdousit*,
/lpjeT/ *lpět* or /lhoStejnī/ *lhostejný*. Before we present our argument, it will be
good to view these forms in a wider perspective.

    The word-initial occurrence of /r/ and /l/ is comparable to /M/ and /j/ (cf.
/MSta/ *msta* and /jho/ *jho*), and all of these phonemes are part of a number of
unique combinations listed in figure III. There have been disputes as to whether
the initial [m], [j], [r] and [l] (by which /M/, /j/, /r/ and /l/ are realized here) constitute separate syllable cores in these combinations. The general consensus is
that they are not (see e.g. Hála 1956: 62, 1961: 123; Palková 1997: 154; Duběda
2005: 132; Krčmová 2008: 177). The controversy springs from disagreements
about the precise definition of the core of the phonic syllable. Generally, it is assumed that it is the segment associated with the peak of sonority (however the

---

9   /umrlTšī/ is analyzed into /um–Mrl–lTšī/, not to /um–mrl–Tšī/ because there is neutrali-
     zation of place of articulation for the nasals in the pre-nuclear context; see §4.5. Hence,
     there is functional amalgamation between /m/ and its archi-phoneme /M/. The same is
     true for the analysis of words like *hamr, humr, žánr, všiml*, i.e. they are analyzed into
     /ham–Mr/, /hum–Mr/, /žān–Mr/ and /Fšim–Ml/, respectively.

With /M/	With /j/	With /r/	With /l/
/Mk/ *mkl* (3rd person sg. of *mknout*)	/jm/ *jméno*	/rv/ *rvát se*	/lp/ *lpí*
/Mz/ *mze* (SSJČ)	/jd/ *jdu*	/rm/ *rmoutit*	/lb/ *lbový* (SSJČ)
/Mš/ *mše*	/jď/ *jdi*	/rt/ *rty*	/lv/ *lvi*
/Mž/ *mžitky*	/js/ *jsi*	/rd/ *rdousit*	/ln/ *lnout*
/Mh/ *mhouřit*	/jh/ *jho*	/rť/ *rtěnka*	/lň/ *lněný*
/Mdl/ *mdlý*	/jMň/ *jmění*	/rď/ *rdít se*	/lz/ *lze*
/Mkn/ *mknout* (SSJČ)	/jsm/ *jsme*	/rz/ *rzi*	/lž/ *lži*
/Mkň/ *mkni* (imp. sg. of *mknout*)	/jSt/ *jste*	/rž/ *ržát*	/lk/ *lkát*
/MSt/ *msta*		/rvj/ *rvěte se*	/lh/ *lhát*
/Mzd/ *mzda*		/rTs/ *rci* (archaic)	/lpj/ *lpět*
/MSť/ *mstít se*		/rTš/ *rčení*	/lSť/ *lstivý*
/MSď/ *mzdě*		(/rp/ *Rpety*)	/lStm/ *lstmi*
/MStn/ *mstný*			/lStn/ *lstný* (SSJČ)
/MStň/ *mstně*			/lStň/ *lstně* (SSJČ)
(/MTs/ *Mcely*)			(/lTš/ *Lčovice*)
			(/lŠť/ *Lštěň*)

FIGURE III: Known "side-syllabic" combinations

sonority is defined).[10] Taking [msta] as an example, such a peak is represented here by the vocoid [a], but the initial [m] corresponds to another peak of sonority, a secondary one, because the immediately neighboring sounds [s] and [t] are allegedly less sonorous. The word *msta* must then be disyllabic under the sonority theory. *Mutatis mutandis*, the same holds for all words in figure III, in particular to those with an initial [r] or [l]. This is, however, in contradiction with how they are treated in Czech (e.g. in verse)—they are not taken to contain any extra syllables.[11]

The whole thing can also be expressed in other words. Irrespective of whether [m], [j], [r] and [l] correspond to separate syllable cores in the words under question, the resulting combinations are problematic because they violate the so-called Sonority Sequencing Principle (= SSP). According to it, the sonority of a syllable increases toward its core, and decreases toward its margins (see e.g. Clements 1990 and references therein). The SSP is sometimes claimed to be a universally valid principle of syllable organization, even though it is well-known that there are many languages which violate it, Czech being one of them.[12] Vari-

---

10 As repeatedly pointed out (e.g. by Clements 1990, Butt 1992, Harris 2006), it is hard (if possible at all) to define sonority on phonetic grounds. Cf. also Lebrun (1966).

11 It has also been confirmed by the test performed by our students (the same test mentioned above).

12 For a long list of other violating languages, see Clements (*op. cit.*) and Blevins (2006).

ous strategies have been put forth to redeem the principle (for a short overview, see Blevins 2006: 334). In the case of Czech the controversy is usually solved by saying that [m], [j], [r], [l] are examples of *pobočná slabika* [side syllable] in such words; the problem is discussed in detail in Skaličková (1954 and 1958), Hála (1956: 59–64, 1961: 120–4) and Krámský (1976: 57–70). It means that the segments are syllabic according to the principle of sonority, but not syllabic according to the way they are treated in the language.

Another common strategy to save SSP is to treat the offending segments as as not belonging to any syllable (i.e. being extrasyllabic). Once they are removed from the domain of the syllable, the resulting syllable does indeed follow SSP. However, the only purpose of such strategies is to evade one obvious fact: languages do not necessarily follow SSP. Moreover, the whole practice is rather dubious. Every time we find a counter-example to our assumption, we declare it to be an exemption and continue to hold the assumption. In the end the assumption is irrefutable because every refutation is rejected by being declared to be an exception. Another problem with the idea of sonority is that there is no agreement as to what it really is and how it is defined. According to some researchers (see references in footnote 10), it does not have any phonetic basis, and so one may rightly wonder whether it has not been arrived at by a circular fashion.[13]

Due to its dubious and speculative nature, the idea of sonority, and hence the Sonority Sequencing Principle, is not used in the work as a criterion. In agreement with Popper's philosophy of science, we operate only with hypotheses in principle refute, which SSP is not (any statement about *all* languages is a speculation). The forms like /MSta/, /jho/, /rti/ or /lpjeT/ will not be analyzed as containing two phonotagms because they are said to violate SSP.[14] The conclusion whether such an analysis is possible must be arrived by other means. As explained in §5.5, a form is poly-phonotagmic if it can be divided into more than one phonotagm. This is not possible in the case of /MSta/, /jho/ and similar forms because there is no evidence that /M/ or /j/ functions as phonotagm nuclei, so they are distributionally dependent on the vowels /a/ and /u/ in these forms.

However, /r/ and /l/ can function as nuclear entities, and so it is important to consider whether forms like /rti/ or /lpjeT/ are divisible into two phonotagms. The answer must be negative. If they contained two phonotagms, one of them would necessarily begin with /r/ or /l/, but this is not possible for the reasons al-

---

13 That is, sonority is used to explain why vocoids are more likely syllabic cores than contoids—because they are more sonorous. However, the conclusion that they are more sonorous can only be derived from the observation that they function as syllable cores more often than contoids. The phenomenon is explained by itself.

14 Moreover, the combinations listed in figure III will not be viewed as deviant in any way. In fact, as we show in the following chapter, they are easily describable on the DU.

ready explained. First, /r/ and /l/ must always be accompanied by at least one phoneme (see (3) above), and if they are to be nuclear, they must be preceded by at least one consonant (see the restriction (8)). Consequently, if /r/ and /l/ occur at the beginning of a PhF of a word followed by a consonant, they are not nuclear.

There is yet another problematic case of the occurrence of /r/ and /l/ must be considered, namely the following forms:

(12) /zrdösiT/ *zrdousit*, realized as [zrdoṳsɪt]
/zlhoStejňeT/ *zlhostejnět*, realized as [zlhostɛjɲɛt]

The word *zrdousit* is derived from *rdousit* "to choke, to strangle (imperfective)". Its meaning is "to put an end to something (especially emotional attitude) by force" (PSJČ) or "to choke, to strangle (perfective)" (SSJČ). The word *zlhostejnět* is a perfective of the imperfective *lhostejnět* "to become indifferent". Both *rdousit* and *lhostejnět* are examples of words which contain a side-syllabic combination, namely /rd/ and /lh/. For the reasons just given, the /r/ and /l/ do not function here as nuclear entities, which is also in agreement with the fact that the initial [r] and [l] are not viewed as syllabic here. The word *rdousit* is realized by two syllables, and *lhostejnět* by three. Their derivates *zrdousit* and *zlhostejnět* are also viewed and treated as having, respectively, two and three syllables, even though [r] and [l] occur between two contoids, which is a situation when they are traditionally said to be syllabic (cf. [zrno] *zrno*, [slza] *slza*). Now, does it mean that the [r] in *zrno* is pronounced differently from the [r] in *zrdousit* and the latter is pronounced like the [r] in *rdousit*, and that the [l] in *slza* is different from the [l] in *zlhostejnět* and *lhostejnět*? As far as we know, no phonetic research has addressed this question.[15] It is nevertheless obvious that [r] and [l] behave (and are perceived) as non-syllabic in the words *zrdousit* and *zlhostejnět*, whereas they behave and are perceived as syllabic in words like *zrno* or *slza*.

The non-syllabic behavior may be shown in verse, as pointed out by Ziková (2008: 143, note 88).[16] She mentions the following example (syllable cores are underlined; phonetic transcription is ours):

(13) *Vlk si zuby brousil, že by ji hned zrdousil.*
[vlk sɪ zubɪ broṳsɪl ʒɛ bɪ jɪ finɛd zrdoṳsɪl]

---

15 Confirmed by Pavel Machač, formerly the Institute of Phonetics, Charles University (personal communication). Machač has recently examined articulatory and acoustic properties of [r] in Czech, but not in these problematic forms (see Machač 2009). He does not think there is any significant difference in them, though.

16 Ziková is one of the few to even mention this problem. Another reference is found in Renský (1960: 93) and Short (1985: 40) for both of whom the *l* in *zlhostejnět* is not syllabic.

The argument is that the line *Vlk si zuby brousil* has the same number of syllables as *že by ji hned zrdousil* because the latter is "součástí říkanky s pravidelným šestislabičným rytmem [part of a rhyme with a regular six-syllable rhythm]" (*ibid.*). Unfortunately, this is not true. Although Ziková does not provide the source of the line, it is most likely from the poem *Vlk vlku vlkem* by the author Valesan.[17] Provided that this is the poem she took the example from, her assessment does not hold, as becomes obvious from the whole verse:

(14) *Na rozcestí slípka bílá* (8 syllables) *bezstarostně lenošila.* (8 syllables)
    Vlk si zuby brousil, (6 syllables) *že by ji hned zrdousil.* (? 6 syllables)
    Slípka se však nezalekla (8 syllables) *a pěkně mu to od plic řekla.* (9 syll.)
    Že ji [sic! *ji*] *vlk nemá žrát,* (6 syllables) *jinak bude litovat.* (7 syllables)
    Vlk se lekl, až mu změkl (8 syllables) *a raději utekl.* (7 syllables)
    Tak chudák vlčici vzal (7 syllables) *a táhli spolu dál.* (6 syllables)

It is apparent that the lines hardly agree in the number of syllables, and so the verse cannot be accepted as a proof that [r] in *zrdousit* is not syllabic.[18] Although her example must be dismissed as not decisive, Ziková's main thesis is correct: *zrdousit* indeed tends to behave as a trisyllabic word in verse. A better example of this behavior can be found in the poem *Váhy* by Bohumil Adámek (transcription is ours):[19]

(15) *Různý kroj se v zástupech těch kasá, mihá;* (12 syllables)
    [ruːzniː kroj se v zaːstupex cɛx kasa: mɪɦaː]
    a kde nezrdousila písně klopot tíha, (? 12 syllables)
    [ʔa gdɛ nɛzrdoṷsɪla piːsɲɛ klopot ciːɦa]
    chvílemi již v řeči cizí (8 syllables)
    [xviːlɛmɪ jɪʒ v rɛʧɪ ʦɪziː]
    domorodý zvuk se ztápí, mizí. (10 syllables)
    [domorodiː zvuk sɛ staːpiː mɪziː]

---

17 Available online (as of 11 March 2013): <http://www.nokturno.net/dilko.php?id=2788>.
18 Another argument is that *r* in *zrdousit* and *l* in *zlhostejnět* are not stressed, the stress being on the adjacent vowel (Ziková *ibid.*, Short *ibid.*), i.e. that the vowels have some phonetic features making them different from the *r* or *l*. However, this is dubious because no stable phonetic correlates of the Czech stress has been found, the stress being rather potential or derived from the overall sound properties of the whole stress unit (Palková 1997: 277ff., Duběda 2002, Palková – Volín 2003, Palková 2004, Duběda – Votrubec 2005). In fact, the argument is rather circular: [r] in *zrdousit* is not syllabic because it is not stressed, and it is not stressed because it is not syllabic. If it were syllabic, it would be stressed because the stress, if realized at all, falls on the first syllable of the stress unit.
19 From the collection *Horské ovzduší*, Prague, 1902, p. 69.

The first two lines agree in the number of syllables provided that *zrd* in *nezrdousila* is not syllabic. Although the next two lines do not agree in the number of syllables, the whole structure of the verse is in accord with remaining verses of the poem (i.e. the first lines contain 12 syllables, the second lines 12 syllables, the third lines 8 syllables, and the fourth lines 10 syllables). Therefore, the author apparently meant *zrd* not to be syllabic.

Another verse, this time containing *zlhostejnělo*, a form of *zlhostejnět*, may be cited (transcription is again ours).[20] If *zlh* is not a separate syllable here, the third line agrees with the second one in the number of syllables (the first one agrees and rhymes with the fourth one).

(16) *Srdce lidu raněné,* (7 syllables)
[srtsɛ lɪdu raɲɛnɛː]
k odvetě byt' na čas zmdlelo, (8 syllables)
[kʔodvɛcɛː bɪc na ʧaz zmdlɛlo]
ochladlo a zlhostejnělo, (? 8 syllables)
[ʔoxladlo ʔa zlhostɛɲɛlo]
nikdy nezapomene. (7 syllables)
[ɲɪgdɪ nɛzapomɛnɛ]

The cited verses show that the words *zrdousit* and *zlhostejnět* are indeed treated in verse as not containing a syllabic [r] and [l].[21] It means that syllabic and non-syllabic [r] and [l] are differentiated in between two contoids, and there is then a difference between words with allegedly non-syllabic liquids and words with allegedly syllabic ones:

(17) ALLEGEDLY NON-SYLLABIC   ALLEGEDLY SYLLABIC
(a) *zrdousit* "to choke"   (a') *zrcadlit* "to mirror"
     zlhostejnět "to become indifferent"   *slza* "tear"
(b) *rty* "lips"   (b') *krtek* "mole"
     lsti "tricks"   *plsti* "felts"
(c) *v rtech* "in the lips"   (c') *vrtech* "drill hole (loc. pl.)"
     v lněném "in linen (clothes)"   *vlněném* "woolen (loc. sg.)"

Thus, *zrdousit* and *zlhostejnět* with allegedly non-syllabic [r] and [l] are different from *zrcadlit* and *slza* which contain allegedly syllabic [r] and [l]. The difference must be the same as that between *rty* and *lsti* on the one hand and *krtek* and

---

20 From the book *Král Ječmínek* by František S. Procházka, Prague, 1906, p. 106.
21 Another confirmation comes from the test dibe by our students: out of 32 students, 26 (81.5 %) viewed *zlhostejněl* (3rd person sg. of *zlhostejnět*) as consisting of three syllables, and 25 (78.1 %) considered *zrdousil* (3rd person sg. of *zrdousit*) to contain two syllables.

plsti on the other. Moreover, the same distinction would then have to exist between *v rty* and *vrty*, and between *v lněném* and *vlněném* where the /r/ in *v rty* and the /l/ in *v lněném* would be allegedly non-syllabic because they are non-syllabic in *rty* and *lněném*. The examples (17c) contain the non-syllabic preposition *v* "in". Although it may be replaced with its syllabic variant *ve* (i.e. *ve rtech, ve lněném*; see §5.3), the syntagms *v rtech* and *v lněném* are possible and attested. They are pronounced as a single unit, and may be viewed as single phonological constituents in which case they can be confronted with single words *vrtech* and *vlněném* where the [r] and [l] are syllabic.

However, it is at all not obvious whether the difference is phonetic or just perceptional. It has not so far been confirmed whether it has some real phonetic basis (in articulation and/or in acoustic characteristics). If it is just a matter of perception, we must be cautious in arriving at any conclusion. The fact that [r] in *zrdousit* and [l] in *zlhostejnět* are viewed as non-syllabic may be and most probably is influenced by our knowledge that these words are derived from *rdousit* and *lhostejnět* where the sounds are non-syllabic. The same could be said *v rtech* and *v lněném*: our perception may be influenced by the knowledge that they consist of two words. If we did not have this information, it is not at all certain whether our perception would be the same.

Let us tentatively assume that there is really some phonetic basis behind the reason the pairs are perceived differently. It may not necessarily be in the syllabicity of [r] and [l], but there can still be a difference in the way the words are pronounced. Phonology should account for this difference because it is obviously relevant for communication: for example, *v rtech* is (by assumption) something other than *vrtech*, and *v lněném* is something other than *vlněném*. We could account for this by postulating two additional phonemes, /R/ and /L/ realized as syllabic [r] and [l] and opposed to /r/ and /l/ realized as non-syllabic [r] and [l]. But this would not be an adequate analysis because the oppositions /R/ × /r/ and /L/ × /l/ would only be relevant in one specific context (at the beginning of a PhF of a word), being neutralized elsewhere.

An alternative analysis may be based on the fact that *zrdousit* or *v rtech* are pronounced as if the [r] was word-initial here, that is to say, their pronunciation is similar to *rdousit* or *rtech* rather than to *zrcadlit* or *vrtech*. The speaker may choose some articulatory means to signal that *zrdousit* consists of two units, *z* (prefix) and *rdousit* "to strangle", and that it is not to be confused with *zrdousit* (a hypothetical word pronounced like *zrcadlit*, that is, where the initial *z* is a prefix). Similarly, he may use certain phonetic means to signal that *v rtech* "in the lips" consists of two units, *v* "in" and *rtech* "lip (loc. pl.)", and that it should not be confused with *vrtech* "drill hole (loc. pl.)". Thus, the phonetic means (whatever they really are) would be employed here in the same manner as the glottal stop in *s ok* "from the eyes" as opposed to *sok* "rival" (see §5.2): the function of both is to signal a boundary between units.[22] Accordingly, the PhF of the words *zrdousit, zlhostejnět, v rtech* etc. could be interpreted as /#z#rdösiT#/, /#z#lhoStejňeT#/, /#v#rteX#/, whereas the PhFs of *zrcadlit, slza, vrtech* etc. as /#zrTsadliT#/, /#slza#/, /#vrteX#/. In the first case the /z/ in /#z#/ and the /v/ in /#v#/ would be instances of a-phonotactic bases (see §5.3 on this notion). It should be stressed that the analysis is not based on the grammatical knowledge, i.e. on the fact that *zrdousit* is a derivate of *rdousit* and *v rtech* consists of two words. It is based on the assumption that there is a phonetic difference which is relevant for communication. But as mentioned, the difference has not been confirmed by phonetic research, so the presented analysis is only tentative.

To conclude the discussion of the nuclearity of /r/ and /l/, we will summarize the conditions under which they fulfill this function. The semiconsonants /r/ and /l/ are nuclear when they are, within a PhF of a word, preceded by a consonant (a necessary condition)[23] and followed by (i) a consonant (as in /prS/ *prs*, /hlT/ *hlt*) or (ii) by a semiconsonant (as in /umrlTši/ *umrlčí*; attested only for /r/) or (iii) by the end of the word (as in /hadr/ *hadr*, /pudl/ *pudl*).

10.3 Position class 'N'

Having dealt with the conditions of the nuclearity of /r/ and /l/, we can now step to discuss their phonotactic properties in the same manner as we did for vowels. When the semiconsonants function as nuclear entities, they do not occur in nuclear position 'n', but occupy instead nuclear archi-position 'N'. This archi-position was introduced to reflect two facts. First, unlike vowels, the semiconsonants are not preceded by five PerPs. Second, unlike vowels, they are not preceded by phonemes occurring in position 'e1', namely by /m/, /n/, /ň/, /j/, /ř/, /r/, /l/. Accordingly, archi-position 'N' is the product of the cancellation of the difference between pre-nuclear position 'e1' and nuclear position 'n', and by this fact, /r/ and /l/ belong both to the pre-nuclear and to the nuclear context. They constitute a separate position class of which they are the only members (see (18)). Since /r/ and /l/ function as nuclear entities, archi-position 'N' is never empty.

(18) *pos* 'N' ∈ {/r/, /l/}

---

22 It is of course not to say that *v rtech* is pronounced with a glottal stop (or glottalization) like *s ok*. We speak here about the *function* of the phonic substance, not of its nature.

23 Note that according to our tentative analysis the /r/ in *zrdousit* or *v rtech* is not preceded by a consonant within one and the same form because /z/ and /v/ belong to another diacreme group (see §5.2 on this notion). Hence, it is not nuclear in these words.

	F0	F1	F2	F3
P1				all
P2				/l/
P3	all	/l/	/l/	all
P4	all	/l/	all	all

FIGURE IV: Phonotactic properties for *pos* 'N' and phonemes for which particular properties are not attested

Phonotactic properties of *pos* 'N' are listed in figure IV. As nuclear /r/, /l/ must be obligatorily preceded by at least one consonant, property 'P0' is redundant for them. Similarly, as they can be preceded by no more than four PerPs, 'P5' is also redundant. Examples are given in appendix D.

The distribution of the semiconsonants is not without limitations, but there is more regularity in comparison to the vowels. The occurrence of /l/ is markedly limited in comparison with /r/. Phonotactic properties 'P3'/'F3', 'P4'/'F2' and 'P4'/'F3' are impossible for both /r/ and /l/, which follows from the discussion in §8.1: no phonotagm can contain more than six non-vowels. The non-attestation of properties 'P3'/'F0' and 'P4'/'F0' will be regularized by the following restriction:

(19) If a nuclear semiconsonant is not followed by any PerP,[24] it cannot be preceded by three or more PerPs.

The absence of property 'P1'/'F3' is interpreted as accidental. Although it may be viewed as an unwarranted decision, it is supported by the fact that property 'P2'/'F3' is attested for /r/ (cf. /šMrnTS/ *šmrnc*), and we see no reason why nuclear /r/, /l/, when followed by three PerPs, could not be preceded just one PerP if they can be preceded by two of them.

---

24   In effect, the semiconsonant occurs at the end of a PhF of a word.

Chapter Eleven: PRE-NUCLEAR DISTRIBUTION

11.1 Introduction

In chapter 7 we introduced five positions and two archi-positions to account for the distribution of PerPs in the pre-nuclear context. In the course of our analysis the phonemes are assigned to these positions of the basis of their phonotactic properties. The final analysis of the pre-nuclear section of the DU is summarized in figure I. It is the purpose of this chapter to discuss details of this analysis.

Phonotactic properties of the individual positions will be examined in the same manner as those of nuclear entities in the previous chapter. We assume that the distribution of phonemes in the pre-nuclear context is not dependent on the distribution of phonemes in the post-nuclear context and vice versa (arguments for this will be given in chapter 17). For that reason, we will only concentrate on the precedence and antecedence of phonemes in the particular context (that is, in the pre-nuclear context in this case). Again, in the tables in this and the next chapter the letter 'P' + number will express how many phonemes can precede a given phoneme, and the letter 'F' + number will express how many phonemes can follow it. In addition, subscripts will be used to specify to which positions the preceding and following phonemes belong. Hence, code 'P1$_{e2}$' means that a phoneme can be preceded by one phoneme from *pos* 'e2' (e.g. /r/ in /vraX/ *vrah*; code 'P2$_{pre1e3}$' means it can be preceded by two phonemes, one of them being from *pos* 'pre1' and the other from *pos* 'e3' (e.g. /a/ in /Stran/ *stran*). The same notation will be used in the next chapter for the distribution of post-nuclear phonemes.

'pre2'	'prel'	'e3'	'e2'	'el'	'n'
P F K X T S Š M j r l v t h (b) Ø	T S Š ř Ø	k g x h t d s z š ž Ø	v M Ø	r l	
				m n ň j ř r l Ø	i e a o u ī ē ā ō ū ë ä ö
		p b f			
		t' d'			

FIGURE I: Pre-nuclear and nuclear section of the main DU and its position classes

		Occurrence in 'el'		Occurrence in 'prel'
/m/	0·0	/moTS/ *moc*	0·1	/Mše/ *mše*
	1·0	/smīX/ *smích*	0·2	/Mdlī/ *mdlý*
	2·0	/StmīvaT/ *stmívat se*	0·3	/MStnī/ *mstný*
	3·0	/FSdmōT/ *vzdmout*		
	4·0	*not found*		
/n/	0·0	/noS/ *nos*		
	1·0	/vnuK/ *vnuk*		
	2·0	/SxnöT/ *schnout*		
	3·0	/lStnī/ *lstný*		
	4·0	*not found*		
/ň/	0·0	/ňiTS/ *nic*		
	1·0	/Mňel/ *měl*		
	2·0	/ShňīT/ *shnít*		
	3·0	/hřMňeT/ *hřmět*		
	4·0	*not found*		
/j/	0·0	/jen/ *jen*	0·1	/jmēn/ *jmén*
	1·0	/pjeT/ *pět*	0·2	/jsme/ *jsme*
	2·0	/kvjeT/ *květ*	0·3	*not found*
	3·0	/FSpjer/ *vzpěr*		
	4·0	/FSkvjeT/ *vzkvět*		
/r/	0·0	/rāj/ *ráj*	0·1	/rtuŤ/ *rtuť*
	1·0	/druX/ *druh*	0·2	/rvjete/ *rvěte*
	2·0	/sMraT/ *smrad*	0·3	*not found*
	3·0	/PŠtroS/ *pštros*		
	4·0	*not found*		
/l/	0·0	/lom/ *lom*	0·1	/lvi/ *lvi*
	1·0	/xlaP/ *chlap*	0·2	/lSťivī/ *lstivý*
	2·0	/FplöT/ *vplout*	0·3	/lStnī/ *lstný*
	3·0	/FStlaK/ *vztlak*		
	4·0	*not found*		

FIGURE II: Differences in the occurrence of /m/, /n/, /ň/, /j/, /r/, /l/ in 'el' and 'prel'

11.2 Position class 'el'

Position 'el' is the first before the nucleus, and so if a phoneme occurs there, it always stands before a vowel. The phonemes belonging to it are listed under (1); the position can also be empty (expressed by 'Ø' in the position class). As neither of these phonemes is phonologically voiceless or voiced, neutralization of voicing does not take place before any of them.

(1) *pos* 'e1' ∈ {/m/, /n/, /ň/, /j/, /ř/, /r/, /l/, Ø}

Except for the nasals, all phonemes of *pos* 'e1' occur in yet another pre-nuclear position. The phonemes /j/, /r/ and /l/ also occur in 'pre2', and /ř/ also occurs in 'pre1'. We will return to the latter when discussing *pos* 'pre1' below in §11.7. The nasals /m/, /n/ and /ň/ occur only in 'e1', which means they always stand before a vowel. In the pre-nuclear context a nasal can also stand before a consonant or a semiconsonant (irrespective of whether the latter functions as the nucleus or not), but in that situation the place of articulation of the nasal is neutralized resulting in the archi-phoneme /M/ which, as shown below, belongs to 'e2' and 'pre2'. Figure II compares the occurrence of the nasals and of /j/, /r/, /l/ in 'e1' and 'pre2'. The distribution of the nasals is also discussed in the next section, and the conditions of the occurrence of /M/, /j/, /r/, /l/ in 'pre2' are discussed in §11.8.

In figure II and similar figures in this and the following chapters, the two-digit number expresses by how many PerPs a given phoneme is followed or preceded. For example, '0·0' means it is not followed or preceded by any PerP, whereas '2·1' means it is preceded by two PerPs and followed by one PerP. There are usually several possibilities as to which positions the preceding and following phonemes belong; this will be specified by other means. The purpose of such figures is only to illustrate and compare occurrences of phonemes. They are also useful because they can be compared to each other. For example, although /v/ occurs in 'e2' and /z/ occurs in 'e3', properties such as '0·0', '1·0', '2·0' or '2·1' hold for both of them.

Now, figure II shows that when standing before a vowel, the phonemes /m/, /n/, /ň/, /j/, /r/ and /l/ can be preceded by none or by one, two or three PerPs; /j/ can in addition be preceded by four PerPs. In all of these situations they belong to position 'e1'. However, the phonemes /j/, /r/ and /l/ can also stand before a PerP in the pre-nuclear context and be followed by one, two or three PerPs. They belong then to 'pre2'.

The information by how many phonemes a certain phoneme can be followed or preceded is important and determines its assignment to a given position, but it is not sufficient. The preceding and following phonemes may belong to several positions. For example, /r/ can be preceded by one PerP, and this phoneme may be either from *pos* 'e2' (cf. /MraK/ *mrak*), or from *pos* 'e3' (cf. /trām/ *trám*), or from *pos* 'E2' (cf. /praK/ *prak*). If it is preceded by two PerPs, then these may belong either to 'e3' and 'e2' (cf. /sMraT/ *smrad*), 'pre1' and 'e3' (cf. /StraX/

	FOn
$P0$	
$P1_{e2}$	
$P1_{e3}$	
$P1_{E2}$	/m/
$P1_{pre1}$	*all*
$P1_{pre2}$	(/j/) /ř/ /r/ /l/
$P2_{e3e2}$	/m/
$P2_{pre1e2}$	/m/ /n/ /ň/ /ř/ /r/ /l/
$P2_{pre2e2}$	/m/ /n/ /ř/ /r/
$P2_{pre1e3}$	/j/
$P2_{pre2e3}$	
$P2_{pre1E2}$	/m/ /n/ /ň/
$P2_{pre2E2}$	/m/ /n/ /ň/
$P2_{pre2pre1}$	/n/ /ň/
$P3_{pre1e3e2}$	/m/ /n/ /ř/ /r/ /l/
$P3_{pre2e3e2}$	/m/ /n/ /ř/ /r/ /l/
$P3_{pre2pre1e2}$	/m/ /n/ /j/ /ř/ /r/ /l/
$P3_{pre2pre1e3}$	/j/
$P3_{pre2pre1E2}$	/m/
$P4_{pre2pre1e3e2}$	/m/ /n/ /ň/ /ř/ /r/ /l/

FIGURE III: Phonotactic properties for *pos* 'e1' and phonemes for which particular properties are not attested (paretheses means that the property is attested only in marginal forms)

strach), 'pre2' and 'e3' (cf. /FkroTšiT/ *vkročit*) and so on. Each of these possibilities refers to a phonotactic property which characterizes position 'e1'. The lists of all phonotactic properties pertinent to 'e1' are given in figure III. The codes express these properties. All phonemes assigned to position 'e1' should in principle display all of them, but this ideal is not reached. In many cases we have no example proving that a given phoneme has a certain phonotactic property. It is our task to determine whether this is accidental or whether there is some regularity behind it. For that reason, it will be again useful to list phonemes which are NOT attested to have some phonotactic property. Some properties are not attested for all members. If it is not found for a certain well-defined class of phonemes, the absence will be viewed as regular, and a collocational restriction accounting for it will be introduced.

Property 'P1$_{pre1}$' is not attested for any phoneme of *pos* 'e1', but since 'P2$_{pre2pre1}$' is attested for /m/, we conclude that phonemes from *pos* 'e1' can be preceded by a phoneme from *pos* 'pre1', that is, by /T/, /S/, /Š/ or /ř/. However, the preceding phoneme may only be /ř/ because the voicing archi-phonemes /T/, /S/ and /Š/ cannot occur before phonemes from *pos* 'el' which do not trigger neutralization of voicing. So they can only be preceded by /ř/, and the only attested combination is /hřm/ in *hřmot*. We see no reason why /řm/ could not be a possible pre-nuclear combination in Czech, too, and property 'Pl$_{pre1}$' is viewed to be possible for the nasals from *pos* 'el'.

However, the mentioned property will not be viewed as possible the sonants /j/, /r/, /l/ and /ř/ neither of which is attested to be preceded by /ř/. In general, the co-occurrence of the sonants in the same section of the DU is quite limited. In the pre-nuclear section there are only three such combinations, and four in the post-nuclear section:

(2) PRE-NUCLEAR   POST-NUCLEAR
(a) /rj/ in *Rjazaň* (foreign place name)   /jr/ in *chejr*
     /lj/ in *Ljuba* (proper name)   /jl/ in *koktejl*
                                             /jř/ in *Kejř* (surname)
                                             /rl/ in *stárl* (see §10.2)
(b) /lpj/ in *lpět*

Several conclusions can be drawn from this. To begin with, the same section of the DU cannot contain /ř/ and /r/ or /l/, which will be regularized as follows:

(3) /ř/ cannot occur in the same section of the DU with a semiconsonant.

It holds irrespective of whether the mentioned phonemes stand in close proximity or separated by other phonemes. Hence, although pre-nuclear combinations like /řvj/ or /hřMň/ are possible, those like /řl/, /řvr/ or /hřMl/ are not. What is more, since archi-position 'N' is the product of cancellation of the difference between positions 'el' and 'n', phonemes occurring there belong both to the pre-nuclear context and to the nuclear context. Consequently, the restriction holds even if the semiconsonant is nuclear, that is, a nuclear semiconsonant cannot be preceded by a combination containing /ř/. Or, which equals to the same, if /r/ or /l/ is the nucleus of a phonotagm, /ř/ cannot occur in its pre-nuclear section.

It is also obvious that if /r/, /l/ or /ř/ co-occurs with /j/, the latter phoneme is always closer to the nucleus; compare /rj/ × /jr/, and /lj/ × /jl/. This will be captured by these restrictions:

(4) (a) If a semiconsonant occurs in the same section of the DU with /j/, the latter occurs in a less peripheral position.
     (b) If /ř/ occurs in the same section of the DU with /j/, the latter occurs in a less peripheral position.

(4b) pertains actually only to the post-nuclear context because in the pre-nuclear context the co-occurrence of /ř/ with /j/ is impossible, which follows from the following more general restriction:

(5)   In the pre-nuclear context, /ř/ cannot co-occur with a sonant (/j/, /ř/, /r/, /l/).

The pre-nuclear section is further limited by the fact that it cannot contain two semiconsonants. In other words, if a pre-nuclear combination contains a semi-consonant, it cannot contain another semiconsonant, although it may contain, for example, two nasals (cf. /MStnī/ *mstný*). This fact is accounted for by restriction (6). Since archi-position 'N' partly belongs to the pre-nuclear section, too, another consequence of the restriction is such that when the nucleus of a phono-tagm is a semiconsonant, it cannot be preceded by a combination which contains another semiconsonant. In the post-nuclear section the restriction does not hold due to the existence of /rl/ in *stárl*.

(6)   The pre-nuclear section of the DU cannot contain two instances of a semi-consonant.

Finally, we should take note of the fact that neither the pre-nuclear section nor the post-nuclear section contains two identical sonants. Thus, the following restriction holds:

(7)   The same section of the DU cannot contain two identical sonants.

Let us discuss further the phonotactic properties of the phonemes from *pos* 'e1'. Figure III allows us to introduce other restrictions on their combinability. The fact that property 'P4$_{pre2pre1e3e2}$' is not attested for /ř/, /r/ and /l/ is regularized by the next restrictions. The first holds only for non-nuclear semiconsonants (i.e. when they occur in 'e1', not in 'N') because the nuclear ones can be preceded by as much as four PerPs (cf. /TŠtvrT/ *čtvrt*). To say it otherwise, if /r/, /l/ or /ř/ stands before a vowel, it can only be preceded by as much as three PerPs (cf. /PŠtroS/ *pštros*, /FShlīžeT/ *vzhlížet*, /FSpřīmenī/ *vzpřímený*).

(8)   (a)   A non-nuclear semiconsonant cannot be preceded by more than three PerPs.
      (b)   /ř/ cannot be preceded by more than three PerPs.

These restrictions say nothing about nasals, even though property 'P4$_{pre2pre1e3e2}$' is also not attested for them, but there is some hint that they may have this property after all, and can be preceded by four PerPs. SSJČ lists the verb *vzdmouti* as a variant of *vzedmouti*. The 2nd person plural imperative of the latter is *vzedměte*, which suggests that the same form for *vzdmouti* could be *vzdměte*. The PhF of the latter would begin with /FSdMň/, that is, with a combination where a nasal is preceded by four PerPs. However, the imperative does not seem to be attested, so the combination is just hypothetical and has not been included in our database, but at the same time it is not declared as impossible.

Yet the distribution of the nasals is not without limitations.[1] Figure III shows that /m/ is not attested to have properties 'P1$_{E2}$', 'P2$_{pre1E2}$', 'P2$_{pre2E2}$' and 'P3$_{pre2pre1E2}$' or, to put it otherwise, it is never found before a phoneme from *pos* 'E2', i.e. /p/, /b/, /f/. Like these, the phoneme /m/ is a labial, but it does not mean that it cannot be preceded by another labial because it is preceded by /v/ as in *vmísit*. However, /v/ belongs to another position class than /p/, /b/, /f/, namely to 'e2'. Accordingly, we propose the following restriction:

(9)   /m/ cannot be preceded by a phoneme from *pos* 'E2' (/p/, b/, /f/).

Let us return to the non-nuclear /r/, /l/ and to /ř/. Besides the restrictions under (8), two others hold for them; see (10). It is a consequence of the fact that properties 'P3$_{pre1e3e2}$', 'P3$_{pre2e3e2}$' and 'P3$_{pre2pre1e2}$' are not attested for them. In contrast, nasals and nuclear semiconsonants have this capacity, cf. /hřMň/ in *hřmět* and /Skvrna/ *skvrna*. In other words, if /ř/ and non-nuclear /r/ and /l/ are preceded by three PerPs 'CCC$_1$', 'C$_1$' is always either from *pos* 'E2' or from 'e3', i.e. it is an occlusive other than palatal or a fricative other than /v/.

(10) (a)   A non-nuclear semiconsonant cannot be preceded by a combination of type 'CCC$_1$' where 'C$_1$' is from *pos* 'e2' (/v/ or /M/).

   (b)   /ř/ cannot be preceded by a combination of type 'CCC$_1$' where 'C$_1$' is from *pos* 'e2' (/v/ or /M/).

Finally, let us have a look at the pre-nuclear occurrence of /j/, in particular at the situation when it is preceded by another PerP. Several such combinations have already been mentioned, namely /lj/ in *Ljuba* and /rj/ in *Rjazaň* (and /lpj/ in *lpět*). Others (but not all of them) are these:

(11) /Mj/ in *Mjachký*

/vj/ in *věk*	/zvj/ in *zvěd*	/Fzvj/ in *vzvěděti* (PSJČ)
/pj/ in *pět*	/Spj/ in *zpět*	/FSpj/ in *vzpěrač*
/bj/ in *běh*	/Fbj/ in *vběhnout*	/FSbj/ in *vzběhnouti* (SSJČ)

---

1   One can notice in figure III that properties 'P2$_{pre1E2}$' and 'P2$_{pre2E2}$' are not attested for any nasal, but this will not be interpreted as a regular phenomenon (except for /m/). The properties could be attested for /n/ and /ň/ in the words *spnouti* and *vpnouti* recorded in NLA. See also chapter 14 under DE3*e*.

/fj/ in *fĕrtošek*
/sj/ in *sjet*
/zj/ in *zjev*   /Fzj/ in *vzjímati* (SSJČ)
/kj/ in *kjariza* (ASCS)

To begin with, /j/ is preceded by /M/, but this is attested only in the surname *Mjachký*. We assume that /M/ occurs here in 'e2', not in 'pre2' because the combination /Mj/ parallels the structure of similar combinations of the 'e1' phonemes with the 'e2' phonemes (see §14.2 under DE2*a* for the combinations). Moreover, /j/ is preceded /v/ which is another member of *pos* 'e2'. The /v/ can be further preceded by other PerPs. Besides the ones given under (11), there is also /FSkvj/ in *vzkvĕt* where four PerPs stand before /j/. The phoneme /v/ is a labial, and /j/ can be preceded by the other labials, /p/, /b/ and /f/. The latter three belong to *pos* 'E2' instead. Note that there are more combinations with /p/ and /b/ (and /v/) than those listed under (11). Finally, /j/ can be preceded by a phoneme from *pos* 'e3', though only four such combinations are attested (all are given under (11)). The combinations /sj/, /zj/ and /Fzj/ are synchronically and diachronically results of prefixation, whereas /kj/ is possible only if the words *kjariza* (ASCS) and the adjective *kjótský* (derived from the foreign place name *Kjóto*) are accepted. The same combination is moreover attested in prepositional syntagms such as *k jídlu* (cf. §5.3). The phoneme /k/ is thus the only non-labial occlusive occurring before /j/. Accordingly, we propose the following restrictions to capture the distribution of /j/:

(12) (a)   /j/ cannot be preceded by an occlusive other than labial or velar.
     (b)   /j/ cannot be preceded by a fricative other than labial or alveolar.

11.3 Position class 'e2'

Position 'e2' is the second position before 'n' or the first position before 'N'. Its position class is given under (13); it can also be empty.

(13) *pos* 'e2' ∈ {/v/, /M/, Ø}

/v/ is a voiced labial fricative; it has other phonotactic properties than its voiceless counterpart /f/; the latter belongs to *pos* 'E2' (see below). /M/ is the nasal archi-phoneme resulting from neutralization of the opposition between /m/, /n/ and /ň/. Like in the case of phonemes from *pos* 'e1', neutralization of voicing does not take place before /v/ or /M/, i.e. both voiceless and voiced consonants can stand before them. Both /v/ and /M/ also occur in 'pre2'. The difference between these occurrences is illustrated in figure IV. They occur in 'e2' if standing

		Occurrence in 'e2'		Occurrence in 'pre2'
/v/	0·0	/vīš/ *výš*	0·1	/vMrŠťïT/ *vmrštit*
	1·0	/tvūj/ *tvůj*	0·2	/vMňeStnaT/ *vměstnat*
	2·0	/SkvoST/ *skvost*	0·3	*not found*
	3·0	/FSkvēST/ *vzkvést*		
	0·1	/vraT/ *vrat*		
	1·1	/svjeT/ *svět*		
	2·1	/Skvjel/ *skvěl*		
	3·1	/FSkvjeT/ *vzkvět*		
/M/	0·0	/MlŠ/ *mlž*	0·1	/MŠe/ *mše*
	1·0	/smrT/ *smrt*	0·2	/MSta/ *msta*
	2·0	*not found*	0·3	/MStnī/ *mstný*
	3·0	*not found*		
	0·1	/MraK/ *mrak*		
	1·1	/sMňer/ *směr*		
	2·1	/hřMňeT/ *hřmět*		
	3·1	(/FSdMňete/ *vzdměte*)		

FIGURE IV: Differences in the occurrence of /v/, /M/ in 'e2' and 'pre2'

right before a nuclear phoneme, or if standing before a phoneme belonging to *pos* 'e1'. In both cases they may be the first phonemes in the phonotagm, or they may be preceded by up to three PerPs. The occurrence of /v/ in 'pre2' is rather limited, and we will return to it in §11.8. As regards /M/, it always occurs in 'pre2' if it stands before two or three PerPs. When standing before one PerP, it may occur in 'e2' as well as 'pre2'. If this phoneme is /m/, /n/, /ň/, /j/, /ř/, /r/ or /l/ (i.e. a phoneme from *pos* 'e1'), we assign /M/ to 'e2'; in other situations it belongs to 'pre2' (for example in /MŠe/ *mše* or /MhöřiT/ *mhouřit*). It follows from the centripetal nature of the DU.

Phonotactic properties of position 'e2' are schematized in figure V (see the next page). Again, the phonemes listed are NOT attested to have the property in question. Some properties are not attested for all members of *pos* 'e2'. Let us note that /M/ could have property 'P3$_{pre2pre1e3}$'/'F1$_{e1}$n' if the form /FSdMňete/ *vzdměte* is accepted (see the previous section). Phonotactic properties 'P1$_{pre1}$'/ 'F0N' and 'P1$_{pre2}$'/F0N' are not possible for /v/ and /M/, that is, the mentioned phonemes cannot be preceded by a phoneme from *pos* 'pre1' or *pos* 'pre2' provided that the nucleus of the phonotagm is a semiconsonant. Since neutralization of voicing does not take place before them, these positions could only be occupied by /ř/ (i.e. 'pre1') or /j/, /r/, /l/, /M/ ('pre2'). Now, it follows from the restrictions introduced above under (3)–(6), that /ř/, /j/, /r/, /l/ cannot occur in the

	F0n	F0N	F1_{e}n
P0	/M/		
P1_{e3}	/M/	/v/	
P1_{pre1}	/M/	all	all
P1_{pre2}	/M/	all	
P2_{pre1e3}	/M/	/M/	
P2_{pre2e3}	/M/	all	
P2_{pre2pre1}	/v/	all	/v/
P3_{pre2pre1e3}	/M/	/M/	/M/

FIGURE V: Phonotactic properties for *pos* 'e2' and phonemes for which particular properties are not attested

pre-nuclear section of the DU provided that a semiconsonant is the nucleus. We are thus left with /M/, that is, the only thinkable combinations are /MM/ and /Mv/. The former can be immediately rejected because Czech does not allow two identical phonemes stand next to each other (see §9.2). The latter will also be rejected, but before doing so, let us look at similar combinations of a nasal + an occlusive or a fricative (all are listed):

(14) NASAL + OCCLUSIVE   NASAL + FRICATIVE
(a) /Mk/ in *mkl*   (c) /Mz/ in *mze*
(b) /MTs/ in *Mcely* (place name)   /Mš/ in *mše*
     /Mdl/ in *mdlo*   /Mž/ in *mžít*
     /Mkn/ in *mknouti*   /Mx/ in *Mchov* (place name)
     /Mkň/ in *mkni*   /Mh/ in *mhouřit*
     /Mkl/ in *mkla*   (d) /MStn/ in *mstný*
                                  /MStň/ in *mstně*

It is obvious from the attested combinations that if /M/ precedes an occlusive or a fricative, the latter can be an alveolar, a palatal or a velar, but it is never a labial. Thus, it is appropriate to introduce the following restriction on which basis the combination /Mv/ is rejected. This explains why properties 'P1_{pre1}'/'F0N' and 'P1_{pre2}'/F0N' are not possible for /v/ and /M/.

(15) In the pre-nuclear context a labial cannot be preceded by a nasal.[2]

---

2   See also p. 215 for the discussion of another restriction pertaining to the labials.

/t/	0·0	/ten/ *ten*	/d/	0·0	/duP/ *dub*
	1·0	/Stan/ *stan*		1·0	/Sdar/ *zdar*
	2·0	/FStāT/ *vstát*		2·0	/FSdāT/ *vzdát*
	0·1	/tma/ *tma*		0·1	/draK/ *drak*
	1·1	/StraX/ *strach*		1·1	/Sdravī/ *zdravý*
	2·1	/FStlaK/ *vztlak*		2·1	/FSdmöT/ *vzdmout*
	0·2	/tMňe/ *tmě*		0·2	/dvje/ *dvě*
	1·2	*not found*		1·2	*not found*
	2·2	*not found*		2·2	(/FSdMňete/ *vzdměte*)
/s/	0·0	/sen/ *sen*	/z/	0·0	/zem/ *zem*
	1·0	/Ksilofōn/ *xylofon*		1·0	/TzinkaT/ *dzinkat*
	2·0	/STsiziT/ *zcizit*		2·0	*not found*
	0·1	/svūj/ *svůj*		0·1	/znāT/ *znát*
	1·1	/Tsval/ *cval*		1·1	/FzňiK/ *vznik*
	2·1	/STsvaknöT/ *scvaknout*		2·1	*not found*
	0·2	/svjeT/ *svět*		0·2	/zMňena/ *změna*
	1·2	/FsMňe/ from *vsměstnati*		1·2	/zvjeTšňiT/ *zvěčnit*
	2·2	*not found*		2·2	*not found*
/š/	0·0	/šaT/ *šat*	/ž/	0·0	/žīT/ *žít*
	1·0	/KšilT/ *kšilt*		1·0	/TžeS/ *džez*
	2·0	/rTšeňī/ *rčení*		2·0	/STžezovaT/ *zdžezovat*
	0·1	/šveTS/ *švec*		0·1	/žvaňiT/ *žvanit*
	1·1	/Tšvero/ *čtvero*		1·1	/FžrāT/ *vžrát*
	2·1	/FTšleň/ *včleň*		2·1	*not found*
	0·2	*not found*		0·2	*not found*
	1·2	*not found*		1·2	*not found*
	2·2	*not found*		2·2	*not found*

FIGURE VIa: The occurrence of /t/, /d/, /s/, /z/, /š/, /ž/ in 'e3'

11.4 Position class 'e3'

Position 'e3' is the third pre-nuclear position. Its position class is given in (16). It contains all voiceless and voiced occlusives and fricatives except for /p/, /b/, /f/ which belong to 'E2', /v/ which belongs to 'e1', and /t'/, /d'/ which belong to 'E3'. The position can also be empty.

(16) *pos* 'e3' $\in$ {/t/, /d/, /s/, /z/, /š/, /ž/, /k/, /g/, /x/, /h/, Ø}

/k/	0·0	/koF/ *kov*	/g/	0·0	/gonK/ *gong*
	1·0	/řka/ *řka*		1·0	/Sga/ from *zgalvanizovat*
	2·0	/FSkaS/ *vzkaz*		2·0	*not found*
	0·1	/kmen/ *kmen*		0·1	/gram/ *gram*
	1·1	/SkvoST/ *skvost*		1·1	/Sglo/ from *zglobalizovat*
	2·1	/FSkvětaT/ *vzkvétat*		2·1	*not found*
	0·2	/kvjeT/ *květ*		0·2	*not found*
	1·2	/Skvjelī/ *skvělý*		1·2	*not found*
	2·2	/FSkvjeT/ *vzkvět*		2·2	*not found*
/x/	0·0	/xuŤ/ *chuť*	/h/	0·0	/hon/ *hon*
	1·0	/Txoř/ *tchoř*		1·0	/Shon/ *shon*
	2·0	/FSxoP/ *vzchop*		2·0	/FShūru/ *vzhůru*
	0·1	/xvoST/ *chvost*		0·1	/hvoST/ *hvozd*
	1·1	/sxváliT/ *schválit*		1·1	/Shřešiт/ *zhřešit*
	2·1	/FSxlīpnöT/ *vzchlípnout*		2·1	/FShlīžeT/ *vzhlížet*
	0·2	/xvjeT/ *chvět*		0·2	/hvjeST/ *hvězd*
	1·2	/Sxvjelī/ *zchvělý*		1·2	/ShvjeSďiT/ *zhvězdit*
	2·2	*not found*		2·2	*not found*

FIGURE VIb: The occurrence of /k/, /g/, /x/, /h/ in 'e3'

The phonemes from *pos* 'e3' do not occupy any other pre-nuclear position, but their archi-phonemes, which represent them, do. The archi-phonemes /T/, /S/, /Š/ occupy 'pre1' and 'pre2', and /K/, /X/ occupy 'pre2'. The comparison of the occurrence of /T/, /S/, /Š/ in 'pre1' and 'pre2' is given in figure XII in §11.7, and examples of the occurrence of /K/, /X/ in 'pre2' is given in figure XV in §11.8. Figure VI (split into two parts, one part on the preceding page) provided in this section illustrates the occurrence of /t/, /d/, /s/, /z/, /š/, /ž/, /k/, /g/, /x/, /h/ in 'e3'. As is obvious, they can be followed by no PerP or by one or two PerPs, and be at the same time preceded by no PerP or by one or two PerPs. Phonotactic properties of position 'e3' are schematized in figure VII. Some properties are not found for all members of this position class. Many of them are not attested for at least some members, but it is always not possible to regularize these absences.

We will start with property 'P2$_{pre2pre1}$'/'F2$_{e2e1}$n' which is attested only for /k/ (cf. /FSkvjeT/ *vzkvět*). It is not attested for velar fricatives, which could be viewed as a regular phenomenon, but we refrain from introducing such a restriction. Historically, /FS/ in *vzkvět* is a prefix, and since there is /xvjeT/ *chvět* on the one hand and /FShl/ *vzhled* on the other, it does not seem appropriate to assume that combinations /FSxvj/ and /FShvj/ are impossible. This conclusion is supported by another fact. The property is also not attested for the alveolar occlusives /t/

	F0n	F0N	F1$_{e2}$n	F1$_{e2}$N	F1$_{e1}$n	F2$_{e2e1}$n
P0		(/š/) (/ž/)		/d/ /ž/ /k/ /g/ /x/ /h/		/š/ /ž/ /g/
P1$_{pre1}$		/z/ /ž/ /g/	/z/ /ž/ /g/ /h/	/d/ /z/ /š/ /ž/ /g/ /x/ /h/	/z/ /ž/	/d/ /s/ /z/ /š/ /ž/ /g/
P1$_{pre2}$		/d/ /z/ /š/ /k/ /g/	/d/ /s/ /š/ /ž/ /g/ /x/ /h/	*all*	/g/	/t/ /d/ /š/ /ž/ /k/ /g/ /x/ /h/
P2$_{pre2pre1}$	/z/ /g/	/d/ /s/ /z/ /ž/ /k/ /g/ /x/ /h/	/d/ /z/ /š/ /ž/ /g/ /h/	/d/ /z/ /š/ /ž/ /k/ /g/ /x/ /h/	/s/ /z/ /ž/ /g/	/t/ /d/ /s/ /z/ /š/ /ž/ /g/ /x/ /h/

FIGURE VII: Phonotactic properties for *pos* 'e3' and phonemes for which particular properties are not attested (parenthesized phonemes are attested only in marginal forms)

and /d/ unless if we accept /FSdMň/ from *vzdměte*, the hypothetical imperative plural of *vzdmouti*. This form suggests that at least /t/ and /d/ could have property 'P2$_{pre2pre1}$'/'F2$_{e2e1}$n', too.

However, in the case of the alveolar fricatives /s/ and /z/ as well as of the palatal fricatives /š/ and /ž/, the absence of property 'P2$_{pre2pre1}$'/'F2$_{e2e1}$n' can be regularized. Let us look at the situation from another perspective. Position 'pre1' can be occupied by /T/, /S/, /Š/ or /ř/, but if 'e3' is occupied by /s/, /z/, /š/ or /ž/, only /T/ occurs in 'pre1'. First of all, /s/ and /z/ cannot be preceded by /S/, and /š/ and /ž/ cannot be preceded by /Š/, as Czech does not allow geminates (see §9.2). Secondly, alveolar fricatives are never preceded by palatal fricatives, although the reverse is possible (cf. /Sš/ in *zšednout*; see §13.3 on such combinations). Finally, we can rule out the situation when /s/, /z/, /š/ /ž/ would be preceded by /ř/ because the only fricative that /ř/ precedes is /v/ (cf. /řv/ in *řvát*). Accordingly, we propose the following restriction which rules out /řs/, /řz/, /rš/ and /rž/:

(17) In the pre-nuclear context, /ř/ cannot be followed by a fricative belonging to *pos* 'e3', i.e. by a fricative other then labial.

Therefore, if 'e3' is occupied by /s/, /z/, /š/ or /ž/, then 'pre1' can be occupied only by /T/, which results in the combinations /Ts/, /Tz/, /Tš/, /Tž/ realized as affricates (see §3.3). As one can further witness in figure VII, property 'P1$_{pre1}$'/ 'F2$_{e2e1}$n' is also not attested for /s/, /z/, /š/, /ž/, and it is the same situation when we would get the mentioned combinations. Consequently, the following restriction holds; we can imply from it that /s/, /z/ cannot be preceded by two PerPs and at the same time followed by two PerPs:

(18) If an alveolar fricative is preceded by an alveolar occlusive (i.e. /T/), it cannot be followed by two PerPs.

The restriction does not say anything about /š/ and /ž/ for which a more general restriction given under (19) holds. The point is that /š/ and /ž/ can only be followed by one PerP either from *pos* 'e2' (cf. /šv/ in *švec*) or from *pos* 'e1' (cf. /žl/ in *žlutý*), but they are never followed by two PerPs.[3] Their distribution is thus more restricted than that of the alveolar fricatives which enter into such combinations (cf. /svj/ in *svět* or /zMr/ in *zmrazit*).[4]

(19) A palatal fricative cannot be followed by two PerPs 'C$_2$C$_1$' where 'C$_2$' is from *pos* 'e2' (/v/, /M/), and 'C$_1$' is from *pos* 'e1' (/m/, /n/, /ň/, /j/, /ř/, /r/, /l/).

The occurrence of /s/ and /z/ is further restricted by another fact. When standing before a nuclear semiconsonant, the alveolar fricatives ('A$_F$') are not preceded by two PerPs. The same is also actually true for all velars ('K'). We regularize it with the restrictions under (20). They do not apply to labials, alveolar occlusives and palatals (see /v/ in /StvrȚ/ *stvrď*, /t/ in /FStrTŠ/ *vstrč* and /š/ in /FTšrtaťi/ *včrtati* (PSJČ)).

(20) (a)   A nuclear semiconsonant cannot be preceded by a combination of type 'CCA$_F$'.

  (b)   A nuclear semiconsonant cannot be preceded by a combination of type 'CCK'.

Finally, let us take note of the restricted occurrence of /z/ and /g/. Neither is found to be preceded by two PerPs, and /g/ is moreover not followed by two PerPs. In the case of /g/ the source of these limitations can be sought in the history of Czech because the phoneme was introduced to modern Czech mostly through loans from other languages. The following collocational restriction will therefore be introduced:

(21) /g/ cannot be preceded or followed by two PerPs.

No such restriction would be appropriate in the case of /z/, that is, we will assume that /z/ can be preceded by two PerPs. It is based on the following reason-

---

3   However, the palatal fricative archi-phoneme is: cf. /ŠTk/ in *štkát*.
4   NLA lists the word *švědlena* with /švj/, but the word is recorded only once as a variant of *švadlena*, and it is moreover a rather dialectal word (see Kott III: 983).

ing. If the word *bzučet* "to buzz" had a derivate such as *vbzučet* meaning "to fly in while buzzing" (*v-* being a prefix meaning "in, into"), the latter would contain the combination /FPz/ where /z/ is preceded by two PerPs. This word has actually been found, though it is apparently a hapax legomenon.[5] Although the combination has not been included in our data in the end, it is viewed as potentially possible, since the *v-* prefixation is a regular process in Czech.

Finally, the phoneme /g/ is limited by another restriction: it is only preceded by a fricative (cf. /Sgr/ in *zgranulovat* and /Fg/ in *vgalvanizovat*). We find it appropriate to capture this limitation by the following restriction (a non-fricative is an occlusive or a nasal or a sonant):

(22) /g/ cannot be preceded by a non-fricative.

11.5 Position class 'E2'

Archi-position 'E2' has been introduced to account for special distribution of the phonemes /p/, /b/ and /f/ which form its position class (see (23)). It has resulted from the suspension of the difference between positions 'e3' and 'e2', which means that the syntagmatic difference between these positions which is otherwise valid for other phonemes is not valid for /p/, /b/ and /f/.

(23) *pos* 'E2' $\in$ {/p/, /b/, /f/}

Except for /b/, these phonemes do not occur in any other pre-nuclear position, though their archi-phonemes do: both /P/ and /F/ belong to 'pre2'. The phoneme /b/ marginally occurs in 'pre2', namely in /břve/ *Břve* (place name); we will return to it in §11.8. A comparison of the occurrence of /p/, /b/ versus /P/, and that of /f/ versus /F/ is provided in figure VIII on the next page.

Before continuing, we must explain one thing. No archi-position in Czech can be empty because there would be no reason for operating with it. Since the emptiness of a position captures the fact that a phoneme occurring there can be omitted without producing an ill-formed phonotagm, this claim must be substantiated when we are confronted with the omission of /p/ in /praK/ (cf. *prak*) resulting in /raK/ (cf. *rak*). However, in /raK/ it is not archi-position 'E2' that is empty, but positions 'e2' and 'e3' because both or one of them can be filled with a phoneme as shown by /zvraT/ *zvrat*, /vraK/ *vrak* and /zraK/ *zrak*. It is schematized in figure IX (the next page). Thus, when a phoneme occurring in an archi-position is left out, it means the positions which the archi-position represents are empty.

---

5   It is found in the 3rd person singular form *vbzučí* in a poem mentioned at this web page: <http://www.lkpb.cz/cinnost/clen_kozubikova.htm> (accessed 13 March 2013).

	Occurrence in 'E2'			Occurrence in 'pre2'	
/p/	0·0	/peS/ pes	/P/	0·1	/PtāK/ pták
	1·0	/SpāT/ spát		0·2	/PSdˇiT/ bzdít
	2·0	/FSpīraT/ vzpírat		0·3	/PŠtroS/ pštros
	0·1	/pjeST/ pěst		0·4	not found
	1·1	/SpjeF/ zpěv			
	2·1	/FSpjer/ vzpěr			
/b/	0·0	/bīT/ být			
	1·0	/TbāT/ dbát			
	2·0	/FSbudˇiT/ vzbudit			
	0·1	/braK/ brak			
	1·1	/Sbraň/ zbraň			
	2·1	/FSbjehnöT/ vzběhnout			
/f/	0·0	/fēn/ fén	/F/	0·1	/FdāT/ vdát se
	1·0	/sföknöT/ sfouknout		0·2	/FStāT/ vstát
	2·0	not found		0·3	/FzMňeˇT/ vzmět'
	0·1	/fraK/ frak		0·4	/FSkvjeT/ vzkvět
	1·1	/SfruKtizovaT/ zfruktizovat			
	2·1	not found			

FIGURE VIII: Comparison of the occurrence of /p/, /b/, /f/ in 'E2' and /P/, /F/ in 'pre2'

'pre2'	'pre1'	'e3'	'e2'	'e1'	'n'	Phonological form
'pre2'	'pre1'	'e3∩e2' / 'E2'	'e1'	'n'		
∅	∅	/p/		/r/	/a/	/prak/ prak
∅	∅	∅	∅	/r/	/a/	/raK/ rak
∅	∅	/z/	∅	/r/	/a/	/zraK/ zrak
∅	∅	∅	/v/	/r/	/a/	/vraK/ vrak
∅	∅	/z/	/v/	/r/	/a/	/zvraT/ zvrat

FIGURE IX: Phonotactic analysis of prak, rak, zrak, vrak and zvrat

Phonotactic properties of archi-position 'E2' are schematized in figure X. We have said that an archi-position is represented as the intersection of two or more adjacent positions. This can now be expressed in a different way: if every position is characterized by a unique set of phonotactic properties, an archi-position is characterized by the intersection of phonotactic properties of two or more adjacent positions. A phoneme occurring in an archi-position has only those phonotactic properties common to two or more adjacent positions. Therefore, phonotactic properties of the phonemes belonging to 'E2' (i.e. to 'e3∩e2') are those and only those that the phonemes from pos 'e3' and pos 'e2' have in common. This is easily verifiable if one makes the intersection of figure V given

	$F0n$	$F0N$	$Fl_{e1}n$
$P0$			
$P1_{pre1}$		/f/	
$P1_{pre2}$	(/f/)	/f/	/f/
$P2_{pre2pre1}$	/f/	/b/ /f/	/f/

FIGURE X: Phonotactic properties for *pos* 'E2' and phonemes for which particular properties are not attested (parenthesized phonemes are attested only in marginal forms)

in §11.3 and figure VII given in §11.4. Let us illustrate it on the phonemes /t/, which belongs to 'e3', /v/, which belongs to 'e2', and /p/, which belongs to 'E2'. The combinatory possibilities of /p/ are equal to those which /t/ and /v/ have in common. See the following examples:

(24) 'Fl_{e1}'   'P1_{pre1}'   'P1_{pre2}'   'P2_{pre2pre1}'
(a) /trām/ *trám*   /StāT/ *stát*   /rti/ *rty*   /FStāT/ *vstát*
(b) /vraX/ *vrah*   /řvāT/ *řvát*   /lvi/ *lvi*   /břve/ *Břve*
(c) /prām/ *prám*   /SpāT/ *spát*   /lpī/ *lpí*   /FSpaŠ/ *vzpaž*

As the examples show, both /t/ and /v/ are followed by a phoneme from 'e1', and so is /p/. Second, both are preceded by a phoneme from 'pre1' or from 'pre2', and so is /p/. Third, both are also preceded by two phonemes from 'pre1' and 'pre2', and again so is /p/. Finally, all of these phonemes are followed by a vowel or a nuclear semiconsonant while not being preceded by any other phoneme (for reasons of space this is not exemplified, but see figure VIII). The phonemes /t/ and /v/ have other properties, but there is no other they have in common, and /p/ has only those they have in common and no other.

To return to figure X, it holds once again that the phonemes listed there are those NOT found to have the respective phonotactic properties. The only noteworthy fact is the limited distribution of /f/ the source of which could, like in the case of /g/, be sought in the history of Czech (except for a few domestic words, /f/ occurs mostly in words borrowed from other languages). To reflect the fact that 'P_{pre2pre1}' is not attested for /f/, the following restriction is introduced:

(25) /f/ cannot be preceded by two PerPs.

11.6 Position class 'E3'

Archi-position 'E3' results from the suspension of the difference between positions 'e3', 'e2' and 'e1'; its position class is given under (26). It holds once again that the syntagmatic difference between the mentioned positions is not

	FOn
P0	
P1_{pre1}	
P1_{pre2}	
P2_{pre2pre1}	

FIGURE XI: Phonotactic properties for *pos* 'E3'

relevant for /t'/ and /d'/. Both are palatal occlusives, and they do not belong to any other pre-nuclear or even to any other post-nuclear position. Their archi-phoneme /Ť/ only occurs in post-nuclear position 'i3'.

(26) *pos* 'E3' ∈ {/t'/, /d'/}

Phonotactic properties of *pos* 'E3' are schematized in figure XI. They are equal to the intersection of the properties of *pos* 'e3', *pos* 'e2' and *pos* 'e1'. Both /t'/ and /d'/ have all of them, and so no collocational restriction is necessary here. Of course, their distribution is restricted by the fact that they can occur only before a vowel and be preceded by up to two PerPs, but this derives from the very nature of archi-position 'E3'. As it is the product of the suspension of the difference between 'e3', 'e2' and 'e1', the phonemes /t'/ and /d'/ have in fact only those phonotactic properties that are common the latter three positions. See the following examples with /s/ occurring in 'e3', /v/ occurring in 'e2', /m/ occurring in 'e1', and /d'/ occurring in 'E3':

(27) 'P0'/'F0'	'P1_{pre1}'	'P1_{pre2}'	'P2_{pre2pre1}'
(a) /sen/ *sen*	/Tsen/ *cen*	/FsaŤ/ *vsad'*	/STseŤ/ *sced'*
(b) /ven/ *ven*	/řvāT/ *řvát*	/lvi/ *lvi*	(/břve/ *Břve*)
(c) /meT/ *med*	not found	/rmöt'iT/ *rmoutit*	/hřmoT/ *hřmot*
(d) /d'eS/ *děs*	/Sd'el/ *sděl*	/rd'īT/ *rdit se*	/FSd'el/ from *vzdělaný*

As we see, a phoneme occurring in 'e3', 'e2' or 'e1' can be followed by a vowel, and so can /t'/ and /d'/. On the other hand, /t'/ and /d'/ cannot be followed by a nuclear semiconsonant, but this property is not common to positions 'e3', 'e2' and 'e1' because phonemes occurring in 'e1' cannot be followed by a nuclear semiconsonant (see §11.2 above). Second, phonemes occurring in the mentioned positions can be preceded by no PerP or by one PerP belonging either to 'pre1' or 'pre2' or by two PerPs belonging to 'pre2' and 'pre1'. All of these apply to /t'/ and /d'/, too, and they do not have any other property, and no other property is common to positions 'e3', 'e2' and 'e1'.

11.7 Position class 'pre1'

Before discussing the occurrence of phonemes in the last two pre-nuclear positions, we would like to explain why they have been called 'pre1' and 'pre2'. The prefix 'pre' stands for *pre-explosive*, and these positions are called PRE-EXPLOSIVE POSITIONS, whereas those so far discussed are EXPLOSIVE POSITIONS. This terminology mirrors the conditions under which 'pre1' and 'pre2' are occupied:

(28) The pre-explosive positions ('pre1', 'pre2') can be occupied by a phoneme if and only if at least one of the explosive positions ('e1', 'e2', 'e3' or 'E2' or 'E3') is occupied by a phoneme.

If all explosive positions are empty, 'pre1' and 'pre2' must also be empty, which follows from the nature of phonemes assigned to them. First, they are occupied by voicing archi-phonemes which, by definition, occur before occlusives or fricatives. All explosive positions being empty, there is logically no occlusive or fricative before which they could occur. Second, they are occupied by phonemes which can also occur in an explosive position, but by the Principle of Lesser Peripherality (see §9.1), such phonemes are assigned to the explosive positions in case there are several possibilities.

Now, position 'pre1' is the first pre-explosive position or the fourth position from nuclear position 'n' or the third position from archi-position 'N'. Its position class is given under (29); it can also be empty.

(29) *pos* 'pre1' ∈ {/T/, /S/, /Š/, /ř/, Ø}

The archi-phonemes /T/, /S/, /Š/ are products of neutralization of /t/ × /d/, /s/ × /z/, and /š/ × /ž/. They occur in 'pre1' as well as 'pre2'. By the convention that phonemes are assigned to less peripheral positions, 'pre1' will be viewed as the primary place of their occurrence. Consequently, their occurrence in 'pre2' is conditioned, and this condition is expressed as follows:

(30) /T/, /S/, /Š/ occur in 'pre2' only if 'pre1' is already occupied by a phoneme.

When /T/, /S/, /Š/ stand before a phoneme from *pos* 'pre1', i.e. before /T/, /S/, /Š/ or /ř/, they occur in 'pre2'. When not preceding such phonemes, they occur in 'pre1'. Their occurrence in these two positions is compared in figure XII (the next page). When standing in 'pre1', they can be followed by one, two or three PerPs while being preceded by none or by one PerP. When standing in 'pre2', they are the first phonemes in the phonotagm and can be followed by two, three or four PerPs, though only /S/ is found to be followed by as much as four.

		Occurrence in 'pre1'		Occurrence in 'pre2'
/T/	0·1	/Txoř/ *tchoř*	0·2	/TřpiT/ *třpyt*
	1·1	/FTkāT/ *vtkát*	0·3	/TŠpjeT/ *čpět*
	0·2	/TknöT/ *tknout*	0·4	*not found*
	1·2	/FTšleňiT/ *včlenit*		
	0·3	/Tkvjel/ *tkvěl*		
	1·3	/STkvjel/ *stkvěl*		
/S/	0·1	/SpāT/ *spát*	0·2	/STkāT/ *stkát*
	1·1	/FStaň/ *vstaň*	0·3	/STklivjeT/ *ztklivět*
	0·2	/SplaF/ *splav*	0·4	/STkvjel/ *stkvěl*
	1·2	/PStruX/ *pstruh*		
	0·3	/Skvjelī/ *skvělý*		
	1·3	/FSkvjeT/ *vzkvět*		
/Š/	0·1	/ŠtˇīT/ *štít*	0·2	/ŠTkāT/ *štkát*
	1·1	/FŠdi/ *vždy*	0·3	/ŠTknöT/ *štknout*
	0·2	/ŠtvāT/ *štvát*	0·4	*not found*
	1·2	/PŠtroS/ *pštros*		
	0·3	*not found*		
	1·3	*not found*		

FIGURE XII: Differences in the occurrence of /T/, /S/, /Š/ in 'pre1' and 'pre2'

Position 'pre1' is also occupied by /ř/. It has already been assigned to 'e1', which is regarded as its primary place of occurrence. Figure XIII compares these occurrences. It occurs in 'e1' if it stands right before a vowel in which case it may be preceded by one, two or three PerPs. Note that by belonging to 'e1', /ř/ could also be preceded by four PerPs, but as no such form has been found, we have declared it impossible (see §11.2 above). The phoneme /ř/ belongs to 'pre1' if it precedes one PerP which is not from *pos* 'e1' (i.e. which is not /m/, /n/, /ň/, /j/, /ř/, /r/ or /l/) or if it precedes two PerPs. In both situations it may be preceded by one PerP (from *pos* 'pre2'). By belonging to 'pre1', it could also be followed by three PerPs, but no form of this has been found (compare it against /T/ and /S/ in figure XII). The following collocational restriction regularizes it:

(31) /ř/ cannot be followed by more than two PerPs.

There is one peculiar thing about /ř/ occurring in 'pre1', already touched upon it in §4.2 in connection with neutralization of voicing. It concerns the nature of the consonant standing before it in 'pre2'. First of all, even though 'pre2' can be occupied by /M/, /j/, /r/, /l/ (see the next section), these phonemes do not precede

Occurrence in 'e1'		Occurrence in 'pre1'	
	0·0 /řāT/ *rád*	0·1	/řvāT/ *řvát*
	1·0 /tři/ *tři*	1·1	/Křťini/ *křtiny*
/ř/	2·0 /StřeT/ *střed*	0·2	/řvjete/ *řvěte*
	3·0 /PStřeň/ *pstřeň* (PSJČ)	1·2	/hřMňeT/ *hřmět*
	4·0 *not found*	0·3	*not found*
		1·3	*not found*

FIGURE XIII: Differences in the occurrence of /ř/ in 'e1' and 'pre1'

	$F1_{e3}n$	$F1_{e3}N$	$F1_{e2}n$	$F1_{e2}N$	$F1_{e1}n$	$F1_{E2}n$	$F1_{E2}N$	$F1_{E3}n$
$P0$		/ř/	/T/ /S/ /Š/	*all*	*all*		/T/ /ř/	/T/ /ř/
$P1_{pre2}$		/ř/	/T/ /S/ /Š/	*all*	/T/ /S/ /S/	/T/	/T/ /Š/ /ř/	/T/

	$F2_{e3e2}n$	$F2_{e3e2}N$	$F2_{e3e1}n$	$F2_{e2e1}n$	$F2_{E2e1}n$	$F3_{e3e2e1}n$
$P0$	/ř/	/ř/	/ř/	/T/ /S/ /Š/	/T/ /ř/	/Š/ /ř/
$P1_{pre2}$	/ř/	/S/ /ř/	/ř/	/T/ /S/ /Š/	/T/ /ř/	/Š/ /ř/

FIGURE XIV: Phonotactic properties for *pos* 'pre1' and phonemes for which particular properties are not attested

/ř/ if it occupies 'pre1'. The phonemes /j/, /r/, /l/ do not combine with /ř/ in any way, and /M/ precedes /ř/ only if the latter occurs in 'e1' (cf. /Mřenka/ *mřenka*). In short, if /ř/ stands in 'pre1', it may only be preceded by occlusives or by fricatives. Now, these consonants are subject to neutralization of voicing *if* they followed by /ř/ which is followed by either a voiceless or a voiced consonant (except for /v/), cf. /Křťini/ *křtiny* and /XřbeT/ *hřbet*. But if /ř/ is followed by a phoneme for which the voicing opposition is irrelevant, there is no neutralization for the occlusives and the fricatives (cf. /hřmoT/ *hřmot*). The point is that all phonemes which precede /ř/ in these situations belong to 'pre2' irrespective of whether the voicing opposition is relevant for them or not. Thus, both /X/ from /XřbeT/ and /h/ from /hřmoT/ occur in 'pre2'. Whether neutralization of voicing takes place in 'pre2' is conditioned by the neighboring phonemes.

Phonotactic properties of 'pre1' are schematized in figure XIV. Examples demonstrating the pre-nuclear occurrence of the phonemes from *pos* 'pre1' have already been given. Once again, the phonemes listed in the figure are those NOT attested to have a given phonotactic property. Some properties are not attested for all members of this position class. The absence of properties '$F1_{e2}N$' (either in combination with 'P0' or '$P1_{pre2}$') and 'P0'/'$F1_{e1}n$' for all members derives from two facts. First of all, we must realize that since phonemes from *pos* 'e2' and *pos* 'e1' do not trigger neutralization of voicing, /T/, /S/ and /Š/ cannot precede them. Hence, 'pre1' could only be occupied by /ř/ in both cases. The impossibility of 'F1$_{e2}$N' for /ř/ derives from the restriction we already introduced in §11.2, namely that /ř/ cannot occur in the same section with a semiconsonant. On the other hand, the absence of 'P0'/'F1$_{e1}$n' is regarded as accidental. The phoneme /ř/ can be followed by a phoneme from *pos* 'e1', which is proven by /hřmoT/ *hřmot*, although in the latter the /ř/ is further preceded by a PerP from *pos* 'pre2'. However, we see no reason why /řm/ could not be possible, too, if /hřm/ is an attested combination in Czech.

Several collocational restrictions will be introduced here reflecting the information from figure XIV. As we said above, /ř/ cannot be followed by more than two PerPs. In addition, it is subject to another restriction:

(32) If /ř/ is followed by two PerPs 'C$_1$C', then 'C$_1$' can be no other than one from *pos* 'e2' (/v/, /M/).

That is, it can be followed by a phoneme from *pos* 'e3' or *pos* 'E2' (cf. /řka/ *řka*, /TřpiT/ *třpyt*), but in that case the latter cannot be further followed by another PerP. On the other hand, if /ř/ is followed by a phoneme from *pos* 'e2', the latter can be followed by another PerP, cf. /hřMňeT/ *hřmět*.

The alveolar occlusive /T/ is not found to be followed by two PerPs 'C$_1$C' provided that 'C$_1$' is from *pos* 'E2' (i.e. /p/, /b/ or /f/), but it is found to be followed by a combination of type C$_1$C' provided that 'C$_1$' is from 'e3' (i.e. /t/, /d/, /s/, /z/, /š/, /ž/, /k/, /g/, /x/, /h/): cf. /Tklivī/ *tklivý*. Also, /T/ cannot be followed by a phoneme from *pos* 'E2' if the latter stands right before a nuclear semiconsonant. These limitations are, however, more general and hold for all occlusives. Accordingly, we propose the restrictions under (33). The first says that combinations like /Tbl/ or /Kbr/ are not possible, and the second implies that combinations like /Tb/ can only stand before a vowel (cf. *dbát*), but not before a nuclear semiconsonant.

(33) (a) An occlusives cannot be followed by two PerPs 'C$_1$C' provided that 'C$_1$' is from *pos* 'E2'.

   (b) A nuclear semiconsonant cannot be preceded by two PerPs 'C$_2$C$_1$' provided that 'C$_2$' is an occlusive and 'C$_1$' is from *pos* 'E2'.

	0·1	/PtāK/ *pták*			0·0	/Kterī/ *který*
/P/	0·2	/PSdīT/ *bzdít*	/K/		1·0	/Křťini/ *křtiny*
	0·3	/PStruX/ *pstruh*			2·0	*not found*
	0·4	*not found*			0·1	*not found*
	0·1	/FpāliT/ *vpálit*			0·1	/Xbitī/ *hbitý*
/F/	0·2	/FSkaS/ *vzkaz*	/X/		0·2	/XřbeT/ *hřbet*
	0·3	/FSpřimiT/ *vzpřimit*			0·3	*not found*
	0·4	/FSkvjeT/ *vzkvět*			0·4	*not found*

FIGURE XV: The occurrence of /P/, /K/, /F/ and /X/ in 'pre2'

11.8 Position class 'pre2'

Pre-explosive position 'pre2' is the very last pre-nuclear position. When a phoneme occurs there, it is the first one in the phonotagm, as no other phoneme can come before it except for the rare accidental appendices (see the next section). Its position class is reproduced under (34); it can also be empty. We will return to /v/, /t/, /h/ and /b/ below. The position class includes all voicing archi-phonemes except for /Ť/ which does not occur in the pre-nuclear context.

(34) *pos* 'pre2' ∈ {/P/, /F/, /K/, /X/, /T/, /S/, /Š/, /M/, /j/, /r/, /l/, Ø} + {/v/, /t/, /h/, (/b/)}

The phonemes belonging to *pos* 'pre2' can be divided into two groups. The first is constituted by phonemes not occurring in any other pre-nuclear position: /P/, /F/, /K/, /X/. Their occurrence in 'pre2' is illustrated in figure XV. All of them are followed by one PerP or by two Pers. /P/ and /F/ are in addition attested to be followed by three PerPs, and /F/ by four.

The second, larger group is constituted by phonemes which occur in another pre-nuclear position. These are /T/, /S/, /Š/ we discussed in the previous section, /M/, which also occurs in 'e2' (see §11.3), and /j/, /r/, /l/, which also occur in 'e1' (see §11.2). However, /M/, /j/, /r/, /l/ have a special status in 'pre2' and occur there only if both of the following conditions hold:

(35) /M/, /j/, /r/, /l/ OCCUR IN 'pre2' WHEN:
(a)   They precede a consonant; in the case of /M/ this consonant must not be a nasal or /j/ or /ř/.
(b)   The nucleus of the phonotagm they belong to is a vowel.

First of all, in order to occur in 'pre2', they must precede at least one PerP. In the case of /j/, /r/ and /l/, it must only be a consonant, not a semiconsonant. It

'pre2'	'pre1'	'e3'	'e2'	'e1'	'n'	Phonological form
/M/	/S/	/t/	Ø	Ø	/a/	/MSta/ *msta*
/F/	/S/	/t/	Ø	Ø	/a/	/FStaX/ *vztah*
/M/	Ø	/d/	Ø	/l/	/o/	/Mdlo/ *mdlo*
/F/	Ø	/d/	Ø	/l/	/ā/	/FdlāŠďiT/ *vdláždit*
/j/	Ø	/h/	Ø	Ø	/o/	/jho/ *jho*
/F/	Ø	/h/	Ø	Ø	/o/	/FhoďiT/ *vhodit*
/j/	Ø	/s/	Ø	/m/	/e/	/jsme/ *jsme*
/F/	Ø	/s/	Ø	/m/	/i/	/Fsmiknöťi/ *vsmyknouti* (SSJČ)
/r/	Ø	/t/	Ø	Ø	/i/	/rti/ *rty*
/K/	Ø	/t/	Ø	Ø	/e/	/Kterī/ *který*
/r/	/T/	/š/	Ø	Ø	/e/	/rTšeňī/ *rčení*
/S/	/T/	/š/	Ø	Ø	/e/	/STšeřiT/ *zčeřit*
/l/	/S/	/t/	Ø	/n/	/ī/	/lStnī/ *lstný*
/T/	/S/	/t/	Ø	/n/	/ī/	/TStnī/ *ctný* (SSJČ)
/l/	Ø	/p/		/j/	/e/	/lpjeT/ *lpět*
/S/	Ø	/p/		/j/	/e/	/Spjex/ *spěch*

FIGURE XVI: The occurrence of /M/, /j/, /r/, /l/ in 'pre2' as compared to other phonemes

follows from the restrictions on the co-occurrence of semiconsonants and /j/ already discussed in §11.2. Note that /M/ is capable of preceding a nasal, /j/ or /ř/ as in /MňeX/ *měch*, /MjaXkī/ *Mjachký* or /Mřenka/ *mřenka*, but in such combinations it belongs to 'e2' due to the Principle of Lesser Peripherality. The same is true when /M/ occurs before /r/ or /l/ as in /MraK/ *mrak* or /MlīT/ *mlít*, but the latter phonemes are semiconsonants, not consonants.

/M/, /j/, /r/ and /l/ have been assigned to 'pre2' in order to account for a specific group of pre-nuclear combinations such as /MSta/ *msta*, /jho/ *jho*, /rti/ *rty*, /lStnī/ *lstný*. They were already discussed in §10.2 in connection with the nucleus of /r/ and /l/. It was said there that these combinations are problematic for those theories operating with the Sonority Sequencing Principle, since they violate it. For our description which does not rely on this principle, the combinations are not problematic at all and can be easily accounted for by the DU. The occurrence of /M/, /j/, /r/ and /l/ in 'pre2' parallels the occurrence of the other phonemes belonging there. It is illustrated by figure XVI. Yet there is one important difference: /M/, /j/, /r/ and /l/ occur in 'pre2' only if the nucleus of the phonotagm is a vowel and not a semiconsonant, but the other phonemes occur in 'pre2' irrespective of what phoneme is the nucleus. This explains the condition (35b) given above.

Let us now turn the attention to /t/, /h/, /b/ and /v/ which also occur in 'pre2'. The occurrence of /t/ and /h/ is in fact restricted to one particular situation: when

/ř/ stands in 'pre1' in the combinations /třm/ and /hřm/ found in *třmen* and *hřmot* and their derivates. The phoneme /b/ also occurs in 'pre2' if 'pre1' is occupied by /ř/, but this occurrence is only attested in the combination /břv/ found in the place names *Břve* and *Břvany*. Finally, as regards the occurrence of /v/ in 'pre2', they occur there in these forms:

(36) (a) /vMlāťiT/ *vmlátit*
     /vMňeStnaT/ *vmněstnat*
     (b) /vMrŠťiT/ *vmrštit*

The examples call for explanation. When analyzing the pre-nuclear combinations /vMl/ and /vMň/, it is reasonable to assign /l/ and /ň/ to 'e1' and /M/ to 'e2' in both cases, since these are the positions where they otherwise occur. The same with /vM/ before the nuclear /r/ in *vmrštit*: /M/ is assigned to 'e2' where it normally occurs.[6] We are thus left with /v/ which normally occurs in 'e2', but this position is already taken up by /M/, so it must occur in another position. It may be either 'e3', 'pre1', 'pre2'. However, before deciding for one of the solutions, we must consider the facts.

First, no other phoneme can precede /v/ in the combinations /vMl/, /vMň/ and /vM/, that is, no combination 'CvMl', 'CvMň' or 'CvM' where 'C' a PerP has been found. Second, no phoneme can come in between /v/ and /M/, which means that no combination 'vCMl', 'vCMr' or 'vCM' has been found. These facts suggest that /v/ should stand in an archi-position equivalent to 'e3', 'pre1' and 'pre2' rather than in any of these positions because the phonotactic difference between positions 'pre2', 'pre1' and 'e3' is apparently suspended for /v/. It seems to be the most logical solution, but there is one important circumstance which should be taken into consideration. If /v/ is assigned to the archi-position equivalent to 'e3', 'pre1' and 'pre2', then it would be the only entity to occur there. All phonemes with which /v/ commutes in the context before /Ml/, /Mň/ or /M/ and which could hence belong to that archi-position occur in other positions: /s/ in /sMňena/ *směna*, /z/ in /zMňena/ *změna*, /t/ in /tMňe/ *tmě*, /d/ in /dMňete/ *dměte* and /s/ in /sMrŠťiT/ *smrštit* all occur in 'e3', and /j/ in /jMňeňī/ *jmění* occurs in 'pre2'. So the archi-position would be occupied only by /v/, and since archi-positions cannot be empty (because they are introduced to account for the occurrence of certain phonemes, not for their absences), the occurrence of /v/ would not be functional. Something is functional if there is a choice between at least two possibilities.

---

6   /vM/ must not be confused with /vm/ found in *vmichat*. The latter occurs before vowels and poses no problem: /m/ belongs to 'e1' and /v/ to 'e2'. However, the nasal place of articulation is neutralized before /r/ or /l/, so *vmrštit* contains the combination /vM/, not /vm/.

'pre2'	'prel'	'e3'	'e2'	'el'	'n'	Phonological form
/t/	/ř/	Ø	Ø	/m/	/e/	/třmen/ třmen
/T/	/ř/		/t'/		/i/	/Třina/ třtina
/h/	/ř/	Ø	Ø	/m/	/o/	/hřmoT/ hřmot
/X/	/ř/	/t/	Ø	Ø	/ā/	/Xřtān/ chřtán
/b/	/ř/	Ø	/v/	Ø	/e/	/břve/ Břve (place name)
/P/	/S/	/t/	Ø	/r/	/u/	/PStruX/ pstruh
/v/	Ø	Ø	/M/	/l/	/a/	/vMlāťiT/ vmlátit
/v/	Ø	Ø	/M/	/ň/	/e/	/vMňeStnat/ vměstnat
/v/	Ø	Ø	/M/	/r/		/vMrŠŤ/ vmršť
/F/	/S/	/t/	Ø	Ø	/ā/	/FStāT/ vstát

FIGURE XVII: The occurrence of /t/, /h/, /b/ and /v/ in 'pre2'

The archi-position is thus not a possible solution for reasons of consistency, and /v/ must be assigned to another position, either to 'e3', 'prel' or 'pre2'. Out of these, 'pre2' is the most appropriate. The phoneme /v/ does not undergo neutralization of voicing, and so we reject 'prel' because the latter is a position where the voicing opposition is always suspended. In 'pre2', neutralization of voicing is dependent on the neighboring consonants.[7] Moreover, a labial, namely the archi-phoneme /F/, has already been shown to belong to 'pre2', whereas no labial consonant occurs in 'prel' or 'e3'. All in all, 'pre2' offers the simplest analysis. Like in the case of the alveolar occlusive in /třmen/ třmen vs. /Třina/ třtina, and of the velar fricative in /hřmoT/ hřmot vs. /Xřtān/ chřtán, the voicing of the labial fricative will be dependent on the neighboring phoneme. To finish the discussion of this problem, we present figure XVII where the phonotactic analysis of the mentioned forms is shown. Note that when neutralization of voicing is not operative in 'pre2', position 'e3' is always empty.

Having discussed conditions of the occurrence of phonemes in 'pre2', we will now examine phonotactic properties of this position; they are schematized in figure XVIII. Again, we list phonemes NOT found to have a certain property; some properties are not attested for all members of the position class. The phonemes /t/, /h/, /b/ and /v/ are not included because their occurrence is very limited (see above). /t/ and /b/ only have property 'F2_{prele2}' (in /třmen/ and /břve/),

---

7   Although there are no combinations like /fMň/ or /fMl/ proving that the opposition /f/ × /v/ is indeed valid here, this fact should not be taken as evidence for the neutralization. Had we interpreted it so, we would have lost the very cause of this neutralization: in Czech the opposition between voiceless and voiced consonants is not valid before a voiceless or a voiced consonant (except for /v/). The archi-phoneme /M/ is neither voiceless nor voiced. Hence, there cannot be neutralization of voicing.

	$F1_{e3}$	$F1_{e3N}$	$F1_{e2}$	$F1_{e2N}$	$F1_{e1}$	$F1_{E2}$	$F1_{E2N}$	$F1_{E3}$
P0	/T/ /S/ /Š/ /X/ /M/ /j/	/P/ /T/ /S/ /Š/ /K/ /X/ /M/ /j/ /r/ /l/	/P/ /F/ /T/ /S/ /Š/ /K/ /X/ /M/ /j/	see text	/P/ /F/ /T/ /S/ /Š/ /K/ /X/ /M/	/P/ /T/ /S/ /Š/ /M/ /j/ /r/	/P/ /T/ /S/ /Š/ /K/ /X/ /M/ /j/ /r/ /l/	/T/ /S/ /Š/ /K/ /M/ /l/

	$F2_{pre1e3}$	$F2_{pre1e3N}$	$F2_{pre1e2}$	$F2_{pre1e2N}$	$F2_{pre1e1}$	$F2_{pre1E2}$	$F2_{pre1E2N}$	$F2_{pre1E3}$
P0	/P/ /l/	/P/ /S/ /Š/ /K/ /X/ /M/ /j/ /r/ /l/	see text	all	all	/P/ /S/ /Š/ /K/ /M/ /j/ /r/ /l/	/P/ /T/ /S/ /Š/ /K/ /X/ /M/ /j/ /r/ /l/	/S/ /Š/ /X/ /j/ /r/

	$F2_{e3e2}$	$F2_{e3e2N}$	$F2_{e3e1}$	$F2_{e2e1}$	$F2_{E2e1}$	$F3_{pre1e3e2}$	$F3_{pre1e3e2N}$
P0	/P/ /T/ /S/ /Š/ /K/ /X/ /M/ /j/ /r/ /l/	all	/P/ /T/ /S/ /Š/ /K/ /X/ /M/ /r/ /l/	/P/ /F/ /T/ /S/ /Š/ /K/ /X/ /M/ /l/	/P/ /T/ /S/ /Š/ /K/ /X/ /M/ /j/ /r/	/P/ /Š/ /K/ /X/ /M/ /j/ /r/ /l/	/P/ /F/ /Š/ /K/ /X/ /M/ /j/ /r/ /l/

	$F3_{pre1e3e1}$	$F3_{pre1e2e1}$	$F3_{pre1E2e1}$	$F3_{e3e2e1}$	$F4_{pre1e3e2e1}$
P0	/K/ /X/ /j/ /r/	see text	/P/ /S/ /Š/ /K/ /X/ /M/ /j/ /r/ /l/	/P/ /T/ /S/ /Š/ /K/ /X/ /M/ /j/ /r/ /l/	/P/ /T/ /Š/ /K/ /X/ /M/ /j/ /r/ /l/

FIGURE XVIII: Phonotactic properties for *pos* 'pre2' and phonemes for which particular properties are not attested

/h/ only properties 'F2$_{pre1e2}$' and 'F3$_{pre1e2e1}$' (in /hřmoT/, /hřMňeT/), and /v/ only properties 'F1$_{e2}$N' and 'F2$_{e2e1}$' (in /vMrŠťiT/, /vMlāťiT/).

The figure allows us to introduce several restrictions limiting the distribution of phonemes from *pos* 'pre2'. We will begin with /j/. Its occurrence in 'pre2' is very limited. All attested combinations are given under (37). All of the mentioned words are often pronounced without the initial *j* (with the exception of *jho* which is rather archaic and hence hardly used in speech), but in the case of *jméno, jdu, jdi* and *jmění* such pronunciation, though common, is not regarded as orthoepic (VSČ: 59, Zeman 2008: 123). In the case of *jsi, jsme* and *jste* (all of them being forms of *být* "to be") the dropping of *j* is allowed (and quite com-

mon), but not at the beginning of a sentence where the full form is required
(VSČ: 59–60, Zeman *ibid.*).

(37) /jm/ in *jméno* "name"   /jMň/ in *jmění* "possession"
/jd/ in *jdu* "I go"   /jsm/ in *jsme* "we are"
/jďi/ in *jdi* "go!"   /jSt/ in *jste* "you (pl.) are"
/js/ in *jsi* "you are"
/jh/ in *jho* "yoke"

Looking closer at these combinations and at the attested phonotactic properties
of /j/, we can notice two important limitations. First, it is not found to be followed by three or more PerPs, which is something it shares with /ř/ (see (31)
above). Second, it can be followed by a phoneme from *pos* 'e3' (cf. /jd/), *pos*
'e2' (cf. /jMň/), *pos* 'e1' (cf. /jm/) and *pos* 'E3' (cf. /jď/), but it is not found to
be followed by a phoneme from *pos* 'E2'. To capture these limitations, the following restrictions are introduced:

(38) (a) /j/ cannot be followed by more than two PerPs.
     (b) /j/ cannot be followed by a phoneme from *pos* 'E2' (/p/, /b/, /f/).

Above we mentioned the special occurrence of /M/, /j/, /r/, /l/ in 'pre2'; when
they occur in this position, the result is a so-called side-syllabic combination
(see figure III in §10.2 for the attested combinations). However, this occurrence
has its limitations. Although 'pre2' is the fifth pre-nuclear position from the nucleus and thus four PerPs could come in between a phoneme occurring in 'pre2'
and a phoneme occurring in the nuclear position, /M/, /j/, /r/ and /l/ do not stand
before so much phonemes. Still, they have distributional properties which unambiguously determine their membership in 'pre2' (see figure XVIII). As we
have pointed out, /j/ cannot stand before three PerPs and before /p/, /b/, /f/. The
phonemes /M/ and /l/ are attested to stand before three PerPs (cf. /MStnī/ *mstný*,
/lStnī/ *lstný*), but /r/ is attested to stand only before two PerPs. We will assume
that /r/ may also occur before three PerPs, though such occurrence is actually not
attested. As /lStn/ shows, at least one member of the semiconsonant class stands
before so many PerPs. However, neither /M/, nor /r/ and /l/ are found to precede
four PerPs. Actually, the inability to stand before four PerPs is not unique to the
mentioned phonemes, but also applies to all occlusives, to all velars and to all
palatals. The latter phonemes occur only before three PerPs (cf. /Tkvj/ in *tkvět*,
/hřMň/ in *hřmět*, /ŠTkn/ in *štknout*), two PerPs (cf. /Třp/ in *třpyt*, /hvj/ in *hvězda*,
/Škr/ in *škrábat*) or one PerP (cf. /Tb/ in *dbát*, /hr/ in *hrad*, /šl/ in *šlapat*). The
only PerPs standing before four other PerPs are labial and alveolar fricatives (cf.
/FSkvj/ in *vzkvět* and /STkvj/ in *stkvěl*). Accordingly, these limitations will be

expressed with the following collocational restrictions (a non-fricative is an occlusive, a nasal and a sonant):

(39) (a) A non-fricative cannot be followed by more than three PerPs.
(b) A velar cannot be followed by more than three PerPs.[8]
(c) A palatal cannot be followed by more than three PerPs.

Furthermore, the nasal /M/ and all sonants (i.e. /j/, /r/, /l/ and /ř/) are not attested to be followed by two types of combinations: first, by combinations of type 'CC$_1$(C)' where 'C$_1$' is from *pos* 'E2' (i.e. /p/, /b/, /f/) or from *pos* 'e2' (i.e. /v/, /M/); second, by combinations of type 'CCC$_1$(C)' where 'C$_1$' is from *pos* 'e2' (i.e. /v/, /M/); in both cases '(C)' is an optional PerP. On the other hand, /F/ or /S/ can, for example, be followed by such combinations, cf. /FSpř/ in *vzpřímený* and /STkv/ in *stkví*. Hence, these restrictions hold:

(40) (a) A nasal cannot be followed by a combination of type 'CC$_1$' where 'C$_1$' is from *pos* 'E2' (/p/, /b/, /f/) or from *pos* 'e2' (i.e. /v/, /M/).
(b) A sonant cannot be followed by a combination of type 'CC$_1$' where 'C$_1$' is from *pos* 'E2' (/p/, /b/, /f/) or from *pos* 'e2' (i.e. /v/, /M/).
(c) A nasal cannot be followed by a combination of type 'CCC$_1$' where 'C$_1$' is from *pos* 'e2' (/v/, /M/).
(d) A sonant cannot be followed by a combination of type 'CCC$_1$' where 'C$_1$' is from *pos* 'e2' (/v/, /M/).

Let us now discuss the distribution of the velar archi-phonemes /K/, /X/. As mentioned in connection with the restrictions under (39), all velars are not followed by more than three PerPs, so a velar can only be followed by three or two PerPs or by one PerPs (or a nuclear phoneme). The following are attested combinations where a velar stands before two or three PerPs:

(41) (a) /kvj/ in *květ*   (b) /Křt/ in *křtu*
/xvj/ in *chvět*   /Křť/ in *křtiny*
/hvj/ in *hvězda*   /KŠť/ in *kštice*
/hřm/ in *hřmot*   /Xřt/ in *chřtán*
/Xřb/ in *hřbet*
(c) /hřMň/ in *hřmět*   /XTs/ in *chce*
/XTš/ in *chčije*

---

8   However, this restriction is violated in prepositional syntagms such as /KPŠtrosovi/ *k pštrosovi*; see §5.4 on this problem.

As is obvious, only /h/ stands before three PerPs. The velar archi-phonemes /K/ and /X/ are not attested in this situation, being capable to precede only two PerPs. Thus, the following holds:

(42) A velar archi-phoneme cannot be followed by more than two PerPs.[9]

As is further obvious from the combinations under (41), the choice of phonemes before which the velars stand is limited. If they are followed by two PePs, the first may only be from *pos* 'pre1', i.e. /T/, /S/, /Š/ or /ř/ (cf. /KŠť/, /XTs/), or from *pos* 'e2', i.e. /v/ or /M/ (cf. /kvj/). This limitation holds actually also for the labial occlusive /P/ (but not for the labial fricative /F/), as can be confirmed by the following attested two- or four-phoneme combinations with this phoneme:

(43) (a)   /PSť/ in *Pština* (place name)   (b)   /PStr/ in *pstruh*
           /PSď/ in *bzdít*   /PStř/ in *pstřeň* (PSJČ)
                                                       /PStr/ in *pštros*

In contrast, labial fricatives, nasals, alveolars and palatals are followed by a phoneme from *pos* 'e3' or from *pos* 'E2': cf. /Ftl/ in *vtlačit* and /Fpr/ in *vpravit*, /Mdl/ in *mdlo*,[10] /Tkl/ in *tklivý* and /Spl/ in *splav*, /Škr/ in *škrábat* and /Špr/ in *šproch*. To capture the mentioned limitations, the following restrictions are proposed:

(44) (a)   A velar cannot be followed by a combination of type 'C_1C' where 'C_1' is from *pos* 'e3' or from *pos* 'E2'.
     (b)   A labial occlusive cannot be followed by a combination of type 'C_1C' where 'C_1' is from *pos* 'e3' or from *pos* 'E2'.

11.9 Accidental appendices

Position 'pre2' is the last one we have introduced for describing the distribution of PerPs in the pre-nuclear context. The occurrence of phonemes in any of the 442 pre-nuclear combinations found in Czech (they are discussed in chapter 14) can be explained on them. However, there are several other occurrences of phonemes which the pre-nuclear section of the DU is not able to account for. Let us look at the following forms:

(45) (a)   /Střmen/ *střmen*
     (b)   /zMdlelī/ *zmdlelý*
           /STŠtvernāsobiT/ *zčtvernásobit*

---

9   This restriction is again violated in prepositional syntagms such as /KStravje/ *k stravě*.
10   /M/ cannot be followed by a labial, hence by a phoneme from *pos* 'E2'.

?	'pre2'	'pre1'	'e3'	'e2'	'e1'	'n'	Example
/S/	/t/	/ř/	Ø	Ø	/m/	/e/	*střmen*
/z/	/M/	Ø	/d/	Ø	/l/	/e/	*zmdlelý*
/S/	/T/	/Š/	/t/	/v/	Ø	/e/	*zčtvernásobit*

FIGURE XIX: Tentative analysis of /Střm/, /zMdl/ and /STŠtv/

The pre-nuclear combinations attested in these words pose a problem for our analysis. It follows from what has been said so far that /t/ in /třm/, /M/ in /Mdl/, and /T/ in /TŠtv/ occur in 'pre2' which is the last pre-nuclear position or, which equals to the same, the very first position of the DU. By the Principle of Mutual Commutability, the mentioned phonemes are assumed to occur in the same positions also in /Střmen/, /zMdlelī/ and /STŠtvernásobiT/. However, it means that the initial phonemes in these forms are left unassigned to any pre-nuclear position as the tentative analysis in figure XIX shows. It suggests that a new position is necessary. Before working out this suggestion, let us have a closer at the words under (45).

According to SSJČ and PSJČ, *střmen* is a rare archaic variant of *třmen* "stirrup". Another variant is *střemen*. The words under (45b) also have a variant with an inserted *e*: *zmdlelý* is an archaic form of *zemdlelý* "quailed" (according to SSJČ and PSJČ), and *zčtvernásobit* is a variant of *zečtvernásobit* "to quadruple",[11] but whereas PSJČ asserts that the latter is more common, SSJČ claims the opposite: *zčtvernásobit* is more common. It is hard to say which of them is really more common because both are quite rare as one can confirm by searching them in the Czech National Corpus or through Google.com.[12] Still, it is obvious that all of these words are somewhat marginal because they are optional variants of other words (whose phonotactic analysis is not problematic at all).

The mentioned words are not the only ones which are problematic for our analysis. In the first place there may be similar words we have overlooked, but we do not have this in mind. We must return to the non-syllabic prepositions *s*, *z*, *k* and *v* that were discussed in §5.3. It was mentioned there that they may adjoin the following word thus creating phoneme combinations not attested at the beginning of a word. Several examples were given there; they are repeated here (= (46a)) and supplemented with new ones (= (46b)):

(46) (a) /SKt/ in *s kterým*   (b) /FPs/ in *v psí*
         /SXřb/ in *z hřbetu*   /SKřt/ in *z křtin*
         /kjm/ in *k jménu*   /KTŠtv/ in *k čtvrtému*

---

11 In both cases *z*- and *ze*- are in origin variants of the same prefix.
12 The situation as of 13 March 2013.

?	'pre2'	'pre1'	'e3'	'e2'	'e1'	'n'	Example
/S/	/K/	Ø	/t/	Ø	Ø	/e/	s kterým
/S/	/X/	/ř/	/b/	Ø	Ø	/e/	z hřbetu
/K/	/P/	/Š/	/t/	Ø	/r/	/o/	k pštrosům
/z/	/r/	Ø	/t/	Ø	Ø	/ū/	z rtů
/F/	/P/	Ø	/s/	Ø	Ø	/ī/	v psí
/K/	/T/	/Š/	/t/	/v/	/r/		k čtvrtému
/s/	/j/	Ø	Ø	/M/	/ň/	/e/	s jměním
/k/	/l/	/S/	/ť/			/i/	k lstivosti

FIGURE XX: Tentative analysis of combinations arising in prepositional syntagms

/KPŠtr/ in *k pštrosům*   /FKŠť/ in *v kštici*
/vMdl/ in *v mdlobách*   /zMSd/ in *z mzdových*
/KTkl/ in *k tklivému*   /sjMň/ in *s jměním*
/zrt/ in *z rtů*   /FTŠk/ in *v Čkyni*
/vlž/ in *v lžíci*   /klSť/ in *k lstivosti*

Many more examples can be added, and we can even get the combinations /Střm/, /zMdl/ and /STšv/ found in the words *střmen* (cf. *s třmenem*), *zmdlelý* (cf. *z mdlého*) and *zčtvernásobit* (cf. *z čtveřice*). If such combinations are to be plotted onto the five pre-nuclear positions posited for Czech, a lot of complications arise. Consequently, the membership of the positions should be reconsidered or a new pre-nuclear position should be introduced. The reasons are still the same as in the case of the words *střmen*, *zmdlelý* and *zčtvernásobit*. A tentative analysis of some combinations from (46) is shown in figure XX.

The prepositional syntagms like those under (46) are not only similar to the mentioned words in being problematic for our phonotactic analysis, but also in the fact they have variants with an inserted *e*: *se kterým* is a variant of *s kterým*, *ze hřbetu* a variant of *z hřbetu*, *ke jménu* a variant of *k jménu* and so on. Both types of variants are assumed to be possible in Standard Czech, though it is said that the vocalized ones are preferable when an unusual combination is to arise. This fact was already mentioned in §5.3, and we also noted there that in some cases the non-vocalized variants are commoner irrespective of whether a difficult combination is the result. Still, the point is that the occurrence of the combinations such as those under (46) is accidental in the sense that they can be avoided. In this respect they are on a par with /Střmen/, /zMdlelī/ and /STŠtvernāsobiT/.

What is more, when the syntactic structure of sentences is considered in the phonological analysis, the combinations such as those under (46) will not be encountered because the prepositions will be recognized as separate words with separate PhFs. In §5.3 we argued that such a mode of analysis is preferable in

Czech due to advantages it offers, but it must be admitted that it is also a way to evade problems of this kind. Thus, if we still wanted to account for the mentioned problematic combinations, we must adjust our analysis. However, for the sake of simplicity and adequacy, we do not find it appropriate to introduce a new pre-nuclear position for the initial phonemes in these forms (that is, for the phonemes given under the slot marked with '?' in figures XIX and XX). Instead, they will be resorted to a special distributional class. Following the suggestion by Mulder (1994: 51) who dealt with a similar phenomenon in English, they will be called ACCIDENTAL APPENDICES. It reflects the fact that the occurrence of such phonemes is accidental (and in fact optional) at the beginning of phonotagms when position 'pre2' is already occupied by a phoneme. The phonemes which belong to this class are listed under (47). If 'pre2' is occupied by an occlusive or a fricative, only /S/, /K/ and /F/ occur as accidental appendices, and if it is occupied by a sonant, then /s/, /z/, /k/, /v/ occur.

(47) Accidental appendices: /s/, /z/, /k/, /v/, /S/, /K/, /F/

Chapter Twelve: POST-NUCLEAR DISTRIBUTION

12.1 Introduction

This chapter continues in the discussion of the distribution of PerPs focusing on the post-nuclear section. Due to neutralization of voicing only voicing archiphonemes together with sonants and nasals occur there. In the main DU, which underlies major-type phonotagms, their distribution is accounted for by three positions 'i1', 'i2', 'i3' and one archi-position 'I', and in the minor DU, which underlies minor-type phonotagm, it is accounted for by positions 'j1' and 'j2', which are discussed in §12.6. The post-nuclear section of the main DU together with position classes for each of the position is reproduced in the left-hand part of figure I, while its right-hand part reproduces that same for the minor DU. It is obvious that some phonemes can occur in more positions. The principle we introduced at the beginning of the previous chapter according to which phonemes occur in a less peripheral position in case there are more possibilities also applies here, but the situation in the post-nuclear context is more complicated. It will be explained in the following sections. Note that when listing phonotactic properties, we use same same conventions introduced in §10.1.

12.2 Position class 'i1'

Position 'i1' is the first post-nuclear position; if a phoneme occurs there, it stands right after a vowel or after a nuclear semiconsonant. It can also be empty. Its position class is given under (1).

(1) *pos* 'i1' ∈ {/P/, /T/, /K/, /m/, /n/, /ň/, /j/, /r/, /l/, Ø}

'i1'	'i2'	'i3'		'j1'	'j2'
j r l P T K m n ň Ø	P T K S Š F X ř Ø	P T K S Š Ť Ø		S r l Ø	p b f t d ť ď k g x
	m n ň r l				

FIGURE I: Post-nuclear section of the main distributional unit and its position classes (left) and the post-nuclear section of the minor distributional unit and its position classes (right)

	0·0	/rej/ *rej*
/j/	0·1	/rorejS/ *rorejs*
	0·2	/vojSK/ *vojsk*

FIGURE II: The occurrence of /j/ in the post-nuclear context

	F0	F1$_{i2}$	F1$_{i3}$	F1$_{i}$	F2$_{i2i3}$
P0n		/ň/	/P/ /T/ /K/ (/m/ /n/) /ň/ (/l/)	/P/ /T/ /K/ /m/ /n/ /ň/	/ň/
P0N	/j/ /r/	/P/ /K/ /m/ /ň/ /j/ /r/ /l/	all	all	/P/ /T/ /K/ /m/ /ň/ /j/ /r/ /l/

FIGURE III: Phonotactic properties for *pos* 'i1' and phonemes for which particular properties are not attested (parenthesized phonemes are attested only in marginal forms)

All phonemes belonging to this class also occur in another position with the exception of /j/ which occurs only in 'i1'. Its distribution is illustrated in figure II. It can be followed by no PerP or by one or two PerPs. In fact, these are properties shared by the other members of *pos* 'i1'. (Recall that in this and similar tables the digits express the number of preceding and following phonemes.)

/P/, /T/, /K/ in addition occur in 'i2' and 'i3'; their occurrence is discussed in the next section. The nasals /m/, /n/, /ň/ and the semiconsonants /r/, /l/ also occur in archi-position 'I', but 'i1' is the primary place of their occurrence in the post-nuclear context; we will return to them in §12.5. It is worth noting that all phonemes occurring in pre-nuclear position 'e1' occur in post-nuclear position 'i1'. The only exception is /ř/ which belongs to 'i2' in the post-nuclear context.

Phonotactic properties of *pos* 'i1' are schematized in figure III. Like in the previous chapter, the phonemes listed are those NOT attested to have a given property. Some properties are not attested for all members of the position class. The occlusives /P/, /T/, /K/ and the nasals /m/, /n/, /ň/ are not attested to be followed by a phoneme from *pos* 'I', i.e. by /m/, /n/, /ň/, /r/, /l/. This is a result of a more general limitation expressed by the collocational restriction under (2). It means that only sonants can be followed by a semiconsonant or by a nasal, cf. /j/ in /xejr/ *chejr* and /r/ in /Tšerň/ *čerň*.

(2)   A non-sonant (i.e. an occlusive, a fricative and a nasal) cannot be followed by a semiconsonant or by a nasal in the post-nuclear context.

Property 'P0N' is not attested for /j/, which means that if a semiconsonant is the nucleus of the phonotagm, it is not followed by /j/; accordingly, we adopt it as restriction (3). Something similar will be introduced for /ř/ in the next section. Figure III also shows that the same property is not attested for /r/, but this absence will be regarded as accidental. We assume that since nuclear /r/ can be followed by /l/ (cf. /Mrl/ in /umrlTse/ *umrlce*), the reverse is possible, too.

(3)   A nuclear semiconsonant cannot be followed by /j/.

The nasal /ň/ is the only member of *pos* 'il' which is not followed by one PerP or even by two PerPs. This requires a commentary. The other nasals are followed by occlusives and fricatives. Let us approach the problem from another angle. When examining the structure of Czech words, we find at the level of phonetic forms the following syllable-final sequences:[1]

(4)   [mp] in *lamp* (gen. pl. of *lampa*)   [ɱf] in *nymf* (gen. pl. of *nymfa*)
      [mt] in *vikomt, perkamt* (SSJČ)   [ms] in *říms* (gen. pl. of *římsa*)
      [nt] in *cement*   [mʃ] in *jímž*
      [ɲk] in *šizuňk*   [mx] in *střemch* (gen. pl. of *střemcha*)
      [ŋk] in *bank* (gen. pl. of *banka*)   [nf] in *tonf* (gen. pl. of *tonfa*)
                                                [ns] in *trans*
                                                [nʃ] in *jenž*

Some of these sequences are problematic. The sequence [mt] is rare and occurs probably only in *vikomt* "viscount", *perkamt* "mining office board" (archaic according to SSJČ and PSJČ) and in a couple of surnames such as *Klimt*. It is still acceptable and will be interpreted as a realization of the combination /mT/. The sequence [nf] may be found in *tonf*, gen. pl. of *tonfa* "tonfa (side-handed police baton)"[2]. We say "may" because although the pronunciation [tonf] is probably the one preferred by the norm of pronunciation for Czech, [tomɱf] could actually be heard when the word is pronounced. Still, we can assume that [nf] can occur, which gives us the ground for regarding /nF/ as a valid combination.

The most problematic of the phonetic sequences is [ɲk]. It is found in two kinds of words: first, in onomatopoeia like *kuňk* (sound of frog) or *žbluňk* (sound of something falling into water), and second, in words like *šizuňk* or *festuňk*, all probably originally borrowed from German.[3] The mentioned words are included in SSJČ. The database NLA lists much more words ending in -*ňk*, but it is not clear whether they should be accepted as part of the Standard Czech vocabulary. What is more, many if not all have a variant ending in -*nk* (i.e. [ŋk]). It is cer-

---

1   We could also think of [nx] in *stěnh*, an assumed gen. pl. of *stěhna* recorded in Kott X: 396, but it is an archaic or a dialectal word.
2   The word is listed in SN1, and its genitive *tonf* is found in the Czech National Corpus.
3   In most cases [ɲk] is part of -*uňk* which functions as a substitution of German -*ung* (cf. *Festung* "fortress").

/F/		/X/		/ř/	
0·0	/leF/ *lev*	0·0	/vraX/ *vrah*	0·0	/tvāř/ *tvář*
0·1	/praFT/ *pravd*	0·1	/neXȚ/ *necht'*	0·1	/buřT/ *buřt*
1·0	/salF/ *salv*	1·0	/arX/ *arch*	1·0	/pePř/ *pepř*

FIGURE IV: The distribution of /F/, /X/, /ř/ in the post-nuclear context

tainly true of *šizuňk, festuňk* as well as of *žbluňk*, though not of *kuňk*. The latter two words are, however, onomatopoeic expressions which are best viewed as belonging to a separate system of communicational means used by Czech. Now, since there is no other post-nuclear combination involving /ň/ (i.e. [ɲ]), it is fair to ask whether the combination /ňK/ should be admitted into the inventory of Standard Czech. In the end we have chosen not to do so, but at the same time we do not find it adequate to declare such combinations impossible. After all, the mentioned examples suggest that they could be possible.

On the other hand, the fact that there is no combination in which /ň/ would be followed by two PerPs will be interpreted as a regular limitation of Czech; see (5). It is to be recalled that collocational restrictions are not "truths" we discovered, but hypotheses about speech phenomena which we find appropriate to postulate and which have not been refuted. Once a refuting example of a form in which /ň/ is followed by two PerPs is found, the hypothesis will be refuted, but until then it is corroborated and accepted.

(5) /ň/ cannot be followed by two PerPs.

12.3 Position class 'i2'

Position 'i2' is the second post-nuclear position. Its position class is given under (6); it can also be empty. Phonemes in the class belong to three groups: First, /F/, /X/ and /ř/ which occur only in 'i2'; second, /S/ and /Š/ which occur in 'i2' and 'i3'; and third, /P/, /T/ and /K/ which occur in 'i1', 'i2' and 'i3'.

(6) *pos* 'i2' ∈ {/F/, /X/, /ř/, /P/, /T/, /K/, /S/, /Š/, Ø}

The distribution of /F/, /X/, /ř/ is illustrated in figure IV. They occur right after a nuclear phoneme while not being preceded by any other PerP. All of them are also followed by one PerP (belonging to 'i1'), or followed by one PerP (belonging to 'i3'), but none of them is both preceded and followed by a PerP. In other words, they are not attested in any three-phoneme post-nuclear combination. This limitation will be expressed by the following collocational restrictions; in the case of /ř/, the adjacent PerP can only be an occlusive (see §13.3):

	Occurrence in 'i2'		Occurrence in 'i3'	
/S/	0·0	/noS/ nos	1·0	not found
	0·1	/moST/ most	1·0	not found
	1·0	/kurS/ kurz	2·0	/prinTS/ princ
	1·1	/teKST/ text		
/Š/	0·0	/muŠ/ muž	1·0	/jiXŠ/ jichž
	0·1	/poŠT/ pošt	1·0	/puTŠ/ puč
	1·0	/jenŠ/ jenž	2·0	/pūjTŠ/ půjč
	1·1	/kumŠT/ kumšt		

FIGURE V: Differences in the occurrence of /S/, /Š/ in 'i2' and 'i3'

(7) (a) In the post-nuclear context, /F/ and /X/[4] cannot be preceded by a PerP
and at the same time followed by a PerP.

(b) In the post-nuclear context, /ř/ cannot be preceded by a PerP and at the
same time followed by a PerP.

As said, /S/ and /Š/ occur both in 'i2' and 'i3'. The two occurrences are compared in figure V. They occur in 'i2' if they stand right after a nuclear phoneme
and are not followed by any PerP (see the '0·0' examples); it follows from the
Principle of Lesser Peripherality. Secondly, they occur in this position when
they are followed by one PerP, which belongs to pos 'i3' (the '0·1' examples).
Thirdly, they occur in 'i2' when they are both preceded and followed by one
PerP (the '1·1' examples). On the other hand, they occur in 'i3' when they are
preceded by two PerPs and are not followed by any (the '2·0' examples).

Besides these straightforward occurrences, they can also be preceded by one
PerP, but the analysis of this situation is dependent on the particular circumstances. It concerns the following attested combinations:

(8) (a)   /mŠ/ in jímž
      /nS/ in tranz
      /jS/ in rorejs   /jŠ/ in jejž
      /rS/ in kurz   /rŠ/ in verš
      /lS/ in puls   /lŠ/ in Tylš (surname)
   (b) /XS/ in Fuchs (surname)   /XŠ/ in jejichž
   (c) /PS/ in zips   /PŠ/ in Hybš (surname)
      /TS/ in pec   /TŠ/ in tyč
      /KS/ in koks   /KŠ/ in jakžtakž

---

4   /F/ and /X/ are the only fricatives occurring only in 'i2'; the other fricatives /S/ and /Š/
     occur in 'i2' and 'i3'.

		Occurrence in 'i1'		Occurrence in 'i2'		Occurrence in 'i3'
/P/	0·0	/xlaP/ *chlap*	1·0	/alP/ *alb*	1·0	(/vīSP/ *výsp*)
	0·1	/pePř/ *pepř*	1·1	/TserPT/ fr. *excerpt*	2·0	/zāTSP/ *zácp*
	0·2	/zāPST/ *zábst*	0·1	/SkriPT/ *skript*		
			0·1	(/hiPŠ/ *Hybš*)		
/T/	0·0	/jeT/ *jet*	1·0	/nārT/ *nárt*	1·0	/buřT/ *buřt*
	0·1	/moTř/ *modř*	1·1	/pūjTŠ/ *půjč*	2·0	/kumŠT/ *kumšt*
	0·2	/pēTST/ *péct*	0·1	*not found*		
			0·1	/puTŠ/ *puč*		
/K/	0·0	/bīK/ *býk*	1·0	/lajK/ *laik*	1·0	/haFK/ fr. *tomahavk*
	0·1	/moKř/ *mokř*	1·1	/junKT/ fr. *adjunkt*	2·0	/vojSK/ *vojsk*
	0·2	/teKST/ *text*	0·1	/aKT/ *akt*		
			0·1	/ŠtaKŠ/ fr. *jakžtakž*		

FIGURE VI: Differences in the occurrence of /P/, /T/, /K/ in 'i1', 'i2' and 'i3'

The analysis of the combinations under (8a) poses no problem because /m/, /n/, /j/, /r/, /l/ can be assigned to 'i1' where they occur in other form and combinations. In these combinations /S/ and /Š/ occur in 'i2' according to the Principle of Lesser Peripherality. Similarly, the analysis of the combinations under (8b) is not problematic: since /X/ occurs in 'i2' (where it otherwise occurs), so /S/ and /Š/ must occur in 'i3'. On the other hand, the combinations under (8c) are ambiguous because /P/, /T/, /K/ could belong here either to 'i1' or to 'i2', and so /S/, /Š/ could belong either to 'i2' or to 'i3'. We must therefore consider first the occurrence of /P/, /T/, /K/.

In the previous section, /P/, /T/ and /K/ were assigned to 'i1', but they also occur in 'i2' and 'i3'. Figure VI shows differences in their distribution. Position 'i1' is their primary place of occurrence; they occur there when standing right after a nuclear phoneme while being the last phonemes in the phonotagm (see the examples under '0·0'). They also occur in this position when they stand right after a nuclear phoneme and are followed by two PerPs (the examples under '0·2'). If they are both preceded and followed by a PerP, they belong to 'i2' (the examples under '1·1'). Finally, if they are preceded by two PerPs while being the last phonemes in the phonotagm, they belong to 'i3' (the examples under '2·0'). In addition, /P/, /T/, /K/ can be either followed by one PerP, or preceded by one PerP. In this case, however, it is not the number of the adjacent phonemes that determines the membership of /P/, /T/, /K/, but their quality.

Let us look at the attested combinations in which /P/, /T/, /K/ are followed by one PerP. In those under (9a) they occur in 'i1', whereas in those under (9b) they occur in 'i2'. The first occurrence will be explained below, and we will start with on the second.

	'n'	'i1'	'i2'	'i3'	Phonological form
A	/e/	/r/	/P/	/T/	/eKSTserPT/ *excerpt*
	/i/	Ø	/P/	/T/	/SkriPT/ *skript*
	/u/	/n/	/K/	/T/	/adjunKT/ *adjunkt*
	/a/	Ø	/K/	/T/	/aKT/ *akt*
B	/i/	Ø	/P/	/Š/	/hiPŠ/ *Hybš* (surname)
	/ū/	/j/	/T/	/Š/	/pūjTŠ/ *půjč*
	/i/	Ø	/T/	/Š/	/tiTŠ/ *tyč*
	/a/	Ø	/K/	/Š/	/jaKŠtaKŠ/ *jakžtakž*
C	/e/	Ø	/P/	/Ť/	/nePŤ/ *nebť*
	/a/	Ø	/K/	/Ť/	/FšaKŤ/ *všakť*

FIGURE VII: Analysis of the occurrence of /P/, /T/, /K/ in 'i2'

(9) (a) /Př/ in *pepř*   /Tř/ in *dovnitř*   /Kř/ in *mokř*
          /PS/ in *zips*   /TS/ in *pec*   /KS/ in *koks*
     (b) /PT/ in *skript*   /KT/ in *akt*
          /PŠ/ in *Hybš*   /TŠ/ in *tyč*   /KŠ/ in *jakžtakž*
          /PŤ/ in *nebť* (SSJČ)   /KŤ/ in *všakť* (SSJČ)

The reason why /P/ and /K/ are assigned to 'i2' in /PT/ and /KT/ (/TT/ is impossible) is in the existence of the combinations /rPT/ and /nKT/ where /r/ and /n/ belong to 'i1', /P/ and /K/ belong to 'i2' and the final /T/ belongs to 'i3'. The same analysis is assumed for /PT/ and /KT/: /P/ and /K/ occur in 'i2' and /T/ in 'i3'. We have no reason to assume any other analysis as long as it is not in conflict with the data. It can be expressed in other words: the combinations /PT/ and /KT/ are expandable from the left because /rPT/ and /nKT/ are attested, but not from the right because no combination /PTC/ or /KTC/ is found (where 'C' is a PerP).[5] Accordingly, we propose the phonotactic analysis as given in the A section of figure VII.

The situation when /P/, /T/, /K/ are followed by /Š/ can be analyzed in the same way. This time the analysis is complicated by the fact that only /TŠ/ is actually attested to be expandable from the left: cf. /TŠ/ in *tyč* as opposed to /jTŠ/ in *půjč* (imp. sg. of *půjčit*). In contrast, /PŠ/ and /KŠ/ are not expandable either from the left or from the right (and both are in fact very rare). Still, for reasons of simplicity, we propose to treat the latter two combinations in the same way as /TŠ/, namely we assign /P/, /T/, /K/ in /PŠ/, /TŠ/, /KŠ/ to 'i2' and assume that /PŠ/ and /KŠ/ are potentially expandable from the left. Their analysis is shown in the B section of figure VII.

---

5   See §13.6 on expandability.

Finally, there are /PŤ/ and /KŤ/ attested in archaic words *nebť* (a variant of *nebot'*) and *všakť* (a variant of *však*).[6] Although neither of them is expandable from the left, /P/ and /K/ are assigned to 'i2' and /Ť/ to 'i3' for reasons of simplicity. Position 'i3' is the slot in which /Ť/ occurs in other forms, so there is no reason to assume other occurrence. Admittedly, the choice may, to a large degree, be arbitrary (though motivated). As an alternative, we could say that the analysis of /PŤ/ and /KŤ/ is ambiguous because /P/ and /K/ could belong either to 'i1' or to 'i2'.[7] The preferred analysis is shown in the C section of figure VII.

Another ambiguous occurrence of /P/, /T/, /K/ is when they are preceded by one PerP while not being preceded by any. See the following combinations:

(10) (a) /mP/ in *lamp*   /mT/ in *vikomt*
	/nT/ in *moment*	/nK/ in *tank*
	/jP/ in *knajp*	/jT/ in *prejt*	/jK/ in *laik*
	/rP/ in *orb*	/rT/ in *nárt*	/rK/ in *park*
	/lP/ in *lamp*	/lT/ in *kolt*	/lK/ in *kalk*
(b)		/řT/ in *buřt*	/řK/ in *ouřk* (SSJČ)
		/FT/ in *pravd*	/FK/ in *tomahavk*
		/XT/ in *ksicht*	
(c) (/SP/ in *výsp*)		/ST/ in *most*	/SK/ in *vosk*
		/ŠT/ in *mošt*	
(d)		/PT/ in *skript*	
		/KT/ in *akt*	

The analysis of the combinations under (10a) is as follows: since /m/, /n/, /j/, /r/, /l/ occur in 'i1' elsewhere, they are assigned to that position even here. /P/, /T/ and /K/ will then be assigned to 'i2' according to the Principle of Lesser Peripherality and also due to the existence of the combinations /rPT/ (in *excerpt*), /lTS/ (in *sulc*) and /rKT/ (in *infarkt*) where they occur in 'i2' without any ambiguity. The analysis of the combinations under (10b) is not problematic, either, because /ř/, /F/ and /X/ have already been assigned to 'i2', so /T/ and /K/ occur in 'i3' (/P/ is not attested to be preceded by /ř/, /F/ or /X/). Similarly, it will be assumed for the combinations under (10c) that the /S/ and /Š/ occur in 'i2' (as there is no evidence that they occur in 'i1'), and hence /P/, /T/, /K/ must occur in 'i3' in such combinations. Finally, the analysis of the combinations under (10d) has already been given in figure VII.

---

6   /TŤ/ is not found and is regarded to be impossible.
7   It is not possible to introduce an archi-position for /P/, /K/ because if they occurred there, they would always be followed by /Ť/, that is, there would be no choice and hence no necessity for a separate position.

	'n'	'i1'	'i2'	'i3'	*Phonological form*
A	/ā/	/P/	/S/	/T/	/zāPST/ *zábst*
	/i/	/P/	/S/	Ø	/ziPS/ *zips*
	/o/	/T/	/S/	/T/	/moTST/ *moct*
	/o/	/T/	/S/	Ø	/moTS/ *moc*
	/e/	/K/	/S/	/T/	/teKST/ *text*
	/o/	/K/	/S/	Ø	/koKS/ *koks*
B	/u/	/l/	/T/	/S/	/sulTS/ *sulc*
	/i/	/n/	/K/	/S/	/SfinKS/ *Sfinx* (brand name)

FIGURE VIII: Analysis of the occurrence of /S/, /Š/, /K/ in 'i2' and 'i3'

We will now return to the occurrence of /S/, /Š/ and to the combinations /PS/, /TS/, /KS/ on the one hand and /PŠ/, /TŠ/, /KŠ/ on the other. Arguments for the analysis of the latter have already been presented: /P/, /T/, /K/ occur in 'i2' and /Š/ in 'i3'. However, /PS/, /TS/, /KS/ cannot be analyzed in the same way. Let us look at the following examples:

(11) /ziPS/ *zips*   /zāPST/ *zábst*
    /moTS/ *moc*   /moTST/ *moct*   /sulTS/ *sulc*
    /koKS/ *koks*   /teKST/ *text*   /SfinKS/ *Sfinx* (brand name)

/TS/ and /KS/ are both expandable from the left and from the right, though /PS/ is only expandable from the left (which is viewed as accidental). In /TST/ the first /T/ occurs in 'i1', /S/ in 'i2' and the second /T/ in 'i3'. In /lTS/ the phoneme /l/ occurs in 'i1', /T/ in 'i2' and /S/ in 'i3'. These combinations show that /T/ can occur both in 'i1' and 'i2', and /S/ both in 'i2' and 'i3'. The same applies to /K/ and /S/. There is no controversy about it, but a problem arises with the analysis of /TS/ and /KS/. As is obvious from what has just been said, there are two analyses possible. Relying on the Principle of Lesser Peripherality, we prefer the analysis according to which /T/ and /K/ occur in 'i1' and /S/ in 'i2'. The combination /PS/ will be analyzed likewise, and the final analysis is reproduced in the A and B sections of figure VIII.

We are now in a position to summarize conditions of the occurrence of /S/, /Š/ in 'i2' and in 'i3':

(12) CONDITIONS FOR THE OCCURRENCE OF /S/, /Š/ IN THE POST-NUCLEAR CONTEXT
(a1) Both occur in 'i2' if they are neither preceded nor followed by a PerP.
(a2) Both occur in 'i2' if they are preceded by /m/, /n/, /ň/, /j/, /r/, /l/ irrespective of whether they are further followed by another PerP.
(a3) /S/ occurs in 'i2' if it is preceded by one PerP which is /P/, /T/ or /K/ irrespective of whether it is further followed by another PerP.

(b1) Both occur in 'i3' if they are preceded by two PerPs.
(b2) Both occur in 'i3' if they are preceded by /X/.
(b3) /Š/ occurs in 'i3' if it is preceded by /P/, /T/, /K/.

The occurrence of /P/, /T/, /K/ in 'i1', 'i2' and 'i3' is summarized as follows:

(13) CONDITIONS FOR THE OCCURRENCE OF /P/, /T/, /K/ IN THE POST-NUCLEAR CONTEXT

(a1) They occur in 'i1' if they are neither preceded nor followed by any PerP.
(a2) They occur in 'i1' if they are followed by /ř/ or /S/ (the /S/ may be further followed by another PerP).
(b1) They occur in 'i2' if they are preceded by /m/, /n/, /ň/, /j/, /r/, /l/ irrespective of whether they are further followed by any another PerP.
(b2) They occur in 'i2' if they are followed by /Š/ irrespective of whether they are preceded by another PerP.
(b3) They occur in 'i2' if they are followed by /T/ or /T̂/ (with the exception of /T/ which cannot be followed by these phonemes).
(b4) They occur in 'i2' if they are both followed and preceded by one PerP (except for /P/ which is not attested in such a situation).
(c1) They occur in 'i3' if they are preceded by two PerPs.
(c2) They occur in 'i3' if they are preceded by /ř/, /F/, /X/, /S/, /Š/.[8]
(c3) /T/ occurs in 'i3' if it is preceded by /P/ or /K/.

Having discussed in detail the occurrence of the phonemes belonging to *pos* 'i2', we can now look at their phonotactic properties. They are schematized in figure IX (on the next page). The occlusives /P/, /T/, /K/ do not have properties 'P0n'/'F0' and 'P0N'/'F0' when they occur in 'i2', but they have them when they occur in 'i1' (see figure III above). The figure allows us to introduce several collocational restrictions limiting the distribution of the phonemes from *pos* 'i2'.

One restriction was already given above under (7) which explains why /ř/, /F/, /X/ are not both followed and preceded by a PerP. In addition, these phonemes are also not followed by a PerP when standing right after a nuclear semiconsonant as opposed to /S/ in /prST/ *prst*. In the case of /ř/ this will be captured by the restriction under (14) which rules out situations when /ř/ would immediately follow a nuclear semiconsonant, and when /ř/ would be separated from it

---

8   This is subject to further restrictions: the combination /FP/ is impossible because a labial can only be preceded by a labial nasal in the post-nuclear context, and the combinations /XK/ is impossible because two velars cannot occur in the same section of the DU. On the other hand, the absence of /řP/, /XP/, /ŠP/ and /ŠK/ is regarded to be accidental. On the combinations /ŠK/, see chapter 15 under DI2*d*.

	F0	*F1ᵢ₃*
P0n	/P/ /T/ /K/	
P0N	/P/ /T/ /K/ /ř/	/P/ /K/ /F/ /X/ /ř/
P1ᵢₗn		/F/ /X/ /ř/
P1ᵢₗN	/P/ /T/ /Š/ /F/ /X/ /ř/	/P/ /K/ /S/ /Š/ /F/ /X/ /ř/

FIGURE IX: Phonotactic properties for *pos* 'i2' and phonemes for which particular properties
are not attested

by another PerP (i.e. combinations /Př/, /Tř/ and /Kř/ can occur only after a
vowel). Let us add that if the nucleus is a semiconsonant, /ř/ does not even occur
in the pre-nuclear section, which was already pointed in §11.2.

(14) If the nucleus of the phonotagm is a semiconsonant, the post-nuclear section cannot contain /ř/.

In the case of /F/ and /X/, there is a more general restriction which pertains to all
labials ('L') and all velars ('K'); it does not apply to alveolars and palatals, as
shown by /T/ in /StrTŠ/ *strč* and /Š/ in /sMrŠŤ/ *smršt'*:

(15) A nuclear semiconsonant cannot be followed by a combination of types
'LC' or 'KC' where 'C' is any PerP.

12.4 Position class 'i3'

Position 'i3' is the last post-nuclear position of the main DU; if a phoneme occurs there, it is the last phoneme in the phonotagm. Its position class is listed
under (16); it can also be empty.

(16) *pos* 'i3' ∈ {/Ť/, /S/, /Š/, /P/, /T/, /K/, Ø}

The occurrence of /P/, /T/, /K/ and of /S/, /Š/ in this position has already been
explained. The remaining phoneme /Ť/ is the only one which occurs in this and
no other position. Besides standing on its own (cf. /xuŤ/ *chut'* or /vrŤ/ *vrt'* (imp.
sg. of *vrtět*), it is attested in the following combinations:

	F0
$P0n$	/P/ /T/ /K/ /S/ /Š/
$P0N$	/P/ /T/ /K/ /S/ /Š/
$P1_{i1}n$	/P/ /T/ /K/ /S/ /Š/
$P1_{i1}N$	all
$P1_{i2}n$	/P/ /S/
$P1_{i2}N$	/P/ /T/ /K/ /S/ /Ť/
$P2_{i1i2}n$	
$P2_{i1i2}N$	/P/ /T/ /K/ /Ť/

FIGURE X: Phonotactic properties for *pos* 'i3' and phonemes for which particular properties are not attested

(17) (a) /mŤ/ in *jsemt'* (archaic) (b) /PŤ/ in *nebt'* (archaic)
　　　　 /nŤ/ in *ont'* (archaic)　　　　　 /KŤ/ in *však t'* (archaic)
　　　　 /jŤ/ in *pojď*　　　　　　　　　 /XŤ/ in *necht'*
　　　　 /rŤ/ in *žerď*　　　　　　　　　 /SŤ/ in *pust'*
　　　　 /lŤ/ in *bylt'* (archaic)　　　　　 /ŠŤ/ in *poušt'*
　　　(c) /TŠŤ/ in *ačt'* (archaic)

Some combinations are problematic because they occur in rather archaic words and should perhaps be excluded from the analysis. Still, they exemplify the combinatory potential of /Ť/, but suggest that is limited in contemporary Czech. There is only one example of a combination in which it is preceded by two PerPs, but the word *ačt'* (particle/conjunction) is archaic, so we should perhaps conclude that /Ť/ cannot be preceded by two PerPs in Modern Czech. However, since /Ť/, by belonging to 'i3', has a potential to be preceded by two PerPs, /TŠŤ/ may be taken as a manifestation of this potential. Its existence is not the only reason why /Ť/ has been assigned to 'i3'. It has two other properties of this position: it is preceded by a phoneme from *pos* 'i1' as shown by the examples under (17a), and it is preceded by a phoneme from *pos* 'i2' as shown by the examples under (17b).

Phonotactic properties of *pos* 'i3' are schematized in figure X. The occlusives /P/, /T/, /K/, and the fricatives /S/, /Š/ cannot have properties 'P0n', 'P0N', 'P1ᵢ₁n' and 'P1ᵢ₁N' provided that they occur in 'i3'. The absence of property 'P2ᵢ₁ᵢ₂N' for all occlusives (i.e. /P/, /T/, /Ť/, /K/) is accounted for by the following restriction (compare it against e.g. /S/ in /šMrnTS/ *šmrnc*):

(18) A nuclear semiconsonant cannot be followed by a combination of type 'CCO' where 'O' is an occlusive and 'C' any PerP.

		Occurrence in '*il*'		Occurrence in '*I*'
/m/	0·0	/zem/ *zem*	1·0	/jilm/ *jilm*
	0·1	/lamP/ *lamp*		
	0·2	/pomST/ *pomst*		
/n/	0·0	/jen/ *jen*	1·0	/hejn/ *hejn*
	0·1	/banK/ *bank*		
	0·2	/adjunKT/ *adjunk*		
/ň/	0·0	/sīň/ *síň*	1·0	/Tšerň/ *čerň*
	0·1	*not found*		
	0·2	*not found*		
/r/	0·0	/mor/ *mor*	1·0	/xejr/ *chejr*
	0·1	/kurS/ *kurz*		
	0·2	/verST/ *verst*		
/l/	0·0	/pil/ *pil*	1·0	/Ktejl/ from *koktejl*
	0·1	/pulS/ *pulz*		
	0·2	/sulTS/ *sulc*		

FIGURE XI: Differences in the occurrence of /m/, /n/, /ň/, /r/, /l/ in '*il*' and '*I*'

12.5 Position class 'I'

Position 'I' is the only archi-position in the post-nuclear context, being the product of the suspension of the difference between positions 'i2' and 'i3'. Phonemes listed under (19) have been assigned to it because the phonotactic difference between these positions is not functional for them (see §7.3). They can only be preceded by a phoneme belonging to *pos* 'i1' in which case they are never followed by any other PerP. The archi-position cannot be empty.

(19) *pos* 'I' ∈ {/m/, /n/, /ň/, /r/, /l/}

All phonemes of this class also occur in '*il*'. Their post-nuclear occurrence is illustrated in figure XI. They occur in '*il*' when they stand right after a nuclear phoneme while not followed by any other PerP or while followed by one PerP or while followed by two PerPs. In contrast, their occurrence in '*I*' is restricted to one particular situation: when they are preceded by a phoneme belonging to '*il*', namely by /j/, /r/, /l/ in the following attested combinations:

(20) /jm/ in *tajm* (SN1)   /rm/ in *šarm*   /lm/ in *jilm*
     /jn/ in *hejn*   /rn/ in *koncern*   /ln/ in *Lincoln* (foreign surname)
                             /rň/ in *čerň*
     /jr/ in *chejr* (SSJČ)
     /jl/ in *koktejl*   /rl/ in *stárl* (see §10.2)

	$F0$
PI_{il}	

FIGURE XII: Phonotactic property for *pos* 'I'

The phonotactic property of position 'I', the only one, is schematized in figure XII. All members of *pos* 'I' have it,[9] and there is no need for collocational restrictions.

12.6 Position classes for the minor distributional unit

As explained at length in §8.2, it is necessary to operate with two types of DU in Czech. What we have so far dealt with was the distribution of phonemes in post-nuclear positions of the main DU. The post-nuclear section of the minor DU is different from it because it contains only two positions, 'j1' and 'j2'.[10] The occurrence of phonemes is limited in this position as is, in fact, limited the occurrence of minor-type phonotagms as a whole.

The position class for 'j1' is given under (21). Unlike 'j2' (see below), this position may be empty. Phonemes occurring there stand always after a nuclear phoneme (of the minor DU) and are always obligatorily followed by a phoneme from *pos* 'j2'; they also undergo neutralization of voicing. /S/ is attested in /trešt'/ from *trest'mi* or in /pošt/ from *post-jugoslávský*; /r/ is attested only in /verb/ from *Verbný* (surname), and /l/ only in /half/ from *halfvolej* (ASCS).

(21) *pos* 'j1' ∈ {/S/, /r/, /l/, Ø}

The position class for 'j2' is reproduced under (22). This position is never empty. The occlusives and fricatives occurring there do not undergo neutralization of voicing. They can stand right after a nuclear phoneme (of the minor DU) or be preceded by one phoneme from *pos* 'j1', but the latter is not very common. In fact, the only attested examples are the already-mentioned /St/, /St'/, /lf/ and /rb/. In other words, /p/, /d'/, /d/, /k/, /g/ and /x/ are only attested to stand right after a nuclear phoneme.

(22) *pos* 'j2' ∈ {/p/, /b/, /f/, /t'/, /d'/, /t/, /d/, /k/, /g/, /x/}

Minor-type phonotagms are always appended to a major-type phonotagm, so the phonemes belonging to *pos* 'j2' are obligatorily followed by a PerP belonging to

---

9   If they did not, they would not belong to this position.
10   The pre-nuclear section of the minor DU is assumed to be the same as that of the main DU.

the adjacent major-type phonotagm; this phoneme is /m/, /n/, /ň/, /v/ or /j/ or it is /M/ provided that the latter is followed by another PerP (cf. /šikMňe/ *šikmě*). Details are discussed in §8.2.

Chapter Thirteen: PROPERTIES OF PRE-NUCLEAR AND POST-NUCLEAR COMBINATIONS

This chapter examines properties of pre-nuclear and post-nuclear combinations (henceforth jointly called *peripheral combinations*) in Czech. They occur at the beginning and at the end of major-type phonotagms attested at the beginning and at the end of words. An early attempt to describe such combinations was made by Hattala (1870), though he only took into account word-initial combinations. A more exhaustive classification was done by Novotná (1972) for Czech and by Tolstaja (1968, 1974) and Sawicka (1974) for all Slavic languages. In addition, Czech peripheral combinations have been included in the analysis of such combinations in 104 languages by Greenberg (1978). Theoretical and methodological foundations of the mentioned descriptions are not the same as ours, so they are not fully compatible. Our aim is to supplement and expand them, but without trying to correct them, though they could be corrected in some cases.

13.1 Length

The most obvious criterion for the classification of combinations is the one according to the number of phonemes in them; we will speak about COMBINATION LENGTH (after Greenberg *op. cit.*). Czech has pre-nuclear combinations the length of which ranges from 2 to 5 phonemes, and post-nuclear combinations of 2 and 3 phonemes. Figure I summarizes how many combinations of a given length have been included in our analysis. The pre-nuclear combinations exceed almost five times the post-nuclear ones. It is also noteworthy that the number of three-phoneme pre-nuclear combinations is a bit higher than the number of two-phoneme

	Combination length				Total
	Five	*Four*	*Three*	*Two*	
Pre-nuclear	2	43 (50)	179 (198)	182 (192)	406 (442)
Post-nuclear	–	–	19 (29)	65 (75)	84 (104)

FIGURE I: The number of peripheral combinations in our database sorted according to their length

ones. The overall number of the combinations is rather maximal in the sense that our database includes also combinations attested in words probably no longer or at best seldom used in present-day Czech. Examples are /Txn/ in *dchnouti* (SSJČ), /Sdm/ in *sdmýchnouti* (PSJČ), /Pstř/ in *pstřeň* (PSJČ) or /FShř/ in *vzhři-žiti* (PSJČ). They have been included as examples of combinatory capacities of Czech, which are vast. The numbers can even be increased by inclusion of combinations found only in place names, proper names and other marginal words like /jř/ in the surname *Kejř*, /lTŠ/ in the place name *Telč* or /Kf/ in the place name *Kfely* and others. Such combinations will be called MARGINAL COMBINATIONS. The values in the parenthesis express the total number of combinations with the marginal combinations included. The same holds for other tables in this chapter.

13.2 Phonematic constituency

As every phoneme belongs to a paradigmatic class defined by distinctive features its members share with each other, another way of looking at phoneme combinations is through their PHONEMATIC CONSTITUENCY. For example, the phonemes /m/, /n/, /ň/ belong to one paradigmatic class because they all have the distinctive feature 'nasal', and /p/, /b/, /f/, /v/, /m/ belong to another class defined by the feature 'labial'. The first type of features refers to various manners of articulations, and the second type to various places of articulation (see chapter 3). Combinations of phonemes can thus be described according to the manner and the place of articulation of their constituents.

From the perspective of the manner of articulation, we distinguish between occlusives (marked as 'O'), fricatives (= 'F'), nasals (= 'N') and sonants (= 'R'), which includes /j/, /ř/ and non-nuclear /r/, /l/. The types of combinations sorted according to the manner of articulation will be called MANNER TYPES. The second way of approaching the combinations is through the place of articulation. We recognize a class of labials (= 'L'), alveolars (= 'A'), palatals (= 'P'), velars (= 'K')[1] and isolated phonemes (= 'I'). The last group includes sonants (they are isolated because they are phonologically neither labial nor palatal nor alveolar nor velar) and the archi-phoneme /M/, which is also not specified as to the place of articulation. Combination types sorted according to the various places of articulation will be called PLACE TYPES.

---

1   Archi-phonemes are put in between slashes, while letters standing for a certain class of phonemes are put into single quotation marks. Therefore, /P/ is the archi-phoneme 'labial occlusive', whereas 'P' is a class of palatals.

	Containing at least one			
	'F'	'O'	'R'	'N'
Pre-nuclear	330 (359)	250 (270)	200 (217)	116 (128)
Post-nuclear	49 (63)	56 (72)	46 (55)	22 (27)
Total	379 (422)	306 (342)	246 (272)	138 (155)

FIGURE II: The number of peripheral combinations containing at least one occlusive ('O'), one fricative ('F'), one nasal ('N') or one sonant ('R')

In the next three sections we examine the phonematic constituency of all peripheral combinations included in our database. By way of introduction, let us look at the combinability of each paradigmatic class.

Figure II shows how many combinations contain at least one occlusive, one fricative, one nasal or one sonant. The most combinable are fricatives, although in the post-nuclear context there are a few more combinations with an occlusive than with a fricative. The least combinable are nasals; it is partly given by the fact that Czech has only three. Yet it does not explain why there are over 100 more combinations with sonants, of which Czech has four (i.e. /j/, /ř/, /r/, /l/). Now, out of the fricatives, the most combinable are alveolars, then labials, palatals, and the least combinable are velars. Out of the occlusives, the most combinable are alveolars, then velars, labials and the least combinable are palatals. Out of the sonants, the most combinable is /l/, then /r/, then /j/, and the least combinable is /ř/, though the combinability of the last two is comparable. Finally, out of the nasals, the most combinable is the nasal archi-phoneme /M/, then come /ň/, /n/ and /m/, though their combinability is comparable. See figure IV below for the exact numbers.

It is worth noting that the pre-nuclear context allows combinations of two or more phonemes of the same manner of articulation. In this respect the most combinable are fricatives. There are combinations of two (cf. /Fz/ in *vzít*, /Šh/ in *žhář*), three (cf. /FSx/ in *vzchopit se*, /FShl/ in *vzhlížet*) as well as of four fricatives, though there is only one attested example of the latter: /FShv/ in *vzchvívati* (PSJČ). The post-nuclear context allows only combinations of two fricatives, but there are just two of them, /XŠ/ in *jejichž* and marginal /XS/ in the surname *Fuchs*. Pre-nuclear combinations of five fricatives as well as post-nuclear combinations of three fricatives are already disallowed by the structure of the DU because not all positions may be occupied by fricatives (namely 'e1' and 'i1'). On the other hand, the DU allows combinations of up to three occlusives,[2] but

---

2   For example, in the pre-nuclear context one occlusive can occur in 'e3', one in 'pre1' and one in 'pre2'. No such combination is attested, though.

	Containing at least one				
	'*A*'	'*I*'	'*L*'	'*K*'	'*P*'
Pre-nuclear	258 (279)	226 (248)	217 (236)	128 (139)	126 (140)
Post-nuclear	48 (62)	46 (55)	26 (31)	23 (31)	19 (27)
Total	306 (341)	272 (303)	243 (267)	151 (170)	145 (167)

FIGURE III: The number of peripheral combinations containing at least one labial ('L'), one alveolar ('A'), one palatal ('P'), one velar ('K') or one isolated consonant ('I')

only combinations of two are attested (e.g. /Tk/ in *tkát* and /KT/ in *akt*). To capture this, we propose the following collocational restriction:[3]

(1)   Three or more occlusives cannot stand in close proximity.

Combinations of three nasals are not possible in any context, which derives from the DU and from the fact that Czech does not allow geminates.[4] Combinations of two nasals occur in the pre-nuclear context (only two of them, /Mn/ in *mnout* and /Mň/ in *město*); the post-nuclear context disfavors even combinations of two nasals. The DU also disallows combinations of three sonants, but those of two are possible, cf. /lj/ in the proper name *Ljuba* and /jr/ in *chejr*.

Figure III shows how many combinations contain at least one labial, one alveolar, one palatal, one velar or one isolated phoneme. Out of these classes, the most combinable are alveolars. Then come isolated consonants, and after them are labials, then velars, and the least combinable are palatals. Out of the alveolars, the most combinable are fricatives, then occlusives, and the least combinable is /n/. Out of the labials, the most combinable are fricatives, then occlusives, and the least combinable is /m/. The high combinability of the labial fricatives derives mostly from the combinability of /v/ and /F/; on the other hand, /f/ is one of the least combinable PerPs in Czech. Curiously enough, in the case of velars the most combinable are not fricatives, but occlusives, and then fricatives (there is no velar nasal). Finally, out of the palatals, it is again fricatives which are most combinable, but then comes /ň/, and the least combinable are occlusives. See figure IV for the exact numbers.

Alveolars are the most combinable place of articulation. In the pre-nuclear context we find combinations of two (/St/ in *stát*), three (/STs/ in *scestný*) and even four alveolars, though there is only one such example of the latter, namely /TStn/ in *ctný*. Combinations of five alveolars are precluded by the structure of

---

3   The restriction is violated by the prepositional syntagm /KTklivému/ *k tklivému*. See §5.3.
4   Due to neutralization of place of articulation of nasals, a combination of three nasals would have to contain two instances of /M/, which is impossible.

	/S/	/F/	/T/	/l/	/r/	/v/	/j/	/Š/	/k/	/ř/	/t/
Pre-nuclear	111 (120)	83 (94)	55 (61)	68 (73)	55 (59)	59 (63)	37 (43)	34 (39)	52 (55)	43 (47)	49
Post-nuclear	23 (33)	7	33 (37)	10 (16)	18 (20)	–	16 (17)	13 (17)	–	5 (6)	–
Total	124 (153)	90 (101)	88 (98)	78 (89)	73 (79)	59 (63)	54 (60)	47 (56)	52 (55)	48 (53)	49

	/M/	/ň/	/m/	/n/	/z/	/p/	/h/	/s/	/K/	/b/	/d/
Pre-nuclear	39 (46)	38 (42)	28 (30)	27 (28)	31 (36)	33 (34)	32 (34)	30 (34)	8 (10)	26 (29)	27 (28)
Post-nuclear	–	1	11 (12)	10 (14)	–	–	–	–	16 (23)	–	–
Total	39 (46)	39 (43)	39 (42)	37 (42)	31 (36)	33 (34)	32 (34)	30 (34)	24 (33)	26 (29)	27 (28)

	/š/	/x/	/P/	/t'/	/ž/	/X/	/Ť/	/ď/	/g/	/f/
Pre-nuclear	26 (29)	23 (26)	11 (13)	14 (20)	15	6	–	9	7 (8)	7 (8)
Post-nuclear	–	–	10 (14)	–	–	7 (8)	6 (11)	–	–	–
Total	26 (29)	23 (26)	21 (27)	14 (20)	15	13 (14)	6 (11)	9	7 (8)	7 (8)

FIGURE IV: The number of peripheral combinations containing at least one particular PerP

the DU. In the post-nuclear context there are combinations of two and three alveolars (cf. /nT/ in *bažant* and /TST/ in *péct*). Combinations of two labials and two palatals are possible in both contexts (cf. /vm/ in *vmáčknout*, /žň/ in *žně*, /mP/ in *lamp*, /ŠŤ/ in *poušt*), but those of three (or more) labials or palatals are not because the DU does not allow such combinations. Noteworthy is the absence of any combination of two or more velars in any context (see the next section).

Finally, let us look at figure IV illustrating the combinability of individual PerPs.[5] The most combinable are /S/ and /F/, which was expected due to the fact

---

5   The combinability of the Czech phonemes is also examined in Ludvíková – Kraus (1966) and Ludvíková (1968), but the authors have employed a different method and a different phonological theory (they do not operate with archi-phonemes). Their distributional domain is a phonological form of a word within which they counted how many phonemes can appear before a given phoneme, and how many can appear after it. Their analysis has shown that /l/, /r/, /b/, /n/, /m/, /t/, /s/, /v/ and /k/ are (in descending order) the most combinable PerPs. — It is also worth noting that according to the analysis by Volín – Churaňová (2010), who analyzed Czech spoken texts, around 55% of consonants (correspond-

that they are often forms of the prefixes s-, z- and v-, either synchronically or in origin. On the other hand, the high combinability of /T/ is interesting because it cannot be correlated with any grammatical element. Also noteworthy is the combinability of /v/. Quantitatively, it is similar to that of sonants, but in contrast to them it does not occur in the post-nuclear context. The least combinable phonematic class is palatals, but the least combinable individual phonemes are /g/ and /f/, which must be given by historical circumstances. Except for a handful of "native" words, they have been introduced into Czech through foreign borrowings.

13.3 Constituency of two-phoneme combinations

In this section the phonematic constituency of combinations of length 2 is examined. Figure V shows attested place and manner types of the pre-nuclear combinations, and figure VI does the same for the post-nuclear ones. The shaded cells indicate that the respective combination is attested, and the blank ones that it is not (e.g. the shaded cell at the intersection of the 'LL' row and the 'FN' column in figure V means that there is an attested pre-nuclear combination of two labials where the first is a fricative and the second a nasal, i.e. /vm/). The symbol '–' indicates that a combination of some type is not possible in principle (e.g. 'FR' cannot be 'LL' because sonants are not specified as to the place of articulation). The same symbol is also used for combinations of two identical phonemes because no two identical phonemes can stand in close proximity within a phonotagm. If a shaded cell contains 'V_R', combinations of such a type occur also before or after nuclear /r/, /l/. If a cell contains 'V_R' and is not shaded, the type is attested only for nuclear /r/, /l/. There are not many combinations of this kind. First of all, it concerns the pre-nuclear combinations /sM/, /zM/, /šM/, /vM/ (in smrt, zmrznout, šmrnc and vmrštit) where the /M/ is the product of neutralization of place of articulation for nasals; similar combinations are found before vowels without neutralization, cf. /vm/ in vmístit or /sn/ in snový. Much more interesting is the combination /Mk/ attested in /Mkl/ mkl, 3rd person sg. of mknouti se (SSJČ); we will return to it in the next section. If a cell is shaded, but does not contain 'V_R', the combination is attested only in the vicinity of vowels. The parentheses '()' in a cell indicate that the respective type is attested only in marginal combinations. The columns and rows headed 'No.' indicate how many combinations of a given type are attested (parentheses include marginal combinations).

---

ing to PerPs in our analysis) participate in consonantal combinations, whereas the remaining 45% occurs as singletons.

	No.	'OO'	'OF'	'ON'	'OR'	'FO'	'FF'	'FN'	'FR'
		7(9)	17(18)	12	19(20)	24(25)	18	25	25
'LL'	3				–	V_R	–		–
'LA'	9				–	V_R	V_R		–
'LP'	10				–				–
'LK'	5			–	–		V_R	–	–
'LI'	16	–	–	–		–	–	V_R	
'PL'	6				–	V_R			–
'PA'	4				–	V_R			–
'PP'	4				–		–		–
'PK'	2				–	V_R		–	–
'PI'	5	–	–	–	–	–	–	V_R	
'AL'	12		V_R		–	V_R	V_R		–
'AA'	8	–	V_R		–	V_R	–		–
'AP'	10		V_R		–				
'AK'	7			–	–	V_R	V_R	–	–
'AI'	16	–	–	–		–	–	V_R	
'KL'	9(10)				–				–
'KA'	6				–				–
'KP'	5(6)	()			–				–
'KI'	11	–	–	–		–	–		

	No.	'NO'	'NF'	'NN'	'NR'	'RO'	'RF'	'RN'	'RR'
		1	4(5)	2	3(4)	11(12)	10	4	0(2)
'IL'	8								–
'IA'	9				–				–
'IP'	9								–
'IK'	6(7)	V_R		–	–			–	–
'II'	3(6)		–	–		–	–	–	()

FIGURE V: Place and manner types of *pre-nuclear* combinations of length 2

Figures V and VI show which combination types are attested, but the unattested ones are of more interest. Some absences must be accidental, whereas others will be regularized by collocational restrictions introduced below. Though postulated in connection with combinations of two PerPs, they have been checked against more complex combinations and apply to them, too.

The pre-nuclear distribution of alveolar and palatal fricatives is limited by the restriction under (2) which rules out the combinations /Šs/ and /Šz/. The reversed combinations are, however, possible, cf. /Sš/ in *zšednout* and /Sž/ in *zženštilý*.[6]

---

6   Greenberg (*op. cit.*: 257) notes that "there is a strong tendency [in the 104 language he examined, Czech included] for different type sibilants, most commonly [s] and [š], not to combine". See also Jaeger – Van Valin (1982: 135–6) on this.

	No.	'OO'	'OF'	'OR'	'FO'	'FF'	'NO'	'NF'
	No.	3(4)	5(6)	3	9(10)	1(2)	5(6)	7
'LL'	2	−		−		−		
'LA'	5			−				
'LP'	1(3)		()	−			()	
'LK'	2			−				
'LI'	1	−	−		−	−	−	−
'PA'	1				−	V_R		
'PP'	1		−		−	V_R	−	
'AL'	1(2)			−		()		
'AA'	4		−	V_R	−	V_R	−	
'AP'	3(4)		V_R	−	V_R		()	
'AK'	2			−	V_R		V_R	
'AI'	1	−	−		−	−	−	−
'KA'	3(4)			−				−
'KP'	4			−				
'KI'	1	−	−		−	−	−	−

	No.	'RO'	'RF'	'RN'	'RR'
	No.	13	11	6	3
'IL'	9				−
'IA'	9				−
'IP'	5(7)				−
'IK'	7			−	−
'II'	3(4)	−	−	−	

FIGURE VI: Place and manner types of *post-nuclear* combinations of length 2

The post-nuclear context is more restricted because the alveolar and palatal fricatives cannot stand there in close proximity, but this is a consequence of a more general restriction on the occurrence of two fricatives in the post-nuclear context; see (9) below.

(2)   In the pre-nuclear context an alveolar fricative cannot be preceded by a palatal fricative.

Although alveolar fricatives can precede palatal fricatives in the pre-nuclear context, such combinations are not very common. Besides the mentioned /Sš/ and /Sž/, there is /FSš/ in archaic *vzšuměti* (SSJČ), /Sšl/ in archaic *zšlechtiti* (PSJČ), and /SŠť/ in archaic *zšťastniti* (PSJČ). There are also several other words (and hence combinations) recorded only in NLA, for example, *zškaredění* (/SŠk/), *zškvařenina* (/SŠkv/), *zšpouliti* (/SŠp/), *zštafirovati* (/SŠt/), *sšklebiti* (/SŠkl/), *sšněrovati* (/SŠň/), *sšplouchati* (/SŠpl/), *sštváti* (/SŠtv/), *sšvagřiti* (/SŠv/), *vzženit se*

(/FSž/). Hardly any of them is used in contemporary Czech, perhaps with the exception of *vzženit se*, which is found (once) in the Czech National Corpus.[7] These combinations have not been included in our analysis, but they suggest that it would not appropriate to introduce additional restrictions on combinations involving the palatal and alveolar fricatives.

Another restriction concerns palatal and alveolar occlusives; it rules out combinations like /Ťť/, /Ťď/. Let us add that the palatal occlusives cannot even be followed by an occlusive, but this is already encoded in the DU: /ť/ and /ď/ occur in archi-position 'E3' which stands right before the nucleus, and /Ť/ occurs in i3' which is the last post-nuclear position.

(3)   A palatal occlusive cannot be preceded by an alveolar occlusive.

The distribution of velars is also limited. The restriction under (4) implies that the combinations /Pk/, /Pg/ and /PK/ are prohibited. In contrast, velar fricatives are preceded by /P/ (cf. /PxāTŠ/ *pcháč*).

(4)   A velar occlusive cannot be preceded by a labial occlusive.

The next two restrictions are very important. (5a) says that a pre-nuclear or a post-nuclear combination cannot contain two instances of a velar irrespective of whether they would stand in close proximity or be separated by another PerP. In this respect the velars are unique because Czech allows combinations of two labials, alveolar or palatals, cf. /Fb/ in *vbodnout*, /St/ in *stát* and /Šť/ in *štěstí*. The restriction is, however, violated by prepositional syntagms such as *k houslím* with /Kh/ or by *k tchyni* with /KTx/ (see §5.3 on this). The second restriction, (5b), is similar, but limited only to labial occlusives. Thus, combinations like /Přb/, /PŠb/, /PSb/, /PSpn/ are impossible due to it.

(5)   (a)   A peripheral combination cannot contain two velars.
      (b)   A peripheral combination cannot contain two labial occlusives.

There are a few other restrictions applicable either to the pre-nuclear context, or to the post-nuclear one. We will start with the former. Coming back to figure V, we can see that place type 'IL' is not attested in the pre-nuclear context when the 'I' is a nasal, i.e. /M/. This restriction was already mentioned in §11.3. It means that labials cannot be preceded by a nasal, and combinations like /Mv/, /Mpl/ are impossible. However, similar combinations with alveolars, palatals

---

7   The word *vzženit se* is used by some as a "gender-correct" equivalent of *vzmužit se* "to pluck up one's courage", as can be confirmed by looking it up via Google.com (the situation as of 18 March 2013). *Muž* means "man" and *žen(a)* "woman".

and velars are possible: /Mz/ in *mze*, /Mdl/ in *mdlý* or /Mh/ in *mhouřit*. There is another restriction applicable to the labials given under (6). As pointed out in §11.2, the labial nasal /m/ cannot be preceded by a phoneme from *pos* 'E2', i.e. by /p/, /b/, /f/. In sum, the only attested pre-nuclear combinations of two labials are /Fp/, /Fb/ and /vm/ (cf. *vpadnout, vbodnout* and *vmísit*) and /Fpr/, /Fbr/, /Fpl/, /Fbl/, /Fpj/, /Fbj/, /Fpř/ and /Fbř/ (cf. *vpravit, vbruslit, vplout, vblízku* (SSJČ), *vpěchovat, vběhnout, vpřed* and *vbřednouti* (SSJČ)).

(6) In the pre-nuclear context a labial fricative cannot be preceded by another labial.[8]

If we examine the combinability of velar fricatives, we will find out that the liminations on their occurrences can be easily expressed in reference to position classes we have introduced for the pre-nuclear context. It is obvious from the attested combinations that they can precede phonemes belonging to *pos* 'e1' (cf. /xr/, /hl/, /xm/, /hň/), phonemes belonging to *pos* 'e2' (cf. /xv/, /hvj/), phonemes belonging to *pos* 'E2' (cf. /Xb/), phonemes belonging to *pos* 'E3' (cf. /Xť/) and phonemes belonging to *pos* 'pre1' (cf. /Xřt/, /XTs/), but they are not found to precede a phoneme belonging to *pos* 'e3', namely /t/, /d/, /s/, /z/, /š/, /ž/, /k/, /g/, /x/, /h/. Accordingly, the following restriction is proposed:

(7) A velar fricative cannot precede a phoneme belonging to *pos* 'e3'.

The distribution in the post-nuclear context is also limited by restrictions applicable only to that domain of distribution. The one under (8) concerns occlusives. Phonotagm-finally, they are only followed by an alveolar (cf. /PT/, /KS/ in *skript*, *koks*) or by a palatal (cf. /PŤ/, /KŠ/ in *nebť, jakžtakž*); thus, combinations like /PF/, /PK/, /TK/, /TF/ are impossible. Note that an occlusive (as well as a fricative) cannot be followed by a nasal in the post-nuclear context.

(8) In the post-nuclear context an occlusive cannot be followed by a labial or a velar.

The next limitation concerns the post-nuclear distribution of fricatives. The only two attested post-nuclear combinations of two fricatives are /XS/ in the surname *Fuchs* and /XŠ/ in *jejichž*. Any other combinations of two fricatives are impossible. This needs a commentary, since the restriction under (9) allows, besides the attested /XS/ and /XŠ/, also /XF/ and /XX/. However, the latter is impossible due to the fact that Czech does not allow geminates within a phonotagm (see

---

8   The restriction was already mentioned in connection with minor-type phonotagms in chapter 8; see p. 126.

§9.2), and the impossibility of /XF/ is actually already encoded in the DU: both /X/ and /F/ occur only in 'i2' and so their occurrence is mutually exclusive. In fact, the DU also rules some other combinations of two fricatives, namely /FF/, /FX/, /SF/, /SX/, /ŠF/, /SX/ and /XX/.

(9)   In the post-nuclear context a fricative cannot be preceded by a non-velar fricative.

Above we touched upon the limited combinability of labials in the pre-nuclear context. In the post-nuclear one, their occurrence is also restricted:.

(10) (a)   In the post-nuclear context a labial cannot be preceded by another labial unless it is a labial nasal.
 (b)   In the post-nuclear context a labial cannot be preceded by a palatal or by a velar.

The import of these restrictions is that a labial is only preceded, in the post-nuclear context, by another labial or by an alveolar. If it is a labial, then it may only be a nasal, namely /mP/ (cf. *lamp*, gen. pl. of *lampa*); to put it otherwise, the combinations /FP/ and /PF/ are impossible (/PP/, /FF/, /Pm/, /Fm/ are impossible by other restrictions). When a labial is preceded by an alveolar, it may not be an occlusive, which is implied from the restriction given above under (8). It can therefore be only a fricative (cf. /SP/ in *výsp*, gen. pl. of *výspa*) or a nasal (cf. /nF/ in *tonf*, gen. pl. of *tonfa*).

The last restriction introduced here refers to the phoneme /ř/ which cannot co-occur with a fricative or a nasal; see (11). In the pre-nuclear context such combinations are possible: /vř/ in *vřít*. Finally, see §12.2 on the impossibility of occlusive, fricatives and nasals to be followed by a semiconsonant or a nasal.

(11) In the post-nuclear context, /ř/ cannot stand in close proximity with a fricative or a nasal.

13.4 Constituency of three-phoneme combinations

We will now move to the constituency of three-phoneme combinations. Figure VII lists manner types of the pre-nuclear combinations, and figure VIII manner types of the post-nuclear ones (the figures are reproduced on the next two pages). The types are arranged according to the number of combinations they underlie. Under every manner type there is a list of place types attested for the respective manner type. For example, manner type 'OFF' corresponds to two place types 'AAL' and 'APL' (namely to /Tsv/ and /Tšv/). If a type is attested to

'FOR'	'FFR'	'FFN'	'FOF'	'OFO'	'FFO'	'FON'	'FNR'	'OFN'	'FFF'
42	28(30)	14(17)	14	8(11)	10(11)	5(7)	5(6)	5	5
'LLI'	'LAI'	'LAL'	'LAL'	'LAP'	*'LAL'*	'LAL'	'LII'	'AAL'	'LAL'
'LAI'	'LPI'	'LAA'	'LAA'	('LPP')	*'LAA'*	'AAL'	'AII'	'APL'	'LAP'
'LKI'	'LKI'	'LAP'	*'LAP'*	'AAL'	'LAP'	'AKA'		'APP'	'LAK'
'ALI'	'ALI'	'LKL'	'LKL'	'AAP'	'LAK'	'AKL'		'AKA'	'AKL'
'AAI'	'API'	'LKP'	*'AAL'*	'APL'	'LPA'	'AKP'		'AKP'	
'AKI'	'AKI'	'ALA'	'AAA'	*'APA'*	'LPP'				
'PLI'	'KLI'	'ALP'	'AAP'	('APK')	'LPK'				
'PAI'		'AKL'	*'AKL'*	'APP'	'APP'				
'PKI'		'AKA'	'PAL'	'KPP'					
		'AKP'	*'PKL'*						
		'PKA'	'KAA'						
		'PKP'	'KAP'						

'NFO'	'OFR'	'ORO'	'FNN'	'FOO'	'ROF'	'RFO'	'FRO'	'OON'	'OFF'
4(5)	4	4	4	3	2(3)	1(3)	2	2	2
'IAA'	'ALI'	'AIL'	'LIP'	'LAK'	'IAA'	('IAA')	'KIA'	'AKA'	*'AAL'*
'IAP'	'AAI'	'AIP'	'AIA'	'AAK'	'IAP'	'IAP'	'KIL'	'AKP'	'APL'
'IPP'	'API'	'KIA'	'AIP'	'PAK'		('IPP')			
	'KLI'	'KIP'							

'NON'	'ONN'	'RFR'	'NOR'	'ORN'	'OOR'	'OOF'	'ROR'	'FRN'	'RFN'
2	2	2	2	1	1	1	1	1	1
'IKA'	'AIP'	'ILI'	'IAI'	'AIL'	'AKI'	'AKL'	'ILI'	'KIL'	'IAL'
'IKP'			'IKI'						

'RNN'	('ORF')	('NOF')
1	0(1)	0(1)
'IIP'	('LIL')	('IAA')

FIGURE VII: Manner types for *pre-nuclear* combinations of length 3

occur before nuclear /r/, /l/, it is written in italics, which means that non-italicized types occur only before vowels. The numbers in the second rows indicate how many combinations are attested for a given type. Parentheses mean that a type is attested only in marginal combinations.

We can draw several conclusions about the manner types. In total, there are 64 logically possible combinations of the classes 'O', 'F', 'N', 'R' (i.e. $4^3 = 64$), but only 33 of them are attested for pre-nuclear combinations and two of them only for marginal combinations (i.e. 'ORF' and 'NOF'; cf. /břv/ in *Břve* and /MTs/ in *Mcely*). These types correspond to 179 (or 198 with marginal combinations) actually found combinations. For the post-nuclear context, only 7 manner types are attested; they underlie 19 combinations (or 29 with marginal combinations). The impossibility of many manner types is already encoded in the struc-

'ROF'	'OFO'	'RFO'	'NFO'	'NOF'	'ROO'	'NOO'
5 (7)	4 (7)	3 (6)	2 (3)	2 (3)	2	1
'IAA'	'LAA'	'IAA'	'LPA'	*'AAP'*	'ILA'	'AKA'
'IAP'	('LAK')	'IAK'	'LAA'	*'AAA'*	'IKA'	
('IKA')	'AAL'		('AAK')	('AKA')		
	'AAA'					
	'AAP'					
	'AAK'					
	'KAA'					

FIGURE VIII: Manner types for *post-nuclear* combinations of length 3

ture of the DU,[9] or derives from the collocational restrictions previously introduced. The absence of some of the remaining types will be taken care of by additional restrictions. Again, though postulated in connection with combinations of length 3, they have general validity and hold for combinations of length 4 and 5 as well.

The collocational restrictions that follow are applicable to the pre-nuclear context only, though some of them pertain to the post-nuclear one, too, due to the fact that the DU does not allow for such post-nuclear combinations.

The first two restrictions given under (12) concern sonants and nasals. Their import is that if a sonant is followed by two phonemes of the same manner of articulation, it can only be two nasals (cf. /jMň/ in *jmění*), whereas a nasal is followed by no such combination. In the post-nuclear context the sonants and the nasals can only be followed by two occlusives (cf. /rPT/ in *excerpt*, /nKT/ in *adjunkt*), but not by two fricatives, nasals or sonants. The fact that they are not followed by nasals and by sonants is already encoded in the DU. Their inability to be followed by two fricatives is a consequence of the limited distribution of fricatives. As is implied from the restriction under (9), if two fricatives stand next to each other, the first is velar, i.e. /X/, but a velar fricative cannot be both followed by another fricative and preceded by a sonant or a nasal because it can either be preceded, or followed by one PerP in the post-nuclear context. See §12.3 on this peculiarity which is also a property of /F/ and /ř/.

(12) (a)   In the pre-nuclear context a sonant cannot be followed by two occlusives or by two fricatives.

      (b)   In the pre-nuclear context a nasal cannot be followed by two phonemes of the same manner of articulation.

---

9   The DU predicts that combinations of types 'ONO', 'FNF', 'NNN', 'ORR', 'FRR', 'NRR', 'RRO', 'RRF', 'RRN' or 'RRR' are impossible, that is, no matter how positions in the DU are filled, the result will never be a combination of such a type.

The next restriction also concerns sonants; it says that sonants ('R') cannot be preceded by a combination of an occlusive ('O') and a nasal ('N'). As is obvious, it does not specify that we are dealing with pre-nuclear combinations. It is intentional because the restriction is more general. To begin with, no such combination is possible in the post-nuclear context, since the DU will never give rise to it. It can only arise in the pre-nuclear context or in the pre-nuclear and nuclear context if the sonant is nuclear /r/ or /l/. In other words, the restriction prohibits combinations like /tMl/, /kMj/, /dMř/ as well as the combinations /tM/, /dM/, /kM/ and /gM/ which would stand before a nuclear semiconsonant (in contrast, combinations like /sM/ or /vM/ occur before a nuclear semiconsonant: /vMršťiT/ *vmrštit*, /sMrT/ *smrt*). It is worth noting that combination of the reversed type are possible before semiconsonants (and only before them—see §13.6), namely /Mkl/ *mkl*, 3rd person sg. of *mknouti* (SSJČ).

(13) Combinations of type 'ONR' are impossible.[10]

The next restrictions under (14) and (15) hold both for the pre-nuclear and post-nuclear combinations, but are in fact relevant only to the pre-nuclear context because combinations of the mentioned types would never arise in the post-nuclear context where neither a nasal nor a sonant may stand in between two PerP or after two PerPs. This fact is already encoded in the DU. Now, starting with the restrictions under (14), their import is as follows: Sonants stand between two PerPs provided that the left one is a nasal; see (14a). If a sonant is preceded by a nasal, it is always followed by a vowel within a single phonotagm. Actually, the only sonant which occurs between two PerPs is /ř/; it stands between two occlusives (cf. /Třť/ in *třtina*), or between an occlusive and a fricative (only in /břv/ attested in the place name *Břve*), or between a fricative and an occlusive (as in /Xřt/ in *chřtán*). However, /ř/ cannot stand between two fricatives ('F'), which is generalized by the restriction under (14b). A similar restriction applies to nasals, namely (14c), which rules out combinations like /rMj/, /řMj/.

(14) (a) Peripheral combinations of type 'NRC' where 'C' is any PerP are impossible.
     (b) Peripheral combinations of type 'FRF' are impossible.
     (c) Peripheral combinations of type 'RNR' are impossible.

In the pre-nuclear context, fricatives cannot stand between a nasal and a sonant, but occlusives can (cf. /Mdl/ in *mdlý*). In contrast, occlusives cannot occur between a sonant and a nasal, but fricatives have this capacity (cf. /jsm/ in *jsme*).

---

10   In the post-nuclear context such combinations are precluded by the structure of the DU.

Moreover, fricatives cannot stand between two nasals, but the occlusives are capable of this, though there are only two examples: /Mkn/ in *mknouti* (SSJČ) and /Mkň/ in *mkni* (imp. sg. of *mknouti*). Hence, the following restrictions hold:

(15) (a) Peripheral combinations of type 'NFR' are impossible.
　　 (b) Peripheral combinations of type 'RON' are impossible.
　　 (c) Peripheral combinations of type 'NFN' are impossible.

Examining phonemes attested for the particular manner types, we will find out that the occurrence of velars is quite limited (recall also the impossibility of there being two velars in a combination; see (5a) above). One restriction is given under (16). Palatals do not have capacity, either, but this is already ruled out by the structure of the DU. In contrast, labials and alveolars are followed by two phonemes of the same manner of articulation (cf. /vMň/ in *vměstnat* and /sMň/ in *směna*). It should be noted that the restriction under (16) is violated in prepositional syntagms such as /kMněStu/ *k městu*, /KTkaňī/ *k tkaní*, /KFšemu/ *k všemu*. However, as explained in §5.3, we treat such velars as if they occurred in a separate PhF.

(16) In the pre-nuclear context, velars cannot be followed by two phonemes of the same manner of articulation.

The next four restrictions pertain to particular combination types involving a velar ('K'). The first implies that it cannot be preceded by a sonant ('R') + an occlusive ('O'), so combinations like /jTx/ are ruled out (cf. /rTš/ in *rčení* with a palatal). The second implies that it cannot be preceded by two occlusives, which is however violated in prepositional syntagms such as *k tkaní* with /KTk/. (17c) says that it cannot be followed by an occlusive + a labial ('L'), which is again violated in prepositional syntagms such as *k dvěma* with /Kdv/. Finally, (17d) says that that a velar cannot be followed by a fricative ('F') + a labial, and this restriction is again violated in prepositional syntagms such as *k svátku* with /Ksv/.

(17) (a) Peripheral combinations of type 'ROK' are impossible.
　　 (b) Peripheral combinations of type 'OOK' are impossible.
　　 (c) Peripheral combinations of type 'KOL' are impossible.
　　 (d) Peripheral combinations of type 'KFL' are impossible.

The next two restrictions apply only to velar fricatives ('F_K') ruling out combinations like /Txř/, /Thv/ and /XSt/. In contrast, velar occlusives enter in such combinations, as is proven by /Tkl/ in *tklivý*, /Tkv/ in *tkví* (3rd person sg. of *tkvět*) and /Kšť/ in *kštice*. Though applying both to the pre-nuclear and post-nuclear context, the restrictions are only relevant for the former, since a velar fricative cannot stand in between two PerPs in the post-nuclear context (see §12.3). Note that the restrictions are again violated by prepositional syntagms such as *k hradu* with /Khr/ and *k hvězdě* with /Khvj/.

(18) (a)   Peripheral combinations of type 'OF$_K$R' are impossible.
    (b)   Peripheral combinations of type 'OF$_K$F' are impossible.
    (c)   Peripheral combinations of type 'F$_K$FO' are impossible.

In the pre-nuclear context, velars and labials are limited by the restrictions under (19) which rule out combinations like /MSk/, /MTh/, /Msm/, /Mtv/. On the other hand, similar combinations ending in an alveolar (cf. /MTs/ in *Mcely*) or a palatal (cf. /MSť/ in *mstít se*) are possible. In the post-nuclear context, combinations of type 'NCK' where 'C' is any PerP are at least marginally possible (cf. /nSK/ in the foreign place name *Smolensk*).

(19) (a)   Pre-nuclear combinations of type 'NCK' are impossible.
    (b)   Pre-nuclear combinations of type 'NCL' are impossible.

Velar fricatives and palatal fricatives ('F$_P$') cannot be preceded by two PerPs of which the first is an occlusive and the second a fricative; see (20). This time the restrictions pertain to the post-nuclear context as well, but the impossibility of such combinations is already captured in the DU (/F/ and /X/ occur in 'i2' which does not allow them to be preceded by two PerPs). In contrast, velar and palatal occlusives are preceded by a group of an occlusive plus a fricative: cf. /TŠk/ in *Čkyně* (place name) and /PSď/ in *bzdít*. Combinations of this pattern are also not found for alveolar fricatives, but it is a consequence of other restrictions. In effect, only the labial fricative /v/ is found in such combinations: cf. /Tsv/ in *cválat* and /Tšv/ in *čvachtat*. The restrictions are again violated in the prepositional syntagms such as *k schodům* with /KSx/ and *k všemu* with /KFš/.

(20) (a)   Peripheral combinations of type 'OFF$_K$' are impossible.
    (b)   Peripheral combinations of type 'OFF$_P$' are impossible.

The palatal fricatives are further limited by the restriction reproduced under (21). Again, though pertaining to both contexts, it is relevant only for the pre-nuclear context because combinations of three fricatives are impossible in the post-nuclear context. Such combinations are also not possible for the velar fricatives, but this is already implied by other restrictions. Consequently, in combinations of three fricatives the leftmost fricative can only be labial or alveolar (cf. /FSx/ in *vzchopit* and /Sxv/ in *schválit*).

'ALI'	'AKI'	'LAI'	'LLI'	'LAL'	'AAL'	'AAI'	'LKI'	'LAP'	'AKL'
18	12	9(10)	8	8	6(8)	7	7	6(7)	6
'OFR'	'OOR'	'FFR'	'FOR'	'FFO'	'OFO'	'OFR'	'FOR'	'OFO'	'OOF'
'FFR'	'FFR'	'FOR'		'FFF'	'OFF'	'FOR'	'FFR'	'FFO'	'FFF'
'FOR'	'FOR'			'FFN'	'OFN'			'FFF'	'FFN'
				'FOF'	'FOF'			'FFN'	'FOF'
				'FON'	'FON'			'FOF'	'FON'

'AIP'	'AKA'	'AII'	'AKP'	'IAP'	'IAA'	'LAA'	'PLI'	'APL'	'LAK'
5	5	4(5)	4(5)	4(5)	3(5)	4	4	4	4
'ORO'	'OON'	'FNR'	'OON'	'ROF'	'ROF'	'FFN'	'FOR'	'OFF'	'FOO'
'ONN'	'OFN'		'OFN'	'RFO'	'RFO'	'FFO'		'OFN'	'FFF'
'FNN'	'FON'		'FFN'	'NFO'	'NFO'	'FOF'		'OFO'	'FFO'
	'FFN'		('FON')		('NOF')				

'AAP'	'KLI'	'ILI'	'LPI'	'APP'	'API'	'LKL'	'PKI'	'KIL'	'AIL'
3	3	3	3	3	1(3)	2	2	2	2
'OFO'	'OFR'	'ROR'	'FFR'	'OFO'	'OFR'	'FFN'	'FOR'	'FRO'	'ORO'
'FOF'	'FFR'	'RFR'		'OFN'	'FFR'	'FOF'		'FRN'	'ORN'
				'FFO'					

'KIA'	('IPP')	'LPP'	'LPK'	'LKP'	'IAI'	'IAL'	'PAK'	'PKA'	'PKL'
2	(2)	1(2)	1	1	1	1	1	1	1
'ORO'	('RFO')	('OFO')	'FFO'	'FFN'	'NOR'	'RFN'	'FOO'	'FFN'	'FOF'
'FRO'	('NFO')	'FFO'							

'PAL'	'PKP'	'KAA'	'KAP'	'KPP'	'KIP'	'AAA'	'AAK'	'AIA'	'IIP'
1	1	1	1	1	1	1	1	1	1
'FOF'	'FFN'	'FOF'	'FOF'	'OFO'	'ORO'	'FOF'	'FOO'	'FNN'	'RNN'

'ALP'	'APA'	'LII'	'LIP'	'LPA'	'PAI'	'IKI'	'IKA'	'IKP'	('LIL')
1	1	1	1	1	1	1	1	1	0(1)
'FFN'	'OFO'	'FNR'	'FNN'	'FFO'	'FOR'	'NOR'	'NON'	'NON'	('ORF')

('APK')	('ALA')
0(1)	0(1)
'OFO'	'FFN'

FIGURE IX: Place types for *pre-nuclear* combinations of length 3

(21) Peripheral combinations of type 'F_PFF' are impossible.

The last restriction applicable to the pre-nuclear context concerns phonemes from *pos* 'e3' and *pos* 'E2', i.e. all occlusives and all fricatives except for /v/, which belongs to *pos* 'e2' (cf. /Tkv/ in *tkvi*). Note that the restriction actually applies to the phonemes from *pos* 'E3', i.e. /t̕/ and /d̕/, but this is already im-

'IAA'	'IAP'	'IAK'	'AAA'	'LAA'	'IKA'	'AKA'	('AAK')	'AAP'	'ILA'
5(6)	2(3)	1(3)	2	2	1(2)	1(2)	0(2)	1	1
'RFO' 'ROF'	'ROF'	'RFO'	'OFO' 'NOF'	'OFO' 'NFO'	'ROO' ('ROF')	'NOO' ('NOF)	('OFO') ('NFO')	'NOF'	'ROO'

'KAA'	'LPA'	'AAL'	('APP')	('LAK')
1	1	1	0(1)	0(1)
'OFO'	'NFO'	'OFO'	('OFO')	('OFO)

FIGURE X: Place types for *post-nuclear* combinations of length 3

plied from the fact that combinations of three occlusives are impossible (see (1) in §13.2 above).

(22) In the pre-nuclear context, phonemes from *pos* 'e3' and *pos* 'E2' cannot be preceded by two occlusives.

Let us now shift the attention to place types for three-phoneme combinations. Figure IX (see the previous page) lists these types for pre-nuclear combinations, and figure X does the same for post-nuclear combinations. Under every place type there is a list of corresponding manner types. In total, there are 125 (= 5^3) logically possible three-phoneme combinations of 'L', 'P', 'A', 'K', 'I', but only 62 are attested for the pre-nuclear context (including 4 attested only for marginal combinations) and only 15 for the post-nuclear context (including 3 only for marginal combinations). Almost one half of the attested types underlie only one combination. The non-occurrence of many types derives from the structure of the DU or from the previously introduced restrictions. In addition, combinations of the following patterns are impossible in the post-nuclear context ('C' is any PerP):

(23) (a)   Post-nuclear combinations of type 'CPK' are impossible.
     (b)   Post-nuclear combinations of type 'CLP' are impossible.
     (c)   Post-nuclear combinations of type 'CKP' are impossible.

The restriction under (23a) says that combinations where a palatal ('P') is followed by a velar ('K') cannot be preceded by another PerP (e.g. /lŠK/, /PŠK/).[11] Compare them for example with /mŠT/ in *kumšt*. The last two restrictions imply that combinations where a labial ('L') or a velar is followed by a palatal cannot be preceded by another PerPs (e.g. /rPŤ/, /mPŠ/, /nKŤ/, /jKŠ/). Compare them against /TŠŤ/ in *ačt* (archaic) or /lTŠ/ in *Telč*. To put it otherwise, two-phoneme

---

11   See chapter 15 under DI2d on the combination /ŠK/.

'FFOR'	'FFFR'	'OFOR'	'RFON'	'FFON'	'OFON'	'FOFR'
10(11)	3(6)	5	3	3	3	3
'LALI'	'AKLI'	'AALI'	'IAAA'	'LAAL'	'AAAL'	'LAPI'
'LAAI'	('LALI')	'APLI'	'IAAL'	'LALA'	'AAAA'	'AAPI'
'LAKI'	'LAKI'	'LAAI'	'IAAP'	'LALP'	'AAAP'	'AKLI'
'LPKI'		'LPAI'				

'FOON'	'NFON'	('FFNN')	'OOFR'	'ORNN'	'OFOF'	'FOOR'
2	2	0(2)	1	1	1	1
'PAKA'	'IAAA'	('LAIP')	'AKLI'	'AIIP'	*'APAL'*	'AAKI'
'PAKP'	'IAAP'					

'FRNN'	'FONN'	'FFOF'	'FOOF'	'FOFF'	('FFFF')
1	1	1	1	1	0(1)
'KIIP'	'AAIP'	'LAKL'	'AAKL'	*'AAAL'*	'LAKL'

FIGURE XI: Manner types for *pre-nuclear* combinations of length 4

post-nuclear combinations of types 'PK', 'LP', 'KP' are regularly non-expandable from the left (see §13.6 on expandability).

Finally, several other types of post-nuclear combinations will be declared impossible. In the post-nuclear context a nasal ('N') is not found to be followed by an alveolar ('A') + a labial ('L') or by a labial + an alveolar, that is, combinations like /mSP/, /nSP/, /mPS/, /nPS/, /mPT/, /nPT/ are not attested. As to the sonants ('R'), they are followed by a labial + an alveolar (cf. /rPT/ in *excerpt*), but not by the reverse, i.e. by an alveolar + a labial, which means that combinations like /jSP/, /lSP/, /rSP/ are not found. Moreover, sonants are not found to be followed by a palatal ('P') + an alveolar, that is, combinations like /lŠT/, /rŠT/, /jŠT/ are not found. The nasals are capable of this, cf. /mŠT/ in *kumšt*. Finally, both nasals and sonants are not found to be followed by two palatals, which means that combinations like /mŠŤ/, /nŠŤ/, /jŠŤ/, /rŠŤ/, /lŠŤ/ are impossible. In fact, the only PerP found to precede two palatals in the post-nuclear context is /T/ in the combination /TŠŤ/ attested in archaic *ačt*. The mentioned limitations are captured by the following collocational restrictions:

(24) (a)   Post-nuclear combinations of type 'NAL' are impossible.
     (b)   Post-nuclear combinations of type 'NLA' are impossible.
     (c)   Post-nuclear combinations of type 'RAL' are impossible.
     (d)   Post-nuclear combinations of type 'RPA' are impossible.
     (e)   Post-nuclear combinations of type 'NPP' are impossible.
     (f)   Post-nuclear combinations of type 'RPP' are impossible.

'LALI'	'LAKI'	'AKLI'	'LAAI'	'LAIP'	'AAAL'	'IAAP'	'IAAA'
5(7)	3(5)	4	4	2	2	2	2
('FFFR') 'FFOR'	'FFOR' 'FFFR'	'OOFR' 'FOFR' 'FFFR'	'OFOR' 'FFOR'	'FFNN'	'FOFF' 'OFON'	'RFON' 'NFON'	'RFON' 'NFON'

'LAKL'	'APAL'	'APLI'	'IAAL'	'AAIP'	'PAKA'	'LAAL'	'LALA'
1(2)	1	1	1	1	1	1	1
('FFFF') 'FFOF'	'OFOF'	'OFOR'	'RFON'	'FONN'	'FOON'	'FFON'	'FFON'

'LALP'	'AAAA'	'AAAP'	'AAKI'	'AAKL'	'AIIP'	'LAPI'	'LPAI'
1	1	1	1	1	1	1	1
'FFON'	'OFON'	'OFON'	'FOOR'	'FOOF'	'ORNN'	'FOFR'	'OFOR'

'LPKI'	'PAKP'	'AALI'	'AAPI'	'KIIP'
1	1	1	1	1
'FFOR'	'FOON'	'OFOR'	'FOFR'	'FRNN'

FIGURE XII: Place types for *pre-nuclear* combinations of length 4

13.5 Constituency of four- and five-phoneme combinations

We now get to manner and place types of four-phoneme and five-phoneme pre-nuclear combinations; there are no combinations of these lengths in the post-nuclear context. Figure XI (see the previous page) summarizes manner types for combinations of length 4. In total, there are 256 logically possible types (i.e. 4^4), but only 20 type are actually attested (two of which only for marginal combinations). It corresponds to 43 (50) actually attested combinations. The absence of many is structurally conditioned, which is a consequence of two facts. First, the DU precludes some of them, for example 'ONOF', 'FNOF', 'FOFO' or 'FFOO' (that is, no matter how positions are filled, combinations of this kind will never arise). Second, others are not possible due to the restrictions introduced in the previous sections. The absence of some other types will be taken care of by additional restrictions.

Some restrictions on the constituency of four-phoneme combinations arise from the fact that certain types of three-phoneme combinations are not expandable. This notion and the restrictions will be discussed in the next section. At this point we will introduce two other restrictions. The first reflects the fact that only combinations of type 'FFFF' are possible (cf. /FSxv/ in *vzchvívati se* (PSJČ)), that is, combinations of types 'OFFF', 'NFFF' and 'RFFF' are not possible.

'FFOFR'	'FOOFR'
1	1
'LAKLI'	'AAKLI'

FIGURE XIII: Manner types for *pre-nuclear* combinations of length 5

(25) Peripheral combinations of type 'C$_1$FFF' where 'C$_1$' is a non-fricative are impossible.

The second restriction (26) concerns occlusives but not fricatives which are followed by two PerPs of the same manner: cf. /FSxv/ in *vzchvívati* (PSJČ) and /FsMň/ in *vzmět'* (PSJČ). It means that peripheral combinations of types 'OOFF' and 'OONN' are impossible. Types 'OOOO', 'OORR', and also 'FFOO', 'FFRR' are already disallowed by the structure of the DU.

(26) Two occlusives cannot be followed by two PerPs of the same manner of articulation.

Finally, it is worth noting that if a nasal or a sonant is the first phoneme of a four-phoneme combination, it is always followed by a fricative ('F') + an occlusive ('O') + a nasal ('N'), that is, only combinations of type 'RFON' and 'NFON' are found. Accordingly, we propose the following restrictions:

(27) (a) A sonant cannot be followed by any other three PerPs than of type 'FON'.

   (b) A nasal cannot be followed by any other three PerPs than of type 'FON'.

Let us briefly look at place types attested for four-phoneme combinations listed in figure XII. Out of 625 logically thinkable combinations (i.e. 5^4), only 29 are found. More than a half of them underlie only one combination.

Finally, figure XIII provides manner and also place types for the two five-phoneme pre-nuclear combinations. Their phonematic constituency is largely dependent on the structure of the DU and on the restrictions previously postulated. Since all pre-nuclear positions are filled in such combinations, the DU predicts, for example, that the rightmost phoneme will only be a nasal or a sonant. Now, as pointed out in §11.2, semiconsonants and /ř/ cannot be preceded by more than three PerPs, so the rightmost phonemes can only be /j/ or a nasal. The latter would be attested in /FSdMň/ provided that it is accepted (see §11.2). It would correspond to manner type 'FFONN' and place type 'LAAIL'.

13.6 Reducibility, resolvability and expandability

In the previous section we referred to the expandability of peripheral combinations. A combination to which another phoneme can be appended so that the result is still a well-formed combination is expandable. Similarly, we can speak about reducibility of a combination if it is possible to remove a phoneme from it, so that the result is again a well-formed combination. To the best of our knowledge, expandability and reducibility of combinations have not been much discussed in literature, but another property similar to (but not identical with) reducibility was: resolvability.[12] In this section we will examine peripheral combinations from all of these perspectives.

By way of introduction let us first turn our attention to the combination /Mk/ attested in /Mkl/, the PhF of *mkl* which is the 3rd person sg. of *mknouti*.[13] Its status may thus be dubious, but if /Mk/ is nevertheless accepted, it is the only peripheral combination of type 'NO' which is, moreover, found only before a nuclear semiconsonant. There is no evidence that such combinations are possible before vowels. /Mkl/ may be compared to /Mdl/ attested in *mdlý*. Both are of the same pattern, 'NOR', the only difference being whether the sonant is nuclear (as in /Mkl/) or non-nuclear (as in /Mdl/). It induces us to conclude that Czech permits combinations of type 'NOR', but not combinations 'NOV' where 'V' is a vowel. This fact is expressed in the following restriction:

(28) A vowel cannot be preceded by a combination of type 'NO'.

In short, combinations of type 'NOR' are possible before vowels (cf. /Mdl/ in *mdlý*), but those of 'NO' are not, which means that if the final /l/ in /Mdl/ is removed from the combination, the result is not a well-formed pre-vocalic combination. In contrast, if the final /l/ in /Stl/ is removed (cf. /Stl/ in *stlát*), the result is a well-formed combination (cf. /St/ in *stan*).

To account for such a difference, we propose the criterion of REDUCIBILITY. Its definition is given below. In the formulas 'C$_1$' and 'C$_2$' are certain specific PerPs, and 'C$_n$' stands for a sequence of two or more PerPs; it is to ensure the definition holds for combinations of lengths 3, 4 and 5, too. For convenience, the combinations 'C$_n$C$_2$' and 'C$_1$C$_n$' will be called *reductions* of 'C$_1$C$_n$C$_2$'. If a com-

12   One of the few linguists to classify combinations in Czech as to their reducibility is Hattala (1870: 72), although he did not use such a term. Resolvability was mentioned by Tolstaja (1974), but no examples were provided.
13   Although *mkl* is explicitly mentioned in SSJČ (under the entry *mknouti*), it does not seem to be recorded elsewhere (in fact, *mknouti* is rather archaic and/or rare, though not marked so in SSJČ).

	Pre-nuclear		
Only right-hand reducible	/třm/ /hřm/ /Křt/ /Xřt/ /Txn/ /Třp/ /Třť/ /Křť/ /Sxn/		
	/třMň/ /hřMň/ /MStn/ /MStň/ /FSpn/ /FSpň/ /TŠpj/		
Only left-hand reducible	/Mdl/ /Mkn/ /XTs/ /XTš/ /MSt/ /MSd/ /lSť/ /MSť/ /MSď/ (/lTš/ /MTs/ /lŠť/)		
	/PStr/ /PStř/ /PŠtr/ /TStm/ /TStn/ /TStň/ /lStm/ /Shvj/		
Irreducible	/lStn/ /lStň/		

FIGURE XIV: Partly reducible and irreducible combinations (parenthesized combinations are attested only in marginal forms)

bination is both left-hand and right-hand reducible, it is completely reducible; otherwise it is only partly reducible. If the leftmost or rightmost phoneme cannot be removed, the combination is left-hand or right-hand irreducible or completely irreducible if neither options is possible.

(29) REDUCIBILITY OF PERIPHERAL COMBINATIONS

(a) '$C_1C_nC_2$' is reducible if it is left-hand reducible and/or right-hand reducible.

(b) '$C_1C_nC_2$' is left-hand reducible if 'C_nC_2' is attested.

(c) '$C_1C_nC_2$' is right-hand reducible if 'C_1C_n' is attested.

All peripheral combinations in our database are at least partly reducible with the exception of /lStn/ and /lStň/ attested in *lstný* and *lstně* (SSJČ). Combinations of length 2 are not taken into account because they cannot naturally be reduced to any other combination. Figure XIV provides a list of partly reducible combinations and the two completely irreducible combinations. If a combination contains an archi-phoneme like /M/ in /vMň/, we regard it as reducible provided that there is attested at least one combination with a phoneme from which the archiphoneme arose; for /vMň/, it is /vm/ or /vn/ or /vň/. It is noteworthy that all postnuclear combinations are completely reducible, although the left-hand reducibility of /TSP/ (in *zácp*, gen. pl. of *zácpa*) is thinkable only after /SP/ (in *výsp*, gen. pl. of *výspa*) is accepted (see chapter 15 under DI2*d*).

Closely related to the idea of reducibility is another concept, RESOLVABILITY; its definition is given under (30). A combination like /FStr/ is completely resolvable in Czech because all of its *m – 1* subsequences are attested, namely /Fs/,[14] /St/, /tr/, /FSt/, /Str/ (cf. *vsadit, stát, trochu, vstát* and *strana*), whereas

---

14 We take /Fs/, not /FS/ or /Fz/, to be included in /FStr/ because the base of the combination is the voiceless /t/. Similarly, /Fz/ is included in /FShř/ because the base is here the voiced /h/.

/PStr/ is partly resolvable because at least one of its $m - 1$ subsequences is not attested, namely /PSt/.

(30) RESOLVABILITY OF PERIPHERAL COMBINATIONS
(a) A pre-nuclear or post-nuclear sequence of phonemes (i.e. a peripheral combination) of length m is resolvable if it contains at least one attested continuous subsequence of length $m - 1$.[15]
(b) It is partly resolvable if at least one but not all such continuous subsequences are attested.
(c) It is completely resolvable if all such continuous subsequences are attested.

The definition of resolvability was adopted from Greenberg (1978: 250), though the original idea should be credited to Hjelmslev (1936: 53). The latter suggested that all peripheral combinations in all languages are completely resolvable, but this assertion was later invalidated by Fischer-Jørgensen (1952: 36) in the case of Russian or Kutenai. Greenberg did not make such a strong claim, but the data he had from 104 languages showed that all combinations in these languages were at least partly resolvable. It is also true for Czech, as our research has confirmed, but it does not of course mean that it would be a universal feature of all languages.

Resolvability is related to reducibility. If a combination is either left-hand or right-hand reducible, it is partly resolvable. Three-phoneme peripheral combinations which are completely reducible are also completely resolvable. Still, resolvability is not the same as reducibility because more complex combinations may be completely reducible while being at the same time only partly resolvable. For example, a four-phoneme combination '$C_1C_2C_3C_4$' is completely reducible if '$C_2C_3C_4$' and '$C_1C_2C_3$' are attested. But such a combination is completely resolvable only if '$C_2C_3C_4$', '$C_1C_2C_3$', 'C_1C_2', 'C_2C_3' and 'C_3C_4' are all attested, so if one of the latter three combinations does not occur, '$C_1C_2C_3C_4$' cannot be completely resolvable. Despite this logical possibility, in Czech it turns out that all completely reducible combinations are also completely resolvable.[16] Hence, all combinations listed in figure XIV are those and only those that are partly resolvable, while the remaining ones are completely resolvable.[17]

---

15 This should naturally be understood as that the combination is attested in the respective context, i.e. either in the pre-nuclear or post-nuclear context.
16 The only combination for which it does not hold is post-nuclear /rŠTŠ/ in *boršč*. It was one of the reasons we excluded it from our database; see §7.4.
17 The number of completely resolvable combinations is much greater than that of partly resolvable ones. Greenberg (*op. cit.*) noted that this was true for all of the 104 languages he had examined.

As we do not claim that our database contains all peripheral combinations of Czech, it may actually happen that some combinations now declared partly reducible and/or resolvable will eventually prove to be completely reducible and/or resolvable. An interesting question is whether there are structural restrictions which prevent combinations from being completely reducible and/or resolvable. A combination whose left-hand or right-hand reduction is not attested is potentially reducible provided that the reduction is not in conflict with any structural rule. It allows us to distinguish between combinations whose reductions are not structurally possible and hence are regularly missing, and combinations whose reductions are structurally possible and hence are missing by accidence.

Out of all partly reducible combinations, only /XTs/, /XTš/, /lSt'/ and /lŠt'/ may be declared to be of the first kind. The right-hand reduction of the first two, /Xt/, was declared impossible in §13.3 because a velar fricative cannot be followed by a phoneme from *pos* 'e3' to which /t/ belongs. As regards /lSt'/ and /lŠt'/, since both end in a voiceless consonant, their right-hand reductions are /ls/ and /lš/. Combinations of this kind are not attested, namely combinations where a non-nuclear semiconsonant is followed by a voiceless fricative. It is appropriate to adopt this as the collocational restriction under (31). Accordingly, /lSt'/ and /lŠt'/ are systematically right-hand irreducible because their reductions violate this restriction which is otherwise valid for other combinations.

(31) In the pre-nuclear context a non-nuclear semiconsonant cannot be followed by a voiceless fricative.

The remaining partly reducible combinations are considered to be accidentally left-hand or right-hand irreducible. For example, /Shvj/ is right-hand irreducible because /Shv/ is not attested, although we see no reason why such a combination could not be possible; combinations of this pattern are attested, namely /Sxv/ in *schválit*. The same holds for the other combinations.

The opposite of reducibility is EXPANDABILITY defined as follows:

(32) EXPANDABILITY OF PERIPHERAL COMBINATIONS
(a) 'C$_n$' is expandable if it is left-hand expandable and/or right-hand expandable.
(b) 'C$_n$' is left-hand expandable if 'C$_1$C$_n$' is attested.
(c) 'C$_n$' is right-hand expandable if 'C$_n$C$_2$' is attested.[18]

The classification of peripheral combinations is more intricate when it comes to their expandability. Some are not expandable because their expandability is ruled out by the structure of the DU. These can be called *anti-expandable*. For exam-

---

18 'C$_n$' is any peripheral combination. 'C$_1$C$_n$' and 'C$_n$C$_2$' are then called *expansions* of 'C$_n$'.

ple, combinations of length 5 are anti-expandable simply because no longer combinations are possible. Second, all pre-nuclear combinations ending in /r/, /l/ or /j/ are right-hand anti-expandable because these phonemes occupy the rightmost pre-nuclear position, i.e. 'e1', so they can only be followed by a vowel in this case.[19] Right-hand anti-expandable combinations are also those ending in /t'/ or /d'/, which occupy archi-position 'E3', because they can only be followed by a vowel. Similarly, all pre-nuclear combinations beginning with /P/, /K/, /F/, /X/ are left-hand anti-expandable because these phonemes occupy the leftmost pre-nuclear position.[20] Similar reasoning can be applied to the post-nuclear context.

Combinations whose expandability is not *a priori* ruled out, but whose expansions are not attested in our database will be called *non-expandable*, either left-hand or right-hand or both. If a combination is non-expandable, it does not necessarily mean that its potential expansion is not structurally possible; we should look out for clearly defined criteria according to which the expansions could be declared impossible. For example, the non-expandability of post-nuclear /Př/, /Tř/, /Kř/ as well as that of /řT/, /řK/ is regular because /ř/ cannot be combined with more than one PerP in the post-nuclear context (see §12.3). On the contrary, the non-expandability of pre-nuclear /fj/ is merely accidental because other combinations of a labial with /j/ are expandable, that is to say, there is no reason a combination like /Sfj/ could not occur (cf. /Spj/, /Sbj/, /svj/, /zvj/).

In connection with the expandability, several restrictions will be introduced; see (33). Thus, three-phoneme pre-nuclear combinations of type 'FFN' and 'FNR' are regularly non-expandable from the left, and those of type 'OFF' are regularly non-expandable from the right. It concerns combinations such as /Sxn/ in *schnout*, /zMr/ in *zmrazit* or /Tsv/ in *cválat*. Finally, combinations of type 'OFN' (e.g. /Tšm/ in *čmárat*) are regularly non-expandable both from the right and from the left.[21] For other restrictions concerning regular non-expandability of combinations of certain types, see the restrictions under (23).

(33) (a)   Peripheral combinations of type 'CFFN' are impossible.

---

19   Position 'e1' is also occupied by /m/, /n/, /ň/ and /ř/. However, combinations ending in /m/, /n/, /ň/ can be expandable because the nasals will be represented there by the archiphoneme /M/. So /tm/, /tň/, /tn/ are all right-hand expandable because /tMň/ is attested. On the other hand, combinations ending in /Mn/ or /Mň/ are right-hand anti-expandable because no other phoneme may be attached to them from the right. Likewise, combinations ending in /ř/ can be expandable because this phoneme can also occur in 'pre1', which allows for expansions (cf. /tř/ in *třít* × /třm/ in *třmen*).

20   We ignore here what we called *accidental appendices* in §11.9.

21   But combinations of type 'FON' are left-hand expandable, cf. /TStnī/ *ctný*, /FSpnöT/ *vzpnout* or /MStnī/ *mstný*.

Expandability		Attested combinations	
Left-hand	*Right-hand*	*Pre-nuclear*	*Post-nuclear*
anti-exp.	anti-exp.	82 (97)	30 (44)
anti-exp.		106 (119)	32 (34)
	anti-exp.	123 (128)	16 (18)
non-exp.	non-exp.	33 (34)	1 (3)
non-exp.		61 (66)	12 (13)
	non-exp.	81 (94)	20 (22)
exp.	exp.	33	2
exp.		92 (94)	7 (8)
	exp.	56 (57)	15

FIGURE XV: Expandability of peripheral combinations

    (b)   Peripheral combinations of type 'CFNR' are impossible.
    (c)   Peripheral combinations of type 'OFFC' are impossible.
    (d)   Peripheral combinations of types 'COFN' and 'OFNC' are impossible.

Figure XV summarizes how many combinations are anti-expandable, non-expandable and expandable in our database. The numbers are quite diverse, but there is a prevalence of anti-expandable combinations over non-expandable ones and over expandable combinations. The pre-nuclear combinations /Ps/ and /Pš/ are right-hand expandable, but only if we add *two* PerPs to the right to get /PStr/ and /PŠtr/; combinations like /PŠt/ or /PŠt/ are not attested. Similarly, /pn/, /pň/, /tn/ and /tň/ do not have an immediate left-hand expansion, but they can be expanded by adding two PerPs to produce /FSpn/, /FSpň/, /TStn/ and /TStň/.[22] The left-hand expansion of /řv/ is attested only in marginal combinations, namely /břv/ in the place name *Břve*.

13.7 Pairedness and mirror effect

Finally, we will discuss two other criteria for the classification of peripheral combinations, though it does not mean that all classificatory possibilities have been exhausted by that.

    The first criterion is PAIREDNESS; it concerns voiceless and voiced consonants occurring in a peripheral combination. There are four types of combinations according to the voicing of phonemes: voiceless combinations, voiced combinations, mixed combinations and indifferent combinations. Remember that the

---

22   Unless we accept the words *spnouti* and *stnouti* mentioned in NLA.

voicing is here a *phonological* property, so only occlusives and fricatives are phonologically voiceless or voiced. The sonants /j/, /ř/, /r/, /l/, the nasals /m/, /n/, /ň/, /M/, and the voicing archi-phonemes are indifferent to this distinction, i.e. they are neither phonologically voiceless nor voiced.

Voiceless combinations contain one and only one voiceless consonant, e.g. /tr/, /St/, /PStr/, and *voiced combinations* contain one and only one voiced consonant, e.g. /dr/, /FSb/, /rd/. *Mixed combinations* are those which contain both a voiceless and a voiced consonant standing next to one another or which contain two or more voiceless consonants or two or more voiced consonants. Such combinations do not seem to be quite common. In the phonetic sense, groups of obstruents tend to be uniform in the voicing, i.e. a phonetically voiceless obstruent does not usually combine with a phonetically voiced obstruent, perhaps because such groups are hard to pronounce. As explained in §4.2, the homogeneity of such combinations may be phonologically interpreted by neutralization of voicing, that is, one of the obstruents is a realization of a phonologically voiceless or voiced consonant, whereas the others are interpreted as archi-phonemes. Still, there are languages where mixed combinations exist. Czech is one of them, since neutralization of voicing does not take place before /v/. For example, /kv/ and /Stv/ are mixed combinations because they contain both a voiceless and voiced consonant. And in order not to complicate the matter, the combinations such as /gv/, /Sdv/, i.e. those containing two (instead of one) voiced phonemes will also be classified under mixed combinations and not under voiced combinations. Finally, the last group is *indifferent combinations* which contain neither a voiceless nor a voiced consonant. Examples are /rm/, /lň/, /jMň/.

In our database there are 206 (223 if marginal combinations are counted, too) voiceless combinations, 144 (156) voiced combinations, 46 (50) mixed combinations, and 10 (13) indifferent *pre-nuclear* combinations. Due to neutralization of voicing, all post-nuclear combinations are indifferent ones. It is obvious there is a great prevalence of voiceless combinations, i.e. those containing one phonological voiceless consonant.

Let us return to the pairedness. A voiceless combination is *paired* if its voiced counterpart is found or *vice versa*. Therefore, /tr/ is paired because /dr/ is also attested. If the corresponding counterpart is not attested, a combination is *single*. Examples are /Ftř/, /Fhm/, /Mdl/, /lpj/ because /Fdř/, /Fxm/, /Mtl/, /lbj/ are not attested. Now, such combinations are not paired either because their corresponding voicing counterparts are impossible due to some restriction or because they have not happened to be found. Czech has combinations of both kinds. For instance, /pn/, /pň/ must be regularly single because their voicing counterparts /bn/, /bň/ are viewed as as structurally impossible (see §8.2 and §14,2 under DE2*a*), but combinations like /Fhm/, /Ftř/ are single by accidence because there is no reason to assume that /Fxm/ and /Fdř/ cannot be valid combinations in Czech. Overall, there are 162 single pre-nuclear combinations (185 with marginal combinations), 234 (244) paired pre-nuclear combinations,[23] and 10 (13) combinations which are neither. Post-nuclear combinations are neither voiceless nor voiced.

The very last classificatory criterion is the MIRROR EFFECT; the idea was suggested by Sigurd (1965: 106). A pre-nuclear combination 'C_2C_1' has a mirror counterpart if a post-nuclear combination 'C_1C_2' is attested. Similarly, a post-nuclear combination 'C_1C_2' has a mirror counterpart if a pre-nuclear combination 'C_2C_1' is attested. Due to neutralization of voicing in the post-nuclear context, we ignore whether a combination is voiceless or voiced. Hence, post-nuclear /rT/ has a mirror counterpart because /dr/ is attested.[24] The idea holds in principle also for more complex combinations, but we cannot speak about mirror effect of four- and five-phoneme combinations because they are possible in the pre-nuclear context only.

In our database there are 106 (or 112 with marginal combinations) pre-nuclear combinations and 61 (69) post-nuclear combinations which have a mirror counterpart.[25] This also includes combinations whose mirror counterparts are attested only in marginal combinations. The remaining combinations do not have a mirror counterpart.

---

23 The numbers include two combinations which are marginally paired because their counterparts are found only in marginal combinations. These are /Tsp/ (cf. /TSb/ in *Dzbel*) and /Pd'/ (cf. /Pt'/ in *Ptice*).

24 Attested is also /tr/, but the point is that at least one of these combinations exists.

25 The numbers are not the same because as we have explained, /tr/ and /dr/ are both mirror counterparts of /rT/.

Chapter Fourteen: PRE-NUCLEAR COMBINATIONS

14.1 Pre-nuclear distributional types

In this chapter the attested pre-nuclear combinations are sorted into five major pre-nuclear distributional types: DE2, DE3, DE4 and DE5. The number indicates how many pre-nuclear positions of the DU are occupied by a phoneme. Except for DE5, we will recognize several subtypes for every major type. Each and every attested pre-nuclear combination belongs to one type or subtype. If the occurrence of a certain combination is attested only in symbols and other marginal forms, it is placed in between round brackets in the tables that follow. If a combination is attested also before nuclear /r/, /l/, it is italicized. If the possibility of a certain combination is precluded by a collocational restriction, the respective table cells are marked by '–'. Finally, empty cells stand for accidentally missing combinations. Under every distributional type we list phonemes which are NOT attested to occur in a given position in a particular distributional type (we use '~'). When a type is valid for the whole position class, '∀' is used.

For the sake of completeness, two other distributional types, DE0 and DE1, are recognized, though they do not underlie any combination. Type DE0 refers to the situation when none of the pre-nuclear positions is filled with a phoneme. Phonotagms of this type are frequent in Czech (cf. /on/ *on*), which means that the language allows phonotagms beginning with a vowel (but not with a nuclear semiconsonant; see §10.2). Distributional type DE1 refers to situations when just one pre-nuclear position is filled with a phoneme. Particular possibilities are given in figure I. Note that positions 'pre1' and 'pre2' cannot be filled with a phoneme if the other pre-nuclear positions are all empty (see §11.7).

a	Ø	Ø	Ø	Ø	e1
b	Ø	Ø	Ø	e2	Ø
c	Ø	Ø	e3	Ø	Ø
d	Ø	Ø	E2		Ø
e	Ø	Ø	E3		

FIGURE I: Subtypes for distributional type DE1

a	Ø	Ø	Ø	e2	e1
b	Ø	Ø	e3	Ø	e1
c	Ø	Ø	E2		e1
d	Ø	pre1	Ø	Ø	e1
e	pre2	Ø	Ø	Ø	e1
f	Ø	Ø	e3	e2	Ø
g	Ø	pre1	Ø	e2	Ø
h	pre2	Ø	Ø	e2	Ø
i	Ø	pre1	e3	Ø	Ø
j	pre2	Ø	e3	Ø	Ø
k	Ø	pre1	E2		Ø
l	pre2	Ø	E2		Ø
m	Ø	pre1	E3		
n	pre2	Ø	E3		

FIGURE II: Subtypes for distributional type DE2

DE1a: 'e1' = ∀, i.e. {/m/, /n/, /ň/, /j/, /ř/, /r/, /l/}.

DE1b: 'e2' = ∀, i.e. {/M/, /v/}.
/M/ occurs only before a nuclear semiconsonant.

DE1c: 'e3' = ∀, i.e. {/t/, /d/, /s/, /z/, /š/, /ž/, /k/, /g/, /x/, /h/}.

DE1d: 'E2' = ∀, i.e. {/p/, /b/, /f/}.

DE1e: 'E3' = ∀, i.e. {/ť/, /ď/}.

14.2 Two-phoneme combinations (type DE2)

Two-phoneme pre-nuclear combinations belong to the distributional type DE2 which refers to the situation when exactly two pre-nuclear positions of the DU are occupied by phonemes. Its subtypes are given in figure II. They stand behind all 182 (or 192 with marginal combinations included) two-phoneme pre-nuclear combinations recorded in our database.

DE2a: 'e1' = ∀, 'e2' = ∀; figure III (next page); 12 (13) combinations.
     All combinations are attested except for /Mm/ which is impossible due to the restriction according to which a labial (/p/, /b/, /f/, /v/ and /m/) cannot be preceded by a nasal in the pre-nuclear context (see §11.3). /Mj/ is attested only in the surname *Mjachký*.

	/m/	/n/	/ň/	/j/	/ř/	/r/	/l/
/v/	/vm/	/vn/	/vň/	/vj/	/vř/	/vr/	/vl/
/M/	–	/Mn/	/Mň/	(/Mj/)	/Mř/	/Mr/	/Ml/

FIGURE III: Two-phoneme pre-nuclear combinations attested for type DE2*a*

	/m/	/n/	/ň/	/j/	/ř/	/r/	/l/
/t/	/tm/	/tn/	/tň/	–	/tř/	/tr/	/tl/
/d/	/dm/	/dn/	/dň/	–	/dř/	/dr/	/dl/
/s/	/sm/	/sn/	/sň/	/sj/	/sř/	/sr/	/sl/
/z/	/zm/	/zn/	/zň/	/zj/	/zř/	/zr/	/zl/
/š/	/šm/	/šn/	/šň/	–	–	/šr/	/šl/
/ž/	/žm/	/žn/	/žň/	–	–	/žr/	/žl/
/k/	/km/	/kn/	/kň/	/kj/	/kř/	/kr/	/kl/
/g/		/gn/				/gr/	/gl/
/x/	/xm/		/xň/	–	/xř/	/xr/	/xl/
/h/	/hm/	/hn/	/hň/	–	/hř/	/hr/	/hl/

FIGURE IV: Two-phoneme pre-nuclear combinations attested for type DE2*b*

DE2b: 'e1' = ∀, 'e3' = ∀; figure IV; 58 combinations.

Although both 'e1' and 'e3' can be filled with all phonemes belonging to those positions, not all conceivable combinations are attested and possible. The most limited are those with /j/, which is a consequence of the fact that /j/ can only be preceded by labial and velar occlusives or by labial or alveolar fricatives (see §11.2). Another important restriction concerns the combinability of /ř/ with the palatal fricatives /š/ and /ž/. As is obvious from figure IV, the combinations /šř/ and /žř/ are not attested. In fact, there is no pre-nuclear or post-nuclear combination in which /ř/ co-occurs with /š/ or /ž/ (or their archi-phoneme /Š/),[1] though it co-occurs with alveolar fricatives, for example /sř/ in *sřeknouti* (SSJČ), /zř/ in *zřídka*, /Stř/ in *střecha*, /PStř/ in *pstřeň* (PSJČ). Accordingly, we propose the following restriction. The same section refers here either to the pre-nuclear or to the post-nuclear context. Recall that, as noted in §11.2, /ř/ cannot even occur in the same section with a semiconsonant.

(1) /ř/ cannot occur in the same section of the DU with palatal fricatives.

DE2c: 'e1' = ~{/m/}, 'E2' = ∀; figure V; 14 combinations.

The absence of /m/ in 'e1' is viewed to be regular and was already mentioned in §11.2. The non-occurrence of /fn/ and /fř/ is accidental from the synchronic perspective. Finally, take note of the non-occurrence of /bn/, /bň/; we

---

1   In the post-nuclear context, /ř/ does not co-occur with any fricative; see §12.2.

	/n/	/ň/	/j/	/ř/	/r/	/l/
/p/	/pn/	/pň/	/pj/	/př/	/pr/	/pl/
/b/	–	–	/bj/	/bř/	/br/	/bl/
/f/		/fň/	/fj/		/fr/	/fl/

FIGURE V: Two-phoneme pre-nuclear combinations attested for type DE2*c*

	/m/	/n/	/ň/	/j/
/j/	/jm/			–
/r/	/rm/			(/rj/)
/l/		/ln/	/lň/	(/lj/)

FIGURE VI: Two-phoneme pre-nuclear combinations attested for type DE2*e*

already mentioned the absence of these combinations in §8.2 when dealing with the analysis of /ŠkrābnöT/ *škrábnout*. Besides /ť/ and /ď/, which do not precede any PerP in the pre-nuclear context, /b/ is the only occlusive not standing before a nasal. In fact, as figures IV and V show, all other fricatives of all places of articulation can occur before at least one nasal. The phoneme /b/ is thus usual in this respect, and it is reasonable to express this peculiarity by the following restriction:

(2)   A nasal cannot be preceded by /b/.

DE2d: 'e1' = ~{/m/, /n/, /ň/, /j/, /ř/, /r/, /l/}, 'pre1' = ~{/T/, /S/, /Š/, /ř/}; no comb.
    This type does not underlie any combination. Voicing archi-phonemes do not occur before phoneme from *pos* 'e1', as the latter do not trigger neutralization of voicing, so they could only combine with /ř/ in this type. However, no such combination is attested unless we accept /řm/ in *řmotný*, /řn/ in *řnouti* or /řň/ in *řňavý*, all recorded in NLA, but all apparently dialectal. These combinations have not been included in our database, but at the same time they are not regarded as impossible. Cf. also /hřm/ in *hřmot* and /třm/ in *třmen* from type DE3*h*.

DE2e: 'e1' = ~{(/j/), /ř/, /r/, /l/}, 'pre2' = ~{/P/, /F/, /T/, /S/, /Š/, /K/, /X/, /M/}; figure VI; 4 (6) combinations.
    As voicing archi-phonemes cannot precede phonemes from *pos* 'e1', the only phonemes attested for 'pre2' are /r/, /l/ and /j/; the phonotagms in which they occur are realized as so-called side syllables (see §10.2). /M/ cannot occur in 'pre2' provided that 'e2' is empty because the latter position is its primary place of occurrence (see §11.3). Position 'e1' cannot be occupied by /ř/, /r/, /l/ due to various restrictions. The combinations /rj/ and /lj/ are attested only in the place name *Rjazaň* (Russian city) and the proper name *Ljuba*.

	/v/	/M/
/t/	/tv/	–
/d/	/dv/	–
/s/	/sv/	/sM/
/z/	/zv/	/zM/
/š/	/šv/	/šM/
/ž/	/žv/	
/k/	/kv/	–
/g/	/gv/	–
/x/	/xv/	–
/h/	/hv/	–

FIGURE VII: Two-phoneme pre-nuclear combinations attested for type DE2*f*

	/v/
/ř/	/řv/

FIGURE VIII: Two-phoneme pre-nuclear combination attested for type DE2*g*

	/v/	/M/
/r/	/rv/	–
/l/	/lv/	–
/v/	–	/vM/

FIGURE IX: Two-phoneme pre-nuclear combinations attested for type DE2*f*

DE2f: 'e2' = ∀, 'e3' = ∀; figure VII; 13 combinations.

/M/ occurs in 'e2' if preceding a nuclear semiconsonant (cf. /sMrT/ *smrt*), hence the combinations /sM/, /zM/, /šM/ are attested only before nuclear /r/ or /l/, although similar combinations exist for vowels, e.g. /sm/, /zn/, /šň/ (see figure IV). The absence of the combinations /tM/, /dM/, /kM/ and /gM/ derives from the fact that combinations of type 'ONR' are not possible (see §13.3). The absence of /xM/ and /hM/ is also regular; see below under DE3*a*.

DE2g: 'e2' = ~{/M/}, 'pre1' = ~{/T/, /S/, /Š/}; figure VIII; 1 combination.

As neutralization of voicing does not take place before /v/ or /M/, it is only /ř/ that can occupy 'pre1' here. The combination /řM/ is impossible because such a combination could only stand before a nuclear semiconsonant, but it was already pointed out in §11.2 that semiconsonants cannot occur in the same section of the DU with /ř/.

DE2h: 'e2' = ∀, for 'pre2', see text; figure IX; 3 combinations.

Since voicing archi-phonemes do not precede phonemes from *pos* 'e2', /M/, /j/, /r/, /l/ are expected to occupy 'pre2' in this type, but only /r/, /l/ are actually attested. The absence of /M/ is a consequence of the fact that a labial cannot be preceded by a nasal (see §11.3), and the combination /MM/ is impossible due to the fact that Czech does not allow geminates. The absence of /j/ in 'pre2' is regarded to be accidental, that is, there is no reason to think that the combination /jv/ should be impossible because /j/ stands in front of other fricatives (cf. /js/ in *jsi* and /jh/ in *jho*). On the other hand, /jM/ is impossible because it would have to stand before a nuclear semiconsonant. However, if /j/ co-occurs with a semi-

	/t/	/d/	/s/	/z/	/š/	/ž/	/k/	/g/	/x/	/h/
/T/	–	–	/Ts/	/Tz/	/Tš/	/Tž/	/Tk/	–	/Tx/	/Th/
/S/	/St/	/Sd/	–	–	/Sš/	/Sž/	/Sk/	/Sg/	/Sx/	/Sh/
/Š/	/Št/	/Šd/	–	–	–	–	/Šk/			/Šh/
/ř/			–	–	–	–	/řk/		–	–

FIGURE X: Two-phoneme pre-nuclear combinations attested for type DE2*i*

consonant, it must occur in a less peripheral position, but in /jM/ it would occur in a more peripheral position (see §11.2).

Besides /M/, /j/, /r/ and /l/, position 'pre2' happens to be occupied by /v/ as in /vMršťiT/ *vmrštit*; see §11.8 on the argument on the occurrence of /v/ in this position. The combinations /rM/ and /lM/, which could occur before a nuclear semiconsonant, are not possible because the same section of the DU cannot contain two semiconsonants (see §11.2).

DE2i: 'e3' = ∀, 'pre1' = ∀; figure X; 20 combinations.

Although the two positions may be filled with all phonemes belonging there, not all conceivable combinations are attested. Many of them are impossible due to various restrictions.

At this point let us say a few words about /T/. It occurs in 'pre1' only if 'e3' is occupied by alveolar or palatal fricatives or by the velars /k/ and /x/. It also precedes /b/, which occupies 'E2' (i.e. /Tb/ in *dbát*; it belongs under type DE2*k*). If /T/ is combined with alveolar or palatal fricatives, we get, at the level of realization, the affricates [ts], [tʃ], [dz] and [dʒ]. As we will see below under subtype DE3*j*, /Ts/ and /Tš/, but not /Tz/ and /Tž/, can be further preceded by /X/ or /S/. Now, /T/ occurs before /k/, /x/, /b/ in some unique combinations: /Tx/ is found probably only in PhFs of three Czech words (and their detivatives): /Txoř/ *tchoř* "polecat", /Txān/ *tchán* "father-in-law" and /Txiňe/ *tchyně* "mother-in-law" (the latter two are historically related). These combinations are expandable by a phoneme from *pos* 'pre2' or from *pos* 'e2' or *pos* 'e1'. On the other hand, /Tk/ is expandable by a phoneme from *pos* 'e2' or *pos* 'e1' (cf. /Tkv/, /Tkvj/, /Tkn/, /Tkň/, /Tkl/) as well as by a phoneme from *pos* 'pre2' (namely /FTk/, /STk/, /ŠTk/, /ŠTkn/, /ŠTkň/, /STkv/, /STkvj/, /STkl/). The occurrence of such combinations is limited, though; they are attested probably only in PhFs of several words and their derivatives (e.g. those derived and related to *tkát*). The last combination /Tb/ probably occurs only in PhF of one word only, in *dbát* (and its derivates, naturally).

	/t/	/d/	/s/	/z/	/š/	/ž/	/k/	/g/	/x/	/h/
/P/	/Pt/		/Ps/	/Pz/	/Pš/	/Pž/	–	–	/Px/	
/F/	/Ft/	/Fd/	/Fs/	/Fz/	/Fš/	/Fž/	/Fk/	/Fg/	/Fx/	/Fh/
/K/	/Kt/	/Kd/	/Ks/		/Kš/	–	–	–	–	
/M/				/Mz/	/Mš/	/Mž/	/Mk/	–	(/Mx/)	/Mh/
/j/		/jd/	/js/					–		/jh/
/r/	/rt/	/rd/	–	/rz/	–	/rž/		–	–	
/l/			–	/lz/	–	/lž/	/lk/	–	–	/lh/

FIGURE XI: Two-phoneme pre-nuclear combinations attested for type DE2*j*

	/p/	/b/	/f/
/T/		/Tb/	
/S/	/Sp/	/Sb/	/Sf/
/Š/	/Šp/	/Šb/	
/ř/		/řb/	

FIGURE XII: Two-phoneme pre-nuclear
combinations attested for type DE2*k*

	/p/	/b/	/f/
/F/	/Fp/	/Fb/	–
/K/		/Kb/	(/Kf/)
/X/		/Xb/	–
/r/	(/rp/)		
/l/	/lp/	/lb/	

FIGURE XIII: Two-phoneme pre-nuclear
combinations attested for type DE2*l*

DE2j: 'e3' = ∀, 'pre2' = ~{/T/, /S/, /Š/, /X/};[2] figure XI; 35 (37) combinations.
The occurrence of /X/ in 'pre2' is very limited in the subtype. In fact, it is attested only in six combinations, /Xb/, /Xť/, /XTs/, /XTš/, /Xřt/ and /Xřb/, but they do not belong to this subtype. In fact, no combination with /X/ is possible for this type because, as mentioned in §13.3, a velar fricative cannot precede a phoneme from *pos* 'e3'. The combinations of /r/ or /l/ + a voiceless fricative were declared impossible in §13.6. /Mx/ is attested only in the place name *Mchov*.

DE2k: 'E2' = ∀, 'pre1' = ∀; figure XII; 7 combinations.
/řb/ is attested only in *řbuchan*, a name of Cirsium oleraceum (from Old Czech *třbuchan*; see Machek 1954: 256, Hattala 1870: 64).

DE2l: 'E2' = ~{(/f/)}, 'pre2' = ~{/P/, /T/, /S/, /Š/, /M/, /j/}; figure XIII; 6 (8) combinations.
/P/, /M/, /j/ cannot occur in 'pre2' because they cannot precede phonemes from *pos* 'E2' (see §11.3 and §11.8). The gaps for /Kp/ and /Xp/ are noteworthy because their voiced counterparts are attested. /Kf/ is attested only in the Czech place name *Kfely*, and /rp/ only in the place name *Rpety*.

---

2   /T/, /S/, /Š/ cannot occur in 'pre2' if 'pre1' is empty; see §11.7.

	/t'/	/d'/
/P/	(/Pt'/)	/Pd'/
/F/	/Ft'/	/Fd'/
/K/	(/Kt'/)	
/X/	/Xt'/	
/j/		/jd'/
/r/	/rt'/	/rd'/

	/t'/	/d'/
/S/	/St'/	/Sd'/
/Š/	/Št'/	/Šd'/

FIGURE XIV: Two-phoneme pre-nuclear combinations attested for type DE2*m*

FIGURE XV: Two-phoneme pre-nuclear combinations attested for type DE2*n*

a	∅	∅	e3	e2	e1
b	∅	pre1	∅	e2	e1
c	pre2	∅	∅	e2	e1
d	∅	pre1	e3	∅	e1
e	pre2	∅	e3	∅	e1
f	∅	pre1	E2		e1
g	pre2	∅	E2		e1
h	pre2	pre1	∅	∅	e1
h	∅	pre1	e3	e2	∅
i	pre2	∅	e3	e2	∅
j	pre2	pre1	∅	e2	∅
k	pre2	pre1	e3	∅	∅
l	pre2	pre1	E2		∅
m	pre2	pre1	E3		

FIGURE XVI: Subtypes for distributional type DE3

DE2m: 'E3' = ∀, 'pre1' = ~{/T/, /ř/}; figure XIV; 4 combinations.
The absence of /ř/ in 'pre1' is accidental because it can occur before a palatal occlusive (cf. /Třt'/ in *třtina*) and, when standing before an occlusive, it need not be preceded by a PerP (cf. /řb/ in *řbuchan*, /řk/ in *řka*). Combining these facts together, we conclude that /řt'/ and /řd'/ are structurally possible. On the other hand, /T/ cannot precede a palatal occlusive (see §13.3).

DE2n: 'E3' = ∀, 'pre2' = ~{/T/, /S/, /Š/, (/K/), /M/, /l/}; figure XV; 7 (9) combinations.
The absence of the combinations with /l/ in 'pre2' is accidental in light of the existence of those with /r/. On the other hand, combinations with /M/ are impossible because combinations of type 'NO' can occur only before a nuclear semiconsonant (see §13.6), but /t'/ and /d'/ never occur before it. /Pt'/ and /Kt'/ are attested only in the place names *Ptice* and *Ktiš*, respectively.

	/n/	/ň/	/j/	/ř/	/r/	/l/
/tM/		/tMň/	–	–	–	–
/dM/		/dMň/	–	–	–	–
/dv/	–	–	/dvj/	–	–	–
/sv/			/svj/		/svr/	/svl/
/zv/	(/zvn/)	/zvň/	/zvj/	/zvř/	/zvr/	/zvl/
/sM/		/sMň/			/sMr/	/sMl/
/zM/	/zMn/	/zMň/		/zMř/	/zMr/	/zMl/
/kv/	–	–	/kvj/	–	–	–
/xv/	–	–	/xvj/	–	–	–
/hv/	–	–	/hvj/	–	–	–

FIGURE XVII: Three-phoneme pre-nuclear combinations attested for type DE3*a*

14.3 Three-phoneme combinations (type DE3)

Three-phoneme combinations are accounted for by the distributional type DE3 which refers to the situation when three pre-nuclear positions are occupied by phonemes. Its subtypes are summarized in figure XVI (reproduced at the preceding page); they correspond to 180 (199) attested three-phoneme combinations.

DE3a: 'e1' = ~{/m/}, 'e2' = ∀, 'e3' = ~{/š/, /ž/, /g/}; figure XVII; 21 combinations.

There are no combinations with /m/ in 'e1', which will be viewed as a regular phenomenon. As we know, 'e2' can be occupied by /M/ or /v/. The combination /Mm/ is impossible, but /vm/ is possible (cf. *vmísit*). The latter is an instance of two labials standing to each other. However, although such combinations are possible, there is no pre-nuclear combination in which two labials ('LL') would be preceded by another PerP. To account for this fact, we propose the following restriction (it holds for the post-nuclear context, too):

(3)   Combinations of type 'CLL' where 'C' is any PerP are impossible.

The palatal fricatives /š/, /ž/ cannot occur in 'e3' in this subtype because they cannot be followed by two PerPs, and the same holds for /g/ (see §11.4).

The absence of other combinations is regular, too. If 'e1' is occupied by a sonant, and 'e2' by /M/, then 'e3' cannot be filled with an occlusive, which follows from the fact that combinations of type 'ONR' are impossible (see §13.4). Second, if 'e1' is filled with /ř/ or with /r/, /l/, and 'e2' with /v/, then 'e3' cannot be occupied by an alveolar occlusive or by any velar. This situation is more complex, and requires the introduction of new restrictions.

As is obvious, there are no combinations in which a nasal ('N') would be preceded by a labial fricative ('L$_F$') which would in turn be preceded by an alveolar occlusive ('O$_A$'); in other words, combinations like /tvm/, /dvn/ or /kvř/ are not found. Moreover, peripheral combinations of this kind are also not found for /ř/ and semiconsonants. Accordingly, we propose the restrictions under (4). It is necessary to specify that the medial fricative is labial due to the existence of /Tšl/ in *člověk* and /Txn/ in *dchnouti* (SSJČ). Note that the restriction speaks about peripheral combinations because combinations of this pattern are possible when the final semiconsonant is nuclear as in /tvrS/ *tvrz*.

(4)   (a)   Peripheral combinations of type 'A$_O$L$_F$N' are impossible.

       (b)   Peripheral combinations of type 'A$_O$L$_F$C$_1$' where 'C$_1$' is a semiconsonant are impossible.

       (c)   Peripheral combinations of type 'A$_O$L$_F$C$_1$' where 'C$_1$' is /ř/ are impossible.

The semiconsonants are also not found to be preceded by a velar ('K') + a fricative ('F'), which is captured by the restriction under (5). In contrast to the previous restriction, this one is more general because the semiconsonant can be both nuclear and non-nuclear, which is to say that the combinations /kM/, /gM/, /xM/ and /hM/ are impossible before nuclear /r/ and /l/. In the case of /kM/ and /gM/, the restriction overlaps with the one introduced in §13.4 prohibiting combinations of type 'ONR' where the final sonant can also be a nuclear or non-nuclear semiconsonant.

(5)   Combinations of type 'KFC$_1$' where 'C$_1$' is a semiconsonant are impossible.

The last two restrictions to be introduced here are similar to the previous one and pertain to all nasals ('N') and to /ř/. Since these phonemes do not function as nuclei, the restrictions are applicable only to the pre-nuclear context (but, actually, no such combinations are found in the post-nuclear context, too, because the DU does not allow for them). The import of the restriction is that a nasal or /ř/ cannot be preceded by a fricative which is itself preceded by a velar, that is, combinations like /kvn/, /xvň/, /kvř/ or /hvř/ are impossible.

(6)   (a)   Peripheral combinations of type 'KFN' are impossible.

       (b)   Peripheral combinations of type 'KFC$_1$' where 'C$_1$' is /ř/ are impossible.

DE3b: 'e1' = ~{/m/, /n/, /ň/, /ř/, /r/, /l/}, 'e2' = ~{/M/}, 'pre1' = ~{/T/, /S/, /Š/}; figure XVIII (see the next page); 1 combination.

Chapter Fourteen

	/ň/	/j/	/l/
/jM/	/jMň/	–	–
/rv/	–	/rvj/	–
/vM/	/vMň/		/vMl/

	/j/
/řv/	/řvj/

FIGURE XVIII: Three-phoneme pre-nuclear combination attested for type DE3*b*

FIGURE XIX: Three-phoneme pre-nuclear combinations attested for type DE3*c*

With neutralization of voicing not taking place before /v/ and /M/, it is only /ř/ that can occupy 'pre1'. The absence of /M/ in 'e2' is accidental because there is no reason to view combinations like /řMň/ as impossible (cf. /hřMň/ in *hřmět*). In contrast, however, combinations like /řvň/ are viewed to be impossible, which follows from more general restrictions given under (7). They say that /ř/ or a semiconsonant cannot be followed by a fricative ('F') + a nasal ('N').

(7)   (a)   Peripheral combinations of type 'C$_1$FN' where 'C$_1$' is a semiconsonant are impossible.

      (b)   Peripheral combinations of type 'C$_1$FN' where 'C$_1$' is /ř/ are impossible.

The absence of /r/, /l/ and /ř/ in 'e1' is also structurally conditioned because they cannot co-occur with /ř/ (standing in 'pre1'); see §11.2.

DE3c: 'e1' = ~{/m/, /n/, /ř/, /r/}, 'e2' = ∀, for 'pre2', see text; figure XIX; 4 combinations.

Position 'pre2' is here occupied by /j/, /r/ and /v/. It cannot be regularly occupied by /M/ which cannot stand before /M/ or /v/. It could also be occupied by /l/, but no such combination has been found; we view it as accidental. The occurrence of /v/ in 'pre2' was discussed in §11.8. The absence of /n/, /ř/ and /r/ in 'e1' is accidental because we find combinations like /vMn/, /vMř/ and /vMr/ as possible. On the contrary, /m/ cannot regularly occur in 'e1' (see (3) above).

DE3d: 'e1' = ~{/j/}, 'e3' = ~{/z/, /ž/}, 'pre1' = ~{/ř/}; figure XX; 41 (45) combinations.

The absence of /j/ in 'e1' is viewed as accidental. Since the combination /kj/ is attested (cf. *kjariza*), we see no reason why there could not be /Skj/ where the initial /S/ might be a form of the prefix *s-* or *z-*. The absence of /z/ and /ž/ in 'e3' is also viewed to be accidental, but this holds only for combinations where they would be preceded by a fricative.[3] However, combinations where they would be

---

3   For example, /Sžň/. Compare with /Sšň/ attested in *sšněrovati* (NLA). As explained in §13.3, /Sšň/ has not been included in our databáze, but is viewed as possible.

	/m/	/n/	/ň/	/ř/	/r/	/l/
/Ts/	/Tsm/					/Tsl/
/Tš/	/Tšm/		/Tšň/	–	(/Tšr/)	/Tšl/
/Tk/		/Tkn/	/Tkň/			/Tkl/
/Tx/		/Txn/	/Txň/			
/St/	/Stm/			/Stř/	/Str/	/Stl/
/Sd/	(/Sdm/)			/Sdř/	/Sdr/	/Sdl/
/Sš/						(/Sšl/)
/Sk/	/Skm/	/Skn/	(/Skň/)	/Skř/	/Skr/	/Skl/
/Sg/					/Sgr/	/Sgl/
/Sx/	/Sxm/	/Sxn/	/Sxň/	/Sxř/	/Sxr/	/Sxl/
/Sh/	/Shm/	/Shn/	/Shň/	/Shř/	/Shr/	/Shl/
/Št/				–	/Štr/	
/Šk/				–	/Škr/	/Škl/
/Šh/		/Šhn/	/Šhň/	–		

FIGURE XX: Three-phoneme pre-nuclear combinations attested for type DE3*d*

preceded by an occlusive will be declared impossible. This impossibility derives from a more general distributional restriction. If we examine the attested pre-nuclear combinations where some PerP is preceded by an occlusive and followed by some other PerP, i.e. combinations of the pattern 'OC$_1$C$_2$', we will find out that the 'C$_1$' phoneme can be /s/, /š/, /x/ (cf. /Tsm/ in *cmunda*, /Tšl/ in *člověk*, /Txn/ in *dchnouti* (SSJČ)), /S/, /Š/ (cf. /TSp/ in *cpát*, /KŠť/ in *kštice*) or /v/ (cf. /dvj/ in *dvě*). To put it otherwise, the 'C$_1$' phoneme is never a voiced consonant except for /v/, but /v/ belongs to another position class than the other voiced consonants. To say in yet other words, the 'C$_1$' is a never a voiced consonant which belongs to *pos* 'e3', i.e. /d/, /z/, /ž/, /g/ and /h/. In fact, it could not even be /b/, which is also voiced and which belongs to *pos* 'E2', but such combinations are already precluded by other collocational restrictions.[4] Therefore, we introduce the following restriction which rules out combinations like /Pdr/, /Tzm/, /Tžl/, /Pgn/, /Thň/.

(8)   Combinations of type 'OC$_1$C' where 'C$_1$' is a voiced consonant from *pos* 'e3' are impossible.

Let us now move to the phonemes belonging to 'pre1', i.e. /T/, /S/, /Š/ and /ř/. We will be particularly interested in /S/ and /Š/ (see DE2*i* on /T/). Out of them, the most combinable is /S/: it can precede an occlusive and a fricative (either from *pos* 'e3' or from *pos* 'E2') or a combination of an occlusive or a fricative

---

4   And it could not be /ď/ either, but this is already predicted by the structure of the DU.

with a phoneme from *pos* 'e1' or from *pos* 'e2' (cf. /Stm/, /Sdv/). However, not all combinations are possible: /S/ does not occur before /s/, /z/, and a few others are not attested: /Stn/, /Stň/, /Sdn/, /Sdň/. There does not seem to be any evidence for the impossibility of such combinations; in fact, /Stn/ would occur in *stnouti* recorded in NLA. Most lacunae are found in combinations with /Š/. In general, combinations with this archi-phoneme are small in number, though it must be mostly by accidence only. Moreover, there are not many combinations where /Š/ is followed by two PerPs. It can be followed by /h/ which is in turn followed by /n/ or /ň/ (i.e. /Šhn/ and /Šhň/ in *žhnout* and *žhni*). /Š/ can also be followed by /t/ or /k/ which is followed only by /r/ or /l/ (i.e. /Štr/ in *štrachat*, /Škr/ in *škrábat* and /Škl/ in *šklebit se*). It can also be followed by /p/ or /b/ which can in turn be followed by /r/ or /l/, but such combinations belong under DE3*f.* If /Š/ is followed by /t/ or /k/, the latter can also be further followed by /v/ (cf. /Štv/ in *štvát*, /Škv/ in *škvařit*), but these belong to subtype DE3*i.* It is possible to think of *žhla* (with /Šhl/) as the 3rd person singular past tense form of this verb. However, even though *žhla* is found in the Czech National Corpus, its variant *žhnul* is much more common; it is also the one regarded as correct.

The combination /Sdm/ is attested only in *sdmýchnouti* (PSJČ), /Sšl/ in *sšlechtiti* (PSJČ)[5] and /Skň/ in *zknižnění* (PSJČ). All of these combinations are marginal because the mentioned words are rather archaic. /Tšr/ is attested in the surname *Črepa*.

DE3e: 'e1' = ∀, 'e3' = ~{/g/}, 'pre2' = ~{/P/, /T/, /S/, /Š/, /K/, /X/, /r/, /l/}; figure XXI; 32 (34) combinations.

The absence of /g/ in 'e3' is accidental because, for example, /Fgr/ could occur in *vgravitovat*, a potential derivate of *gravitovat* (found in the Czech National Corpus). /P/, /K/ and /X/ cannot occur in 'pre2' because when they are followed by two PerPs, the first of them cannot be from *pos* 'e3' (see §11.8). The non-occurrence of /r/, /l/ in 'pre2' is not straightforward. If /r/ and /l/ occurred in 'pre2' in this subtype, the result would be combinations of the type *semiconsonant – occlusive/fricative – sonant*. Combinations of this pattern are found, namely /lpj/ and /rvj/, although they belong under DE3*c* and DE3*g*, respectively, so similar combinations could be possible for this subtype, too. Moreover, /r/ and /l/ could also occur in combinations of the type *sonant – fricative – nasal* to which belongs /jsm/ attested for this subtype. Actually, the combination /lsň/ could be found in *lsníti se* recorded in NLA. However, due to the marginality of this word, the combination is not included in our database, but it suggests that it could be possible.

---

5   See §13.3 on such combinations.

	/m/	/n/	/ň/	/j/	/ř/	/r/	/l/
/Ft/	/Ftm/			–	/Ftř/	/Ftr/	/Ftl/
/Fd/	/Fdm/			–		/Fdr/	/Fdl/
/Fs/	/Fsm/		/Fsň/				/Fsl/
/Fz/	/Fzm/	/Fzn/	/Fzň/	/Fzj/	/Fzř/	/Fzr/	/Fzl/
/Fš/			(/Fšň/)	–	–	/Fšr/	/Fšl/
/Fž/				–	–	/Fžr/	
/Fk/					/Fkř/	/Fkr/	/Fkl/
/Fx/				–			/Fxl/
/Fh/	(/Fhm/)		/Fhň/	–	/Fhř/	/Fhr/	/Fhl/
/Md/				–			/Mdl/
/Mk/		/Mkn/	/Mkň/	–			/Mkl/
/js/	/jsm/			–	–	–	–

FIGURE XXI: Three-phoneme pre-nuclear combinations attested for type DE3*e*

	/j/	/ř/	/r/	/l/
/Sp/	/Spj/	/Spř/	/Spr/	/Spl/
/Sb/	/Sbj/	/Sbř/	/Sbr/	/Sbl/
/Sf/			/Sfr/	/Sfl/
/Šp/		–	/Špr/	/Špl/
/Šb/		–	/Šbr/	/Šbl/

FIGURE XXII: Three-phoneme pre-nuclear combinations attested for type DE3*f*

Position 'pre2' can also be occupied by /F/, though many combinations with it are missing. Notable is the non-occurrence of /Ftn/, /Ftň/, /Fdn/ and /Fdň/, which could be compared to the non-occurrence of similar combinations with /S/, i.e. of /Stn/, /Stň/, /Sdn/ and /Sdň/ on the one hand (see figure XX), and /Spn/, /Spň/ on the other (see figure XXII). However, NLA mentions the words *spnouti* and *vpnouti* which would contain the combinations /Spn/ and /Fpn/. Compare also /Skn/ and /Skň/ attested in *sknotiti* (SSJČ) and *zknižnění* (PSJČ), respectively (see figure XX), against missing /Fkn/ and /Fkň/. The combination /Fhm/ is only attested in *vhmatávati*, and /Fšň/ in *všňořiti*. Both words are listed in PSJČ, but both are rather archaic.

DE3f: 'e1' = ~{/m/, /n/, /ň/}, 'E2' = ∀, 'pre1' = ~{/T/, /ř/}; figure XXII; 14 combinations.

/m/ cannot occur in 'e1' because it cannot be preceded by a phoneme from *pos* 'E2', but the absence of /n/, /ň/ must be accidental in light of the existence of /pn/, /pň/ and /FSpn/, /FSpň/, i.e. there is no reason to think a combination like /Spn/ is impossible (cf. *spnouti* mentioned in the previous type). The same reasoning applies to the next type. The absence of /ř/ and /T/ in 'pre1' is regular.

	/j/	/ř/	/r/	/l/
/Fp/	/Fpj/	/Fpř/	/Fpr/	/Fpl/
/Fb/	/Fbj/	/Fbř/	/Fbr/	/Fbl/
/lp/	/lpj/	–	–	–

	/m/
/tř/	/třm/
/hř/	/hřm/

FIGURE XXIII: Three-phoneme pre-nuclear combinations attested for type DE3*g*.

FIGURE XXIV: Three-phoneme pre-nuclear combinations attested for type DE3*h*

DE3g: 'e1' = ~{/m/, /n/, /ň/}, 'E2' = ~{/f/}, 'pre2' = ~{/P/, /T/, /S/, /Š/, /K/, /X/, /M/, /j/, /r/}; figure XXIII; 9 combinations.

See the previous type on the nasals. The non-occurrence of /f/ in 'E2' is accidental. /P/, /K/, /X/, /M/, /j/ cannot regularly occur in 'pre2' due to various restrictions. The combinations /lpl/, /lpř/ and /lpr/ are impossible because a semi-consonant cannot combine, within a peripheral combination, with another semi-consonant or /ř/ (see §11.2). Finally, considering /lpj/, we regard the non-occurrence of /r/ in 'pre2' as accidental, i.e. /rpj/ could be possible.

DE3h: 'e1' = ~{/n/, /ň/, /j/, /ř/, /r/, /l/}, 'pre1' = ~{/T/, /S/, /Š/}, for 'pre2', see text; figure XXIV; 2 combinations.

The two attested combinations are unique for two reasons. First, both end in /m/ and there is no evidence for similar combinations ending in another nasal, but they are viewed as possible. On the contrary, similar combinations ending in /j/, /ř/, /r/ or /l/ are impossible due to the very same restrictions mentioned at the previous type. Second, there is no neutralization of voicing in 'pre2', a fact discussed in §11.7.

DE3i: 'e2' = ~{/M/}, 'e3' = ~{/z/, /ž/, /g/, /h/}, 'pre1' = ~{/ř/}; figure XXV; 9 combinations.

/M/ cannot regularly occur in 'e2', and the same is true about /ř/ in 'pre1'. The non-occurrence of /z/, /ž/, /g/, /h/ in 'e3' is accidental, but see also the restriction (8) above. At least, /Shv/ is indirectly attested in *zhvízdati* mentioned in NLA, but is not included in our database.

DE3j: 'e2' = ~{/M/}, 'e3' = ~{/d/, /s/, /š/, /ž/, /g/, /x/, /h/}, 'pre2' = ~{/P/, /T/, /S/, /Š/, /K/, /X/, /M/, /j/, /r/, /l/}; figure XXVI; 3 combinations.

There are only three combinations attested, and they are probably found only in *vtvořiti* (SŞJČ), *vzvolati* (SSJČ), *vkvapiti* (PSJČ) which are very rare words. The absence of /d/, /s/, /š/, /ž/, /g/, /x/ and /h/ in 'e3' is accidental. On the other hand, the absence of /P/, /K/, /X/, /M/, /j/, /r/, /l/ in 'pre2' is regular due to various restrictions.

	/v/
/Ts/	/Tsv/
/Tš/	/Tšv/
/Tk/	/Tkv/
/St/	/Stv/
/Sd/	/Sdv/
/Sk/	/Skv/
/Sx/	/Sxv/
/Št/	/Štv/
/Šk/	/Škv/

FIGURE XXV: Three-phoneme pre-nuclear combinations attested for type DE3*i*

	/v/
/Ft/	/Ftv/
/Fz/	/Fzv/
/Fk/	/Fkv/

FIGURE XXVI: Three-phoneme pre-nuclear combinations attested for type DE3*j*

	/v/
/bř/	(/břv/)

FIGURE XXVII: Three-phoneme pre-nuclear combinations attested for type DE3*k*

	/t/	/d/	/s/	/š/	/ž/	/k/	/x/	/h/
/FT/	–	–	/FTs/	/FTš/		/FTk/		
/FS/	/FSt/	/FSd/	–	/FSš/		/FSk/	/FSx/	/FSh/
/FŠ/		/FŠd/	–	–	–	/FŠk/		
/TŠ/	/TŠt/		–	–	–	(/TŠk/)		
/ST/	–	–	/STs/	/STš/	/STž/	/STk/		
/ŠT/	–	–				/ŠTk/		
/Kř/	/Křt/		–	–	–	–	–	–
/XT/	–	–	/XTs/	/XTš/		–	–	–
/Xř/	/Xřt/		–	–	–	–	–	–
/rT/	–	–	(/rTs/)	/rTš/				
/lT/	–	–		(/lTš/)				
/MT/	–	–	(/MTs/)					
/MS/	/MSt/	/MSd/	–					
/jS/	/jSt/		–					

FIGURE XXVIII: Three-phoneme pre-nuclear combinations attested for type DE3*l*

DE3k: 'e2' = ~{/M/}, 'pre1' = ~{/T/, /S/, /Š/}, for 'pre2', see text; figure XXVII; (0) 1 combination.

The only one combination attested for this type is found in the Czech place names *Břve* and *Břvany*. Other combinations are missing by accident. For instance, /přv/ could be accepted as a potential counterpart of /břv/.

DE3l: 'e3' = ~{/z/, /g/}, 'pre1' = ∀, 'pre2' = ~{/P/, (/l/)}; figure XXVIII; 25 (29) combinations.

The absence of /z/ in 'e3' and that of /P/ in 'pre1' are accidental (we regard combinations like /STz/ or /Přt/ as possible). In contrast, the absence of /g/ in 'e3' is regular because this phoneme cannot be followed or preceded by two

	/p/	/b/
/FS/	/FSp/	/FSb/
/TS/	/TSp/	(/TSb/)
/TŠ/	/TŠp/	/TŠb/
/Tř/	/Třp/	
/Xř/		/Xřb/

FIGURE XXIX: Three-phoneme pre-nuclear combinations attested for type DE3*m*

Perps. The combination /TŠk/ is only attested in the place name *Čkyně*,[6] /MTs/ only in the place name *Mcely*[7] and /lTš/ only in *Lčovice*. The combination /rTs/ occurs only in the archaic word *rci*. It is also worth noting that no combination of /TS/ + a phoneme from *pos* 'e3' is attested in this type, even though /TStm/ exists (from *ctmi*).

DE3m: 'E2' = ~{/f/}, 'pre1' = ~{/T/}, 'pre2' = {/P/, /S/, /Š/, /K/, /M/, /j/, /r/, /l/}; figure XXIX; 7 (8) combinations.

The absence of /f/ in 'E2' is regular because this phoneme cannot be preceded by two PerPs. On the other hand, the absence of /T/ in 'pre1' is accidental because there is no reason to think that combinations like /FTb/ or /STb/ could not be possible. Similarly accidental is the absence of /P/, /K/, /S/, /Š/ in 'pre2', On the contrary, the absence of /M/, /j/, /r/, /l/ is regular due to various restrictions. The combination /TSb/ is attested only in the place name *Dzbel*.

DE3n: 'E3' = ∀, 'pre1' = ~{/T/}, 'pre2' = ~{/S/, /Š/, /X/, /j/, /r/}; figure XXX; 12 (16) combinations.

The absence of /T/ in 'pre1' is regular because this archi-phoneme cannot precede palatal occlusives. Consequently, the non-occurrence of /S/, /Š/ in 'pre2' must also be regarded as regular because these phonemes occupy 'pre2' only if 'pre1' is filled with /T/. Regular is also the absence of /X/ in 'pre2' because, as mentioned in §13.4, a velar fricative cannot be followed by a fricative + an occlusive. On the othe hand, the absence of /j/ in 'pre2' is viewed to be accidental. The combination /PŠť/ occurs only in *Pština*, which is a Czech name for Polish *Pszczyna*; /SŠť/ only in archaic and rare *zšťastniti* (PSJČ; see §13.3 on such combinations); /lŠť/ occurs only in the place name *Lštěň*. Finally, /MŠť/ is attested in the Czech place name *Mštěnovice*.

---

6   NLA also mentions archaic *čkáti* "to wait". It is obsolete now.
7   Its variant is *Mčely* which would give the combination /MTš/.

	/t'/	/d'/
/PS/		/PSď/
/PŠ/	(/PŠt'/)	
/FS/	/FSt'/	/FSď/
/FŠ/	/FŠt'/	
/TS/	/TSt'/	
/TŠ/	/TŠt'/	
/SŠ/	(/SŠt'/)	
/Tř/	/Třt'/	
/KŠ/	/KŠt'/	
/Kř/	/Křt'/	
/lS/	/lSt'/	
/lŠ/	(/lŠt'/)	
/MS/	/MSt'/	/MSď/
/MŠ/	(/MŠt'/)	

a	Ø	pre1	e3	e2	e1
b	pre2	Ø	e3	e2	e1
c	pre2	pre1	Ø	e2	e1
d	pre2	pre1	e3	Ø	e1
e	pre2	pre1	E2		e1
f	pre2	pre1	e3	e2	Ø

FIGURE XXX: Three-phoneme pre-nuclear combinations attested for type DE3*n*

FIGURE XXXI: Subtypes for distributional type DE4

14.4 Four-phoneme combinations (type DE4)

Four-phoneme pre-nuclear combinations belong under the distributional type DE4 which refers to the situation when as many as four positions are occupied by phonemes. Its subtypes are given in figure XXXI; they correspond to 43 (50) actually attested combinations.

DE4a: 'e1' = ~{/m/, /n/, /ř/, /r/, /l/}, 'e2' = ∀, 'e3' = ~{/d/, /s/, /z/, /š/, /ž/, /g/}, 'pre1' = ~{/Š/, /ř/}; figure XXXII (see the next page); 5 combinations.

All combinations under this subtype involve /tMň/, /kvj/, /xvj/ or /hvj/ on which see DE3*a*; the same restrictions mentioned there apply here as well. The absence of /d/ from 'e3' is accidental (cf. /dMň/ in figure XVII above). The phonemes /s/, /z/, /š/, /ž/ as well as /g/ cannot occur in 'e3' (cf. §11.4). Finally, the absence of /Š/ in 'pre1' is accidental,[8] but that of /ř/ is regular.

DE4b: 'e1' = ~{/m/, /n/, (/ň/), (/j/), /ř/, /r/, /l/}, 'e2' = ~{(v/), (/M/)}, 'e3' = ~{/t/, /d/, (/s/), (/z/), /š/, /ž/, /k/, /g/, /x/, /h/}, 'pre2' = ~{/P/, /T/, (/F/), /S/, /Š/, /K/, /X/, /M/, /j/, /r/, /l/}; figure XXXIII (see the next page); 0 (3) combinations.

---

8   SSJČ and PSJČ list a dialectal word *škvěčeti* (i.e. with /Škvj/) where /Š/ is followed by three PerPs. While it does not mean that such a combination is possible in Standard Czech, it suggests that it may not appropriate to assume that the absence of /Š/ in regular in 'pre1' in this subtype.

	/ň/	/j/
/Tkv/	–	/Tkvj/
/StM/	/StMň/	–
/Skv/	–	/Skvj/
/Shv/	–	/Shvj/
/Sxv/	–	/Sxvj/

	/ň/	/j/
/FsM/	(/FsMň/)	–
/Fzv/		(/Fzvj/)
/FzM/	(/FzMň/)	

FIGURE XXXII: Four-phoneme pre-nuclear combinations attested for type DE4*a*

FIGURE XXXIII: Four-phoneme pre-nuclear combinations attested for type DE4*b*.

	/ň/
/třM/	/třMň/
/hřM/	/hřMň/

FIGURE XXXIV: Four-phoneme pre-nuclear combinations attested for type DE4*c*

The three marginal combinations attested for this type are found in *vsměstnati*, *vzmět*' and *vzvěděti*, all recorded in PSJŠ and marked as rare. We should perhaps conclude that combinations falling under type DE4*b* are not possible in present-day Czech. Several more combinations such as /FsMl/, /Fsvl/, /FsMn/ were possible in older Czech (Hattala 1870: 84).

DE4c: 'e1' = ~{/m/, /n/, /j/, /ř/, /r/, /l/}, 'e2' = ~{/v/}, 'pre1' = ~{/T/, /S/, /Š/}, for 'pre2', see text; figure XXXIV; 2 combinations.

Neutralization of voicing does not obtain for 'pre2' here (see §11.8). Only two combinations have been found, though others are potentially possible, e.g. /dřMň/ or /xřMň/. The phonemes /ř/, /r/, /l/ cannot regularly occur in 'e1' in this subtype because they cannot co-occur with /ř/ (see §11.2).

DE4d: 'e1' = ~{/j/}, 'e3' = ~{/s/, /z/, /ž/, /g/}, 'pre1' = ~{/ř/}, 'pre2' = ~{/K/, /X/, /j/, /r/}; figure XXXV; 23 (25) combinations.

The absence of /j/ in 'e1' and the absence of /s/, /z/, /ž/ in 'e3' is viewed to be accidental, but that of /g/ regular because it cannot be preceded by two PerPs (see §11.4). We could have assumed that alveolar fricatives cannot be preceded by two PerPs and be at the same time followed by a phoneme from *pos* 'e1', but we do not find such a restriction appropriate because of the existence of /STsv/ (in *scvaknout*). In the latter combination, /s/ is preceded by two phonemes and followed by a phoneme from *pos* 'e2'. We will not assume that it could not be followed by a phoneme from *pos* 'e1', too. Similarly accidental is the absence of /r/ in 'pre2' in light of /lStn/. But the absence of /K/, /X/ and /j/ in 'pre2' is regular for this subtype.

	/m/	/n/	/ñ/	/ř/	/r/	/l/
/PSt/				/PStř/	/PStr/	
/PŠt/				–	/PŠtr/	
/FTš/				–		/FTšl/
/FSt/				/FStř/		/FStl/
/FSd/	/FSdm/					
/FSk/				/FSkř/		/FSkl/
/FSx/						(/FSxl/)
/FSh/				(/FShř/)		/FShl/
/FŠk/				–	/FŠkr/	
/STk/						/STkl/
/STš/				–		/STšl/
/ŠTk/		/ŠTkn/	/ŠTkň/	–		
/TSt/	/TStm/	/TStn/	/TStň/			
/lSt/	/lStm/	/lStn/	/lStň/	–	–	–
/MSt/		/MStn/	/MStň/			

FIGURE XXXV: Four-phoneme pre-nuclear combinations attested for type DE4*d*

/TStm/ is attested only in *ctmi*, instr. pl. of *čest* "virtue". /TStn/ is attested only in *ctnost* "virtuousness" and archaic *ctný* "virtuous" (SSJČ). Finally, /TSTň/ is attested only in *ctni* "virtuous (pl.)". All these words are ultimately derivatives of the same root. The Czech orthoepy allows two pronunciations for *ctnost*:[9] [ʦtnost] and [ʦnost] (VSČ: 63, Zeman 2008: 123). The former is a full, unreduced pronunciation recommended for recitation, and the latter is a simplified pronunciation supposedly preferred in casual speech. Thus, the combinations /TStn/ and /TStň/ should perhaps be excluded from our database if they can be reduced to /Tsn/ and /Tsň/ without any change in meaning, but they are certainly examples of possibilities of the system and they, moreover, parallel /TStm/ in structure.

There are numerous accidental gaps in figure XXXV; many combinations are structurally possible, and several of them such as /FSkr/, /FStr/, /FSdr/, /FSdř/, /FShr/, /FShň/ or /FSxr/ were possible in older Czech (Hattala 1870: 83).

DE4e: 'e1' = ~{/m/}, 'E2' = ~{/f/}, 'pre1' = ~{/T/, /ř/}, 'pre2' = ~{/P/, /S/, /Š/, /K/, /X/, /M/, /j/, /r/, /l/}; figure XXXVI (next page); 9 (10) combinations.

As a consequence of various restrictions, /m/ cannot occur in 'e1', /f/ in 'E2', /T/, /ř/ in 'pre1', and /K/, /X/, /M/, /j/, /r/, /l/ in 'pre2'. Several other combinations were found in older Czech, e.g. /FŠpl/ (Hattala *op. cit.*: 83–4). /FSbř/ is attested only in *vzbředlý* (PSJČ, rare).

---

9   Presumably also for *ctný* and *ctni*, but apparently not for *ctmi*.

	/n/	/ň/	/j/	/ř/	/r/	/l/
/FSp/	/FSpn/	/FSpň/	/FSpj/	/FSpř/	/FSpr/	/FSpl/
/FSb/	–	–	/FSbj/	(/FSbř/)		
/TSp/			/TSpj/			
/TŠp/			/TŠpj/	–		

FIGURE XXXVI: Four-phoneme pre-nuclear combinations attested for type DE4*e*

	/v/
/FSk/	/FSkv/
/FSx/	(/FSxv/)
/TŠt/	/TŠtv/
/STs/	/STsv/
/STk/	/STkv/

	/j/
/FSkv/	/FSkvj/
/STkv/	/STkvj/

FIGURE XXXVII: Four-phoneme pre-nuclear combinations attested for type DE4*f*

FIGURE XXXVIII: Five-phoneme pre-nuclear combinations attested for type DE5

DE4f: 'e2' = ~{/M/}, 'e3' = ~{/d/, /z/, /š/, /ž/, /g/, (/x/), /h/}, 'pre1' = ~{/ř/}, 'pre2' = ~{/P/, /Š/, /K/, /X/, /M/, /j/, /r/, /l/}; figure XXXVII; 4 (5) combinations.

Again, as a consequence of various restrictions, /M/ cannot occur in 'e2'; /š/, /ž/ in 'e3'; /ř/ in 'pre1'; and /P/, /K/, /X/, /M/, /j/, /r/, /l/ in 'pre2'. The absence of /d/, /z/, /h/ in 'e3' is accidental, but that of /g/ regular. Although there are only a few combinations attested, we assume more are potentially possible (e.g. /FStv/, /FSdv/ or /FShv/).

15.5 Five-phoneme combinations (type DE5)

In this final distributional type all pre-nuclear positions are occupied by phonemes. There is only one possible configuration: the one in which all pre-nuclear positions are occupied, which corresponds only to two attested combinations.

DE5: 'e1' = ~{/m/, /n/, /ň/, /ř/, /r/, /l/}, 'e2' = ~{/M/}, 'e3' = ~{/t/, /d/, /s/, /z/, /š/, /ž/, /g/, /x/, /h/}, 'pre1' = ~{/Š/, /ř/}, 'pre2' = ~{/P/, /T/, /Š/, /K/, /X/, /M/, /j/, /r/, /l/}; figure XXXVIII; 2 combinations.

As a consequence of various restrictions, /ř/, /r/, /l/ cannot occur in 'e1'; /s/, /z/, /š/, /ž/, /g/ in 'e3'; /ř/ in 'pre1'; and /P/, /T/, /K/, /Š/, /X/, /M/, /j/, /r/, /l/ in 'pre2'. On the other hand, accidental is the absence of /m/, /n/, /ň/ in 'e1', of /M/ in 'e2', of /t/, /d/, /x/, /h/ in 'e3', and of /Š/ in 'pre1'. That is to say, there is no reason combinations like /FStvj/, /FShvj/, /FSxvj/ could not be possible. Moreover, a combination /FSdMň/ could be at least hypothetically possible; see §11.2.

Chapter Fifteen: POST-NUCLEAR COMBINATIONS

15.1 Post-nuclear distributional types

In this chapter we continue in the discussion of peripheral combinations, turning now our attention to the post-nuclear context. In order to account for such combinations, we distinguish between two major post-nuclear distributional types: DI2 and DI3 where the number again expresses how many positions are filled with a phoneme. Several subtypes are recognized for type DI2. Every attested post-nuclear combination belongs to one and only one subtype. We list again phonemes which are NOT attested to occur in a given subtype. The notation used in this chapter is the same as the one in the previous chapter.

We can also, for the sake of completeness, refer to two other distributional types which do not underlie any combination: DI0 and DI1. In type DI0 none of the post-nuclear positions is occupied by a phoneme. Such phonotagms are numerous in Czech (cf. /Sto/ *sto* or /hr/ *hr* from *být hr*). In type DI1, only one post-nuclear position is filled with a phoneme. There are three possibilities how this is achieved; see figure I. The fourth type, DI1*d*, is impossible because 'I' is only filled with a phoneme if 'i1' is filled with one (see §12.5).

DI1a: 'i1' = ∀, i.e. {/P/, /T/, /K/, /m/, /n/, /ň/, /j/, /r/, /l/}.

DI1b: 'i2' = ~{/P/, /T/, /K/}.
/P/, /T/, /K/ cannot occur in 'i2' if the other post-nuclear positions are empty (see §12.3). Hence, the position can be filled with /F/, /X/, /ř/, /S/ or /Š/.

DI1c: 'i3' = ~{/P/, /T/, /K/, /S/, /Š/}.
This position can only be filled with /Ť/ because /P/, /T/, /K/, /S/, /Š/ do not occur in 'i3' if the other post-nuclear positions are empty (see §12.3).

a	i1	Ø	Ø
b	Ø	i2	Ø
c	Ø	Ø	i3
d	Ø		I

FIGURE I: Subtypes for distributional type DI1

a	i1	i2	Ø
b	i1	Ø	i3
c	i1		I
d	Ø	i2	i3

FIGURE II: Subtypes for distributional type DI2

	/P/	/T/	/K/	/m/	/n/	/j/	/r/	/l/
/P/	–	–	–	/mP/		/jP/	/rP/	/lP/
/T/	–	–	–	/mT/	/nT/	/jT/	/rT/	/lT/
/K/	–	–	–		/nK/	/jK/	/rK/	/lK/
/S/	/PS/	/TS/	/KS/	/mS/	/nS/	/jS/	/rS/	/lS/
/Š/	–	–	–	/mŠ/	/nŠ/	/jŠ/	/rŠ/	(/lŠ/)
/ř/	/Př/	/Tř/	/Kř/	–	–	(/jř/)	–	–
/F/	–	–	–	/mF/	/nF/	/jF/	/rF/	/lF/
/X/	–	–	–	/mX/		/jX/	/rX/	/lX/

FIGURE III: Two-phoneme post-nuclear combinations attested for type DI2*a*

15.2 Two-phoneme combinations (type DI2)

Two-phoneme post-nuclear combinations are accounted for by the distributional type DI2 which refers to the situation when exactly two post-nuclear positions are filled with a phoneme. It has four subtypes listed in figure II. They correspond to 65 (75) actually attested combinations.

DI2a: 'i1' = ~{/ř/}, 'i2' = ∀; figure III; 37 (39) combinations.
  /ř/ cannot combine with /r/, /l/ (see §11.2), with nasals and with fricatives (see §12.2). In fact, in the post-nuclear context, /ř/ combines with occlusives only or with /j/ as in /jř/, but the latter is attested only in the surname *Kejř*. As explained in §12.3, if the occlusives /P/, /T/, /K/ occur in 'i1', they cannot be followed by /P/, /T/, /K/ or /Š/. Although the combinations /PT/, /KT/, /PŠ/, /TŠ/ and /KŠ/ are attested, they belong under DI2*d*. The combinability of /P/, /T/, /K/ is further limited on which see §12.2. See there also on the absence of combinations with /ň/.

DI2b: 'i1' = ~{/P/, /T/, /K/, (/m/, /n/, /l/)}, 'i3' = ~{/P/, /T/, /K/, /S/, /Š/}; figure IV; 2 (5) combinations.
  /P/, /T/, /K/ do not occur in 'i1' if 'i2' is empty, and in 'i3' if 'i2' is empty (see §12.3), which is true even for /S/, /Š/. The combinations /mŤ/, /nŤ/, /lŤ/ are parenthesized because they occur in PhFs of markedly archaic words *jsemť*, *onť* and *bylť*, these being *jsem* "I am", *on* "he" and *byl* "he was" plus the suffix -*ť*. They nevertheless show a combinatorial potential.

	/m/	/n/	/j/	/r/	/l/
/ť/	(/mť/)	(/nť/)	/jť/	/rť/	(/lť/)

FIGURE IV: Two-phoneme post-nuclear combinations attested for type DI2*b*

	/j/	/r/	/l/
/m/	/jm/	/rm/	/lm/
/n/	/jn/	/rn/	(/ln/)
/ň/		/rň/	
/r/	/jr/	–	/rl/
/l/	/jl/		–

FIGURE V: Two-phoneme post-nuclear combinations attested for type DI2*c*

	/P/	/T/	/K/	/S/	/Š/	/F/	/X/	/ř/
/P/	–	–		(/SP/)		–		–
/T/	/PT/	–	/KT/	/ST/	/ŠT/	/FT/	/XT/	/řT/
/K/	–	–	–	/SK/		/FK/	–	/řK/
/S/	–	–	–	–	–	–	(/XS/)	–
/Š/	(/PŠ/)	/TŠ/	/KŠ/	–	–		/XŠ/	–
/ť/	/Pť/	–	/Kť/	/Sť/	/Šť/		/Xť/	

FIGURE VI: Two-phoneme post-nuclear combinations attested for type DI2*d*

DI2c: 'i1' = ~{/P/, /T/, /K/, /m/, /n/, /ň/}, 'I' = ∀; figure V; 9 (10) combinations.
/P/, /T/, /K/, /m/, /n/, /ň/ cannot occur in 'i1' in this subtype because they cannot be followed by a sonant or a nasal (see §12.2). /rl/ occurs in /Stārl/ *stárl* on which see §10.2. /ln/ is attested in the foreign surname *Lincoln*.

DI2d: 'i2' = ∀, 'i3' = ~{(/P/)}; figure VI; 17 (21) combinations.
The combinations marked with a dash in figure VI are impossible due to various restrictions. A note should be given to /SP/. It is attested only in *výsp*, gen. pl. of *výspa*. Although *výsp* is found in the Czech National Corpus and through Google.com (the situation as of 19 March 2013), there are disagreements whether it is correct in Standard Czech. The most recent grammar (MSČ, 2010, p. 173) states that the only correct genitive plural is *výsep*, and so does MČ2 (1986, p. 325).[1] On the other hand, PMČ (1996, p. 257) mentions only *výsp*. Phonologically, there is no reason to declare /SP/ invalid. First, it fits the pattern of /ST/, /SK/ and /Sť/, i.e. it is of the type *alveolar fricative + occlusive*. If /SP/ is rejected, /P/ would be the only occlusive which is not preceded by /S/ in the post-nuclear context. Second, /SP/ is also attested as part of the post-nuclear combination /TSP/ (found in *zácp*, gen. pl. of *zácpa*). Considering these facts, we regard the combination /SP/ as structurally possible, but, due to the problems mentioned, we classify it under marginal combinations.

---

1   *výsep* is also mentioned as the only genitive plural of *výspa* in Internet Language Reference book (accessed 19 March 2013).

	/P/	/T/	/K/	/m/	/n/	/j/	/r/	/l/
/PT/	–	–	–	–			/rPT/	
/TS/	–	–	–		/nTS/	/jTS/	/rTS/	/lTS/
/TŠ/	–	–	–		/nTŠ/	/jTŠ/	/rTŠ/	(/lTŠ/)
/KT/	–	–	–		/nKT/		/rKT/	
/KS/	–	–	–		(/nKS/)		(/rKS/)	
/SP/		/TSP/		–	–	–	–	–
/ST/	/PST/	/TST/	/KST/	/mST/		/jST/	/rST/	(/lST/)
/SK/	(/PSK/)		(/TSK/)		(/nSK/)	/jSK/	(/rSK/)	(/lSK/)
/ŠT/				/mŠT/		–	–	–
/ŠŤ/		(/TŠŤ/)			–	–	–	–

FIGURE VII: Three-phoneme post-nuclear combinations attested for type DI3

The combination /XS/ is only attested in the surname *Fuchs*, and /PŠ/ only in the surname *Hypš*. We could also include the combination /ŠK/ attested in *tamaryšk*, a rare variant of *tamaryšek* according to PSJČ. This combination is also found in e.g. *lašk* recorded in NLA. As it occurs in rare words, it has not been included in our database.

15.3 Three-phoneme combinations (type DI3)

Three-phoneme post-nuclear combinations are account for by the distributional type DI3 which refers to the situation when all post-nuclear positions are occupied by a phoneme. It underlies 19 (29) combinations.

DI3: 'i1' = ~{/ň/}, 'i2' = ~{/ř/, /F/, /X/}, 'i3' = ~{/Ť/}; figure VII; 19 (29) combinations.
    The absence of /ň/ in 'i1' is regarded as structurally conditioned; see §12.2. The non-occurrence of /ř/, /F/, /X/ in 'i2' is also regular; see §12.3.
    Many combinations are attested only in proper names and other symbols: /rKS/ and /lST/ in the surnames *Marx*, *Holst*; /lTŠ/ in the Czech place name *Telč*; and /nKS/ in the brand name *Sfinx*. To these we could add /rSK/, /lSK/, /nSK/, /PSK/, /TSK/[2] found in the foreign (Russian) place names *Magnitogorsk, Tobolsk, Smolensk, Vítebsk, Kuzněck*. Although they fit the pattern of the other combinations for this subtype, their status may be doubtful due to the origin of the mentioned words. Finally, /TŠŤ/ is attested in the archaic form *ačt*.

---

2   /TSK/ is also attested in *kuck* which is, according to PSJČ, an onomatopoeic word for choking.

Chapter Sixteen: COMBINATIONS OF NUCLEAR AND PERIPHERAL PHONEMES

Nuclear phonemes do not combine with each other within a single major-type phonotagm because there can only be one such phoneme in it. If a group of two nuclear phonemes occurs, they belong to separate phonotagms like the ones in /idea/ *idea* or in /abēovē/ *abbéové* (see Mathesius 1931b on such combinations). Within a single phonotagm the nuclear phonemes combine only with PerPs. In this chapter we discuss such combinations.

16.1 'CV' combinations

We will start with the situation when the short vowels /i/, /e/, /a/, /o/, /u/ are preceded by a single PerP. They can be preceded by all PerPs (except for the voicing archi-phonemes which do not occur before nuclear phonemes, and except for /M/ which do not occur before vowels). Examples of words with such combinations are given in figure I. This assertion must, however, be confronted with claims by other researchers.

There is a long tradition of phonological descriptions of Czech questioning the combinability of the back vowels /o/, /u/, /ö/ with the palatals /ť/, /ď/, /š/, /ž/, /ň/, with /j/, /ř/, and with the affricates [ts] and [ʧ] interpreted here as /Ts/ and /Tš/, respectively. The idea goes back at least to Mathesius (1931a), and is repeated by other linguists (Ludvíková 1968: 61, Vachek 1968: 89, Těšitelová et al. 1985: 18–9, Grygarová-Rechzieglová 1993: 265, Krčmová 2008: 111). Mathesius (*ibid.*) argued that such combinations are encountered only in the following situations:[1]

---

1   Mathesius (*ibid.*) also questioned the ability of the velars /k/, /h/, /x/ to combine with the vowel /e/, but this claim can be at once dismissed because at least /k/ and /h/ do combine with /e/ in "neutral" words such as *ke, keř, kedluben, herec, hezký, hebký*. It is only /xe/ which has limited combinability because it occurs mostly in words originally borrowed from foreign languages such as *chemie* "chemistry" (but there is also a genuine Czech place name *Cheb*, and also the word *chechtat*, although the latter, one might argue, is onomatopoeic in origin). — See also the commentary on Mathesius' observations in Rech-zieglová (1998).

	/i/	/e/	/a/	/o/	/u/
/p/	pil	pes	pak	pot	puk
/b/	byl	bez	bar	bok	bude
/f/	film	fena	fakt	fot'	funkce
/v/	vid	ven	vana	vor	vulkán
/m/	myš	med	mast	moč	muset
/t/	tyč	teď	tak	to	tu
/d/	diktát	den	dar	do	duch
/s/	syn	sen	sad	sok	sud
/z/	zima	zem	zase	zorný	zub
/n/	nyní	nes	nad	noc	nutit
/ť/	tis	tělo	ťal	šťovík	ťuhýk
/ď/	div	děs	ďas	ďobat	see text
/š/	šik	šel	šaty	šotek	šum
/ž/	živý	žena	žací	žok	žula
/ň/	nic	něco	ňadra	žňový	šňupat
/k/	kytka	keř	kaz	koza	kus
/g/	gymnázium	gel	galantní	golf	guma
/x/	chyba	chemie	chata	chod	chuť
/h/	hynout	hezký	had	hod	hudba
/j/	jiný	jen	jak	jogurt	junák
/ř/	řinout	řez	řada	křoví	křupat
/r/	rys	rej	rak	roj	rub
/l/	lis	let	lak	loj	luk

FIGURE I: Attested 'CV' combinations with a short vowel

(1) (a) Across morphological boundaries (e.g. rtuťový, sleďů, mužů, pňový, bojovat, křovina).
     (b) In words of foreign origin (e.g. čokoláda "chocolate", jód "jodine", žok "hopsack").
     (c) In "domestic" words of onomatopoeic origin or in emotionally colored words (e.g. křupat, ťukat, fňukat, kňourat, šoupati, ďobati).

Although observations of this kind have undoubtedly some importance, they are somewhat overestimated. The fact that two phonemes are split between PhFs of two morphemes may be of some significance, but it is dependent on the way pleremes are morphologically analyzed. However, as the morphological analysis is dependent on the phonological one, there is a danger of circularity. It is phonology that tells us that the form of keř "shrub" is identifiable with the form of *kř* in *křovina* "shrubbery", so that they are interpreted as allomorphs of one moneme (morpheme) rather than synonymous monemes (morphemes).[2]

Similarly, the determination of the foreign or onomatopoeic origin of a word may be problematic. Some linguists (Mathesius 1932: 231, Vachek 1968: 31, 89) are apparently of the opinion that certain words are so phonologically marked that we can deduce they are synchronically foreign without knowing their origin, but the reasoning seems to be circular. For example, knowing that the word *jód* was borrowed to Czech from a foreign language, we can say that it contains a combination /jō/. On the examination of its distribution we find out that /jō/ occurs only in words about which we could claim they were borrowed from foreign languages, and we conclude that /jō/ is a mark of foreignness. But could this conclusion be reached without our prior knowledge of the origin of the words it occurs in? We can at most list such words (and how can we be sure we have listed all of them?), but so can we list words containing e.g. /je/. One of them is *jed*; now, what is the phonological difference between *jed* and *jód*? Unless we know their history, there is none. The whole argument is furthermore dubious because the conclusion that /jō/ occurs only in words of foreign origin rests upon our ability to say they are indeed words of foreign origin. What makes a certain word domestic in origin? Such a question cannot have a definitive answer, and the answer could not even be decisive because Modern Czech contains a number of words (such as *kalhoty* or *košile*) once borrowed from foreign languages, but since then fully "domesticated".

Thus, it is not relevant whether a combination is attested in a certain group of words only, but whether it is attested at all. To return to the combinability of the short vowels with PerPs, we repeat that every short vowel can be preceded by every possible PerP. Figure I gives examples of words in which they combine with the palatals /ť/, /ď/, /š/, /ž/, /ň/ and with /ř/, /j/. Although some combinations are rare, they are still existent (like /ťa/ in *ťal*). Others are only attested in more complex combinations such as /ťo/ which has been found only as part of /šťo/ in *šťovík*. Similarly, /ňo/ is attested only as part of /žňo/ in *žňový*, /ňu/ as part of /šňu/ in *šňupat*, /řu/ as part of /křu/ in *křupat*, and /ďu/ found only in *shromažďuje*. It does not, however, mean that words beginning just with /ťo/, /ďu/, /ňo/, /ňu/, /řu/ are impossible in Czech. In fact, such words (except those beginning with /ňo/) exist, but they are, some might argue, of onomatopoeic or other origin (cf. *ťopkat*, *ďubka*, *ňuhňat*, *řupoň*), and some of them (e.g. *ďubka*) may not even belong to Standard Czech.

---

2   Another thing is that there is no universal morphological analysis, so that English *blackbird* consists of two morphemes in some analyses, while others treat it, more appropriately, as a single morpheme/moneme (Mulder – Hervey 1980: 122–44).

	/ī/	/ē/	/ā/	/ō/	/ū/
/p/	pít	péct	pás	pór	půst
/b/	být	bérec	bát se	bójka	bůh
/f/	fík	fén	fáma	fór	fúze
/v/	víc	vést	vát	kvóta	vůl
/m/	mýt	mést	mást	móda	může
/t/	týl	téct	tát	tón	tůň
/d/	dým	déle	dál	dóm	důl
/s/	sít	séct	sám	sója	sůl
/z/	zívat	zévnatka	zábst	zóna	zůstat
/n/	nýbrž	nést	náš	nóbl	nůž
/ť/	tít	–	šťáva	–	zeťů
/ď/	díl	–	ďábel	–	sleďů
/š/	šit	šéf	šál		hrabošů
/ž/	žít	pasažér	žák	demižón	mužů
/ň/	níž	–	tučňák	–	šňůra
/k/	kýchat	kéž	kát se	kód	kůl
/g/	angína	génius	gáže	gól	kolegů
/x/	chýše	schéma	chátrat	chór	chůze
/h/	hýbat se	hélium	hák	cirhóza	hůl
/j/	jíst		já	jód	pokojů
/ř/	říct	(Břéťa)	řád		lékařů
/r/	rýt	réva	rám	rómština	růže
/l/	lýko	léto	lán	lóže	lůžko

FIGURE II: Attested 'CV' combinations with a long vowel

The situation is more interesting in the case of the long vowels /ī/, /ē/, /ā/, /ō/, /ū/. Figure II provides examples of words where such combinations are attested. An empty cell means the respective combination has not been found. The dash indicates a given combination is not structurally possible; for these, we will postulate several collocational restrictions below. As is obvious, labials, alveolars, velars and /r/, /l/ combine with the long vowels, but the combinability of the palatals /ť/, /ď/, /š/, /ž/, /ň/ and of /ř/, /j/ requires a commentary.

First of all, /řē/ has been found only in the proper name Břéťa. The word tučňák, whose PhF is /tuTšňāK/, shows that the combination /ňā/ is possible. Since /Tšň/ is not a well-formed post-nuclear combination, /ň/ must belong to the same phonotagm as /ā/. Other combinations are also attested only word-internally, namely /ťū/ in zeťů, /ďū/ in sleďů, /šū/ in hrabošů, /žē/ in pasažér, /žō/ in demižón, /žū/ in mužů, /gī/ in angína and /gū/ in kolegů, but their acceptable is dependent on the way we analyze the PhFs of the mentioned words.

Let us take *zeťů* as an example. Since it contains two phonemes which elsewhere function as nuclear entities (i.e. /e/ and /ū/), it is appropriate to assume that its PhF /zeťū/ consists of two phonotagms. The medial /ť/ could be ascribed to the first or to the second, i.e. two possible analyses are /zeť–ū/ and /zeŤ–ťū/ (the second with functional amalgamation). The first analysis is problematic for its assumption of /zeť/ with no final neutralization of voicing, which is a characteristic of all attested major-type phonotagms. Still, /zeť/ may be a minor-type phonotagm for which neutralization of voicing is not the necessary condition. However, as we argued in §8.2, the category of minor-type phonotagms is assumed in case alternative analyses are demonstrably less simple and less adequate. For /zeťū/, the alternative is /zeŤ–ťū/. Still, even the latter is not without problems because there is no direct evidence that /ťū/ is a well-formed combination within a single phonotagm, but it is simpler to permit this kind of combinations rather than to introduce another bundle of minor-type phonotagms to which /zeť/ would belong. It is simpler to account for most phenomena with just one model (i.e. with the major-type phonotagm) than to work with several models. Finally, if the analysis /zeť–ū/ were chosen, the combination /ťū/ would have to be declared impossible because we would not have any evidence of the contrary. Thus, we would not only have to operate with a new type of phonotagms, but also with an additional collocational restriction. In comparison to this, the division /zeŤ–ťū/ offers a much simpler analysis. The same argument can be applied to the other mentioned combinations.

The same reasoning is, however, not possible in the case of /lēkařū/ *lékařů* and /pokojū/ *pokojů* which contain an inter-nuclear sonant. If /ť/ in /zeťū/ cannot stand the end of a phonotagm due to neutralization of voicing, then the sonants /j/ and /ř/ can do so (cf. /māj/ *máj* and /keř/ *keř*), and so it is possible to analyze PhFs of the given words into /lēK–kař–ū/ and /poK–koj–ū/. Hence, they do not, strictly speaking, provide evidence that /jē/, /řū/ and /jū/ are possible combinations within one phonotagm, but lacking any indication of the opposite, we do not find it appropriate to introduce a distributional rule which declares /řū/ and /jū/ impossible. Doing so requires that we can single out a unique property that either the phonemes /j/ and /ř/, or the phonemes /ē/ and /ū/ have in common, and which, in both cases, are not shared by other phonemes. We cannot think of any. Furthermore, there is some evidence that at least /jū/ is possible, namely in /jūlinka/ *Jůlinka* (proper name). Note also that /jē/ is attested /jēgroFki/ *jégrovky* (obsolete according to SSJČ).

Figure II further shows that the combinations /ťē/, /ťō/, /ďē/, /ďō/, /šō/,[3] /ňē/, /ňō/ and /řō/ are also not found. The absence of /ťē/, /ťō/, /ďē/, /ďō/, /ňē/ and /ňō/

---

3   Unless we accept *kapišónek* (SSJČ) with the phonotagm /šōn/ or *šógun* (ASCS) with /šō/.

	/ĕ/	/ä/	/ö/
/p/	terapeut	pauza	pouta
/b/		bauxit	bouda
/f/	feudál	fauna	foukat
/v/			vousy
/m/		mauzoleum	mouka
/t/	(Teuton)	tautologie	touha
/d/	deuterium	(Poldauf)	doufat
/s/		sauna	soud
/z/	zeugma	tezaurus	zout se
/n/	neuron	nausea	nouze
/t'/			šťouchat
/ď/		ďaur	slaďoučký
/š/		(Šaur)	šourek
/ž/			lžou
/ň/			kňour
/k/		kauce	koule
/g/		gauner	kolegou
/x/		(Dachau)	choutky
/h/	heuristika	hausbót	houba
/j/			(Jouza)
/ř/			dřou
/r/		raut	roura
/l/	leukémie	laureát	louka

FIGURE III: Attested 'CV' combinations with a diphthongal vowel

	/r/	/l/
/p/	prst	plsť
/b/	brk	blb
/f/	frnknout	troufl
/v/	vrch	vlk
/m/	–	–
/t/	trn	pletl
/d/	drť	vedl
/s/	srp	slza
/z/	zrno	vezl
/t'/	–	–
/ď/	–	–
/š/	(Kutlvašr)	(Litomyšl)
/ž/	plunžr	(Pížl)
/ň/	–	–
/k/	krk	klk
/g/	bagr	triangl
/x/	chrt	uprchl
/h/	hrb	hlt
/j/	–	–
/ř/	–	–
/r/	–	–
/l/		–
/M/	mrkat	mlž

FIGURE IV: Attested 'CV' combinations with a semiconsonant

is of particular interest. Such combinations have not even been found word-internally, which means that there is no evidence whatsoever for their well-formedness. We conclude they are impossible and introduce the following simple collocational restriction (a palatal non-fricative being a palatal occlusive and a palatal nasal):

(2)   A long mid vowel (i.e. /ē/, /ō/) cannot be preceded by a palatal non-fricative.

No such restriction can be introduced for the missing /šō/ and /řō/ because /š/ and /ř/ do not constitute any well-defined class either with /t'/, /ď/, /ň/ or with each other (i.e. they have phonologically nothing in common). Consequently, their absence is regarded as accidental.

Let us now move to the diphthongal vowels. Their ability to combine with pre-nuclear phonemes is shown in figure III.[4] The combinability is quite limited, though these limitations concern mostly /ë/ and /ä/ which, diachronically speaking, were introduced to Czech relatively recently through loan words, whereas /ö/ arose through regular development of Czech from Common Slavic. But facts like these should not have any bearings on a synchronic analysis.

A more serious problem is with /ë/, realized as [ɛu̯]. In the Czech orthography this sound is spelled as *eu*. However, not every *eu* sequence is pronounced as the [ɛu̯] diphthong. Elsewhere, it is pronounced as two syllables, [ɛ.u] (e.g. in *muzeum*, phonologically /muzeum/, not /muzëm/). In some other cases there is apparently free variation between the monosyllabic and disyllabic pronunciation (and hence between /ë/ and /eu/), though *eu* is probably always pronounced monosyllabically in some words (e.g. in *euro*).[5] Unfortunately, the latter cannot be said about the words included in figure III because all of them may be pronounced both with monosyllabic or disyllabic *eu*. Due to these problems, it is difficult to draw conclusions from the figure. Yet there is at least one apparent restriction on the combinability of /ë/ with palatals; no palatal has been found before this vowel, which may simply be a consequence of the fact that no word has been borrowed from a language where such a combination occurs. Since the other two diphthongal vowels combine with palatals, we have decided not to introduce any collocational restriction here.

Finally, the combinability of the nuclear semiconsonants /r/ and /l/ will be examined. Figure IV provides examples of words where they are preceded by a PerP. The words *troufl, pletl, vedl, vezl, Kutlvašr, Litomyšl, plunžr* (SSJČ), *Pížl, bagr, triangl* and *uprchl* are analyzed in the same way as *zeťů* discussed above; see also §10.2 on the phonotagm-final nuclear /r/, /l/. The combinations /šl/, /šr/ and /žl/ have only been found in proper names such as *Litomyšl, Kutlvašr* and *Pížl*. The nuclear semiconsonants cannot be preceded by /m/, /n/, /ň/ because of neutralization of place of articulation for the nasals—they are preceded by /M/ instead. They are also not preceded by /ť/, /ď/, which is already encoded in the DU. They cannot combine with /ř/ (see §11.2). Finally, /rr/ and /ll/ are impossible because Czech does not allow geminates (see §9.2). The dash is also used for combinations with /j/ because these are impossible because a nuclear semiconsonant cannot be followed by /j/ (see §12.2)

---

4   See above on *zeťů* for the argument behind the analysis of *terapeut, sladoučký, kolegou, Poldauf* and *Dachau*. The words *Teuton, Poldauf, Šaur, Dachau* and *Jouza* are proper names. The combination /ňä/ has only been found in the onomatopoeic expression *mňau*, and /jä/ only in onomatopoeic *jau*; they are not included in the table.

5   This seems to be true for all words beginning with *eu*.

	/i/	/e/	/a/	/o/	/u/
/P/	hřib	sklep	chlap	strop	strup
/F/	vliv	lev	splav	kov	smluv
/m/	podzim	lem	klam	strom	rum
/T/	byt	let	plat	plot	prut
/S/	lis	les	klas	kos	kus
/n/	syn	ven	stan	slon	kun
/Ť/	sviť	teď	lať	hoď	chuť
/Š/	myš	lež	až	koš	kuš
/ň/	zhyň	změň	dlaň	jabloň	fuň
/K/	smyk	vlek	lak	mlok	kluk
/X/	zdvih	mech	strach	hloh	pluh
/j/	pij	rej	kraj	kroj	sluj
/ř/	miř	keř	vař	oř	nekuř
/r/	sekyr	per	dar	mor	chmur
/l/	myl	měl	kal	kol	mul

FIGURE V: Attested 'VC' combinations with a short vowel

16.2 'VC' combinations

This section discusses combinations of the nuclear phonemes with single post-nuclear phonemes. The combinability with the short vowels is quite straightforward because all combinations are attested; see figure V. However, the combinability of the long vowels is not so neat—see figure VI. There are several missing combinations, but failing to find any regularity behind them, we conclude they are missing by accidence. The words *gróf*, *takéť*, *čikóš* are archaic according to SSJŠ. The PhF /drūPki/ (i.e. *drůbky*) must be analyzed into /drūP/ and /ki/ because /Pk/ is not a possible pre-nuclear combination.

In comparison with the short and the long ones, the diphthongal vowels are quite defective in their co-occurrence with post-nuclear phonemes; see figure VII (see p. 268). The most defective is again /ë/: we are aware of only two words where it is followed by a single PerP, namely *terapeut*[6] and *eur* (gen. pl. of *euro*). Since it is not possible to tell why out of all PerPs only /T/ and /r/ could follow /ë/, the absence of the other 'VC' combinations is regarded as accidental—with one important exception to be given presently. Similarly, the gaps in the combinations with /ä/ are accidental because no regularity can be discerned. The words *šturmhaub*, *lauf* and *šlauch* are slightly archaic or colloquial, but they might be included (all are listed in SSJČ). The word *Rosenbaum* is a proper name.

---

6   Provided that it is pronounced as [tɛrapɛu̯t], not as [tɛrapɛ.ut] (see Romportl et al. 1978).

	/ī/	/ē/	/ā/	/ō/	/ū/
/P/	cíp	chléb	dráp	rób	drůbky
/F/	dřiv	chlév	páv	gróf	sův
/m/	vím	krém	rám	dóm	dům
/T/	mít	portrét	vát	kód	úd
/S/	peníz	fréz	vás	próz	vůz
/n/	vín	fén	pán	tón	trůn
/Ť/	piď	takéť	záď		
/Š/	výš	též	náš	čikóš	nůž
/ň/	skřiň		stráň		tůň
/K/	vík	lék	mák	jóg	
/X/	líh		hrách		bůh
/j/	šíj		ráj	gój	svůj
/ř/	uhlíř	bankéř	lhář		hůř
/r/	výr	pér	pár	pór	dvůr
/l/	víl	podél	sál	pól	půl

FIGURE VI: Attested 'VC' combinations with a long vowel

The exception we have alluded to is the absence of the combinations with /j/ running through all diphthongal vowels, which can be generalized in this collocational restriction (compare it against /a/ in /kraj/ *kraj* or /ā/ in /rāj/ *ráj*):

(3)   A diphthongal vowel cannot be followed by /j/.

Finally, figure VIII (reproduced on the next page) examplifies the ability of the nuclear semiconsonants to combine with post-nuclear phonemes. They cannot regularly be followed by /ř/ and /j/. The combinations /rr/ and /ll/ are again impossible because Czech does not allow geminates. The absence of the other combinations is accidental. See §10.2 on the word *umrlce*.

16.3 Combinability of nuclear phonemes with peripheral combinations

If the combinability of the nuclear phonemes with single PerPs could be relatively easily described, the situation is more complicated with peripheral combinations. It is difficult to examine their combinability in the same manner, that is, to find out whether each and every peripheral combination can co-occur with each and every nuclear phoneme because there are as much as 442 pre-nuclear combinations and 104 post-nuclear combinations (marginal combinations in-

	/ë/	/ä/	/ö/
/P/		šturmhaub	sloup
/F/		lauf	houf
/m/		(Rosenbaum)	
/T/	terapeut	aut	pout
/S/		aplaus	vous
/n/		klaun	letoun
/ř/			pout'
/Š/		flauš	souš
/ň/			letouň
/K/			brouk
/X/		šlauch	rouch
/j/	–	–	–
/ř/			kouř
/r/	eur	aur	kocour
/l/		aul	kotoul

	/r/	/l/
/P/	vrb	blb
/F/	ponejprv	
/m/	hrm	
/T/	chrt	hlt
/S/	prs	slz
/n/	trn	vln
/ř/	vrt'	pohlt'
/Š/	strž	plž
/ň/	vrň	plň
/K/	krk	vlk
/X/	vrch	plch
/j/	–	–
/ř/	–	–
/r/		–
/l/	umrlce	–

FIGURE VII: Attested 'VC' combinations with a diphthongal vowel

FIGURE VIII: Attested 'VC' combinations with a semiconsonant

cluded). Some are attested only before one particular nuclear phoneme like /FSkvj/ attested only before /e/ in *vzkvět* or /Kt/ only before /e/ in *který*; the same is true for post-nuclear combinations, e.g. /PST/ is attested only after /ä/ in *zábst*. Tables demonstrating this type of combinability would not only run through many pages, but would also contain many gaps. Such absences must be accidental in many cases, yet they are sometimes governed by regular collocational restrictions (see below). As argued in §5.4, in order to determine whether a certain non-occurrence is regular, we must find out whether it pertains to some well-defined class of entities or features.

We have failed to discern any restriction affecting the co-occurrence of the short vowels with pre-nuclear combinations, by which we conclude that any short vowel has the capacity to be preceded by any pre-nuclear combination. It is supported by two facts. One is that any short vowel can be preceded by any single PerP (see above). The other is a fact mentioned in §10.1, namely that the short vowels can be preceded by any number of PerPs (but, of course, only up to five of them). The only exception is combinations of type 'NO' which cannot occur before any vowel (such combinations are possible before nuclear semiconsonants, cf. /Mkl/ *mkl*, 3rd person sg. form of *mknouti* (SSJČ); see §13.6).

On the other hand, the combinability of the long vowels with pre-nuclear combinations is limited by several collocational restrictions. It follows from the restriction introduced above under (2) that the long mid vowels /ē/, /ō/ cannot be preceded by any pre-nuclear combination ending in a palatal non-nasal (e.g. by /Křť/, /FSď/, /šň/). Having examined the constituency of PhFs of Czech words, we may introduce another restriction limiting the combinability of the palatals ('P') and /j/ with the long vowels, but also with the diphthongal vowels ('C_n' is any number of PerPs):

(4) (a) A non-short vowel cannot be preceded by a combination of type 'C_nCP'.

(b) A non-short vowel cannot be preceded by a combination of type 'C_nCC$_1$' where 'C_1' is /j/.

The consequence is that the long and diphthongal vowels cannot be preceded by combinations like /FSď/, /Spj/, /zMň/, /FSkvj/, whereas the short vowels have this capacity. The combinability of the long vowels is further restricted by a fact already mentioned in §10.1: They cannot be preceded by more than four PerPs. Similarly, the diphthongal vowels cannot be preceded by more than three PerPs (see again §10.1).

In comparison with the vowels, the ability of nuclear /r/, /l/ to be preceded by pre-nuclear combinations is very limited. They cannot be preceded by five pre-nuclear phonemes, which is already encoded in the DU. Many other restrictions are deducible from the DU, too, and also from the restrictions which hold for /r/, /l/ in general. In §10.2 it was mentioned that the word-final nuclear semiconsonants were not preceded by three or more PerPs, although they have this capacity when not being final (cf. /TŠtvrT/ *čtvrt*). Some restrictions pertaining to the nuclear semiconsonants were already mentioned in previous chapters. Several other restrictions can be introduced once we return to the properties of peripheral combinations discussed in chapter 13. We mentioned there which types of peripheral combinations were attested to occur before or after a nuclear semiconsonant, but we did not discuss them in detail. We would like to pay this dept here and to introduce several collocational restrictions:

(5) (a) A nuclear semiconsonant cannot stand in close proximity with a combination of type 'OO'.

(b) A nuclear semiconsonant cannot be preceded by a combination of types 'CCN' and 'CCCN'.[7]

(c) A nuclear semiconsonant cannot be preceded by a combination of type 'LP'.

(d) A nuclear semiconsonant cannot be preceded by a combination of type 'KP'.

---

7   It does not hold for dialectal words such as *čmrkat* "to scribble" containing /TšM/.

(e) A nuclear semiconsonants cannot be preceded by a combination of type 'KA'.

These restrictions can be compared to vowels for which they do not hold. In contrast to (5a) the vowels are preceded and followed by two occlusives ('OO'; cf. /TkāT/ *tkát* or /SkriPT/ *skript*). Let us add that the nuclear semiconsonants cannot also be preceded by a combination of type 'ON', whereas vowels can (cf. /tma/ *tma*); this was already pointed out in §13.4. Furthermore, as the restriction under (5b) says, the semiconsonants cannot be preceded by a nasal ('N') which is itself preceded by two or three other PerPs; the vowels have this capacity (cf. /TšňīT/ *čnít* and /lStmi/ *lstmi*). Finally, the semiconsonants cannot be followed by a labial ('L') + a palatal ('P'), by a velar ('K') + a palatal, and by a velar + an alveolar ('A'), whereas the vowels are followed by such combinations (cf. /hiPŠ/ *Hybš* (surname), /jaKŠtaKŠ/ *jakžtakž*, /faKT/ *fakt*, respectively).

We will now move to the ability of the nuclear phonemes to co-occur with post-nuclear combinations. We have not been able to discern any restriction limiting the combinability of the short and long vowels. This conclusion must be confronted with claims made by Trnka (1961), who is one of the few to consider the distribution of vowel length in Czech.[8] On examining occurrences and co-occurrences of the long vowels in Czech words, he (*op. cit.*: 12) made the following observations (Trnka's terminology and transcription are retained):

(6) (a) Long vowels do not occur before homomorphemic consonant clusters other than *st, sť, sk, zd, zď, šť, žď, tr, tř, dr, dř, rt, rť, mň*.
     (b) Long vowels are non-occurrent in the first syllable of disyllabic morphemes.
     (c) When in homomorphemic hiatus, vowels are only short.
     (d) The opposition *i|í* and *u|ú* is neutralized before *j* and before the tautosyllabic *m*.

Although Trnka's claims are confirmed by examples he gave, they are all dubious except for the claim under (6a). As regards (6d), the oppositions /i/ × /ī/ and /u/ × /ū/ can indeed be neutralized in the mentioned environments (cf. Krčmová 2008: 135, 137, 200), but this phenomenon is not regarded to be orthoepic, and the length is required to be retained in Standard Czech (Palková 1997: 264, 323, Zeman 2008: 36).

---

8   The distribution of the length of Czech vowels has also been discussed in reference to certain types of words and their derivatives (see Bethin 2003a, 2003b, Scheer 2001, 2003, 2004, and Sukač 2013). However, the distribution seems to be conditioned grammatically rather than phonologically in this case.

The dubiousness of Trnka's other claims stems from his references to *homomorphemic clusters, disyllabic morphemes* and *homomorphemic hiatus*. As already pointed out in §16.1, whether something belongs to one or to two morphemes must be decided, in the first place, on morphological criteria, not on phonological ones. Morphological boundaries can be phonologically signaled, but it is the morphological analysis that tells us what kind of morphological units the phonological signals mark or whether the marked boundaries are boundaries of morphological units at all. But even if we employed morphological criteria, we would still have to make recourse to the history of Czech to find out whether some words contain a morphological boundary and others not. Synchronically speaking, it is hardly possible to say that *základ* "basis" contains two morphemes *zá* and *klad* or that *vážka* "dragon-fly" is built of *váž* and *ka*;[9] words like these thus contradict the claim (6a). It is also contradicted by *úct*, gen. pl. of *úcta* or by *půjč*, imper. sg. of *půjčit*. Even if the list of the exceptional combinations mentioned under (6a) were extended to contain some more such as *kl*, *ct* or *jč*, it would still be of no avail. The rule is simply not valid in present-day Czech, at least in this form.[10]

Similarly, it is hardly possible to maintain that *důvod* "reason" or *kámen* "stone" contain synchronically two morphemes. Therefore, the claim (6b) cannot be valid, either. Finally, the claim (6c) can only be valid provided that we know where a morphological boundary falls (i.e. that there is a morphological boundary in *abbéové* "abbots" or *třietapový* "three-period") or provided that the words *příušnice* "mumps" and *náušnice* "earrings" can be synchronically shown to contain a morphological boundary between *pří* and *ušnice* and *ná* and *ušnice*; the fact that both words are associated with and were originally derived from *uši* "ears" does not mean they contain, synchronically, any such morpheme.

The bottom line is that the claims under (6) have no validity in our description. Ergo, the combinability of the long vowels does not seem to be limited in any obvious way in Czech, though the issue still requires further investigation. Nevertheless, the combinability of the diphthongal vowels is limited: They cannot be followed by /j/, which means that they cannot also be followed any post-nuclear combination where /j/ stands in close proximity with them. Aside from this, however, we have not been able to discern any other restriction.

The ability of nuclear /r/, /l/ to be followed by post-nuclear combinations is subject to many restrictions. Like the diphthongal vowels, they cannot be fol-

---

9   *vážka* is ultimately derived from *váž-*, *váha* "weight", but this origin is utterly obscured in Modern Czech.

10   It is noteworthy that in Trnka (1982: 188), where Trnka (1961) is reprinted, the list of exceptions here reproduced under (6a) was reduced and does not include *šť* and *žď*.

lowed by /j/, hence they cannot be followed by any post-nuclear combination with /j/. They cannot be followed by two occlusives as mentioned earlier in this section. In addition, they are subject to the following new restriction: they cannot be followed by a nasal ('N') + a fricative ('F'), which is possible for vowels (cf. /nimF/ *nymf*).

(7)   A nuclear semiconsonant cannot be followed by a combination of type 'NF'.

16.4 'CVC' combinations

In this final section we explore 'C_1VC_2' combinations within single phonotagms in order to find out whether the selection of a PerP or a peripheral combination in the 'C_1' place affects the selection of a PerP or a peripheral combination in the 'C_2' place, and *vice versa*. Thus, strictly speaking, we will not deal with combinations of peripheral and nuclear phonemes, but with the interaction between pre-nuclear and post-nuclear phonemes and their combinations.

Until now it has been assumed that the pre-nuclear context and the post-nuclear context are mutually independent domains of distributions. It is arguably much easier to deal with the distribution and combinations of PerPs in such a way (which has in fact been a practice of many other linguists), but we must keep in mind that it is a hypothesis and not a fact. There may be and are languages where it is not so. For example, Hervey (1978) cites an example of Kamali Arabic where the occurrence of a consonantal combination in either the pre-nuclear or the post-nuclear context precludes the occurrence of a consonantal combination in the other context. So, whereas the phonotagms like /nmal/ and /malx/[11] are well-formed in this language, the form /nmalx/ is not because a vowel cannot be both preceded and followed by a consonantal combination. Similar examples could no doubt be found in other languages, though there are usually rather tendencies to avoid certain combinations than strict restrictions (cf. Davis – Baertsch 2011). For example, Cairns (1988) discusses several pan-syllabic constraints (as he calls them) limiting the co-occurrence of pre-nuclear combinations and post-nuclear combinations in English. Earlier, Fudge (1969: 279ff.) mentioned that English avoids syllables both beginning and ending with combinations containing /l/ or /r/ (the first violated by *flail*), and the very same tendency has been cited for Norwegian (Vogt 1942: 22). Similarly, German and Swedish tend to avoid syllables both beginning and ending with /r/, /l/, /m/ or /n/ (Twaddell 1940–41: 41, Sigurd 1958: 47). To the best of our knowledge, the

---

11   These are phonological forms of words with the meaning "to be fed-up with" and "to cause damage to", respectively.

same thing has not been examined for Czech, and it is the purpose of this section to pay the debt—at least partly because we will not be primarily interested in whether there is some tendency in Czech words to avoid a certain 'CVC' combination, that is, whether some combinations are more frequent than the others, but whether such combinations are possible at all.

Figures IX and X (see the next two pages)[12] provide examples of words in which a given 'CVC' combination occurs. Note that the choice of the nuclear phoneme is irrelevant here except for the rows with the nasal archi-phoneme /M/ which appears only before nuclear semiconsonants. The combinations /M_j/ and /M_ř/ in which a nuclear semiconsonant is preceded by /M/ and followed by /j/ or /ř/ are impossible due to the restrictions introduced in the previous section.

When compiling the tables, we have first attempted to find a word with a PhF corresponding exactly to a given 'CVC' combination; the majority of such words have been found. If not, we have looked for words where a given combination occurs, but where one of the PerPs is further preceded or followed by another PerP. Thus, /lvūF/ *lvův* attests the combinability of the pre-nuclear /v/ and the post-nuclear /F/ because there is no reason to think a word with the PhF /vūF/ is impossible in Czech. All these words have a mono-phonotagmic PhF. However, some 'CVC' combinations have only been found in words with poly-phonotagmic PhFs. For example, the combination of the pre-nuclear /f/ and the post-nuclear /F/ is found in *šéfův*.[13] If its PhF /šēfūF/ is to be analyzed into individual phonotagms, the second of them is /fūF/ because the medial /f/ must be assigned to the second. The same holds for several other combinations: *xenofob* containing /foP/, *doufáš* containing /fāŠ/, *marketingář* (SN1) containing /gāř/, *cukrář* containing /rář/, and others. The PhF /přiřTšeno/ (*přiřčeno*) attests /řiř/ because it is not possible to divide it into /při-řTšeno/, /řTš/ not being a possible pre-nuclear combination (/ř/ would have to occur here in 'pre2', not in 'pre1' where it belongs). Similarly with /jiřSkī/ *jiřský* (SSJČ): the only possible analysis is /jiř–Skī/. A little problematic is the word *pravděpodobně* whose PhF /praFďepodobňe/ might contain the phonotagm /ďeP/ showing the combination /ď_P/ is possible. We are aware of no other example, and there is no reason not to accept it. Finally, several combinations seem to occur only in proper names such

---

12 A few notes to the tables: The word *váb* is poetic accordingly to SSJČ. /ď_P/ is attested only in *pravděpodobně*. The word *nán* is gen. pl. of *nána*. /ď_ň/ is also attested in the place name *Bdin*, and /š_ň/ also in the place name *Všeň*. /g_ř/ is attested probably only *marketingář*. /x_j/ is also attested in the vulgarism *chuj*. The word *mln* is gen. pl. of *mlna* (SSJČ). Finally, the combination /Mrl/ is attested in /umrlTse/ (see §10.2). For the other empty cells, no example has been found. Many words in the tables are in genitive plural forms or in the imperative singular forms.

13 There is also a surname *Foff*, i.e. /foF/.

	/P/	/F/	/T/	/S/	/Ř/	/Š/	/K/	/X/
/p/	pop	páv	pot	pas	pouť	piš	puk	puch
/b/	bab	byv	bot	bos	buď	buš	bok	bůh
/f/	xenofob	šéfův	fit	fis	foť	doufáš	fík	foch
/v/	váb	lvův	vod	vaz	voď	výš	vak	vah
/m/	map	domov	mít	maz	meť	myš	mák	much
/t/	tep	tav	tát	tas	teď	tuž	tak	tah
/d/	dob	dav	dát	dóz	vždyť	dáš	dek	duh
/s/	sob	sov	sít	(Sas)	síť	suš	sok	sáh
/z/	zub	název	zad	zas	záď	vozíš	vozík	vrazích
/n/	neb	nov	nad	nás	nať	nůž	nok	nach
/ť/	vtip	návštěv	tít	tis	štiť	tíž	tik	tíh
/ď/	see text	div	dít	děs		díž	dík	zdích
/š/	šíp	šéf	šat	šos	šeď	koušeš	šik	šach
/ž/	žup	živ	žít	úžas	složitě	lžeš	žok	žeh
/ň/	hňup	niv	nit	kněz	niť	niž	vznik	nich
/k/	kup	kov	kat	kaz	káď	kuš	skok	řekách
/g/	(Egypt)	kolegův	fregat	vágus	fregatě	langoš	pedagog	ligách
/x/	chyb	chov	chod	chas	choď	chýš	(Machek)	plochých
/h/	hub	háv	had	has	hať	jehož	hák	hoch
/j/	(Jób)	jev	jít	jas	jeď	již	jak	jich
/ř/	řep	řev	řád	říz	řiť	řež	řek	hřich
/r/	ryb	rév	rád	ráz	raď	růž	rak	roh
/l/	líp	lev	let	les	leť	lež	lok	lih
/M/		mrv	smrdutý	mls	mrť	mlž	mrkat	mlh

FIGURE IX: Examples of words where 'CVC' combinations are attested

as *Machek* attesting /xeK/, *Jób* attesting /jōP/, *Sas* attesting /saS/,[14] *Lštěň* attesting /ťeň/, and *Kníř* attesting /ňīř/. Although these words only provide indirect evidence, they suggest that the respective 'CVC' combinations are possible in Czech.

Empty cells in figures IX and X mean that no such 'CVC' combination has been found. It holds for /ď_Ť/, /ď_ň/, /ň_ň/, /j_ň/, /ř_r/, /r_r/, /M_P/ and /M_r/ (the last two refer to the situation when a nuclear semiconsonant is preceded by /M/ and followed by /P/ or /ř/). The question we should now ask is whether their absence can be regularized or whether they are missing by accident. Having found no regularity, we assume the latter. Moreover, /ď_Ť/ could be attested in /ďīťe/ if we analyze it as /ďīŤ–ťe/ with functional amalgamation. Similarly, /ď_ň/ could occur in /hoďiňe/ *hodině* if we analyzed it as /hoŤ–ďiň–ňe/; /ň_ň/ in

---

14   Unless we accept *ses*, a variant of *se* with -*s* shortened from *jsi*.

	/m/	/n/	/ň/	/j/	/ř/	/r/	/l/
/p/	*pum*	*pán*	*peň*	*pyj*	*spoř*	*par*	*pel*
/b/	*bomb*	*bon*	*báň*	*boj*	*boř*	*bor*	*bol*
/f/	*fám*	*fén*	*fuň*	*trofej*	*šafář*	*fór*	*faul*
/v/	*vám*	*ven*	*voň*	*voj*	*vař*	*vor*	*val*
/m/	*mám*	*min*	*míň*	*máj*	*miř*	*mor*	*mír*
/t/	*tam*	*ten*	*tůň*	*taj*	*čtyř*	*tur*	*týl*
/d/	*dám*	*den*	*daň*	*dej*	*dař*	*dar*	*dál*
/s/	*sám*	*sen*	*saň*	*sej*	*tesař*	*sýr*	*sel*
/z/	*zem*	*zón*	*vězeň*	*zuj*	*zář*	*vzor*	*zel*
/n/	*nám*	*nán*	*naň*	*hnůj*	*snář*	*nor*	*nul*
/t'/	*tím*	*stín*	*(Lštěň)*	*chtěj*	*rytíř*	*štír*	*těl*
/d'/	*dím*	*hodin*		*děj*	*hmoždíř*	*děr*	*děl*
/š/	*šum*	*výšin*	*vášeň*	*šij*	*šíř*	*šár*	*šel*
/ž/	*lžim*	*žen*	*žeň*	*žij*	*lyžař*	*žer*	*žal*
/ň/	*ním*	*(Knín)*		*něj*	*(Kniř)*	*knír*	*snil*
/k/	*kým*	*kin*	*kůň*	*kyj*	*keř*	*kur*	*kal*
/g/	*gum*	*gen*	*kolegyň*	*reaguj*	see text	*figur*	*gel*
/x/	*uchem*	*tchán*	*kuchyň*	*nechej*	*tchoř*	*chýr*	*chyl*
/h/	*jhem*	*han*	*hoň*	*háj*	*hoř*	*her*	*hol*
/j/	*jím*	*jen*		*jej*	*jiřský*	*jer*	*jel*
/ř/	*třem*	*křen*	*dřeň*	*hřej*	*přiřčeno*		*přál*
/r/	*rám*	*ran*	*roň*	*ráj*	*cukrář*		*ryl*
/l/	*lom*	*lan*	*laň*	*lej*	*sklář*	*lir*	*lil*
/M/	*mrmlat*	*mln*	*mrně*	–	–		*umrlce*

FIGURE X: Continuation of figure IX

/koňiňe/ *konině* (i.e. /koň–ňiň–ňe/); /j_ň/ in /jiňí/ *jiní* (i.e. /jiň–ňí/); /ř_r/ in /přiroda/ *příroda* (i.e. /přīr–roT–da/); /r_r/ in /erár/ *erár* (i.e. /er–rār/). Admittedly, such analyzes are doubtful exactly because there is no evidence such phonotagms are possible in Czech. At the same time, however, there is no indication of the opposite, so we will assume that they are possible. In contrast, the combinations /M_j/ and /M_ř/ are impossible because a nuclear semiconsonant cannot be followed by /j/ or /ř/ (see §12.2 and §12.3).

Thus, to sum it up, there is no restriction on the combinability of the pre-nuclear and post-nuclear phonemes within a phonotagm. In the combination 'C₁VC₂' the occurrence of a single 'C₁' does not limit or determine the occurrence of a single 'C₂' and the other way round: the occurrence of a single 'C₂' does not limit or determine the occurrence of a single 'C₁'. Something else is preferences. It is obvious that Czech prefers to avoid the combinations /d'_Ť/, /d'_ň/, /ň_ň/, /j_ň/, /ř_r/, /r_r/, which have not been directly found, and also the combinations /t'_ň/, /ň_n/, /ň_ř/, /x_K/, /g_P/, /j_P/, which have only been found in symbols (such as proper or place names). Some other combinations are furthermore little frequent, especially those involving /g/ and /f/ or combinations involving the same phonemes (e.g. /n_n/, /l_l/).

So far, we have purposely talked about single 'C₁' and 'C₂' because the situation is different with peripheral combinations. First of all, it is obvious that if, for example, the combination /ň_n/ has not been found, then there is no phonotagm containing a pre-nuclear combination ending in /ň/ (such as /Fzň/) and a post-nuclear combination beginning with /n/ (such as /nK/), that is, there is no phonotagm like /FzňenK/. However, it does not necessarily mean that it is not possible. The point is to find out whether certain types of pre-nuclear combinations cannot occur with certain types of post-nuclear combinations. One such important regularity was already noted in §8.1: No phonotagm in Czech can contain more than six non-vowel phonemes. It follows from it that if a nuclear phoneme is preceded by a four-phoneme combination, it cannot be followed by a three-phoneme combination because phonotagms of type 'CCCCVCCC' are impossible due to the mentioned restriction. Likewise, if a nuclear phoneme is preceded by a five-phoneme combination, it cannot be followed by two or more PerPs because phonotagms of types 'CCCCCVCC' and 'CCCCCVCCC' are also impossible due to that restriction. If the nucleus of a phonotagm is a nuclear semiconsonant, which is a non-vowel, the co-occurrence of pre-nuclear and post-nuclear combinations is even more limited. If a semiconsonant is preceded by a four-phoneme combination, then it can only be followed by one post-nuclear phoneme. If it is preceded by a three-phoneme combination, it can be followed by up to two phonemes and so on.

Chapter Seventeen: CONCLUSION

The purpose of this final chapter is to supplement and justify the analysis presented in our book. Basically, we have dealt with two areas: the occurrence of
phonemes in Czech, and their combinations. This book is not the only description of these areas, but it has strived to overcome the existing analyses. In the
second area our analysis excels over the others in providing a more detailed and
comprehensive account of phoneme combinability in Czech. And in what follows we want to show that even in the first area our analysis has advantages over
the other accounts. There is actually only one comparable alternative: Henry
Kučera's description of the occurrence of Czech phonemes within the syllable.
Published in 1961 in his book *The Phonology of Czech*, it has gained currency
and been referred to both by domestic and foreign linguists. In the next section
we briefly outline his analysis and point out its problems. Besides the brevity
and lack of detail, Kučera's analysis suffers from the methodological perspective. In §17.2 we offer an alternative analysis of phonotagms inspired by Kučera's approach, and in §17.3 we justify why we have not chosen such an approach and based our analysis of the notion of DU. Finally, we will show how
our model can used for the calculation of potential combinations, which is something Kučera's model is not capable or at least the capacity is much limited.

17.1 Kučera's analysis of the syllable in Czech

Kučera bases his phonotactic description on the syllable which he, following
Haugen (1956b), defines as "the smallest unit of recurrent phonemic sequences
which makes it possible to describe the distribution of segmental phonemes and
configurative phonemic entities [roughly: suprasegmental features] most eco-
nomically" (1961: 71–2). In the 1961 book he does not provide any guidelines
how the syllable is to be analyzed or how its structure is to be determined, but
the procedure is outlined in Kučera – Monroe (1968: 41): the syllable is a constituent of a microsegment (see below), and "[t]he minimum requirement for a
phonological syllable is that it contain a *syllabic nucleus* which serves [...] as
the center of stress and of intonational levels". However, despite giving such a
definition, Kučera does not follow it or if he does, his analysis seems to be circular. First of all, the center of stress and of intonational levels is of course the syl-

lable nucleus, which makes the definition circular. Secondly, /r/ and /l/ are nuclear even in unstressed environments (e.g. in *vítr* and *vedl*, the stress being on
the first syllable); and nuclear /m/, which Kučera also operates with, is never
found under stress (actually, it is found only in *sedm* and *osm* and their derivatives and a couple of proper names).[1] Moreover, as we showed in §10.2, /r/ and
/l/ must be obligatorily preceded by a consonant if they are to be nuclear. It is
not certain how Kučera would deal or dealt with these issues, and his analysis is
thus both vague and methodologically dubious.

The syllable is a constituent of a microsegment which roughly equates with
the PhF of a word. The agreement is not absolute because Kučera recognizes so-
called isolated consonantal microsegments /s/, /z/, /v/, /vz/ and /k/ which are not
part of the syllable and constitute pre-syllabic segments. They correspond to the
prepositions *s* "with", *z* "from", *v* "in" and *k* "to" *as well as* to the prefixes *s-, z-,
v-, vz-* and *k-*. While the treatment of the prepositions as a special phonotactic
category is justified in Czech (see the discussion in §5.3), the separation of the
prefixes is unwarranted. Kučera does not explain when the word-initial *s-, z-, v-*
and *k-* are prefixes and when they are part of the root because in many cases this
can only be decided when we know the origin of the word.[2] Although a synchronic morphological analysis may recognize such prefixes (e.g. in *smýt* "to
wash off" × *mýt* "to wash"), there are words in which the prefix is identifiable
only diachronically, that is, such combinations are synchronically unanalyzable.
One example is *smilovat* "to have mercy" as opposed to *milovat* "to love". Both
are historically derived from the same base, i.e. the initial *s* is historically a prefix, but synchronically hardly any relation can be set between *smilovat* and *milovat*. Kučera's analysis is even more problematic in excluding the word-initial
vz- which used to be a productive suffix in older Czech but which is no longer
productive in Modern Czech. In some cases it could perhaps be synchronically
identified as a prefix, e.g. in *vzbudit* "to wake up" × *budit* "to wake", but in
words like *vzdor* "defiance", *vzpoura* "mutiny" or *vztek* "anger" such an analysis
is possible only diachronically (for example, *vztek* is related to *téci* "to flow").

It is not clear how Kučera would analyze the words mentioned in the preceding paragraph, but we may expect that at least *smyl* (past tense of *smýt* "to
wash off") will have a different phonotactic structure than *smil* (a kind of plants
of the genus Helichrysum) despite the fact that they are pronounced identically
and contains the same phonemes. The word *smyl* will consist of the isolated con-

---

1   See §3.5 for reasons we do not operate with nuclear /m/.
2   Kučera marks the boundary between the microsegments /s/, /z/, /v/, /vz/, /k/ and the fol-
    lowing syllable by an internal disjuncture, but since, as he notes (p. 63), the disjuncture
    may be realized by zero, it cannot be used for discerning the boundary.

Onset				Peak	Coda		
O_{44}	O_{43}	O_{42}	O_{41}		C_{31}	C_{32}	C_{33}
	O_{33}	O_{32}	O_{31}	N	C_{21}	C_{22}	
		O_{22}	O_{21}	N_1N_2	C_{11}		
			O_{11}				

FIGURE I: Kučera's model of the syllable

sonantal microsegment /s/ (corresponding to the prefix s- in smyl) and the sylla-ble /mil/, whereas smil will consist of the syllable /smil/. In our analysis both have the same phonotactic structure, i.e. they correspond to the phonotagm /smil/, which is by far a more realistic and consistent analysis. On the other hand, Kučera's analysis of the vz- words is completely uncertain. For example, vztek might be either said to correspond to the isolated consonantal microseg-ment /vz/ + the syllable /tek/ or just the syllable /fstek/ (note that Kučera does not operate with neutralization of voicing). The choice between these analyses depends on whether the vz- portion is recognized as a prefix, which is doubtful. In our analysis, vztek corresponds unambiguously to one phonotagm /FSteK/. Besides the dubiousness of such an approach, Kučera's decision to separate the isolated consonantal microsegments /s/, /z/, /v/, /vz/ and /k/ is in addition arbi-trary. If he excludes these prefixes from the syllable, why does he not do the same with suffixes such as the infinitival -t as in zábst "to freeze"? We are not given an answer.

In Kučera's view the syllable is a bundle of positions just as our DU is, but his conception of the position is quite dissimilar to the one followed in this work. In order to make the comparison easier we will use the term place for the position in Kučera's sense. Now, a place (i.e. a position for Kučera) refers to relative placement of a phoneme within the syllable. He distinguishes between peak places, onset places and coda places, but since the places are relative, they are defined (and numbered) in reference to the number of phonemes within a syllable. Thus, when a syllable begins with one PerP, there is only one onset place; when it begins with two PerPs, there are two onset places and so on. Kučera posits as much as two peak places because he views diphthongs a com-binations of two vowels (for problems connected with this analysis, see §3.4). The largest onset has four places, and the largest coda contains three places.

The model of Kučera's syllable is reproduced in figure I. It has been adopted from Kučera (1961), but the numbering has been taken over from Kučera – Monroe (1968).[3] The places are indexed with a two-digit number in which the

---

3   In the 1961 book Kučera uses combinations of letters and numbers.

first digit refers to the length of a combination in which a phoneme belonging to that place occurs, and the second to the relative placement of the phoneme within that combination. For example, /l/ in /len/ *len* occurs in 'O_{11}', but in /hlen/ *hlen* it occurs in 'O_{21}'. The membership of the places is reproduced under (1). It should be remembered that we interpret the phonematic system of Czech differently from Kučera, so his phonemes are only remotely comparable to ours.

(1) MEMBERSHIP OF PLACES IN KUČERA'S MODEL (KUČERA 1961: 80)

(a) *Peak places*
'N' = all vowels + /r/, /l/, /m/
'N_1' = /e/, /a/, /o/
'N_2' = /u/

(b) *Onset places*
'O_{11}' = C (i.e. consonants) + /j/[4]
'O_{21}' = C – /g/
'O_{22}' = C – /ṭ/, /ḍ/, /n/, /ṇ/[5]
'O_{31}' = /p/, /t/, /ṭ/, /k/, /b/, /d/, /ḍ/, /h/, /m/, /n/, /ṇ/, /l/, /r/, /ř/, /v/, /j/
'O_{32}' = obstruents – /ṭ/, /ḍ/, /g/, /f/, /č/ + /m/, /ř/, /v/
'O_{33}' = obstruents – /p/, /ṭ/, /ḍ/, /g/ + /m/, /l/, /v/, /j/
'O_{41}' = /n/, /ṇ/, /r/, /ř/, /v/, /j/
'O_{42}' = /p/, /t/, /k/, /m/, /v/
'O_{43}' = /t/, /k/, /s/, /š/, /ř/
'O_{44}' = /p/, /t/, /f/, /s/, /h/, /m/, /j/

(c) *Coda places*
'C_{11}' = C[6]
'C_{21}' = obstruents – /ṭ/, /ḍ/, /č/ + (sonorants – /ṇ/) + /ř/, /v/
'C_{22}' = C – /r/, /j/
'C_{31}' = /k/, /p/, /g/, /b/, /m/, /n/, /r/, /j/
'C_{32}' = /k/, /s/, /š, /g/, /z/, /ž/
'C_{33}' = /t/, /k/, /s/, /d/, /g/, /z/

Kučera's syllable has only four onset places because the PhFs of *vzkvět* and *stkvěl*, which we have taken as evidence that Czech allows five-phoneme pre-nuclear combinations, are presumably interpreted as containing isolated conso-

---

4   /j/ is a semivowel for Kučera, for purely phonetic reasons.
5   /ṭ/, /ḍ/, /ṇ/ are palatal stops.
6   Although Kučera recognizes that the voicing difference is suspended in the coda, he in-
    cludes both voiceless and voiced consonants in the coda places because "this will later
    simplify the procedure for dividing interludes [i.e. intervocalic combinations] in codas
    and onsets" (1961: 80).

nantal microsegments. Thus, in his analysis a word (i.e. a microsegment) can begin with five consonants, but not a syllable. Another consequence of the exclusion of the isolated consonantal microsegments is that the membership of some places is reduced because certain phonemes occur there only in PhFs of prefixed words. For example, place 'O_{21}' is said to be occupied by all consonants except for /g/ because this phoneme is preceded by another consonant only in prefixed words (such as *zgalvanizovat*). Similarly, 'O_{31}' is said not to be occupied by /x/ (i.e. /x/ cannot be preceded by two consonants) because words like *vzchopit* are treated as containing an isolated consonantal microsegment which is not part of the syllable.

It may be argued that an advantage of Kučera's analysis is its ability to say that certain combinations are possible only in non-prefixed words and others only in prefixed words.[7] However, his analysis does only a half of this. Although it implies that syllables in non-prefixed words do not begin with five consonants, we are not told whether such combinations are possible in prefixed words. For instance, the analysis implies that /g/ cannot be preceded by a consonant or that /x/ cannot be preceded by two consonants in non-prefixed words, but no indication is given as to whether it is possible in prefixed words. Kučera's analysis is limited in this respect because although he supplements it with 26 rules restricting and generalizing the combinability of phonemes within the syllable (1961: 75–9), he notes that these constraints "do not apply across syllable boundaries and, consequently, across microsegment boundaries" (*op. cit.*: 80). Thus, besides being questionable from the methodological point of view, the exclusion of the isolated consonantal microsegments also considerably diminishes the adequacy of the analysis by not providing some important details.

17.2 Alternative analysis of phonotagms in Czech

Although Kučera's analysis is problematic, its basic idea has its worth. It starts from the assumption that self-contained phonotactic entities (be they called phonotagms or syllables) can be described upon a network of points where each of these points expresses the relative placement of the phoneme occurring there. It permits us to distinguish, for example, the class of PerPs which occur before a nuclear phoneme, and which are not preceded by any other PerP from the classes of PerPs which also occur before a nuclear phoneme, but which are at the same time preceded by one or two or three PerPs. One may expect, and Kučera's analysis confirms it for Czech, that the membership of these classes will not be

---

7   Our analysis does not do this because of the difficulties in determining whether something is synchronically a prefix or not.

Onset places					Peak places	Coda places		
O_{55}	O_{54}	O_{53}	O_{52}	O_{51}		C_{31}	C_{32}	C_{33}
	O_{44}	O_{43}	O_{42}	O_{41}	P_v	C_{21}	C_{22}	
		O_{33}	O_{32}	O_{31}	P_s	C_{11}		
			O_{22}	O_{21}				
				O_{11}				

FIGURE II: Kučera-inspired model of the phonotagm

the same and that the number of phonemes in these classes will decrease with the increase of the number of co-occurring phonemes. In this respect, Kučera's syllable model is superior to the DU because the latter does not readily provide information of this kind, although it can be inferred from phonotactic properties of particular phonemes tabulated in chapters 11 and 12. In order to compensate for this drawback, we offer an alternative, Kučera-inspired analysis of phonotagms in Czech, that is, an analysis based on the notion of place.

Figure II schematizes the alternative model. It contains as much as five onset places, one peak place and as much as three coda places. Commentaries on the membership of the places follow. The digits again indicate the relative placement of a phoneme in a combination of a given length.

Peak places
'P_v' = all vowels
'P_s' = /r/, /l/

Two types of peak place are distinguished for convenience: 'P_v' occupied by vowels, and 'P_s' occupied by semiconsonants. The distinction is useful because the nuclear semiconsonants can only be preceded by four PerPs, so onset places 'O_{55}' through 'O_{51}' are irrelevant for them. Furthermore, non-short vowels are only preceded by four PerPs, so places 'O_{55}' through 'O_{51}' are also irrelevant for them (see §10.1).

Onset places
1) The occurrence of SINGLE pre-nuclear phonemes
'O_{11}' = all PerPs except for the voicing archi-phonemes
The place is occupied by all phonemes capable of occurring in such a situation, that is, /p/, /b/, /t/, /d/, /t'/, /d'/, /k/, /g/, /f/, /v/, /s/, /z/, /š/, /ž/, /x/, /h/, /m/, /n/, /ň/, /j/, /ř/, /r/, /l/, /M/. If the nucleus of the phonotagm is /r/ or /l/, the archi-phoneme /M/ occurs instead of the nasals /m/, /n/, /ň/. The same holds for the other places standing right before the nucleus.

2) The occurrence of phonemes in TWO-PHONEME pre-nuclear combinations
'O_{21}' = the same as 'O_{11}'
The place is occupied by the same phonemes as 'O_{11}' because unlike Kučera we acknowledge that /g/ can be preceded by one PerP as in *zgalvanizovat*.
'O_{22}' = all PerPs except for /t'/, /d'/, /m/, /n/, /ň/ and /Ť/
The palatal occlusives do not occur in this place because they cannot precede a non-vowel, and the same is true for the three nasals (the latter are represented by /M/ in such a situation).

3) The occurrence of phonemes in THREE-PHONEME pre-nuclear combinations
'O_{31}' = all PerPs except for /g/, /f/, /z/ and voicing archi-phonemes
The fact that /g/ cannot be preceded (as well as followed) by two PerPs was mentioned in §11.4 and was interpreted there as a regular phenomenon. The same was denied to /z/, that is, it is viewed to be accidental that it is not found to be preceded by two PerPs. Similarly, /f/ cannot regularly be followed by two PerPs (see §11.5).
'O_{32}' = all PerPs except for /t'/, /d'/, /j/, /r/, /l/, /P/, /Ť/, /K/, /F/, /X/
The non-occurrence of /j/, /r/, /l/, /P/, /K/, /F/, /X/ is regularized in the DU itself: these phonemes cannot be preceded by any PerP provided that they are also followed by at least one (in other words, they belong to 'pre2'). Likewise, the palatal occlusives cannot regularly occur in such a situation, which is also encoded in the DU (/Ť/ does not occur in the pre-nuclear context at all, and /t'/, /d'/ occur only before a vowel). Thus, all phonemes capable of appearing in this situation do indeed appear there.
'O_{33}' = all PerPs except for /p/, /t'/, /d'/, /g/, /f/, /š/, /ž/, /Ť/
The non-occurrence of /t'/, /d'/ and /Ť/ is regular for the reasons already given. The inability of /g/ to be followed by two PerPs was regularized in §11.4, and in the same section we concluded that /š/ and /ž/ cannot be followed by two PerPs. In contrast, the non-occurrence of /p/ and /f/ in 'O_{33}' is best viewed as accidental because /b/ can only in such a situation, though only marginally in the place name *Břve*.

4) The occurrence of phonemes in FOUR-PHONEME pre-nuclear combinations
'O_{41}' = /v/, /m/, /n/, /ň/, /j/, /ř/, /r/, /l/
The DU predicts that this place can only be occupied by phonemes belonging to *pos* 'e1' or *pos* 'e2' because no other place can be preceded by three PerPs. All of them occur in this place except for /M/, which is a consequence of the fact that combinations of type 'CCN' and 'CCCN' (where 'C' is a PerP and 'N' is a nasal) cannot occur before a nuclear semiconso-

nant (which was mentioned in §16.3). In other words, the non-occurrence of the other PerPs in this place is regular.

'O_{42}' = /p/, /b/, /t/, /d/, /k/, /v/, /s/, /š/, /x/, /h/, /M/

Similarly, the DU predicts that the only phonemes capable of occurring in this place are those from *pos* 'e3' and *pos* 'e2' because no other phonemes can be preceded by two PerPs while followed by one PerP. The phonemes from these position classes which do not occur in 'O_{42}' are /z/, /ž/, /g/ and /f/, but it is only the absence of /g/ which we regard as regular (see above).

'O_{43}' = /t/, /k/, /s/, /z/, /x/, /h/, /ř/, /T/, /S/, /Š/

The DU predicts that only phonemes from *pos* 'e3' and *pos* 'pre1' can occur in this place. The absent ones are /d/, /g/, /š/, /ž/. The non-occurrence of /g/, /š/ and /ž/ is regular (see above), while that of /d/ is accidental.[8]

'O_{44}' = /t/, /h/, /l/, /P/, /T/, /F/, /S/, /Š/, /M/

The DU predicts that only phonemes belonging to *pos* 'pre1' and *pos* 'pre2' can occur in this place. The absence of /K/ and /X/ was regularized in §11.8. The absence of /r/ is accidental (cf. /l/ in *lstný*). Finally, the phonemes /t/ and /h/ occur in 'O_{44}' in /třMň/ (*třmět*) and /hřMň/ (*hřmět*), which suggests that we could expect there also /d/ and /x/. See §11.8 on the occurrence of /t/ and /h/ in this situation.

5) The occurrence of phonemes in FIVE-PHONEME pre-nuclear combinations
'O_{51}' = /j/

The DU predicts that only phonemes from *pos* 'e1' can occur in this place, but /ř/, /r/ and /l/ were said to be regularly incapable of this in §11.2. On the other hand, the absence of the nasals /m/, /n/, /ň/ is viewed to be accidental because of the potential combination /FSdMň/ in *vzdměte*.

'O_{52}' = /v/

Only phonemes from *pos* 'e2' can occur here, though /M/ could occur here, too (see the previous place).

'O_{53}' = /k/

Only phonemes from *pos* 'e3' can occur here. The absence of /t/ and /d/ is accidental, which implies from what is said under 'O_{51}'. On the other hand, the absence of /s/, /z/, /š/, /ž/ and /g/ was regularized in §11.4.

'O_{54}' = /T/, /S/

The DU predicts that only phonemes from *pos* 'pre1' can occur here. The absence of /Š/ is viewed as accidental, whereas that of /ř/ has been interpreted as a regular phenomenon (see §11.7).

---

8   NLA mentions the word *zdmouti* whose hypothetical plural imperative would be *zdměte* with /SdMň/.

'O_{55}' = /F/, /S/

Finally, the DU predicts that only phonemes from *pos* 'pre2' can occur in this place. However, in §11.8 we concluded that /P/, /T/, /K/, /X/, /M/, /j/, /r/ and /l/ cannot be followed by four PerPs, so their absence is regular here. Similarly, the non-occurrence of /Š/ is viewed as regular because palatals cannot be followed by more than three PerPs (see §11.8).

Coda places

1) The occurrence of SINGLE post-nuclear phonemes

'C_{11}' = all PerPs capable of occurring in the post-nuclear context

That is, the place can be occupied by the sonants /m/, /n/, /ň/, /j/, /ř/, /r/, /l/, and by the voicing archi-phonemes (due to neutralization of voicing).

2) The occurrence of phonemes in TWO-PHONEME post-nuclear combinations

'C_{21}' = the same as 'C_{11}' except for /Ť/ and /ň/

All PerPs capable of occurring in the post-nuclear context can be followed by one PerP except for /Ť/ and /ň/. The absence of /Ť/ is encoded in the DU (it can only be a phonotagm-final phoneme), whereas that of /ň/ is viewed to be accidental. See §12.2 on the combination /ňK/ in words like *šizuňk*.

'C_{22}' = the same as 'C_{11}' except for /j/

The non-occurrence of /j/ in this place is encoded in the DU (it does not occur in a position allowing for such occurrence). Except for this one, all PerPs capable of occurring in the post-nuclear context occur here, even the sonants /r/, /l/, /m/, /n/, /ň/ (cf. *chejr, koktejl, jilm, koncern, čerň*).

3) The occurrence of phonemes in THREE-PHONEME post-nuclear combinations

'C_{31}' = {/P/, /T/, /K/, /m/, /n/, /j/, /r/, /l/}

The DU predicts that only phonemes from *pos* 'i1' can occur in this place, and out of them it is only /ň/ that is missing, which was interpreted as a regular phenomenon in §12.2.

'C_{32}' = {/P/, /T/, /K/, /S/, /Š/}

Only phonemes from *pos* 'i2' can occur in this place, but the absence of /F/, /X/ and /ř/ was regularized in §11.3 (they cannot be both preceded and followed by a PerP).

'C_{33}' = {/P/, /T/, /Ť/, /K/, /S/, /Š/}

Finally, the DU predicts that only phonemes from *pos* 'i3' can occur in this place, and all of them do.

17.3 Justifying our analysis

Having laid out the alternative way of describing phonotagms in Czech, we must now justify our decision not to base our overall analysis on such a model. It is as consistent with the theory as the distributional unit is,[9] but the choice has been a matter of adequacy and simplicity. While the degree of simplicity is comparable, we are convinced that the DU offers a more detailed analysis than the Kučera-inspired one.

The advantage lies in the concept of the position. In contrast to the places of the alternative model, the positions of the DU do not express the relative placement of phonemes within certain combinations, but combinatory potentials of phonemes. A phoneme is assigned to a position if it shares distributional and combinatory properties of other phonemes occurring there. This is of course true of the places, too, because all phonemes occurring in, say, 'O_{31}' can be preceded by two PerPs, but the places express only this kind of information. In contrast, the membership of a phoneme in, say, position 'e2' expresses that the phoneme may be preceded by three PerPs or by two PerPs or by one PerP or by no PerP at all, while it may be at the same time followed by one PerP or no PerP at all. It is again true that this kind of information is also retrievable from the Kučera-inspired model by comparing and intersecting particular places, but positions provide this information immediately.

It must be acknowledged that although the positions tell us by how many and by which phonemes a certain phoneme can be followed or preceded, they say nothing about whether it actually is followed or preceded by them. The membership of a phoneme in a position which is followed by two other positions does not necessarily depend on the phoneme's ability to be followed by two other phonemes, although it has this capacity in most cases. It may be sufficient that it is followed by a phoneme from both of the two following positions.[10] In contrast, this kind of information is immediately obvious from the membership of a phoneme in a certain place because a phoneme belongs to some place if and only if it is preceded or followed by a given number of phonemes. Nevertheless, the drawback is advantageous in the end. Examples will help.

We have said that place 'O_{43}' is not attested to be occupied by /d/, that is, there is no phonotagm in which this phoneme is preceded by one PerP while followed by two PerPs. The DU predicts that such combinations could be possible because /d/ occurs in a position which allows for them, but the Kučera-inspired

---

9   AF does not explicitly works with such a model, but the theory does not rule it out.

10   For example, /g/ belongs to 'e3', even though it is not followed by two PerPs, but it can be followed by a phoneme from *pos* 'e2' and a phoneme from *pos* 'e1'; see §11.4.

model does not give us any ground for such a prediction. At most, we could say that since /t/ occurs in this place, its voiced counterpart /d/ could occur there, too, but this reasoning is unwarranted because phonemes in the voicing pairs need not have the same distribution, as is true in the case of /f/ and /v/.

Another example is provided by pre-nuclear combinations of five phonemes. Two such combinations are attested, /FSkvj/ and /STkvj/, and the Kučera-inspired model captures both of them. However, it does not tell us much about potentially possible five-phoneme combinations. At most, we can assume from it that /FTkvj/ could be possible, but that is about all. On the other hand, the DU model has a greater predictive power. By calculating possibilities of the occurrence of phonemes in particular positions and by checking them against collocational restrictions, we will arrive at the following combinations about which we can claim that they are potentially possible because they follow the rules of the combinatorics of Czech phonemes:

(2) /FStMn/, /FStMň/, /FSdMn/, /FSdMň/, /FStvj/, /FSdvj/, /FSxvj/, /FShvj/, /FTkvj/, /FŠtMn/, /FŠtMň/, /FŠdMn/, /FŠdMň/, /FŠkvj/, /FŠtvj/, /FŠdvj/, /SŠtMn/, /SŠtMň/, /SŠdMn/, /SŠdMň/, /SŠtvj/, /SŠdvj/, /SŠkvj/,[11] /ŠTkvj/

We do not claim that if new words are coined or derived, Czech will make use of all of these combinations; what we claim is that they are more likely than some others because their structure is in accord with the ways phonemes occur and combine in Czech. What is more, the possibility of at least of one of them is confirmed by other means, namely /FSdMň/ in potential *vzdmĕte* (see §11.2). The alternative model fails to predict this combination, and it tells us nothing about whether it is possible or not.

In general, the ability to predict new combinations is the greatest advantage of the DU model in comparison to the Kučera-inspired model. This ability has also manifested otherwise. The DU has naturally been set up on the basis of the existing phonotagms, but since the vocabulary of Czech is enormous, we were not aware of all words some of which could contain brand new phonotagms or phoneme combinations. We still are not in fact. Generalizing the structure of the known phonotagms, we made hypotheses about the DU. We assumed a certain number of positions and their membership. When we became aware of new phonotagms or combinations, we tested them against the DU. If the model was not able to account for them, the hypothesis was rejected, and a new form of the DU was postulated. At some point, however, no new combination could invalidate our model, and all newly discovered combinations were describable on the

---

11 The last four may appear strange due to the /SŠ/ combination, but see §13.3 on similar combinations.

DU. It means that the model predicted the possibility of some combinations which were later confirmed to exist.

17.4 Freight-yard schemes

The demonstration the DU's ability to predict potential combinations can also be done in reference to the schemes reproduced in figures III and IV (see p. 290). The first is for the pre-nuclear context of the DU and the other for its post-nuclear context. They should ideally be combined, but it is more convenient to have them split. The first scheme can have a variant for phonotagms with nuclear /r/ or /l/; in that case the scheme will not include position 'e1' and archi-position 'E3'. Both schemes have been redrawn from our model of the DU.

The schemes of this kind have been called *freight yard schemes*, and it is quite an apt name.[12] Imagine they represent maps of a route of a train. Every position can be viewed as a station where a wagon is hitched to the train. Every train must have a machine. This is the nuclear entity occurring in the nuclear position. A train can carry as much as five wagons if it goes through the route in the first scheme (or four if going through the scheme for the nuclear semiconsonants), and as much as three wagons if going through the route in the second scheme. At every station a wagon is not only hitched to the train, but the wagon can also be loaded with some goods, although it may remain empty in some stations. That is, all those five (or four) pre-nuclear and all those three post-nuclear positions can be filled with a phoneme, but some positions may remain empty.

In the schemes the lines represent routes the train can take. If we start in station 'n', the machine can go either to station 'e1' or to the station marked 'E3', that is, to the first archi-position. In the latter case the train loads /t'/ or /d'/ skipping stations 'e1', 'e2' and 'e3', and going directly to station 'pre1'. In station 'E3' the wagon must always be loaded, i.e. an archi-position is always occupied by a phoneme. But if the train goes to station 'e1', the wagon it takes can be loaded with /m/, /n/, /ñ/, /j/, /ř/, /r/ or /l/, or it remains empty. Then it can go either to station 'e2' or to station 'E2', that is, to the second archi-position. Once again, if choosing station 'E2', it skips 'e2' and 'e3', and goes straight to 'pre1'. In station 'E2' it loads /p/ or /b/ or /f/. If the train goes instead to station 'e2', the wagon can be loaded with /v/ or /M/ or remain empty. It continues then to station 'e3' where it can take on /t/, /d/, /s/, /z/, /š/, /ž/, /k/, /g/, /x/ or /h/, or the wagon can remain empty. Either way, the train continues to station 'pre1' where it could get even if it went through stations 'E3' or 'E2'. At station 'pre1' the

---

12   The term has been adopted from Hockett (1958: 290–1); see also Goldsmith (2011: 184–7) on finite state automata.

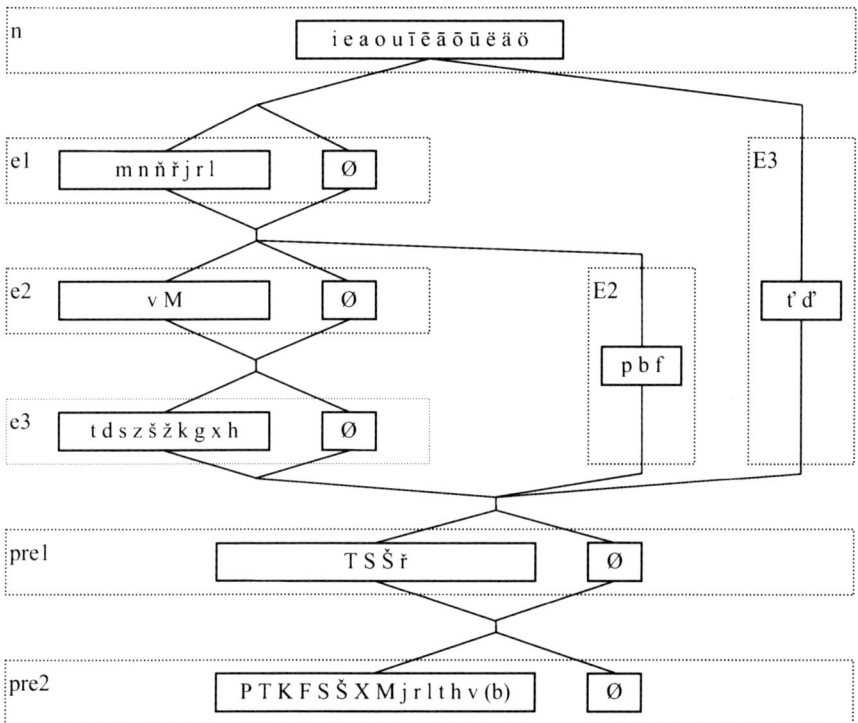

FIGURE III: Freight-yard scheme for the pre-nuclear context of the main distributional unit

wagon can be loaded with /T/, /S/, /Š/ or /ř/ or it can remain empty; a phoneme can be loaded in this station only if it has been loaded at least one at the previous stations. Finally, the train continues to station 'pre2', the end of its route; the last wagon can be loaded with /P/, /F/, /K/, /X/, /T/, /S/, /Š/, /X/, /r/, /l/, /j/ or /M/, and in some cases even with /t/, /h/, /v/ or /b/, but again only if it loaded at least one wagon in the previous stations. The wagon could also remain empty, though. If the wagon in station 'pre1' remains empty, the wagon in station 'pre2' cannot be loaded with /T/, /S/ or /Š/ because these phonemes are primarily loaded in the former, that is, 'pre1' is their primary place of occurrence.

    In the post-nuclear scheme (see figure IV) the situation is a little more complicated particularly as regards the occurrence of /P/, /T/, /K/, /S/ and /Š/ (see §12.3 where it was discussed in detail). It is possible to incorporate the peculiarities into the scheme to get a more accurate one, but it will result in a graphically complex scheme, which is rather a drawback of two-dimensional drawings than the scheme itself. In the post-nuclear context the train we used as a simile

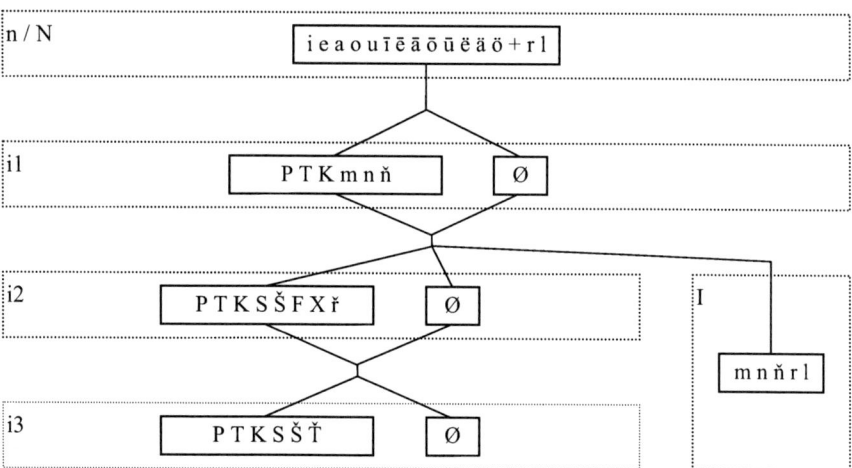

FIGURE IV: Freight-yard scheme for the post-nuclear context of the main distributional unit

can take up no more than three wagons. At the start the machine may only go through station 'i1' where the wagon is loaded with /P/, /T/, /K/, /m/, /n/, /ň/ or remains empty. In the latter case the train cannot go to station 'I' because this archi-position is only occupied if 'i1' is occupied. If it goes there, it skips stations 'i2' and 'i3', and the wagon can be loaded with /j/, /r/, /l/, /m/, /n/ or /ň/. If the train goes to 'i2' instead (irrespective of whether the wagon was loaded in 'i1'), the wagon can be loaded there with /P/, /T/, /K/, /S/, /Š/, /F/, /X/, /ř/, or it can remain empty. Some of these phonemes can be loaded under special conditions. For example, if /r/ or /l/ is loaded in 'i2', /ř/ cannot be loaded in 'i2' because they do not co-occur. The train continues to station 'i3' where its last wagon can be loaded with /P/, /T/, /K/, /S/, /Š/, /Ť/ or remain empty. Again, some of the phonemes can be loaded under special conditions or it may even happen that they are not loaded at all. The latter takes place when the wagon is loaded with a phoneme at 'i1' and with /F/, /X/ or /ř/ at 'i2' because these phonemes can only occur in two-phoneme combinations (see §12.3).

Now, since the DU contains a finite number of positions which can be occupied by a finite number of phonemes (including zero for an empty position), there is a finite number of routes the train can take and a finite number of ways the wagons can be occupied. In other words, there is a finite number of phonotagms the model will generate. A fairly simple algorithm can be, on the basis of the freight-yard schemes, written to handle all the ways the positions can be filled. However, and this is important, the output must be further subject to collocational restrictions filtering out combinations which have been declared impossible. The final result is a set of combinations the subset of which contains all attested combinations. To be specific, the output of the pre-nuclear scheme includes all 442 directly attested combinations, and that of the post-nuclear scheme includes 104 directly attested combinations. There is no attested combination which cannot be calculated from the model. If there were, the model would be invalidated, which is not a possibility we do not rule out, but which we have not been able to achieve.[13]

The remaining combinations are those which are not attested (or which we have overlooked), but which can be claimed to be potentially possible in Czech because they follow the pattern of the attested combinations. Besides the actually attested combinations, the pre-nuclear freight-yard scheme supplemented with filters generates 789 potential combinations, and the post-nuclear scheme will generate 46 combinations. They are listed in appendix C. As we already pointed out in the preceding section, Czech will hardly make use of all these combinations when new words are coined, derived or borrowed from other languages. It does not even seem probable given the high number of such combinations. We also admit that some of these combinations seem to be likelier candidates than others, for example, those beginning with /F/, /v/, /S/, /s/ or /z/ because they could arise from the prefixation of *v-*, *s-* or *z-*, while some other combinations would be at once viewed with suspicion (for example, pre-nuclear /řď/, /Kž/, /jxm/, /zřň/). However, if the strange combinations are confronted with the attested combinations of a similar pattern (cf. /Křť/ in *křtiny*, /Pž/ in *bžunda*, /jsm/ in *jsme*, /hřm/ in *hřmot*), it may be hard to say why they look strange (apart from the fact that they are not attested). It would be possible to lower the number of potential combinations by introducing additional collocational restrictions, but we must realize that every additional restriction limits the combinatory potential of Czech. It is obvious from the attested combinations, which are of various patterns, that this potential is great. We have said that an advantage of languages in contrast with other semiotic systems is their ability to combine means of expression for the creation of new means. Czech is a language where this ability is exploited considerably, but where the whole potential is far from exhausted.

---

13 The point is that the DU is a set of hypotheses which are accepted not because they are true facts, but because we have failed to refute them.

Appendix A: COLLOCATIONAL RESTRICTIONS

This appendix summarizes all collocational restrictions introduced in our analysis. The numbers in square brackets refer to sections where a restriction was introduced and discussed. Since restrictions generally involve at least two classes of phonemes, it is obvious that even though mentioned under a certain heading, they may apply to other phonemes, too.

1 Restrictions on the general structure of the phonotagm

R1 Two identical phonemes cannot stand in close proximity. [§9.2]

R2 A voiceless or a voiced consonant cannot stand in close proximity with a voicing archi-phoneme of the same place and manner of articulation. [§9.2]

R3 No phonotagm can contain more than six non-vowels. [§8.1]

2 Restrictions on the phonemes from pos 'e2' (i.e. /v/, /M/)

R4 A nasal cannot be followed by a combination of type 'CCC$_1$' where 'C$_1$' is from *pos* 'e2'. [§11.8]

R5 A sonant cannot be followed by a combination of type 'CCC$_1$' where 'C$_1$' is from *pos* 'e2'. [§11.8]

2.1 Restrictions on the phonemes from pos *'e2' and* pos *'E2' (i.e. /p/, /b/, /f/)*

R6 A nasal cannot be followed by a combination of type 'CC$_1$' where 'C$_1$' is from *pos* 'E2' or from *pos* 'e2'. [§11.8]

R7 A sonant cannot be followed by a combination of type 'CC$_1$' where 'C$_1$' is from *pos* 'E2' or from *pos* 'e2'. [§11.8]

3 Restrictions on the occlusives

R8 Three or more occlusives cannot stand in close proximity. [§13.2]

R9 An occlusive cannot be followed by two PerPs 'C$_1$C' provided that 'C$_1$' is from *pos* 'E2'. [§11.7]

R10 Two occlusives cannot be followed by two PerPs of the same manner of articulation. [§13.5]

R11 Peripheral combinations of type 'OFF$_P$' are impossible. [§13.4]

R12 Peripheral combinations of type 'OFF$_K$' are impossible. [§13.4]

R13 Peripheral combinations of type 'OFFC' are impossible. [§13.6]

R14   Peripheral combinations of type 'OC$_1$C' where 'C$_1$' is a voiced consonant from *pos* 'e3' are impossible. [§14.3 under DE3d]

R15   In the pre-nuclear context, phonemes from *pos* 'e3' and *pos* 'E2' cannot be preceded by two occlusives. [§11.4]

R16   In the post-nuclear context an occlusive cannot be followed by a labial or by a velar. [§13.3]

3.1 Restrictions on the labial occlusives

R17   A labial occlusive cannot be followed by a combination of type 'C$_1$C' where 'C$_1$' is from *pos* 'e3' or *pos* 'e2' or from *pos* 'E2'. [§11.8]

R18   A peripheral combination cannot contain two labial occlusives. [§13.3]

3.2 Restrictions on the alveolar occlusives

R19   Peripheral combinations of type 'A$_O$L$_F$N' are impossible. [§14.3 under DE3*a*]

R20   Peripheral combinations of type 'A$_O$L$_F$C$_1$' where 'C$_1$' is a semiconsonant are impossible. [§14.3 under DE3*a*]

R21   Peripheral combinations of type 'A$_O$L$_F$C$_1$' where 'C$_1$' is /ř/ are impossible. [§14.3 under DE3*a*]

3.3 Restrictions on the palatal occlusives

R22   A palatal occlusive cannot be preceded by an alveolar occlusive. [§13.3]

3.4 Restrictions on the velar occlusives

R23   A velar occlusive cannot be preceded by a labial occlusive. [§13.3]

3.4.1 Restrictions on /g/

R24   /g/ cannot be preceded or followed by two PerPs. [§11.4]

R25   /g/ cannot be preceded by a non-fricative. [§11.4]

4 Restrictions on the fricatives

R26   Peripheral combinations of type 'NFN' are impossible. [§13.4]

R27   Peripheral combinations of type 'C$_1$FN' where 'C$_1$' is a semiconsonant are impossible. [§14.3 under DE3*b*]

R28   Peripheral combinations of type 'C$_1$FN' where 'C$_1$' is /ř/ are impossible. [§14.3 under DE3*b*]

R29   Peripheral combinations of types 'COFN' and 'OFNC' are impossible. [§13.6]

R30   In the post-nuclear context a fricative cannot be preceded by a non-velar fricative. [§13.3]

4.1 Restrictions on the labial fricatives

R31   In the pre-nuclear context a labial fricative cannot be preceded by another labial. [§13.3]

4.1.1 Restrictions on /f/

R32   /f/ cannot be preceded by two PerPs. [§11.5]

4.2 Restrictions on the alveolar fricatives

R33   An alveolar fricative cannot be preceded by a palatal fricative. [§13.3]

R34   If an alveolar fricative is preceded by an alveolar occlusive, it cannot be followed by two PerPs. [§11.4]

4.3 Restrictions on the palatal fricatives

R35   A palatal fricative cannot be followed by two PerPs 'C$_2$C$_1$' where 'C$_2$' is from *pos* 'e2', and 'C$_1$' is from *pos* 'e1'. [§11.4]

R36   Peripheral combinations of type 'F$_P$FF' are impossible. [§13.4]

4.4 Restrictions on the velar fricatives

R37   A velar fricative cannot precede a phoneme from *pos* 'e3'. [§13.3]

R38   Peripheral combinations of type 'OF$_K$R' are impossible. [§13.4]

R39   Peripheral combinations of type 'OF$_K$F' are impossible. [§13.4]

R40   Peripheral combinations of type 'F$_K$FO' are impossible. [§13.4]

4.5 Restrictions on /F/ and /X/

R41   In the post-nuclear context, /F/ and /X/ cannot be preceded by a PerP and at the same time followed by a PerP. [§12.3]

5 Restrictions on the nasals

R42   A nasal cannot be preceded by /b/. [§14.2 under DE2*c*]

R43   A nasal can be followed by no other three PerPs than of type 'FON'. [§13.5]

R44   In the pre-nuclear context a nasal cannot be followed by two phonemes of the same manner of articulation. [§13.4]

R45   Peripheral combinations of type 'RNR' are impossible. [§13.4]

R46   Peripheral combinations of type 'NFR' are impossible. [§13.4]

R47   Peripheral combinations of type 'CFFN' are impossible. [§13.6]

R48   Peripheral combinations of type 'CFNR' are impossible. [§13.6]

R49   Pre-nuclear combinations of type 'NCL' are impossible. [§11.4]

5.1 Restrictions on /m/

R50   /m/ cannot be preceded by a phoneme from *pos* 'E2'. [§11.2]

5.2 Restrictions on /ñ/

R51   In the post-nuclear context, /ñ/ cannot be followed by two PerPs. [§12.2]

6 Restrictions on the non-fricatives

R52   A non-fricative cannot be followed by more than three PerPs. [§11.8]

R53   Peripheral combinations of type 'C₁FFF' where 'C₁' is a non-fricative are impossible. [§13.5]

7 Restrictions on the non-sonants

R54   In the post-nuclear context, a non-sonant cannot be followed by a semi-consonant or by a nasal. [§12.2]

8 Restrictions on the labials

R55   In the pre-nuclear context a labial cannot be preceded by a nasal. [§11.3]

R56   Pre-nuclear combinations of type 'CLL' are impossible. [§14.3 under DE3*a*]

R57   In the post-nuclear context a labial cannot be preceded by another labial unless it is a labial nasal. [§13.3]

R58   In the post-nuclear context a labial cannot be preceded by a palatal or by a velar. [§13.3]

9 Restrictions on the palatals

R59   A palatal cannot be followed by more than three PerPs. [§11.8]

R60   Post-nuclear combinations of type 'CLP' are impossible. [§13.4]

R61   Post-nuclear combinations of type 'CPK' are impossible. [§13.4]

R62   Post-nuclear combinations of type 'CKP' are impossible. [§13.4]

10 Restrictions on the velars

R63   A peripheral combination cannot contain two velars. [§13.3]

R64   A velar cannot be followed by more than three PerPs. [§11.8]

R65   A velar cannot be followed by a combination of type 'C₁C' where 'C₁' is either from *pos* 'e3' or from *pos* 'E2'. [§11.8]

R66   Peripheral combinations of type 'OOK' are impossible. [§13.4]

R67   Peripheral combinations of type 'KOL' are impossible. [§13.4]

R68   Peripheral combinations of type 'KFL' are impossible. [§13.4]

R69   Peripheral combinations of type 'KFN' are impossible. [§14.3 under DE3*a*]

R70   Peripheral combinations of type 'KFC₁' where 'C₁' is /ř/ are impossible. [§14.3 under DE3*a*]

R71   Combinations of type 'KFC₁' where 'C₁' is a semiconsonant are impossible. [§14.3 under DE3*a*]

R72   A velar archi-phoneme cannot be followed by more than two PerPs. [§11.8]

R73   Pre-nuclear combinations of type 'NCK' are impossible. [§11.4]

11 Restrictions on the sonants

R74   The same section of the DU cannot contain two identical sonants. [§11.1]

R75   Combinations of type 'ONR' are impossible.[1] [§13.4]

R76   Peripheral combinations of type 'RON' are impossible. [§13.4]

R77   Peripheral combinations of type 'ROK' are impossible. [§13.4]

R78   Peripheral combinations of type 'NRC' are impossible. [§13.4]

R79   Peripheral combinations of type 'FRF' are impossible. [§13.4]

R80   A sonant cannot be followed by any other three PerPs than of type 'FON'. [§13.5]

R81   In the pre-nuclear context a sonant cannot be followed by two occlusives or by two fricatives. [§13.4]

11.1 Restrictions on /ř/

R82   /ř/ cannot be followed by more than two PerPs. [§11.7]

R83   /ř/ cannot be preceded by more than three PerPs. [§11.2]

R84   /ř/ cannot occur in the same section with a semiconsonant. [§11.2]

R85   /ř/ cannot occur in the same section with a palatal fricative. [§14.2 under DE2*b*]

R86   If /ř/ is followed by two PerPs 'C$_1$C', then 'C$_1$' can be no other than one from *pos* 'e2'. [§11.7]

R87   /ř/ cannot be followed by a fricative belonging to *pos* 'e3'. [§11.3]

R88   In the pre-nuclear context, /ř/ cannot be preceded by a combination of type 'CCC$_1$' where 'C$_1$' is from *pos* 'e2'. [§11.2]

R89   In the pre-nuclear context, /ř/ cannot co-occur with a sonant. [§11.2]

R90   In the post-nuclear context, /ř/ cannot stand in close proximity with a fricative or a nasal. [§13.3]

R91   In the post-nuclear context, /ř/ cannot be preceded by a PerP and at the same time followed by a PerP. [§12.3]

11.2 Restrictions on /j/

R92   /j/ cannot be preceded by an occlusive other than labial or velar. [§11.2]

R93   /j/ cannot be preceded by a fricative other than labial or alveolar. [§11.2]

R94   /j/ cannot be followed by more than two PerPs. [§11.8]

R95   /j/ cannot be followed by a phoneme from *pos* 'E2'. [§11.8]

---

1   This restriction holds also for nuclear semiconsonants!

R96   If a semiconsonant occurs in the same section with /j/, the latter occurs in a less peripheral position. [§11.2]

R97   If /ř/ occurs in the same section with /j/, the latter occurs in a less peripheral position. [§11.2]

11.3 Restrictions on the semiconsonants

R98   The pre-nuclear section cannot contain two instances of a semiconsonant. [§11.2]

11.3.1 Restrictions on the non-nuclear semiconsonants

R99   A non-nuclear semiconsonant cannot be preceded by more than three PerPs. [§11.2]

R100   A non-nuclear semiconsonant cannot be followed by a voiceless fricative. [§13.6]

R101   In the pre-nuclear context a non-nuclear semiconsonant cannot be preceded by a combination of type 'CCC$_1$' where 'C$_1$' is from *pos* 'e2'. [§11.2]

11.3.2 Restrictions on the nuclear semiconsonants

R102   A nuclear semiconsonant must be preceded by at least one consonant. [§10.2]

R103   If a nuclear semiconsonant is followed by any PerP, it cannot be preceded by three or more PerPs. [§10.3]

R104   A nuclear semiconsonant cannot stand in close proximity with a combination of type 'OO'. [§16.3]

R105   A nuclear semiconsonant cannot be preceded by a combination of type 'CCA$_F$'. [§11.4]

R106   A nuclear semiconsonant cannot be preceded by a combination of type 'CCK'. [§11.4]

R107   A nuclear semiconsonant cannot be preceded by a combination of types 'CFN' and 'CCFN'. [§16.3]

R108   A nuclear semiconsonant cannot be preceded by a combination of type 'LP'. [§16.3]

R109   A nuclear semiconsonant cannot be preceded by a combination of type 'KP'. [§16.3]

R110   A nuclear semiconsonant cannot be preceded by a combination of type 'KA'. [§16.3]

R111   A nuclear semiconsonant cannot be preceded by a combination of type 'CCA$_F$'. [§11.4]

R112   A nuclear semiconsonant cannot be preceded by a combination of type 'CCK'. [§11.4]

R113   A nuclear semiconsonant cannot be preceded by two PerPs 'C_2C_1' provided that 'C_2' is an occlusive and 'C_1' is from *pos* 'E2'. [§11.7]

R114   A nuclear semiconsonant cannot be followed by /j/. [§12.2]

R115   If the nucleus of the phonotagm is a semiconsonant, the post-nuclear section cannot contain /ř/. [§12.3]

R116   A nuclear semiconsonant cannot be followed by a combination of type 'NF'. [§16.3]

R117   A nuclear semiconsonant cannot be followed by a combination of types 'LC' or 'KC'. [§12.3]

R118   A nuclear semiconsonant cannot be followed by a combination of type 'CCO'. [§12.4]

12 Restrictions on the vowels

R119   A vowel cannot be preceded by a combination of type 'NO'. [§13.6]

12.1 Restrictions on the long mid vowels

R120   A long mid vowel cannot be preceded by a palatal non-fricative. [§16.1]

12.2 Restrictions on the non-short vowels

R121   A non-short vowel cannot be preceded by more than four PerPs. [§10.1]

R122   A non-short vowel cannot be preceded by a combination of type 'C_nCP'. [§16.3]

R123   A non-short vowel cannot be preceded by a combination of type 'C_nCC_1' where 'C_1' is /j/. [§16.3]

12.3 Restrictions on the diphthongal vowels

R124   A diphthongal vowel cannot be followed by /j/. [§16.2]

Appendix B: PERIPHERAL COMBINATIONS AND THEIR PROPERTIES

This appendix provides a complete listing of 442 pre-nuclear and 104 post-nuclear combinations analyzed in this work; they are tabulated in chapters 14 and 15. Every combination is given a series of analytical properties; they are discussed in chapter 13.

Explanations:
COLUMN
Com *The combinations*
  Parenthesized combinations are attested only in symbols and other marginal words.
  Italicized combinations are attested also before or after nuclear semiconsonants.
MT *Manner type*
  O = occlusive
  F = fricative
  N = nasal
  R = sonant
PT *Place type*
  L = labial
  A = alveolar
  P = palatal
  K = velar
  I = isolated consonant or semiconsonant
DT *Distributional type*
E *Expandability*
  L = left-hand expandable
  R = right-hand expandable
  L! = left-hand expandable, but not immediately expandable
  R! = right-hand expandable, but not immediately expandable
  X = left-hand or right-hand non-expandable
  (X) = marginally left-hand or right-hand non-expandable
  - = left-hand or right-hand anti-expandable

R   *Reducibility*
            L = left-hand reducible
            R = right-hand reducible
            X = left-hand or right-hand (depending on position) non-redu-
            cible
            - = left-hand or right-hand anti-reducible
Rs   *Resolvability*
            P = partly resolvable
            C = completely resolvable
            - = resolvability not applicable
P   *Pairedness* (not applicable to post-nuclear combinations)
            P = paired
            S = single
            - = pairedness not applicable
V   *Voicing of the combination* (not applicable to post-nuclear com-
            binations)
            + = voiced combination
            – = voiced combination
            M = mixed combination
            I = indifferent combination
M   *Mirror effect*
            Y = has a mirror counterpart
            N = does not have a mirror counterpart
Example   Examples of words where a combination is attested. If attested
            only in PSJČ or SSJČ, it is mentioned.

Pre-nuclear combinations (442)

Com	MT	PT	DT	E	R	Rs	P	V	M	Example
/Ml/	NR	II	DE2a	L-	--	-	-	I	Y	*mlok*
/Mn/	NN	IA	DE2a	L-	--	-	-	I	N	*mnout si*
/Mň/	NN	IP	DE2a	L-	--	-	-	I	N	*město*
/Mr/	NR	II	DE2a	L-	--	-	-	I	Y	*mrak*
/Mř/	NR	II	DE2a	L-	--	-	-	I	N	*mříže*
(/Mj/)	NR	II	DE2a	X-	--	-	-	I	Y	*Mjachký* (surname)
/vj/	FR	LI	DE2a	L-	--	-	P	+	Y	*vědět*
/vl/	FR	LI	DE2a	L-	--	-	P	+	Y	*vlast*
/vm/	FN	LL	DE2a	XR	--	-	S	+	Y	*vmísit se*
/vn/	FN	LA	DE2a	LR	--	-	S	+	Y	*vnuk*
/vň/	FN	LP	DE2a	LR	--	-	P	+	N	*vnější*

/vr/	FR	LI	DE2a	L-	--	-	P	+	Y	*vrata*
/vř/	FR	LI	DE2a	L-	--	-	S	+	N	*vřít*
/dl/	OR	AI	DE2b	L-	--	-	P	+	Y	*dlouho*
/dm/	ON	AL	DE2b	LR	--	-	P	+	Y	*dmout*
/dn/	ON	AA	DE2b	XR	--	-	P	+	Y	*dnes*
/dň/	ON	AP	DE2b	XR	--	-	P	+	N	*dni*
/dr/	OR	AI	DE2b	L-	--	-	P	+	Y	*drahý*
/dř/	OR	AI	DE2b	L-	--	-	P	+	Y	*dřevo*
/gl/	OR	KI	DE2b	L-	--	-	P	+	Y	*glazura*
/gn/	ON	KA	DE2b	XX	--	-	P	+	Y	*gnoseologický*
/gr/	OR	KI	DE2b	L-	--	-	P	+	Y	*granule*
/hl/	FR	KI	DE2b	L-	--	-	P	+	Y	*hlava*
/hm/	FN	KL	DE2b	LX	--	-	S	+	Y	*hmat*
/hn/	FN	KA	DE2b	LX	--	-	P	+	N	*hnát*
/hň/	FN	KP	DE2b	LX	--	-	P	+	N	*hnít*
/hr/	FR	KI	DE2b	L-	--	-	P	+	Y	*hrách*
/hř/	FR	KI	DE2b	L-	--	-	P	+	N	*hřešit*
/kl/	OR	KI	DE2b	L-	--	-	P	−	Y	*klobouk*
/km/	ON	KL	DE2b	LX	--	-	S	−	N	*kmet*
/kn/	ON	KA	DE2b	LX	--	-	P	−	Y	*knot*
/kň/	ON	KP	DE2b	LX	--	-	S	−	Y	*kniha*
/kj/	OR	KI	DE2b	L-	--	-	S	−	Y	*kjariza* (ASCS)
/kr/	OR	KI	DE2b	L-	--	-	P	−	Y	*krádež*
/kř/	OR	KI	DE2b	L-	--	-	S	−	Y	*kříž*
/sj/	FR	AI	DE2b	X-	--	-	P	−	Y	*sjezd*
/sl/	FR	AI	DE2b	L-	--	-	P	−	Y	*sláma*
/sm/	FN	AL	DE2b	LR	--	-	P	−	Y	*smát se*
/šm/	FN	PL	DE2b	LX	--	-	P	−	Y	*šmíra*
/sn/	FN	AA	DE2b	LR	--	-	P	−	Y	*snář*
/sň/	FN	AP	DE2b	LR	--	-	P	−	N	*snít*
/sr/	FR	AI	DE2b	X-	--	-	P	−	Y	*srub*
/šl/	FR	PI	DE2b	L-	--	-	P	−	Y	*šlépěj*
/šn/	FN	PA	DE2b	XX	--	-	P	−	Y	*šnek*
/šň/	FN	PP	DE2b	LX	--	-	P	−	N	*šněrovat*
/sř/	FR	AI	DE2b	X-	--	-	P	−	N	*sřezat*
/šr/	FR	PI	DE2b	X-	--	-	P	−	Y	*šramot*
/tl/	OR	AI	DE2b	L-	--	-	P	−	Y	*tlak*
/tm/	ON	AL	DE2b	LR	--	-	P	−	Y	*tma*
/tn/	ON	AA	DE2b	L!R	--	-	P	−	Y	*tnout*
/tň/	ON	AP	DE2b	L!R	--	-	P	−	N	*tni* (imp. sg. of *tnout*)
/tr/	OR	AI	DE2b	L-	--	-	P	−	Y	*tráva*

/tř/	OR	AI	DE2b	L-	--	-	P	–	Y	*třeba*
/xl/	FR	KI	DE2b	L-	--	-	P	–	Y	*chlap*
/xm/	FN	KL	DE2b	LX	--	-	P	–	Y	*chmury*
/xň/	FN	KP	DE2b	LX	--	-	P	–	N	*chňapnout*
/xr/	FR	KI	DE2b	L-	--	-	P	–	Y	*chrápat*
/xř/	FR	KI	DE2b	L-	--	-	P	–	N	*chřípí*
/zj/	FR	AI	DE2b	X-	--	-	P	+	Y	*zjev*
/zl/	FR	AI	DE2b	L-	--	-	P	+	Y	*zlatý*
/žl/	FR	PI	DE2b	X-	--	-	P	+	Y	*žlutý*
/zm/	FN	AL	DE2b	LR	--	-	P	+	Y	*zmatek*
/žm/	FN	PL	DE2b	XX	--	-	P	+	Y	*žmoulat*
/zn/	FN	AA	DE2b	LR	--	-	P	+	Y	*znak*
/zň/	FN	AP	DE2b	LR	--	-	P	+	N	*zničit*
/žn/	FN	PA	DE2b	XX	--	-	P	+	Y	*žnout*
/žň/	FN	PP	DE2b	XX	--	-	P	+	N	*žně*
/zr/	FR	AI	DE2b	L-	--	-	P	+	Y	*zrak*
/zř/	FR	AI	DE2b	L-	--	-	P	+	N	*zřejmě*
/žr/	FR	PI	DE2b	X-	--	-	P	+	Y	*žrát*
/bj/	OR	LI	DE2c	L-	--	-	P	+	Y	*běloba*
/bl/	OR	LI	DE2c	L-	--	-	P	+	Y	*bláto*
/br/	OR	LI	DE2c	L-	--	-	P	+	Y	*bratr*
/bř/	OR	LI	DE2c	L-	--	-	P	+	N	*bříza*
/fj/	FR	LI	DE2c	X-	--	-	P	–	Y	*fěrtoch* (SSJČ)
/fl/	FR	LI	DE2c	L-	--	-	P	–	Y	*flám*
/fň/	FN	LP	DE2c	X-	--	-	P	–	N	*fňukat*
/fr/	FR	LI	DE2c	L-	--	-	P	–	Y	*frak*
/pj/	OR	LI	DE2c	L-	--	-	P	–	Y	*pět*
/pl/	OR	LI	DE2c	L-	--	-	P	–	Y	*plat*
/pn/	ON	LA	DE2c	L!-	--	-	S	–	N	*pnout*
/pň/	ON	LP	DE2c	L!-	--	-	S	–	N	*pni* (imp. sg. of *pnout*)
/pr/	OR	LI	DE2c	L-	--	-	P	–	Y	*práce*
/př/	OR	LI	DE2c	L-	--	-	P	–	N	*příbor*
/rm/	RN	IL	DE2e	-X	--	-	-	I	N	*rmoutit*
(/lj/)	RR	II	DE2e	--	--	-	-	I	Y	*Ljuba* (proper name)
(/rj/)	RR	II	DE2e	--	--	-	-	I	Y	*Rjazaň* (place name)
/jm/	RN	IL	DE2e	-R	--	-	-	I	N	*jméno*
/ln/	RN	IA	DE2e	-X	--	-	-	I	N	*lnout*
/lň/	RN	IP	DE2e	-X	--	-	-	I	N	*lněný*
/dv/	OF	AL	DE2f	LR	--	-	P	M	Y	*dva*
/gv/	OF	KL	DE2f	XX	--	-	P	M	Y	*guajak* (SSJČ)
/hv/	FF	KL	DE2f	XR	--	-	P	M	N	*hvozd*

/kv/	OF	KL	DE2f	LR	--	-	P	M	Y	*kvést*
/sM/	FN	AI	DE2f	X-	--	-	P	–	Y	*smrt*
/sv/	FF	AL	DE2f	LR	--	-	P	M	N	*svatba, svrbět*
/šM/	FN	PI	DE2f	X-	--	-	S	–	Y	*šmrnc*
/šv/	FF	PL	DE2f	LR	--	-	P	M	N	*švagr, Švrček* (surname)
/tv/	OF	AL	DE2f	LX	--	-	P	M	Y	*tvůj, tvrz*
/xv/	FF	KL	DE2f	LR	--	-	P	M	N	*chvíle*
/zM/	FN	AI	DE2f	X-	--	-	P	+	Y	*zmrznout*
/zv/	FF	AL	DE2f	LR	--	-	P	M	N	*zvát, zvrhlík*
/žv/	FF	PL	DE2f	XX	--	-	P	M	N	*žvanit*
/řv/	RF	IL	DE2g	(X)R	--	-	S	+	N	*řvát*
/rv/	RF	IL	DE2h	-R	--	-	S	+	N	*rvát*
/lv/	RF	IL	DE2h	-X	--	-	S	+	N	*lvi*
/vM/	FN	LI	DE2h	--	--	-	S	+	Y	*vmrštit*
/řk/	RO	IK	DE2i	XX	--	-	S	–	Y	*řka* (archaic form of *říct*)
/Sd/	FO	AA	DE2i	LR	--	-	P	+	Y	*zdát, zdržet*
/Sg/	FO	AK	DE2i	XR	--	-	P	+	Y	*zgalvanizovat*
/Sh/	FF	AK	DE2i	LR	--	-	P	+	Y	*shon, shrnout*
/Sk/	FO	AK	DE2i	LR	--	-	P	–	Y	*skákat, skrz*
/Sš/	FF	AP	DE2i	XX	--	-	P	–	N	*zšednout*
/St/	FO	AA	DE2i	LR	--	-	P	–	Y	*stát, strmý*
/Sx/	FF	AK	DE2i	LR	--	-	P	–	Y	*schod, zchrtlý* (PSJČ)
/Sž/	FF	AP	DE2i	XX	--	-	P	+	N	*zženštilý*
/Šk/	FO	PK	DE2i	LR	--	-	S	–	Y	*škola, škrt*
/Št/	FO	PA	DE2i	LR	--	-	P	–	Y	*štáb, štrbské*
/Šd/	FO	PA	DE2i	LX	--	-	P	+	Y	*ždáti* (SSJČ)
/Šh/	FF	PK	DE2i	XR	--	-	S	+	Y	*žhář*
/Th/	OF	AK	DE2i	XX	--	-	P	+	Y	*dharma* (SSJČ)
/Tk/	OO	AK	DE2i	LR	--	-	S	+	Y	*tkát*
/Ts/	OF	AA	DE2i	LR	--	-	P	–	Y	*cena, crčet*
/Tš/	OF	AP	DE2i	LR	--	-	P	–	Y	*čelo, črta*
/Tx/	OF	AK	DE2i	XX	--	-	P	–	Y	*tchoř*
/Tz/	OF	AA	DE2i	XX	--	-	P	+	Y	*dzinkati* (SSJČ)
/Tž/	OF	AP	DE2i	LX	--	-	P	+	Y	*džus*
/Fd/	FO	LA	DE2j	-R	--	-	P	+	N	*vdát se*
(/Fg/)	FO	LK	DE2j	-X	--	-	P	+	N	*vgalvanisovati* (PSJČ)
/Fh/	FF	LK	DE2j	-R	--	-	P	+	N	*vhodit, vhrnout*
/Fk/	FO	LK	DE2j	-R	--	-	P	–	N	*vkus*
/Fs/	FF	LA	DE2j	-R	--	-	P	–	N	*vsadit, vsrknout*
/Fš/	FF	LP	DE2j	-R	--	-	P	–	N	*všechno*
/Ft/	FO	LA	DE2j	-R	--	-	P	–	N	*vtom, vtrhnout*

/Fx/	FF	LK	DE2j	-R	--	-	P	−	N	vcházet, vchrstnout
/Fz/	FF	LA	DE2j	-R	--	-	P	+	N	vzít
/Fž/	FF	LP	DE2j	-R	--	-	P	+	N	vžít se
/jd/	RO	IA	DE2j	-X	--	-	S	+	N	jde
/jh/	RF	IK	DE2j	-X	--	-	S	+	N	jho
/js/	RF	IA	DE2j	-R	--	-	S	−	N	jsi
/Kd/	OO	KA	DE2j	-X	--	-	P	−	N	kdo
/Ks/	OF	KA	DE2j	-X	--	-	S	−	Y	xylofon
/Kš/	OF	KP	DE2j	-R	--	-	S	−	N	kšandy
/Kt/	OO	KA	DE2j	-X	--	-	P	+	N	který
/lh/	RF	IK	DE2j	-X	--	-	S	+	N	lhostejný
/lk/	RO	IK	DE2j	-X	--	-	S	−	N	lkát
/lz/	RF	IA	DE2j	-X	--	-	S	+	N	lze
/lž/	RF	IP	DE2j	-X	--	-	S	+	N	lži
/Mš/	NF	IP	DE2j	-X	--	-	P	−	N	mše
/Mz/	NF	IA	DE2j	-X	--	-	S	+	N	mze (SSJČ)
/Mž/	NF	IP	DE2j	-X	--	-	P	+	N	mžitky
/Mk/	NO	IK	DE2j	-R	--	-	S	−	N	mkl (3rd p. sg. of mknouti)
(/Mx/)	NF	IK	DE2j	-X	--	-	S	−	Y	Mchov (Czech place name)
/Ps/	OF	LA	DE2j	-R!	--	-	P	−	Y	psát
/Pš/	OF	LP	DE2j	-R!	--	-	P	−	N	pšenice
/Pt/	OO	LA	DE2j	-X	--	-	S	+	N	pták
/Px/	OF	LK	DE2j	-X	--	-	S	−	N	pcháč
/Pz/	OF	LA	DE2j	-X	--	-	P	+	Y	bzukot
/Pž/	OF	LP	DE2j	-X	--	-	P	+	N	bžunda
/rd/	RO	IA	DE2j	-X	--	-	P	+	N	rdousit
/rt/	RO	IA	DE2j	-R	--	-	P	−	N	rty
/rz/	RF	IA	DE2j	-X	--	-	S	+	N	rzi
/rž/	RF	IP	DE2j	-X	--	-	S	+	N	ržát
/Mh/	NF	IK	DE2j	-X	--	-	S	+	N	mhouřit
/řb/	RO	IL	DE2k	LX	--	-	S	+	Y	řbuchan (Machek 1957: 256)
/Sb/	FO	AL	DE2k	LR	--	-	P	+	Y	sbírat, zbrklý
/Sf/	FF	AL	DE2k	XR	--	-	S	−	N	sfouknout
/Sp/	FO	AL	DE2k	LR	--	-	P	−	Y	spát, sprcha
/Šb/	FO	PL	DE2k	LR	--	-	P	+	Y	žbublati, žbrdolek (SSJČ)
/Šp/	FO	PL	DE2k	LR	--	-	P	−	Y	špatný, šplhat
/Tb/	OO	AL	DE2k	XX	--	-	S	−	Y	dbát
/Fb/	FO	LL	DE2l	-R	--	-	P	+	N	vbodnout, vbrzku
/Fp/	FO	LL	DE2l	-R	--	-	P	−	N	vpadnout, vpršeti (PSJČ)
(/Kf/)	OF	KL	DE2l	-X	--	-	S	−	Y	Kfely (Czech place name)
/Kb/	OO	KL	DE2l	-X	--	-	S	−	N	kbelík

/lb/	RO	IL	DE21	-X	--	-	P	+	N	*lbový* (SSJČ)
/rp/	RO	IL	DE21	-X	--	-	S	–	N	*Rpety* (place name)
/lp/	RO	IL	DE21	-R	--	-	P	–	N	*lpí*
/Xb/	FO	KL	DE21	-X	--	-	S	+	N	*hbitý*
/Sť/	FO	AP	DE2m	L-	--	-	P	–	N	*stín*
/Sď/	FO	AP	DE2m	L-	--	-	P	+	N	*zdědit*
/Šť/	FO	PP	DE2m	L-	--	-	P	–	N	*šťavnatý*
/Šď/	FO	PP	DE2m	X-	--	-	P	+	N	*ždímat*
/Pď/	OO	LP	DE2n	--	--	-	(P)	–	N	*bdít*
(/Pť/)	OO	LP	DE2n	--	--	-	P	+	N	*Ptice* (Czech place name)
(/Kť/)	OO	KP	DE2n	--	--	-	S	+	N	*Ktiš* (Czech place name)
/Fť/	FO	LP	DE2n	--	--	-	P	–	N	*vtělený*
/Fď/	FO	LP	DE2n	--	--	-	P	+	N	*vděčný*
/jď/	RO	IP	DE2n	--	--	-	S	+	N	*jdi*
/rď/	RO	IP	DE2n	--	--	-	P	+	N	*rdít se*
/rť/	RO	IP	DE2n	--	--	-	P	–	N	*rtěnka*
/Xť/	FO	KP	DE2n	--	--	-	S	–	N	*chtít*
/dMň/	ONN	AIP	DE3a	X-	LR	C	P	+	N	*dměte* (imp. pl. of *dmout*)
/dvj/	OFR	ALI	DE3a	X-	LR	C	S	M	N	*dvě*
/hvj/	FFR	KLI	DE3a	L-	LR	C	P	M	N	*hvězda*
/kvj/	OFR	KLI	DE3a	L-	LR	C	S	M	N	*květ*
/sMl/	FNR	AII	DE3a	X-	LR	C	P	–	N	*smlouva*
/sMň/	FNN	AIP	DE3a	L-	LR	C	P	–	N	*směna*
/sMr/	FNR	AII	DE3a	X-	LR	C	P	–	N	*smrad*
/svj/	FFR	ALI	DE3a	X-	LR	C	P	M	N	*svět*
/svl/	FFR	ALI	DE3a	X-	LR	C	P	M	N	*svlak*
/svr/	FFR	ALI	DE3a	X-	LR	C	P	M	N	*svrab*
/tMň/	ONN	AIP	DE3a	L-	LR	C	P	–	N	*tmě*
/xvj/	FFR	KLI	DE3a	L-	LR	C	P	M	N	*chvět*
/zMl/	FNR	AII	DE3a	X-	LR	C	P	+	N	*zmlátit*
/zMn/	FNN	AIA	DE3a	X-	LR	C	S	+	N	*zmnohonásobit*
/zMň/	FNN	AIP	DE3a	L-	LR	C	P	+	N	*změna*
/zMr/	FNR	AII	DE3a	X-	LR	C	P	+	N	*zmrazit*
(/zMř/)	FNR	AII	DE3a	X-	LR	C	S	+	N	*zmřížiti* (PSJČ)
/zvj/	FFR	ALI	DE3a	L-	LR	C	P	M	N	*zvěd*
/zvl/	FFR	ALI	DE3a	X-	LR	C	P	M	N	*zvlášť*
(/zvn/)	FFN	ALA	DE3a	X-	LR	C	S	M	N	*zvnaditi* (PSJČ)
/zvň/	FFN	ALP	DE3a	X-	LR	C	S	M	N	*zvnějšku*
/zvr/	FFR	ALI	DE3a	X-	LR	C	P	M	N	*zvracet*
/zvř/	FFR	ALI	DE3a	X-	LR	C	S	M	N	*zvředovatět*
/řvj/	RFR	ILI	DE3b	X-	LR	C	S	+	N	*řvěte*

/vMň/	FNN	LIP	DE3c	--	LR	C	S	M	N	*vměstnat se*
/vMl/	FNR	LII	DE3c	--	LR	C	S	M	N	*vmlátiti* (SSJČ)
/rvj/	RFR	ILI	DE3c	--	LR	C	S	+	N	*rvěte se*
/jMň/	RNN	IIP	DE3c	--	LR	C	-	I	N	*jmění*
/Sdl/	FOR	AAI	DE3d	X-	LR	C	P	+	Y	*zdlouhavý*
(/Sdm/)	FON	AAL	DE3d	LX	LR	C	P	+	Y	*sdmýchnouti* (PSJČ)
/Sdr/	FOR	AAI	DE3d	X-	LR	C	P	+	Y	*zdraví*
/Sdř/	FOR	AAI	DE3d	X-	LR	C	P	+	N	*zdřímnout si*
/Sgl/	FOR	AKI	DE3d	X-	LR	C	P	+	N	*zglajchšaltovat*
/Sgr/	FOR	AKI	DE3d	X-	LR	C	P	+	Y	*zgranulovat*
/Shl/	FFR	AKI	DE3d	L-	LR	C	P	+	N	*zhloupnout*
/Shm/	FFN	AKL	DE3d	XX	LR	C	P	+	N	*zhmotnit se*
/Shn/	FFN	AKA	DE3d	XX	LR	C	P	+	N	*zhnusit*
/Shň/	FFN	AKP	DE3d	XX	LR	C	P	+	N	*shnít*
/Shr/	FFR	AKI	DE3d	X-	LR	C	P	+	N	*zhroutit se*
/Shř/	FFR	AKI	DE3d	L-	LR	C	P	+	N	*zhřešit*
/Skl/	FOR	AKI	DE3d	L-	LR	C	P	–	N	*sklon*
/Skm/	FON	AKL	DE3d	XX	LR	C	S	–	N	*skmotřiti se* (SSJČ)
/Skn/	FON	AKA	DE3d	XX	LR	C	S	–	Y	*sknotiti se* (SSJČ)
(/Skň/)	FON	AKP	DE3d	XX	LR	C	S	–	N	*zknižnění* (PSJČ)
/Skr/	FOR	AKI	DE3d	X-	LR	C	P	–	Y	*zkrachovat*
/Skř/	FOR	AKI	DE3d	L-	LR	C	S	–	N	*zkřížit*
(/Sšl/)	FFR	API	DE3d	X-	LR	C	S	–	N	*zšlechtiti* (PSJČ)
/Stl/	FOR	AAI	DE3d	L-	LR	C	P	–	Y	*stlačit*
/Stm/	FON	AAL	DE3d	LR	LR	C	P	–	N	*stmívat se*
/Str/	FOR	AAI	DE3d	L-	LR	C	P	–	Y	*ztratit se*
/Stř/	FOR	AAI	DE3d	L-	LR	C	P	–	N	*střádat*
/Sxl/	FFR	AKI	DE3d	L-	LR	C	P	–	N	*schlíplý*
/Sxm/	FFN	AKL	DE3d	XX	LR	C	P	–	N	*zchmuřovat*
/Sxn/	FFN	AKA	DE3d	XX	XR	C	P	–	N	*schnout*
/Sxň/	FFN	AKP	DE3d	XX	LR	C	P	–	N	*schni*
/Sxr/	FFR	AKI	DE3d	X-	LR	C	P	–	N	*schránka*
/Sxř/	FFR	AKI	DE3d	X-	LR	C	P	–	N	*zchřadnout*
/Štr/	FOR	PAI	DE3d	L-	LR	C	S	–	Y	*štrachat*
/Škr/	FOR	PKI	DE3d	X-	LR	C	S	–	N	*škrábat*
/Škl/	FOR	PKI	DE3d	X-	LR	C	S	–	N	*šklebit se*
/Šhn/	FFN	PKA	DE3d	XX	LR	C	S	+	N	*žhnout*
/Šhň/	FFN	PKP	DE3d	XX	LR	C	S	+	N	*žhni*
/Tkl/	OOR	AKI	DE3d	L-	LR	C	S	–	N	*tklivý*
/Tkn/	OON	AKA	DE3d	LX	LR	C	S	–	Y	*tknout*
/Tkň/	OON	AKP	DE3d	LX	LR	C	S	–	N	*tkni*

/Tsl/	OFR	AAI	DE3d	X-	LR	C	S	–	Y	*clona*
/Tšl/	OFR	API	DE3d	L-	LR	C	S	–	N	*člověk*
(/Tšr/)	OFR	API	DE3d	L-	LR	C	S	–	N	*Črepa* (surname)
/Tsm/	OFN	AAL	DE3d	XX	LR	C	S	–	Y	*cmunda*
/Tšm/	OFN	APL	DE3d	XX	LR	C	S	–	Y	*čmárat*
/Tšň/	OFN	APP	DE3d	XX	LR	C	S	–	N	*čnět*
/Txn/	OFN	AKA	DE3d	XX	XR	C	S	–	N	*dchnouti* (SSJČ)
/Txň/	OFN	AKP	DE3d	XX	LR	C	S	–	N	*dchni* (imp. sg. of *dchnouti*)
/Fdl/	FOR	LAI	DE3e	--	LR	C	P	+	N	*vdláždit*
/Fdm/	FON	LAL	DE3e	-X	LR	C	P	+	N	*vdmýchnouti* (SSJČ)
/Fdr/	FOR	LAI	DE3e	--	LR	C	P	+	N	*vdrápati se* (SSJČ)
/Fhl/	FFR	LKI	DE3e	--	LR	C	P	+	N	*vhled*
(/Fhm/)	FFN	LKL	DE3e	-X	LR	C	S	+	N	*vhmatávati se* (PSJČ)
/Fhň/	FFN	LKP	DE3e	-X	LR	C	S	+	N	*vhníst*
/Fhr/	FFR	LKI	DE3e	--	LR	C	S	+	N	*vhrabat se*
/Fhř/	FFR	LKI	DE3e	--	LR	C	S	+	N	*vhřížiti* (SSJČ)
/Fkl/	FOR	LKI	DE3e	--	LR	C	S	–	N	*vklouznout*
/Fkr/	FOR	LKI	DE3e	--	LR	C	S	–	N	*vkrádat se*
/Fkř/	FOR	LKI	DE3e	--	LR	C	S	–	N	*vkřiknouti* (SSJČ)
(/Fzj/)	FFR	LAI	DE3e	--	LR	C	S	+	N	*vzjímati* (SSJČ)
/Fsl/	FFR	LAI	DE3e	--	LR	C	P	–	N	*vsled* (SSJČ)
/Fšl/	FFR	LPI	DE3e	--	LR	C	P	–	N	*všlehati* (SSJČ)
/Fsm/	FFN	LAL	DE3e	-R	LR	C	P	–	N	*vsmýknouti* (SSJČ)
(/Fsň/)	FFN	LAP	DE3e	-R	LR	C	P	–	N	*vsníti* (PSJČ)
/Fšr/	FFR	LPI	DE3e	--	LR	C	P	–	N	*všroubovat*
/Ftl/	FOR	LAI	DE3e	--	LR	C	P	–	N	*vtlačit*
/Ftm/	FON	LAL	DE3e	-X	LR	C	P	–	N	*vtmelit*
/Ftr/	FOR	LAI	DE3e	--	LR	C	P	–	N	*vtrousit*
/Ftř/	FOR	LAI	DE3e	--	LR	C	S	–	N	*vtřískat*
/Fxl/	FFR	LKI	DE3e	--	LR	C	P	–	N	*vchlípenina*
/Fzl/	FFR	LAI	DE3e	--	LR	C	P	+	N	*vzlétnout*
/Fzm/	FFN	LAL	DE3e	-R	LR	C	P	+	N	*vzmužit se*
/Fzn/	FFN	LAA	DE3e	-R	LR	C	S	+	N	*vznášet se*
/Fzň/	FFN	LAP	DE3e	-R	LR	C	P	+	N	*vznik*
/Fzr/	FFR	LAI	DE3e	--	LR	C	P	+	N	*vzruch*
/Fzř/	FFR	LAI	DE3e	--	LR	C	S	+	N	*vzření*
/Fžr/	FFR	LPI	DE3e	--	LR	C	P	+	N	*vžráti se* (SSJČ)
/jsm/	RFN	IAL	DE3e	-X	LR	C	S	–	N	*jsme*
/Mdl/	NOR	IAI	DE3e	--	LX	P	S	+	N	*mdlý*

/Mkl/	NOR	IKI	DE3e	--	LR	C	S	–	N	*mkla*[1]
/Mkn/	NON	IKA	DE3e	-X	LR	C	S	–	N	*mknouti* (SSJČ)
/Mkň/	NON	IKP	DE3e	-X	LR	C	S	–	N	*mkni* (imp. sg. of *mknouti*)
/Sbj/	FOR	ALI	DE3f	L-	LR	C	P	+	N	*sběr*
/Sbl/	FOR	ALI	DE3f	X-	LR	C	P	+	N	*zbláznit se*
/Šbl/	FOR	PLI	DE3f	X-	LR	C	P	+	N	*žbluňkat*
/Sbr/	FOR	ALI	DE3f	X-	LR	C	P	+	N	*zbrázděný*
/Sbř/	FOR	ALI	DE3f	L-	LR	C	P	+	N	*zbřidličnatět*
/Sfl/	FFR	ALI	DE3f	X-	LR	C	S	–	N	*zflákati* (SSJČ)
/Sfr/	FFR	ALI	DE3f	X-	LR	C	S	–	N	*zfruktizovati* (SSJČ)
/Spj/	FOR	ALI	DE3f	L-	LR	C	P	–	N	*spěchat*
/Spl/	FOR	ALI	DE3f	L-	LR	C	P	–	N	*splav*
/Spr/	FOR	ALI	DE3f	L-	LR	C	P	–	N	*správa*
/Spř/	FOR	ALI	DE3f	L-	LR	C	P	–	N	*spřízněný*
/Špr/	FOR	PLI	DE3f	X-	LR	C	P	–	N	*šproch*
/Šbr/	FOR	PLI	DE3f	X-	LR	C	P	+	N	*žbrunda*
/Špl/	FOR	PLI	DE3f	X-	LR	C	P	–	N	*šplouchat*
/Fbj/	FOR	LLI	DE3g	--	LR	C	P	+	N	*vběhnout*
/Fbl/	FOR	LLI	DE3g	--	LR	C	P	+	N	*vblízku* (SSJČ)
/Fbr/	FOR	LLI	DE3g	--	LR	C	P	+	N	*vbruslit*
/Fbř/	FOR	LLI	DE3g	--	LR	C	P	+	N	*vbřednouti* (SSJČ)
/Fpj/	FOR	LLI	DE3g	--	LR	C	P	–	N	*vpěchovat*
/Fpl/	FOR	LLI	DE3g	--	LR	C	P	–	N	*vplout*
/Fpr/	FOR	LLI	DE3g	--	LR	C	P	–	N	*vpravit*
/Fpř/	FOR	LLI	DE3g	--	LR	C	P	–	N	*vpřed*
/lpj/	ROR	ILI	DE3g	--	LR	C	S	–	N	*lpět*
/třm/	ORN	AIL	DE3h	-R	XR	P	S	–	N	*třmen*
/hřm/	FRN	KIL	DE3h	-R	XR	P	S	+	N	*hřmot*
/Sdv/	FOF	AAL	DE3i	XX	LR	C	P	M	N	*zdvojit*
/Skv/	FOF	AKL	DE3i	XR	LR	C	S	M	N	*skvost, skrvna*
/Stv/	FOF	AAL	DE3i	XX	LR	C	P	M	N	*stvořit, stvrdit*
/Sxv/	FFF	AKL	DE3i	LR	LR	C	S	M	N	*schválit*
/Škv/	FOF	PKL	DE3i	XX	LR	C	S	M	N	*škvařit se, škvrně*
/Štv/	FOF	PAL	DE3i	LX	LR	C	S	M	N	*štvát*
/Tkv/	OOF	AKL	DE3i	LR	LR	C	S	M	N	*tkví*
/Tšv/	OFF	APL	DE3i	XX	LR	C	S	M	N	*čvachtat*
/Tsv/	OFF	AAL	DE3i	LX	LR	C	S	M	N	*cválat, cvrnkat*
/Ftv/	FOF	LAL	DE3j	-X	LR	C	S	M	N	*vtvořiti* (SSJČ)
/Fzv/	FFF	LAL	DE3j	-R	LR	C	S	M	N	*vzvolati* (SSJČ)

---

1   3rd person feminine singular of *mknouti* (SSJČ).

/Fkv/	FOF	LKL	DE3j	-X	LR	C	S	M	N	*vkvartýrovati* (PSJČ)
(/břv/)	ORF	LIL	DE3k	-X	LR	C	S	M	N	*Břve* (Czech place name)
/FSd/	FFO	LAA	DE3l	-R	LR	C	P	+	N	*vzdálit se*
/FŠd/	FFO	LPA	DE3l	-R	LR	C	S	+	N	*vždy*
/FSh/	FFF	LAK	DE3l	-R	LR	C	P	+	N	*vzhůru*
/FSk/	FFO	LAK	DE3l	-R	LR	C	S	–	N	*vzkázat*
/FŠk/	FFO	LPK	DE3l	-R	LR	C	S	–	N	*vškatulkovati* (SSJČ)
/FSš/	FFF	LAP	DE3l	-R	LR	C	S	–	N	*vzšuměti* (SSJČ)
/FSt/	FFO	LAA	DE3l	-R	LR	C	P	–	N	*vstát, vstrčit*
/FSx/	FFF	LAK	DE3l	-R	LR	C	P	–	N	*vzchopit se*
/FTk/	FOO	LAK	DE3l	-X	LR	C	S	–	N	*vtkát*
/FTs/	FOF	LAA	DE3l	-X	LR	C	S	–	N	*vcelku*
/FTš/	FOF	LAP	DE3l	-R	LR	C	S	–	N	*včera, včrtati* (PSJČ)
/jSt/	RFO	IAA	DE3l	-X	LR	C	S	–	N	*jste*
/Křt/	ORO	KIA	DE3l	-X	XR	P	S	–	N	*křtu*
(/TŠk/)	OFO	APK	DE3l	-X	LR	C	S	–	N	*Čkyně* (Czech place name)
/MSd/	NFO	IAA	DE3l	-X	LX	P	P	+	N	*mzda*
/MSt/	NFO	IAA	DE3l	-R	LX	P	P	–	N	*msta*
(/MTs/)	NOF	IAA	DE3l	-X	LX	P	S	–	N	*Mcely* (Czech place name)
(/rTs/)	ROF	IAA	DE3l	-X	LR	C	S	–	N	*rci* (archaic form of *říct*)
/rTš/	ROF	IAP	DE3l	-X	LR	C	S	–	N	*rčení*
(/lTš/)	ROF	IAP	DE3l	-X	LX	P	S	–	N	*Lčovice* (Czech place name)
/STk/	FOO	AAK	DE3l	-R	LR	C	S	–	N	*stkát*
/STs/	FOF	AAA	DE3l	-R	LR	C	S	–	N	*scestný*
/STš/	FOF	AAP	DE3l	-X	LR	C	P	–	N	*zčeřit*
/STž/	FOF	AAP	DE3l	-X	LR	C	P	+	N	*zdžezovati* (SSJČ)
/ŠTk/	FOO	PAK	DE3l	-R	LR	C	S	–	N	*štkát*
/TŠt/	OFO	APA	DE3l	-R	LR	C	S	–	N	*čte, čtrnáct*
/Xřt/	FRO	KIA	DE3l	-X	XR	P	S	–	N	*chřtán*
/XTs/	FOF	KAA	DE3l	-X	LX	P	S	–	N	*chce*
/XTš/	FOF	KAP	DE3l	-X	LX	P	S	–	N	*chčije*
/FSb/	FFO	LAL	DE3m	-R	LR	C	P	+	N	*vzbudit*
/FSp/	FFO	LAL	DE3m	-R	LR	C	P	–	N	*vzpažit, vzprchnouti* (PSJČ)
/Třp/	ORO	AIL	DE3m	-X	XR	P	S	–	N	*třpyt*
/TŠb/	OFO	APL	DE3m	-X	LR	C	P	+	N	*džbán*
/TSp/	OFO	AAL	DE3m	-X	LR	C	(P)	–	Y	*cpát se*
(/TSb/)	OFO	AAL	DE3m	-X	LR	C	P	+	Y	*Dzbel* (Czech place name)
(/TŠp/)	OFO	APL	DE3m	-R	LR	C	P	–	N	*čpí*
/Xřb/	FRO	KIL	DE3m	-X	LR	C	S	+	N	*hřbitov*
/PSď/	OFO	LAP	DE3n	--	LR	C	S	+	N	*bzditi* (SSJČ)
(/PŠť/)	OFO	LPP	DE3n	--	LR	C	S	–	N	*Pština* (Czech place name)

/FSď/	FFO	LAP	DE3n	--	LR	C	P	+	N	vzdělaný
/FSť/	FFO	LAP	DE3n	--	LR	C	P	–	N	vstěhovati (SSJČ)
/FŠť/	FFO	LPP	DE3n	--	LR	C	S	–	N	vštípit
/Křť/	ORO	KIP	DE3n	--	XR	P	S	–	N	křtiny
/KŠť/	OFO	KPP	DE3n	--	LR	C	S	–	N	kštice
/lSť/	RFO	IAP	DE3n	--	LX	P	S	–	N	lstivý
(/MŠť/)	NFO	IPP	DE3n	--	LR	P	S	–	Y	Mštěnovice (Cz. place name)
(/lŠť/)	RFO	IPP	DE3n	--	LX	P	S	–	N	Lštěň (Czech place name)
/MSď/	NFO	IAP	DE3n	--	LX	P	P	+	N	mzdě
/MSť/	NFO	IAP	DE3n	--	LX	P	P	–	N	mstít se
/Třť/	ORO	AIP	DE3n	--	XR	P	S	–	N	třtina
/TSť/	OFO	AAP	DE3n	--	LR	C	S	–	N	ctí
/TŠť/	OFO	APP	DE3n	--	LR	C	S	–	N	čti
(/SŠť/)	FFO	APP	DE3n	--	LR	C	S	–	N	zšťastniti (PSJČ)
/Tkvj/	OOFR	AKLI	DE4a	X-	LR	C	S	M	N	tkvět
/StMň/	FONN	AAIP	DE4a	X-	LR	C	S	–	N	stmělý (SSJČ)
/Skvj/	FOFR	AKLI	DE4a	L-	LR	C	S	M	N	skvělý
/Shvj/	FFFR	AKLI	DE4a	X-	LX	P	P	M	N	zhvězditi (SSJČ)
/Sxvj/	FFFR	AKLI	DE4a	X-	LR	C	P	M	N	schvělý (SSJČ)
(/FsMň/)	FFNN	LAIP	DE4b	--	LR	C	P	–	N	vsměstnati (PSJČ)
(/Fzvj/)	FFFR	LALI	DE4b	--	LR	C	S	M	Y	vzvěděti (PSJČ)
(/FzMň/)	FFNN	LAIP	DE4b	--	LR	C	P	+	N	vzměť (PSJČ)
/třMň/	ORNN	AIIP	DE4c	--	XR	P	S	–	N	třměti (SSJČ)
/hřMň/	FRNN	KIIP	DE4c	--	XR	P	S	+	N	hřmět
/FSdm/	FFON	LAAL	DE4d	-X	LR	C	S	+	N	vzdmýchati (SSJČ)
/FShl/	FFFR	LAKI	DE4d	--	LR	C	P	+	N	vzhlížet
(/FShř/)	FFFR	LAKI	DE4d	--	LR	C	S	+	N	vzhřížiti (PSJČ)
/FSkl/	FFOR	LAKI	DE4d	--	LR	C	S	–	N	vzkličit
/FSkř/	FFOR	LAKI	DE4d	--	LR	C	S	–	N	vzkřísit
/FŠkr/	FFOR	LPKI	DE4d	--	LR	C	S	–	N	vškrábat se
/FStl/	FFOR	LAAI	DE4d	--	LR	C	S	–	N	vztlak
/FStř/	FFOR	LAAI	DE4d	--	LR	C	S	–	N	vstřícný
(/FSxl/)	FFFR	LAKI	DE4d	--	LR	C	P	–	N	vzchlípiti (PSJČ)
/FTšl/	FOFR	LAPI	DE4d	--	LR	C	S	–	N	včlenit
/lStm/	RFON	IAAL	DE4d	-X	LX	P	S	–	N	lstmi
/lStn/	RFON	IAAA	DE4d	-X	XX	P	S	–	N	lstný
/lStň/	RFON	IAAP	DE4d	-X	XX	P	S	–	N	lstně
/MStn/	NFON	IAAA	DE4d	-X	XR	P	S	–	N	mstný (SSJČ)
/MStň/	NFON	IAAP	DE4d	-X	XR	P	S	–	N	mstně (PSJČ)
/PStr/	OFOR	LAAI	DE4d	--	LX	P	S	–	N	pstruh
/PStř/	OFOR	LAAI	DE4d	--	LX	P	S	–	N	pstřeň (PSJČ)

/PŠtr/	OFOR	LPAI	DE4d	--	LX	P	S	-	N	*pštros*
/STšl/	FOFR	AAPI	DE4d	--	LR	C	S	-	N	*sčleniti* (SSJČ)
/STkl/	FOOR	AAKI	DE4d	--	LR	C	S	-	N	*ztklivět*
/ŠTkn/	FOON	PAKA	DE4d	-X	LR	C	S	-	N	*štknout*
/ŠTkň/	FOON	PAKP	DE4d	-X	LR	C	S	-	N	*štkni*
/TStm/	OFON	AAAL	DE4d	--	LX	P	S	-	N	*ctmi*
/TStn/	OFON	AAAA	DE4d	--	LX	P	S	-	N	*ctný* (SSJČ)
/TStň/	OFON	AAAP	DE4d	--	LX	P	S	-	N	*ctně*
/FSbj/	FFOR	LALI	DE4e	--	LR	C	P	+	N	*vzběhnouti* (SSJČ)
(/FSbř/)	FFOR	LALI	DE4e	--	LR	C	P	+	N	*vzbředlý* (PSJČ)
/FSpj/	FFOR	LALI	DE4e	--	LR	C	P	-	N	*vzpěrač*
/FSpl/	FFOR	LALI	DE4e	--	LR	C	S	-	N	*vzplanout*
/TŠpj/	OFOR	APLI	DE4e	--	LX	P	S	-	N	*čpět*
/FSpn/	FFON	LALA	DE4e	--	XR	P	S	-	N	*vzpnouti se* (SSJČ)
/FSpň/	FFON	LALP	DE4e	--	XR	P	S	-	N	*vzpni se*
/FSpr/	FFOR	LALI	DE4e	--	LR	C	S	-	N	*vzpruha*
/FSpř/	FFOR	LALI	DE4e	--	LR	C	P	-	N	*vzpřímený*
/TSpj/	OFOR	AALI	DE4e	--	LR	C	S	-	N	*cpěte se*
/TŠpj/	OFOR	APLI	DE4e	--	XR	P	S	-	N	*čpět*
/FSkv/	FFOF	LAKL	DE4f	-R	LR	C	S	M	N	*vzkvétat*
(/FSxv/)	FFFF	LAKL	DE4f	-X	LR	C	S	M	N	*vzchvívati se* (PSJČ)
/TŠtv/	OFOF	APAL	DE4f	-X	LR	C	S	M	N	*čtvero, čtvrtek*
/STsv/	FOFF	AAAL	DE4f	-X	LR	C	S	M	N	*scvaknout, scvrknout*
/STkv/	FOOF	AAKL	DE4f	-X	LR	C	S	M	N	*stkví*
/FSkvj/	FFOFR	LAKLI	DE5	--	LR	C	S	M	N	*vzkvět*
/STkvj/	FOOFR	AAKLI	DE5	--	LR	C	S	M	N	*stkvěl*

Post-nuclear combinations (104)

Com	MT	PT	DT	E	R	Rs	M	Example
/jF/	RF	IL	DI2a	-X	--	-	Y	*sejf*
/jK/	RO	IK	DI2a	-X	--	-	Y	*laik*
/jP/	RO	IL	DI2a	-X	--	-	Y	*knajp* (gen. pl. of *knajpa*)
/jS/	RF	IA	DI2a	-R	--	-	Y	*rorejs*
/jŠ/	RF	IP	DI2a	-X	--	-	N	*jejž*
/jT/	RO	IA	DI2a	-R	--	-	N	*prejt*
/jX/	RF	IK	DI2a	-X	--	-	N	*cejch*
(/jř/)	RR	II	DI2a	-X	--	-	N	*Kejř* (surname)
/lF/	RF	IL	DI2a	-X	--	-	Y	*salv*
/lK/	RO	IK	DI2a	-X	--	-	Y	*kalk*

/lP/	RO	IL	DI2a	-X	--	-	Y	*alb* (gen. pl. of *album*)
/lS/	RF	IA	DI2a	-R	--	-	Y	*pulz*
/lT/	RO	IA	DI2a	-R	--	-	Y	*kolt*
/lX/	RF	IK	DI2a	-X	--	-	Y	*valch*
(/lŠ/)	RF	IP	DI2a	-X	--	-	Y	*Tylš* (surname)
/mF/	NF	LL	DI2a	-X	--	-	Y	*nymf* (gen. pl. of *nymfa*)
/mP/	NO	LL	DI2a	-R	--	-	N	*lamp*
/mS/	NF	LA	DI2a	-R	--	-	Y	*říms* (gen. pl. of *římsa*)
/mŠ/	NF	LP	DI2a	-R	--	-	Y	*jímž*
/mT/	NO	LA	DI2a	-X	--	-	Y	*vikomt* (SSJČ)
/mX/	NF	LK	DI2a	-X	--	-	Y	*střemch* (gen. pl. of *střemcha*)
/nF/	NF	AL	DI2a	-X	--	-	Y	*tonf* (gen. pl. of *tonfa* (SN1))
/nK/	NO	AK	DI2a	-R	--	-	Y	*tank, cvrnkat*
/nS/	NF	AA	DI2a	-R	--	-	Y	*tranz*
/nŠ/	NF	AP	DI2a	-X	--	-	Y	*jenž*
/nT/	NO	AA	DI2a	-R	--	-	Y	*moment*
/rF/	RF	IL	DI2a	-X	--	-	Y	*harf*
/rK/	RO	IK	DI2a	-R	--	-	Y	*park*
/rP/	RO	IL	DI2a	-R	--	-	Y	*orb* (gen. pl. of *orba*)
/rS/	RF	IA	DI2a	-R	--	-	Y	*kurz*
/rŠ/	RF	IP	DI2a	-X	--	-	Y	*verš*
/rT/	RO	IA	DI2a	-R	--	-	Y	*nárt*
/rX/	RF	IK	DI2a	-X	--	-	Y	*arch*
/Př/	OR	LI	DI2a	X-	--	-	Y	*pepř*
/PS/	OF	LA	DI2a	XR	--	-	Y	*zips*
/Tř/	OR	AI	DI2a	-X	--	-	Y	*dovnitř*
/TS/	OF	AA	DI2a	LR	--	-	Y	*pec, mudrc*
/Kř/	OR	KI	DI2a	X-	--	-	Y	*mokř* (SSJČ)
/KS/	OF	KA	DI2a	LR	--	-	Y	*koks*
/jŤ/	RO	IP	DI2b	--	--	-	N	*pojď*
(/lŤ/)	RO	IP	DI2b	--	--	-	N	*bylť* (archaic form)
(/mŤ/)	NO	LP	DI2b	--	--	-	N	*jsemť* (archaic form)
(/nŤ/)	NO	AP	DI2b	--	--	-	N	*onť* (archaic form)
/rŤ/	RO	IP	DI2b	--	--	-	N	*žerď*
/jl/	RR	II	DI2c	--	--	-	Y	*koktejl*
/jm/	RN	IL	DI2c	--	--	-	Y	*Sejm* (SSJČ), *tajm* (SN1)
/jn/	RN	IA	DI2c	--	--	-	N	*hejn* (gen. pl. of *hejno*)
/jr/	RR	II	DI2c	--	--	-	Y	*chejr* (SSJČ)
/lm/	RN	IL	DI2c	--	--	-	Y	*jilm*
(/ln/)	RN	IA	DI2c	--	--	-	Y	*Lincoln* (surname)
/rl/	RR	II	DI2c	--	--	-	N	*stárl*

/rm/	RN	IL	DI2c	--	--	-	Y	*šarm*
/rn/	RN	IA	DI2c	--	--	-	Y	*koncern*
/rň/	RN	IP	DI2c	--	--	-	Y	*čerň*
/FK/	FO	LK	DI2d	X-	--	-	Y	*tomahavk*
/FT/	FO	LA	DI2d	X-	--	-	Y	*pravd*
/PT/	OO	LA	DI2d	LX	--	-	Y	*skript* (gen. pl. of *skriptum*)
/PŤ/	OO	LP	DI2d	L-	--	-	Y	*nebť* (SSJČ)
(/PŠ/)	OF	LP	DI2d	XX	--	-	Y	*Hybš* (surname)
/TŠ/	OF	AP	DI2d	L-	--	-	Y	*meč, mlč*
/KŠ/	OF	KP	DI2d	XX	--	-	Y	*jakžtakž*
/KT/	OO	KA	DI2d	LX	--	-	Y	*akt*
/KŤ/	OO	KP	DI2d	L-	--	-	N	*všakť* (SSJČ)
/řK/	RO	IK	DI2d	X-	--	-	Y	*ouřk* (SSJČ), *Pyřk* (surname)
/řT/	RO	IA	DI2d	X-	--	-	Y	*buřt*
/SK/	FO	AK	DI2d	L-	--	-	Y	*lesk, prsk* (SSJČ)
/ST/	FO	AA	DI2d	L-	--	-	Y	*dost, prst*
/SŤ/	FO	AP	DI2d	X-	--	-	N	*pusť, prsť*
(/SP/)	FO	AL	DI2d	L-	--	-	Y	*výsp* (gen. pl. of *výspa*)
/ŠT/	FO	PA	DI2d	L-	--	-	Y	*mošt, obršt* (SSJČ)
/ŠŤ/	FO	PP	DI2d	X-	--	-	N	*poušť, smršť*
(/XS/)	FF	KA	DI2d	X-	--	-	Y	*Fuchs* (surname)
/XŠ/	FF	KP	DI2d	X-	--	-	Y	*jejichž*
/XT/	FO	KA	DI2d	X-	--	-	Y	*ksicht* (SSJČ)
/XŤ/	FO	KP	DI2d	X-	--	-	N	*nechť*
/jSK/	RFO	IAK	DI3	--	LR	C	N	*vojsk*
/jST/	RFO	IAA	DI3	--	LR	C	N	*gajst* (SSJČ)
/jTS/	ROF	IAA	DI3	--	LR	C	N	*AIDS* (pronounced [ajts])
/jTŠ/	ROF	IAP	DI3	--	LR	C	N	*půjč*
/KST/	OFO	KAA	DI3	--	LR	C	N	*text*
/lTS/	ROF	IAA	DI3	--	LR	C	Y	*sulc*
/mST/	NFO	LAA	DI3	--	LR	C	Y	*pomst*
/mŠT/	NFO	LPA	DI3	--	LR	C	Y	*kumšt*
/nKT/	NOO	AKA	DI3	--	LR	C	Y	*adjunkt*
/nTS/	NOF	AAA	DI3	--	LR	C	N	*princ, šmrnc*
/nTŠ/	NOF	AAP	DI3	--	LR	C	N	*pomeranč*
/PST/	OFO	LAA	DI3	--	LR	C	Y	*zábst*
/rKT/	ROO	IKA	DI3	--	LR	C	Y	*infarkt*
/rPT/	ROO	ILA	DI3	--	LR	C	N	*excerpt* (SSJČ)
/rST/	RFO	IAA	DI3	--	LR	C	N	*verst* (gen. pl. of *versta*)
/rTS/	ROF	IAA	DI3	--	LR	C	Y	*herc*
/rTŠ/	ROF	IAP	DI3	--	LR	C	Y	*terč*

/TSP/	OFO	AAP	DI3	--	LR	C	N	*zácp* (gen. pl. of *zácpa*)
/TST/	OFO	AAA	DI3	--	LR	C	N	*péct*
(/TŠŤ/)	OFO	APP	DI3	--	LR	C	N	*ačť* (archaic)
(/lSK/)	RFO	IAK	DI3	--	LR	C	N	*Tobolsk* (foreign place name)
(/lST/)	RFO	IAA	DI3	--	LR	C	Y	*Holst* (surname)
(/lTŠ/)	ROF	IAP	DI3	--	LR	C	N	*Telč* (Czech place name)
(/nKS/)	NOF	AKA	DI3	--	LR	C	Y	*Sfinx* (brand name)
(/nSK/)	NFO	AAK	DI3	--	LR	C	N	*Smolensk* (foreign place name)
(/PSK/)	OFO	LAK	DI3	--	LR	C	N	*Vitebsk* (foreign place name)
(/rKS/)	ROF	IKA	DI3	--	LR	C	Y	*Marx* (surname)
(/rSK/)	RFO	IAK	DI3	--	LR	C	N	*Magnitogorsk* (for. place name)
(/TSK/)	OFO	AAK	DI3	--	LR	C	N	*Kuzněck* (foreign place name)

Appendix C: POTENTIAL PRE-NUCLEAR AND POST-NUCLEAR COMBINATIONS

Pre-nuclear combinations (789)

Pd	Kž	Xď	Mt	řt	jť	jz	rn
Tp	gm	Šf	Md	řd	řť	jš	jn
Kp	gň	Šx	Mť	lt	řď	jž	jň
Kď	gř	Xf	Mď	ld	rk	rh	řn
Ph	gj	fn	Ms	jt	jk	jx	řň
Tf	Šg	xn	rb	lť	řf	lm	rň
Kz	Xp	fř	řp	lď	jv	řm	

Tkm	Tsň	křv	Fgv	Fkň	Fgl	Fsv	svň
Tkj	Tšn	přm	STz	Spn	Fgr	FSž	Sfň
Tkr	Txm	břm	STx	Spň	Fgř	Fšv	Sšm
Tkř	tvj	přn	STh	Stn	Fkj	Fžv	Sžm
PSt	Tsj	břn	Sgv	Sdn	Sgj	FŠh	Sšn
PSd	Tsr	přň	Šdv	Stň	Sgř	FŠx	Sžn
PSť	Tsř	břň	ŠTs	Sdň	Skj	Fxv	Sšň
PSk	tMn	dřm	ŠTz	Sgm	Šbj	Fhv	Sžň
PŠt	dMn	třn	ŠTš	Sgn	Špj	Sšv	Šfn
PŠd	Přd	dřn	ŠTž	Sgň	Šdl	Sžv	Šfň
PŠď	Přt	třň	ŠTx	Špn	Šdr	SŠx	Šxm
PŠk	Přť	dřň	ŠTh	Špň	Štl	SŠh	Šhm
TSt	Přď	křm	Šgv	Štm	Šgj	Shv	Šxn
TSd	Přk	křn	XTz	Šdm	Šgl	Fsn	Šxň
TSď	Třb	křň	XTž	Štn	Šgr	Fšm	Fsj
TSk	Třt	FTp	Fpn	Šdn	Škj	Fžm	Fsr
TŠd	Třd	FTb	Fpň	Štň	FŠp	Fšn	Fsř
TŠď	Třď	STp	Ftn	Šdň	FŠb	Fžn	Fžl
KSt	Třk	STb	Fdn	Škm	FŠt	Fšň	Fxr
KSd	Křp	ŠTp	Fdň	Šgm	FŠď	Fžň	Fxř
KSť	Křb	ŠTb	Ftň	Škn	SŠb	Fxm	svř
KSď	Křd	Fdv	Fgm	Šgn	SŠp	Fhn	Sfj
KŠt	Křď	FTz	Fkm	Škň	SŠd	Fxn	Sfř
KŠd	přv	FTž	Fgn	Šgň	SŠt	Fxň	Sšr
KŠď	třv	FTx	Fkn	Fdř	SŠď	svn	Sžl
Tsn	dřv	FTh	Fgň	Fgj	SŠk	Sfn	Sžr

Šfj	xMř	Xřd	xřň	jTs	jSť	jŠk	jhn
Šfl	hMř	Xřť	MTz	jTz	jSď	lŠk	jxň
Šfr	xMr	Xřď	MTš	lTs	lSď	rŠk	jhň
Šxl	hMr	vřm	MTž	lTz	rSť	jvn	lvj
Šhl	Fřp	fřm	Mtn	rTz	rSď	jvň	rzj
Šxr	Fřb	vřn	Mdn	jTš	jSk	jzm	lzj
Šhr	Fřt	fřn	Mtň	jTž	lSk	jsn	jMn
vMn	Fřd	fřň	Mdň	lTž	rSk	jzn	lMn
sMn	Fřť	vřň	Mdr	rTž	jŠt	jsň	rMn
vMj	Fřď	sřm	Mdř	lbj	jŠd	jzň	řMn
vMr	Fřk	zřm	Mtl	rpj	lŠt	jšm	lMň
vMř	Sřp	sřn	Mtr	rbj	lŠd	jžm	rMň
sMj	Sřb	zřn	Mtř	lkj	rŠt	jšn	řMň
sMř	Sřt	sřň	Mkj	rkj	rŠd	jžn	
zMj	Sřd	zřň	Mkr	jSd	jŠť	jšň	
xMj	Sřť	xřm	Mkř	lSt	jŠď	jžň	
hMj	Sřď	hřn	MŠt	lSd	lŠď	jxm	
xMl	Sřk	xřn	MŠd	rSt	rŠť	jhm	
hMl	Xřp	hřň	MŠď	rSd	rŠď	jxn	

PStv	PŠtň	PSdř	TSkj	třMn	FTšv	ŠTšr	FSdň
PSdv	PŠkm	PStl	TSkl	dřMn	STšv	Škvj	FSkm
PSkv	PŠkn	PSkj	TSkr	dřMň	ŠTsv	FtMn	FSkn
PŠtv	PŠkň	PSkl	TSkř	křMn	ŠTšv	FdMn	FSkň
PŠdv	TSpn	PSkr	TŠbj	křMň	Ftvj	FtMň	FŠpn
PŠkv	TSpň	PSkř	TŠpl	FTkv	Fdvj	FdMň	FŠpň
TStv	TSdm	PŠtl	TŠbl	ŠTkv	FTsj	StMn	FŠtm
TSdv	TSdn	PŠdl	TŠpr	FTkm	FTsl	SdMn	FŠdm
TSkv	TSdň	PŠdr	TŠbr	FTkn	FTsr	ŠtMň	FŠtn
TŠdv	TSkm	PŠkj	TŠtl	FTkň	FTsř	ŠdMň	FŠdn
TŠkv	TSkn	PŠkl	TŠdl	STkm	FTšr	SdMň	FŠtň
PSdm	TSkň	PŠkr	TŠtr	STkn	Fkvj	ŠtMn	FŠdň
PStm	TŠpn	TSpl	TŠdr	STkň	Stvj	ŠdMn	FŠkm
PSdn	TŠpň	TSpr	TŠkj	ŠTkm	Sdvj	FStv	FŠkn
PStn	TŠtm	TSpř	TŠkl	FTkj	STsj	FSdv	FŠkň
PSdň	TŠdm	TSbl	TŠkr	FTkl	STsl	FŠtv	SŠpn
PStň	TŠtn	TSbj	přvj	FTkr	STsr	FŠdv	SŠpň
PSkm	TŠdn	TSbř	břvj	FTkř	STsř	FŠkv	SŠtm
PSkn	TŠtň	TSbr	třvj	STkj	STšr	SŠtv	SŠdm
PSkň	TŠdň	TStl	dřvj	STkr	Šdvj	SŠdv	SŠtn
PŠdm	TŠkm	TSdl	křvj	STkř	Štvj	SŠkv	SŠdn
PŠtm	TŠkn	TStr	přMn	ŠTkj	ŠTsj	FStm	SŠtň
PŠdn	TŠkň	TStř	břMn	ŠTkl	ŠTsl	FStn	SŠdň
PŠtn	PSdl	TSdr	přMň	ŠTkr	ŠTsr	FSdn	SŠkm
PŠdň	PSdr	TSdř	břMň	FTsv	ŠTšl	FStň	SŠkn

SŠkň	FŠbr	SŠtl	FSxr	FzMn	MSdn	rStň	rŠtn
FSbr	FŠtl	SŠdl	FShr	fřMn	MSdň	rSdň	rŠdn
FSbl	FŠdl	SŠdr	FSxř	vřMn	MŠdm	lSdň	lŠtň
FSdl	FŠtr	SŠkl	FŠxr	fřMň	MŠtm	lSkm	lŠdn
FStr	FŠdr	SŠkj	FŠhl	vřMň	MŠdn	rSkm	rŠtň
FSdr	FŠkj	SŠkr	FŠxl	sřMn	MŠtn	rSkn	rŠdň
FSdř	FŠkl	FSšv	FŠhr	zřMn	MŠdň	lSkn	lŠdň
FSkj	SŠpr	FSžv	Fxvj	sřMň	MŠtň	rSkň	rŠkm
FSkr	SŠbr	FShv	Fhvj	zřMň	rStm	lSkň	lŠkm
FŠpj	SŠpl	Fsvj	SŠxl	xřMn	rSdm	lŠtm	lŠkn
FŠbj	SŠbl	FSšl	SŠxr	hřMn	lSdm	rŠtm	rŠkn
FŠpl	SŠpj	FSšr	SŠhr	xřMň	rStn	rŠdm	lŠkň
FŠbl	SŠbj	FSžl	SŠhl	MSdm	rSdn	lŠdm	rŠkň
FŠpr	SŠtr	FSžr	FsMn	MStm	lSdn	lŠtn	

FTkvj	FSdvj	FŠkvj	SŠkvj	FStMň	FŠdMn	SŠtMn	SŠdMň
ŠTkvj	FŠtvj	SŠtvj	FStMn	FSdMň	FŠtMň	SŠdMn	FSxvj
FStvj	FŠdvj	SŠdvj	FSdMn	FŠtMn	FŠdMň	SŠtMň	FShvj

Post-nuclear combinations (46)

FŤ	mK	ňT	ňK	ňS	ňX	řŤ	lň
ŠK	nP	ňŤ	nX	ňŠ	řP	jň	lr

PSP	TSŤ	KŠŤ	mKS	nSŤ	lKT	rPS	lSŤ
PSŤ	TŠT	mKT	mSŤ	nŠT	jKT	lKS	rSŤ
PŠT	KSŤ	mTS	mSK	jPT	jPS	jKS	
PŠŤ	KŠT	mTŠ	nST	lPT	lPS	jSŤ	

Appendix D: DISTRIBUTION OF NUCLEAR PHONEMES

This appendix provides examples of words in which phonotactic properties of nuclear phonemes are attested; they are discussed in chapter 10. Phonological representation is given only when necessary.

/i/	F0	F1	F2	F3
P0	i	Ir	Ind	
P1	ti	/miŠ/ myš	/ñiXŠ/ nichž	(Minsk)
P2	zdi	/pliŠ/ plyš	/KsiXT/ ksicht	instikt
P3	vždy	vznik	/FStiTŠ/ vztyč	
P4		vstřik		
P5				

/e/	F0	F1	F2	F3
P0		es	erb	
P1	ne	jet	jenž	verst
P2	vře	/vjeT/ vět	/xřeST/ chřest	
P3	jsme	/kvjeT/ květ	/StřemX/ střemch	
P4	/lStňe/ lstně	vzhled		
P5		/STkvjel/ stkvěl		

/a/	F0	F1	F2	F3
P0	a	až	akt	
P1	na	pak	tank	infarkt
P2	kra	mrak	start	
P3	skla	/StraX/ strach	/StlaTŠ/ stlač	/SxramST/[1]
P4		vztlak		
P5				

/o/	F0	F1	F2	F3
P0	o	on	orb	
P1	to	tok	most	vojsk
P2	sto	/StoX/ stoh	sport	
P3	sklo	vzdor	skvost	
P4		pštros	/TStnoST/ ctnost	
P5				

---

1 Extracted from *schramstnout*.

/u/	F0	F1	F2	F3
P0	*u*	*už*	*uzd*	
P1	*tu*	*tuž*	*kurt*	*kumšt*
P2	*mnu*	*stud*	*špunt*	
P3	*mzdu*	*vzmuž (se)*	/StluTŠ/ *stluč*	
P4		*pstruh*		
P5				

/ī/	F0	F1	F2	F3
P0				
P1	*jí*	*jít*	*míst*	/řīTST/ *říct*
P2	*spí*	*znít*	*sníst*	/zřīTST/ *zříct*
P3	*tkví*	/SkrīT/ *skrýt*	*zhníst*	
P4	*stkví*	/lStnīX/ *lstných*	/FStřīTS/ *vstříc*	
P5				

/ē/	F0	F1	F2	F3
P0		*ér*		
P1	*té*	*fén*	*lézt*	/pēTST/ *péct*
P2	*své*	*sfér*	*plést*	/StēTST/ *stéct*
P3	*mdlé*	*mdlém*	*vznést*	/svlēTST/ *svléct*
P4	/TStnē/ *ctné*	/TStnēm/ *ctném*	*vzkvést*	
P5				

/ā/	F0	F1	F2	F3
P0		*ár*		
P1	*já*	*náš*	*nárt*	*zábst*
P2	*svá*	*zdát*	*zmást*	
P3	*mdlá*	/Xřtān/ *chřtán*	*střást*	
P4	/TStnā/ *ctná*	*vzplát*		
P5				

/ō/	F0	F1	F2	F3
P0		*ód*		
P1	/tō/ fr. *šapitó*	*gól*		
P2	/grō/ *gros*	/xlōr/ *chlór*		
P3				
P4				
P5				

/ū/	F0	F1	F2	F3
P0		*úl*	*úst*	/ūTST/ *úct*
P1		*kůl*	*půst*	
P2	*rtů*	*stůl*	*vrůst*	
P3	*křtů*	*stvůr*	*vzrůst*	
P4				
P5				

/ë/	F0	F1	F2	F3
P0		/ër/ *eur*		
P1	/lë/ *leu*²	/zëK/ fr. *zeugma*		
P2				
P3				
P4				
P5				

/ä/	F0	F1	F2	F3
P0		/äT/ *aut*		
P1	/tä/ *tau*	/räT/ *raut*	/gäTŠ/ *gauč*	
P2	/Tšä/ *čau*	/SkäT/ *skaut*		
P3				
P4				
P5				

/ö/	F0	F1	F2	F3
P0				
P1	/mö/ *mou*	/pöŤ/ *pouť*	/pöŠŤ/ *poušť*	
P2	/dvö/ *dvou*		/xröST/ *chroust*	/tlöTST/ *tlouct*
P3	/Mdlö/ *mdlou*	/FplöT/ *plout*		/StlöTST/ *stlouct*
P4	/TStnö/ *ctnou*			
P5				

/r/	F0	F1	F2	F3
P1	hr	*vrt*	*prst*	
P2	/Str/ from *mistr*	*šprt*	*smršť*	/šMrnTS/ *šmrnc*
P3		*skvrn*	/FStrTŠ/ *vstrč*	
P4		/TŠtvrT/ *čtvrt*		

/l/	F0	F1	F2	F3
P1	/hl/ from *vrhl*	*mlž*	*plst*	
P2	/Sxl/ from *uschl*	*šplh*	/sMlTŠ/ *smlč*	
P3				
P4				

---

2   The name of the Romanian currency.

REFERENCES

Akamatsu, Tsutomu. 1988. *The Theory of Neutralization and the Archiphoneme in Functional Phonology*. John Benjamins Publishing Company.
—. 1992. *Essentials of Functional Phonology*. Peeters.
Algeo, John. 1978. "What consonant clusters are possible?". *Word* 29.206–24.
Appel, Wilhelm. 1957–8. "Energiebasis – Artikulationsbasis". *Wiener slavistisches Jahrbuch* 6.73–104.
Arnold, Gordon F. 1955–6. "A phonological approach to vowel, consonant and syllable in modern French". *Lingua* 5.253–87.
—. 1964. "Vowel and consonant: a phonological definition re-examined". *In Honour of Daniel Jones* (eds. David Abercrombie et al.), 16–25. Longmans.
ASCS = *Akademický slovník cizích slov I–II* [Academic dictionary of foreign words]. Academia, 1995.
Awedyk, Wiesław. 1975. *The Syllable Theory and Old English Phonology*. Wydawnictwo Polskiej akademii nauk.
Bagemihl, Bruce. 1991. "Syllable structure in Bella Coola". *Linguistic Inquiry* 22:4.589–646.
Bárkányi, Zsuzsanna – Kiss, Zoltán. 2010. "A phonetic approach to the phonology of *v*: A case study from Hungarian and Slovak". *Turbulent Sounds. An Interdisciplinary Guide* (eds. Susanne Fuchs – Martine Toda – Margena Żygis), 103–42. de Gruyter.
Bartoň, Tomáš et al. 2009. *Statistiky češtiny*. Nakladatelství Lidové noviny – Ústav Českého národního korpusu.
Bell, Alan. 1976. "The distributional syllable". *Linguistic Studies Offered to Joseph Greenberg, Vol. 2: Phonology* (ed. Alphonse Juilland), 249–62. Anma Libri.
—. 1978. "Syllabic consonants". *Universals of Human Language, Vol. 2: Phonology* (ed. Joseph Greenberg), 153–201. Stanford University Press.
Bell, Alan – Hooper, Joan. 1978. "Issues and evidence in syllabic phonology". *Syllables and Segments* (eds. Alan Bell – Joan B. Hooper), 3–22. North-Holland Publishing Company.
Bermel, Neil. 2010. "O tzv. české diglosii v současném světě". *Slovo a slovesnost* 71.5–30.

Bethin, Christina Y. 2003a. "Prosodic effects in Czech morphology". *American Contributions to the Thirteenth International Congress of Slavists, Ljubljana* (eds. Robert Maquire – Alan Timberlake), 9–22. Slavica.

—. 2003b. "Metrical quantity in Czech: Evidence from hypocoristics". *Formal Approaches to Slavic Linguistics 11: The Amherst Meeting 2002* (eds. Wayles Browne et al.), 63–82. Michigan Slavic Materials.

Bičan, Aleš. 2008a. *Phonematics of Czech: An Axiomatic-functionalist View.* Masaryk University. Unpublished PhDr. thesis, available online: <http://www.phil.muni.cz/linguistica/art/bican/bic-rigo.pdf>.

—. 2008b. "Accent and diaereme in Czech". *La Linguistique* 44:2.45–66.

—. 2010. "Čím je *Petr* zvláštní aneb kombinovatelnost slabičného /r/ v češtině". *Karlík a továrna na lingvistiku* (eds. Aleš Bičan et al.), 49–68. Host – Masarykova univerzita.

—. 2011a. "Distribution and combinations of Czech consonants". *Zeitschrift für Slawistik* 56:2.153–71.

—. 2011b. "Structure of syllables in Czech". *Formalization of Grammar in Slavic Languages* (eds. Peter Kosta – Lilia Schürks), 13–28. Peter Lang.

—. 2011c. "Distribuční a kombinační vlastnosti /ř/ v současné češtině". *m*OST 2009. Österreichische StudierendenTagung für SlawistInnen* (ed. Dagmar Heeg), 36–42. Verlag Otto Sagner.

—. 2011d. "Distributional unit: Hypothesis and testing". *Axiomatic Functionalism: Theory and Application* (eds. Aleš Bičan – Paul Rastall), 103–42. Peter Lang.

—. 2011e. *Phonotactics of Czech.* Masaryk University. PhD. thesis.

Bičan, Aleš – Rastall, Paul (eds.). 2011. *Axiomatic Functionalism: Theory and Application.* Peter Lang.

Blevins, Juliette. 1995. "The syllable in phonological theory". *The Handbook of Phonological Theory* (ed. John Goldsmith), 206–44. Blackwell.

—. 2003. "Independent nature of phonotactic constraints". *The Syllable in Optimality Theory* (eds. Caroline Féry – Ruben van de Vijver), 375–403. Cambridge University Press.

—. 2006. "Syllable: typology". *Encyclopedia of Language and Linguistics, Vol. 12* (ed. Keith Brown), 333–7. Elsevier.

Bosch, Anna R. K. 2011. "Syllable-internal structure". *The Blackwell Companion to Phonology* (eds. Marc van Oostendorp – Colin J. Ewen – Elizabeth Hume – Keren Rice), 781–98. Wiley-Blackwell.

Breen, Gavan – Pensalfini, Rob. 1999. "Arrernte: a language with no syllable onsets". *Linguistic Inquiry* 30.1–25.

Butskhrikidze, Marika. 2002. *The Consonant Phonotactics of Georgian.* LOT.

Butt, Matthias. 1992. "Sonority and the explanation of syllable structure". *Linguistische Berichte* 137.45–67.

Cairns, Charles. 1988. "Phonotactics, markedness and lexical representation". *Phonology* 5.209–36.

Cairns, Charles – Raimy, Eric. 2011. "Introduction". *Handbook of the Syllable* (eds. Charles Cairns – Eric Raimy), 1–30. Brill.

Chlumský, Josef. 1911. "Une varieté peu connue de l'*r* linguale (le ř tcheque)". *Revue de phonétique* 1.5–39.

Cholin, Joana. 2011. "Do syllables exist? Psycholinguistic evidence for the retrieval of syllabic units in speech productions". *Handbook of the Syllable* (eds. Charles Cairns – Eric Raimy), 225–53. Brill.

Chomsky, Noam. 1964. *Current Issues in Linguistic Theory*. Mouton.

Clements, George. 1990. "The role of the sonority cycle in core syllabification". *Papers in Laboratory Phonology I: Between the Grammar and Physics of Speech* (eds. John Kingston – Mary E. Beckman), 283–333. Cambridge University Press.

Clements, George – Keyser, Samuel Jay. 1983. *CV Phonology: A Generative Theory of the Syllable*. MIT Press.

Coleman, John. 2001. "The phonetics and phonology of Tashlhiyt Berber syllabic consonants". *Transactions of the Philological Society* 99:1.29–64.

Côté, Marie-Helène. 2012. "The role of the syllable in the organization and realization of sound systems". *The Oxford Handbook of Laboratory Phonology* (eds. Abigail C. Cohn – Cécile Fougeron – Marie K. Huffman), 232–42. Oxford University Press.

Cvrček, Václav – Cvrčková, Ludmila. 2011. *Velký slovník rýmů*. Nakladatelství Lidové noviny.

Čermák, František. 2011. *Morfémika a slovotvorba češtiny*. Nakladatelství Lidové noviny.

Český národní korpus [Czech National Corpus]. Institute of the Czech National Corpus, Charles University. Available online: <http://ucnk.ff.cuni.cz/>.

Daneš, František. 1957. *Intonace a věta ve spisovné češtině*. Nakladatelství Československé akademie věd.

Databáze heslářů [Database of glossaries]. Institute of the Czech Language, Academy of Sciences of the Czech Republic. Available online: <http://lexiko.ujc.cas.cz/heslare/>.

Davidsen-Nielsen, Niels. 1978. *Neutralization and Archiphoneme. Two Phonological Concepts and Their History*. Akademisk Forlag.

Davis, Stuart – Baertsch, Karen. 2011. "On the relationship between codas and onset clusters". *Handbook of the Syllable* (eds. Charles Cairns – Eric Raimy), 71–97. Brill.

Dell, François – Elmedlaoui, Mohamed. 2002. *Syllables in Tashlhiyt Berber and in Moroccan Arabic.* Kluwer Academic Press.

Deme, L. 1966. "Ein slawistischer Beitrag zu der Frage der Silbe". *Studia Slavica* 12.69–79.

Dickins, James. 1998. *Extended Axiomatic Functionalism.* Mouton de Gruyter.

—. 2007. *Sudanese Arabic: Phonematics and Syllable Structure.* Otto Harrassowitz.

Dickins, Tom. 1998. "Prepositional vocalization in Contemporary Czech". *The Slavonic and East European Review* 76:2.201–33.

Dixon, R. M. W. 1980. *The Languages of Australia.* Cambridge University Press.

Duanmu, San. 2008. *Syllable Structure: The Limits of Variation.* Oxford University Press.

Duběda, Tomáš. 2002. "Structural and quantitative properties of stress units in Czech and French". *Phonetics and its Applications: Festschrift for Jens-Peter Köster on the Occasion of his 60th Birthday* (eds. A. Braun – H. R. Masthoff), 26–9. Steiner.

—. 2005. *Jazyky a jejich zvuky.* Karolinum.

Duběda, Tomáš – Votrubec, Jan. 2005. "Acoustic analysis of Czech stress: intonation, duration and intensity revisited". *INTERSPEECH-2005*, 1429–32. Lisabon.

El-Shakfeh, Fawzi. 1987. *The Phonematics, Phonotactics and Para-phonotactics of Southern Standard British English.* University of St. Andrews. Unpublished PhD. thesis, available online via the EThOS service: <http://ethos.bl.uk>.

Fidler, Masako. 2010. "Onomatopoeia as an embryonic word: Sound and submorphemic properties of Czech onomatopoeic expressions". *Karlík a továrna na lingvistiku* (eds. Aleš Bičan et al.), 138–55. Host – Masarykova univerzita.

Firchow, Irwin – Firchow, Jacqueline. 1969. "An abbreviated phoneme inventory". *Anthropological Linguistics* 11.9:271–6.

Fischer-Jørgensen, Eli. 1952. "On the definition of phoneme categories on a distributional basis". *Acta Linguistica* 7.8–39.

Frinta, Antonín. 1909. *Novočeská výslovnost.* Nákladem České akademie věd císaře Františka Josefa pro vědy, slovesnost a umění.

—. 1916. *Fonetická povaha a historický vývoj souhlásky "v" ve slovanštině.* Nákladem České akademie věd císaře Františka Josefa pro vědy, slovesnost a umění.

Fudge, Erik. 1969. "Syllables". *Journal of Linguistics* 5.253–86.

Gabjanda, James D. 1976. *An Axiomatic Functionalist Analysis of the Phonology of Yulu.* University of St. Andrews. Unpublished PhD. thesis, available online via the EThOS service: <http://ethos.bl.uk>.

Gardner, Sheena. 1985. *Parasyntax and the Sentential Level in Axiomatic Functionalism.* University of St. Andrews. Unpublished PhD. thesis, available online via the EThOS service: <http://ethos.bl.uk>.

Gardner, Sheena – Hervey, Sándor. 1983. "Structural sentences types". *La Linguistique* 19:2.3–19. [Reprinted in Bičan – Rastall 2011.]

Garvin, Paul. 1948. "Kutenai I: Phonemics". *International Journal of American Linguistics* 14:1.37–42.

Goldsmith, John. 2011. "The syllable". *The Handbook of Phonological Theory* (eds. John Goldsmith – Jason Riggle – Alan C. L. Yu), 164–96. Wiley-Blackwell.

Greenberg, Joseph. 1962. "Is the vowel–consonant dichotomy universal?". *Word* 18.73–81.

—. 1978. "Some generalizations concerning initial and final consonant clusters". *Universals of Human Language, Vol. 2: Phonology* (ed. Joseph Greenberg), 243–79. Stanford University Press.

Grygarová-Rechzieglová, Adela. 1993. "K otázce měkkosti a kombinatoriky českých fonémů". *Slovo a slovesnost* 54.255–69.

Haas, William. 1957. "Zero in linguistic description". *Studies in Linguistic Analysis (Special volume of the Philological Society),* 33–53. Basil Blackwell.

Haiman, John. 1980. *Hua: A Papuan Language of the Eastern Highlands of New Guinea.* John Benjamins.

Hála, Bohuslav. 1956. *Slabika, její podstata a vývoj.* Nakladatelství Československé akademie věd.

—. 1961. "La syllabe, sa nature, son origine et ses transformations". *Orbis* 10:1.69–143.

—. 1962. *Uvedení do fonetiky češtiny na obecně fonetickém základě.* Nakladatelství Československé akademie věd.

Harris, John. 2006. "The phonology of being understood: further arguments against sonority". *Lingua* 116.1483–94.

Hattala, Martin. 1870. *Počátečné skupeniny souhlásek československých.* Tiskem dra. Ed. Grégra.

Haugen, Einar. 1956a. "Syllabification in Kutenai". *International Journal of American Linguistics* 22:3.196–201.

—. 1956b. "The syllable in linguistic description". *For Roman Jakobson* (eds. Morris Halle et al.), 213–21. Mouton.

Havránek, Bohuslav – Jedlička, Alois. 1988₆. *Česká mluvnice.* Státní pedagogické nakladatelství.

Hjelmslev, Louis. 1936. "On the principles of phonematics". *Proceedings of the Second International Congress of Phonetic Sciences* (eds. Daniel Jones – D. B. Fry), 49–54. Cambridge University Press.

—. 1961. *Prolegomena to a Theory of Language* (trans. by Francis J. Whitfield). The University of Wisconsin Press.

Hervey, Sándor. 1972. "Mulder's 'axiomatic' linguistics". *Lingua* 28.348–79.

—. 1978. "On the extrapolation of phonological forms". *Lingua* 45.37–63.

—. 1982. *Semiotic Perspectives*. George Allen & Unwin.

—. 1990. "Sentences and linguistic data". *La Linguistique* 26:1.17–27.

—. 1996. "Functionalism, Axiomatic". *Concise Encyclopedia of Syntactic Theories* (eds. Keith Brown – Jim Miller), 110–3. Pergamon Press.

Heselwood, Barry. 2007. "Schwa and the phonotactics of RP English". *Transactions of the Philological Society* 105.148–87.

—. 2008. "Simultaneous phonemes in English". *Linguistica* ONLINE, <http://www.phil.muni.cz/linguistica/art/heselwood/hes-001.pdf>.

Hoard, James. 1966. "Juncture and syllable structure in English". *Phonetica* 15. 96–109.

Hockett, Charles. 1955. *A Manual of Phonology*. Indiana University Publications in Anthropology and Linguistics.

—. 1958. *A Course in Modern Linguistics*. The Macmillan Company.

Holdeman, Jeffrey D. 2000. "Czech preposition vocalization: Towards an articulatory approach". *Brown Slavic Contributions XIII: Modern Czech Studies* (eds. Alexander Levitsky – Masako U. Fidler), 53–64. Brown University.

Hooper, Joan. 1972. "The syllable in phonological theory". *Language* 48.525–40.

Howkins, Douglas William. 1972. *The Phonology of San Martín Quechua*. University of St. Andrews. Unpublished doctoral thesis, available online via the EThOS service: <http://ethos.bl.uk>.

Hulst, Harry van der – Ritter, Nancy A. 1999. "Theories of the syllable". *The Syllable. Views and Facts* (eds. Harry van der Hulst – Nancy A. Ritter), 13–52. Mouton de Gruyter.

Hůrková, Jiřina. 1995. *Česká výslovnostní norma*. Scientia.

Hůrková, Jiřina – Hlaváč, Sáva. 1981. "K výzkumu českých souhlásek likvidních". *Slovo a slovesnost* 42.269–79.

Hyman, Larry M. 2008. "Universals in phonology". *The Linguistic Review* 25.83–137.

—. 2011. "Does Gokana really have no syllables? Or: what's so great about being universal?". *Phonology* 28.55–85.

Jaeger, Jeri J. – Van Valin, Robert D. 1982. "Initial consonant clusters in Yateé Zapotec". *International Journal of American Linguistics* 48:2.125–38.

Internetová jazyková příručka. [Internet Language Reference Book] Institute of the Czech Language, Academy of Sciences of the Czech Republic. Available online: <http://prirucka.ujc.cas.cz/>.

Jakobson, Roman – Halle, Morris. 1956. *Fundamentals of Language.* Mouton

Jensen, John T. 2000. "Against ambisyllabicity". *Phonology* 17.187–235.

Jones, Daniel. 1931. "The 'word' as a phonetic entity". *La Maître Phonétique* 36.60–65.

—. 1956. "The hyphen as a phonetic sign". *Zeitschrift für Phonetik* 9:2.99–107.

Kahn, Daniel. 1976. *Syllable-based Generalizations in English Phonology.* Unpublished Ph.D. Thesis, Massachusetts Institute of Technology. Available online: <http://dspace.mit.edu/handle/1721.1/16397>.

Kelih, Emmerich. 2012. *Die Silbe in slawischen Sprachen.* Verlag Otto Sagner.

Key, Harold. 1961. "Phonotactics of Cayuvava". *International Journal of American Linguistics* 27:2.143–50.

Kott = Kott, František. 1878–1893. *Česko-německý slovník I–VIII.* Tiskem a nákladem tiskárny Josefa Koláře.

Krakow, Rena. 1999. "Physiological organization of syllables: a review". *Journal of Phonetics* 27.23–54.

Krámský, Jiří. 1976. *Papers in General Linguistics.* Mouton.

Krčmová, Marie. 2008₃. *Úvod do fonetiky a fonologie pro bohemisty.* Ostravská univerzita v Ostravě.

Kučera, Henry. 1961. *The Phonology of Czech.* Mouton & Co.

—. 1963. "Entropy, redundancy and functional load in Russian and Czech". *American Contributions to the Fifth International Congress of Slavists*, 191–219. Mouton & Co.

Kučera, Henry – Monroe, George. 1968. *A Comparative Quantitative Phonology of Russian, Czech, and German.* American Elsevier Publishing Company.

Kuryłowicz, Jerzy. 1948. "Contribution à la théorie de la syllabe". *Bulletin de la Société Polanaise de Linguistique* 8.80–114.

Lebrun, Y. 1966. "Sur la syllabe, sommet de sonorité". *Phonetica* 14.1–15.

Lehiste, Ilse. 1960. "An acoustic-phonetic study of internal open juncture". *Phonetica, Supplementum ad Vol. 5.*

—. 1965. "Juncture". *Proceedings of the Fifth International Congress of Phonetic Sciences* (ed. E. Zwirner – W. Bethre), 172–200. S. Kager.

Lekomceva, M. I. 1968. *Tipologija struktur sloga v slavjanskix jazykax.* Nauka.

Lin, Yen-Hwei. 1997. "Syllabic and moraic structures in Piro". *Phonology* 14.403–36.

Lowenstamm, Jean. 1996. "CV as the only syllable type". *Current Trends in Phonology: Models and Methods* (eds. Jacques Durand – Bernard Laks), 419–42. ESRI.

Ludvíková, Marie. 1968. "Kombinatorika českých fonémů z kvantitativního hlediska". *Slovo a slovesnost* 29.56–65.

—. 1972a. "Quantitative syllable analysis of words in Czech". *Prague Studies in Mathematical Linguistics* 3.27–34.

—. 1972b. "Some quantitative aspects of the Czech syllables". *Prague Studies in Mathematical Linguistics* 4.141–54.

—. 1976. "On some statistical differences in two spoken texts on the syllabic level". *Prague Studies in Mathematical Linguistics* 5.91–104.

—. 1978. "On the occurrence of syllables in different word positions". *Prague Studies in Mathematical Linguistics* 6.39–45.

Ludvíková, Marie – Kraus, Jiří. 1966. "Kvantitativní vlastnosti soustavy českých fonémů". *Slovo a slovesnost* 26.334–44.

Machač, Pavel. 2009. "Implications of acoustic variation for the segmentation of the Czech trill /r/". *Cross-Modal Analysis of Speech, Gestures, Gaze and Facial Expressions, Lecture Notes in Artificial Intelligence 5641* (eds. Anna Esposito – Robert Vích), 173–81. Springer-Verlag.

Machač, Pavel – Skarnitzl, Radek. 2004. "Selected acoustic properties of the Czech palatal plosives". *13th Czech-German Workshop – Speech Processing* (ed. Robert Vích), 29–35. Ústav radiotechniky a elektroniky AV ČR.

—. 2009. *Principles of Phonetic Segmentation*. Epocha Publishing House.

Machek, Václav. 1957. *Česká a slovenská jména rostlin*. Nakladatelství Československé akademie věd.

Malmberg, Bertil. 1964. "Juncture and syllable division". *In Honour of Daniel Jones* (eds. David Abercrombie et al.), 116–9. Longmans.

—. 1967₂. *Structural Linguistics and Human Communication*. Springer-Verlag.

Martinet, André. 1956. *La description phonologique avec application au parler franco-provençal d'Hauteville (Savoie)*. Librairie Droz.

—. 1965. *La linguistique synchronique*. Presses universitaires de France.

—. 1977. "Some basic principles of functional linguistics". *La Linguistique* 13:1.7–14.

—. 1991₃. *Éléments de linguistique générale*. Armand Colin.

Mathesius, Vilém. 1929. "La structure phonologique du lexique du tchèque modern". *Travaux du Cercle Linguistique de Prague* 1.67–84.

—. 1931a. "O výrazové platnosti některých českých skupin hláskových". *Naše řeč* 15.38–40.

—. 1931b. "Několik slov o hiátu v dnešní češtině". *Naše řeč* 15.219–21.

—. 1931c. "Zur problem der Belastungs- und Kombinationsfähigkeit der Phoneme". *Travaux du Cercle Linguistique de Prague* 4.148–52.

—. 1932. "Cizí slova se stanoviska synchronického". *Časopis pro moderní filologii* 18.231–9.

Matteson, Esther. 1965. *The Piro (Arawakan) Language*. University of California Press.

Mazlová, Věra. 1946. "Jak se projevuje zvuková stránka češtiny v hláskových statistikách". *Naše řeč* 30.101–11, 146–51.

MČ1 = Dokulil, Miloš – Horálek, Karel – Hůrková, Jiřina – Knappová, Miloslava (eds.). 1986. *Mluvnice češtiny 1*. Academia.

MČ2 = Komárek, Miroslav – Kořenský, Jan – Petr, Jan (eds.). 1986. *Mluvnice češtiny 2*. Academia.

Meynadier, Yohann. 2001. "La syllabe phonétique et phonologique: une introduction". *Travaux Interdisciplinaires du Laboratoire Parole et Langage* 20. 91–148.

Mills, Elizabeth. 1984. *Senoufo Phonology, Discourse to Syllable*. Dallas: Summer Institute of Linguistics – the University of Texas at Arlington. Available online: <http://www.ethnologue.com/show_work.asp?id=18838>.

Mulder, Jan W. F. 1968. *Sets and Relations in Phonology: An Axiomatic Approach to the Description of Speech*. Clarendon Press.

—. 1987. Effective methodology and effective phonological description". *La Linguistique* 23.19–42. [Reprinted in Bičan – Rastall 2011.]

—. 1989. *Foundations of Axiomatic Linguistics*. Mouton de Gruyter.

—. 1993. "Negativism as an effective methodology in linguistic description". *Linguistics and Philosophy. The Controversial Interface* (eds. Rom Harré – Roy Harris), 179–97. Pergamon Press.

—. 1994. "Written and spoken languages as separate semiotic systems". *Semiotica* 101:1–2.41–72.

—. 1996. "Methodology and description". *La Linguistique* 32:1.17–34.

—. 1998. "Epistemology and linguistics: Anatomy of an approach". *Productivity and Creativity: Studies in General Linguistics in Honour of E. M. Uhlenbeck* (ed. Mark Janse), 115–60. Mouton de Gruyter.

Mulder, Jan W. F. – Hervey, Sándor G. J. 1972. *Theory of the Linguistic Sign*. Mouton.

—. 1980. *The Strategy of Linguistics*. Scottish Academic Press.

—. 2009. "Postulates for Axiomatic Functionalism". *Linguistica* ONLINE, <http://www.phil.muni.cz/linguistica/art/mulderhervey/muh-001.pdf>.

Mulder, Jan W. F. – Hurren, Antony. 1968. "The English vowel-phonemes from a functionalist point of view, and a statement of their distribution". *La Linguistique* 1.43–60.

Mulder, Jan W. F. – Rastall, Paul. 2005. *Ontological Questions in Linguistics*. Lincom.

MSČ = Cvrček, Václav et al. 2010. *Mluvnice současné češtiny 1*. Karolinum.

References

Nejedlý, Petr. 2009. "Neznámý kurtoazní výraz ve staré češtině". *Studia etymologica Brunensia 6* (eds. Ilona Janyšková – Helena Karlíková), 275–80. Nakladatelství Lidové noviny.

NLA = *Novočeský lexikální archiv* [Lexical archive of new Czech]. Available online (after signing in) as part of Databáze heslářů [Database of glossaries], <http://lexiko.ujc.cas.cz/heslare/>. Institute of the Czech Language, Academy of Sciences of the Czech Republic.

Novotná, Jiřina. 1962. "K přepisu zvukové podoby některých hláskových skupin v češtině". *Naše řeč* 45.82–7.

—. 1972. "Kombinační schopnost českých konsonantických fonémů". *Studia z filologii polskiej i słowiańskiej* 12.269–84.

Novotná-Hůrková, Jiřina. 1974. "K výslovnosti některých souhláskových skupin a tzv. rázu v češtině". *Slovo a slovesnost* 35.113–20.

—. 1980. "Selected problems of consonant clusters". *Phonetica Pragensia* 6.89–95.

O'Connor, J. D. – Trim, J. L. M. 1953. "Vowel, consonant, and syllable – a phonological definition". *Word* 9:2.103–22.

Ondráčková, Jana. 1967. "Monosyllables in the rhythmical structure of the utterance (on the anacrusis in Czech)". *Phonetica* 16.1–13.

Padgett, Jaye. 2002. "Russian voicing assimilation, final devoicing, and the problem of [v]". Ms. University of California, Santa Cruz. Available online: <http://people.ucsc.edu/~padgett/locker/newvoice.pdf>.

Palková, Zdena. 1997₂. *Fonetika a fonologie češtiny*. Karolinum.

—. 2004a. "Přízvukový takt ve struktuře češtiny". *Čeština – univerzália a specifika 5* (eds. Zdeňka Hladká – Petr Karlík), 399–408. Nakladatelství Lidové noviny.

—. 2004b. "The set of phonetic rules as a basis for the prosodic component of an automatic TTS synthesis in Czech". *Phonetica Pragensia* 10.33–46.

—. 2012. "Rytmus řeči a verše v češtině". *Česká literatura* 3 (2012).338–54.

Palková, Zdena – Volín, Jan. 2003. "The role of F0 contours in determining foot boundaries in Czech". *Proceedings of the 15th International Congress of Phonetic Sciences, Vol. 2*, 1783–6. Causal Productions Pty Ltd.

Pavlík, Radoslav. 2009. "A study of the trilled character of the Czech ř in three speech genres". *Linvistika a lingvodidaktika na školách filologického zamerania I: Zborník príspevkov* (ed. Daniel Lančarič), 31–55. Z-F Lingua.

Pike, Kenneth. 1947. *Phonemics: A Technique for Reducing Languages to Writing*. University of Michigan Press.

PMČ = Karlík, Petr – Nekula, Marek – Rusínová, Zdenka (eds.). 1996₂. *Příruční mluvnice češtiny*. Nakladatelství Lidové noviny.

Podlipský, Václav Jonáš. 2009. *Reevaluating Perceptual Cues: Native and Non-native Perception of Czech Vowel.* Palacký University. Unpublished Ph.D. thesis.

Podlipský, Václav Jonáš – Skarnitzl, Radek – Volín, Jan. 2009. "High front vowels in Czech: a contrast in quantity or quality?". *Interspeech 2009*, 132–5. ISCA.

Popper, Karl. 2002a. *The Logic of Scientific Discovery.* Routledge Classics.

—. 2002b. *Conjectures and Refutations.* Routledge Classics.

Profous, Antonín. 1951. *Místní jména v Čechách III.* Česká akademie věd a umění.

PSJČ = *Příruční slovník jazyka českého I–VIII* [Coincise Dictionary of the Czech Language]. Státní nakladatelství, 1935–1957. Available online: <http://bara.ujc.cas.cz/psjc/>.

Pulgram, Ernst. 1970. *Syllable, Word, Nexus, Cursus.* Mouton.

Rastall, Paul. 1991. "Complete utterances". *La Linguistique* 30:2.81–91.

—. 1993. *Empirical Phonology and Cartesian Tables.* Mellen Press.

—. 2000. *A Linguistic Philosophy of Language.* Mellen Press.

—. 2011. "'Theory' in linguistics: Strengths and weaknesses in Axiomatic Functionalism". *Axiomatic Functionalism: Theory and Application* (eds. Aleš Bičan – Paul Rastall), 255–74. Peter Lang.

—. 2012. "Czech phonology and Axiomatic Functionalist approach". *Linguistica* ONLINE, <http://www.phil.muni.cz/linguistica/art/rastall/ras-004.pdf>.

Rechzieglová, Adela. 1998. "K fonologii expresivity v češtině". *Slavica Pragensia ad tempora nostra*, 129–34. Univerzita Karlova.

Renský, Miroslav. 1960. "Funkce slabiky v jazykovědném systému". *Slovo a slovesnost* 21.86–95.

Ridouane, Rachid. 2008. "Syllables without vowels: phonetic and phonological evidence from Tashlhiyt Berber". *Phonology* 25.321–59.

Romportl, Milan. 1973. *Studies in Phonetics.* Academia.

Romportl, Milan et al. 1978. *Výslovnost spisovné češtiny.* Academia.

Romportl, Simeon. 1984. "Úloha rázu a jeho ekvivalentů při signalizování předělu". *Slovo a slovesnost* 45.104–120.

Saporta, Sol – Olson, Donald. 1958. "Classification of intervocalic clusters". *Language* 34:2.261–6.

de Saussure, Ferdinand. [1916] 1972. *Cours de linguistique générale* (édition critique préparée par Tullio de Mauro). Payot.

Sawicka, Irena. 1974. *Struktura grup spółgłoskowych w językach słowiańskich.* Wydawnictwo Polskiej akademii nauk.

—. 1985. "Syllable structure in Slavic languages". *Rocznik slawistyczny* 45.3–9.

—. 2009. "Segmental clusters in the Slavic languages". *Die slavischen Sprachen / The Slavic Languages, Part 1* (eds. Sebastian Kempgen et al.), 52–67. Mouton de Gruyter.

Scheer, Tobias. 2001. "The rhythmic law in Czech: vowel final prefixes". *Current Issues in Formal Slavic Linguistics* (eds. Gerhild Zybatow et al.), 37–48. Peter Lang.

—. 2003. "The key to Czech vowel length: templates". *Investigations into Formal Slavic Linguistics* (eds. Peter Kosta et al.), 97–118. Peter Lang.

—. 2004. "O samohláskové délce při derivaci v češtině". *Čeština – univerzália a specifika 5* (eds. Zdeňka Hladká – Petr Karlík), 224–339. Nakladatelství Lidové noviny.

—. 2012. *Direct Interface and One-Channel Translation.* De Gruyter Mouton.

Schütz, Albert. 1981. "A reanalysis of the Hawaiian vowel system". *Oceanic Linguistics* 20:1.1–43.

Selkirk, Elizabeth. 1982. "The syllable". *The Structure of Phonological Representations, Vol. 2* (eds. Harry van der Hulst – Norval Smith), 337–83. Foris.

Short, David. 1985. "Some notes on the distribution of /l/ in Czech – with special reference to butterflies". *Phonetica Pragensia* 7.35–41.

Shrager, Miriam. 2012. "Neutralization of word final voicing in Russian". *Journal of Slavic Linguistics* 20:1.71–99.

Sigurd, Bengt. 1958. "Tendencies in the combination of prevocal and postvocal consonants in Swedish monosyllables". *Studia Linguistica* 12.27–51.

—. 1965. *Phonotactic Structures of Swedish.* Uniskol.

—. 1968. "Phonotactic aspects of the linguistic expression". *Manual of Phonetics* (ed. Bertil Malmberg), 450–463. North-Holland.

Silverman, Daniel. 2012. *Neutralization.* Cambridge University Press.

Skaličková, Alena. 1954. "K otázce podstaty slabiky". *Slovo a slovesnost* 15.19–24.

—. 1958. "A contribution to the problem of the syllable". *Zeitschrift für Phonetik* 11.160–5.

Skarnitzl, Radek. 2004. "Acoustic categories of nonmodal phonation in the context of the Czech conjunction 'a'". *Phonetica Pragensia* 10.57–68.

—. 2011. *Znělostní kontrast nejen v češtině.* Nakladatelství Epocha.

—. 2012. "Dvojí i v české výslovnosti". *Naše řeč* 95:3.141–53.

SN1 = *Nová slova v češtině, Slovník neologizmů 1* [New Words in Czech, Dictionary of Neologisms]. Academia, 1998.

Spang-Hanssen, Hennig. 1958. "Typological and statistical aspects of distribution as a criterion in linguistic analysis". *Proceedings of the Eighth International Congress of Linguists*, 182–213. Oslo University Press.

—. 1959. *Probability and Structural Classification in Language Description*. Rosenkilde and Bagger

SSČ = *Slovník spisovné češtiny* [Dictionary of Literary Czech]. Academia, 2003₃.

SSJČ = *Slovník spisovného jazyka českého I–IV* [Dictionary of the Literary Czech Language]. Academia, 1960–1971. Available online: <http://bara.ujc.cas.cz/ssjc/>.

Studenovský, David. 2008. "Změny intenzity v rámci průběhu českých jednoduchých vokálů a diftongů". *Phonetica Pragensia* 11.145–53.

—. 2010. "Comparison of Czech diphthongs with the corresponding short simple vowels". *Phonetica Pragensia* 12.37–48.

Studenovský, David – Trpák, Jindřich. 2004. "The duration of the Czech diphthong [ou] in comparison with vowel-vowel sequences". *Phonetica Pragensia* 10.69–77.

Sukač, Roman. 2013. "Fish and its fisherman. Paradigmatic and derivative length in Czech". *Zeitschrift für Slavistik* 58:1.72–101.

Szigetvári, Péter. 2011. "Syllables". *Continuum Companion to Phonology* (eds. Nancy C. Kula – Bert Botma – Kuniya Nasukawa), 64–94. Continuum.

Šefčík, Ondřej. 2004. "Alternace konsonantů v češtině – fonotaktické a morfologické modelování systému". *Čeština – univerzália a specifika 5* (eds. Zdeňka Hladká – Petr Karlík), 441–7. Nakladatelství Lidové noviny.

Šimáčková, Šárka – Podlipský, Václav Jonáš – Chládková, Kateřina. 2012. "Czech spoken in Bohemia and Moravia". *Journal of the International Phonetic Association* 42:2.225–32.

Tabain, Marija – Breen, Gavan – Butcher, Andrew. 2004. "VC vs. CV syllables: a comparison of Aboriginal languages with English". *Journal of the International Phonetic Association* 34:2.175–200.

Těšitelová, Marie et al. 1985. *Kvantitativní charakteristiky současné češtiny*. Academia.

Tolstaja, Cvetlana M. 1968. "Fonologičeskoe rasstojanie i sočetaemosť soglasnyx v slavjanskix jazykax". *Voprosy jazykoznanija* 3.66–81.

—. 1974. "K xarakteristike konsonatnyx sočetanij v slavjanskix jazykax (načalo i konec slova). *Slavia* 43.113–33.

Trávníček, František. 1951. *Mluvnice spisovné češtiny I*. Slovanské nakladatelství.

Trnka, Bohumil. 1937. *Pokus o vědeckou teorii a praktickou reformu těsnopisu*. Filosofická fakulta.

—. 1966. "The distribution of vowel length and its frequency in Czech". *Prague Studies in Mathematical Linguistics* 1.11–6.

—. 1972. "On the frequency and distribution of consonant clusters in Czech". *Prague Studies in Mathematical Linguistics* 3.9–14.

—. 1982. *Selected Papers in Structural Linguistics* (ed. Vilém Fried). Mouton Publishers.

Trubetzkoy, Nikolai. 1939. *Grundzüge der phonologie*. = *Travaux du Cercle Linguistique de Prague* 7.

Twaddell, William F. 1939. "Combinations of consonants in stressed syllables in German". *Acta Linguistica* 1.189–99.

—. 1940–41. "Combinations of consonants in stressed syllables in German (continued)". *Acta Linguistica* 2.31–50.

Uhlenbeck, Eugenius M. 1950. "The structure of the Javanese morpheme". *Lingua* 2.239–70.

Vachek, Josef. 1932. "Fonologický poměr hlásek *i* a *j* v češtině a v slovenštině". *Slavia* 11.265–73.

—. 1940. "Poznámky k fonologii českého lexika". *Listy filologické* 67.395–402.

—. 1968. *Dynamika fonologického systému současné spisovné češtiny*. Academia.

Vestergaard, Torben. 1967. "Initial and final consonant combinations in Danish monosyllables". *Studia Linguistica* 11.37–66.

Vogt, Hans. 1942. "The structure of the Norwegian monosyllables". *Norsk tiddsskrift for sprogvidenskap* 12.5–29.

—. 1954. "Phoneme classes and phoneme classification". *Word* 10.28–34.

—. 1958. "Structure phonémique du géorgien". *Norsk tiddsskrift for sprogvidenskap* 18.5–90.

Volín, Jan. 2002. "Čtyři scénáře vývoje české laterály". *Čeština doma a ve světě* 1 (2002).7–13.

—. 2010. "Fonetika a fonologie". *Mluvnice současné češtiny 1* (eds. Václav Cvrček et al.), 35–64. Karolinum.

—. 2012. "Jak se v Čechách 'rázuje'". *Naše řeč* 95.51–4.

Volín, Jan – Churaňová, Eliška. 2010. "Probabilities of consonantal sequences in continuous Czech texts". *Phonetica Pragensia* 12.49–62.

Volín, Jan – Skarnitzl, Radek. 2005. "Czech voiced labiodental continuant discrimination from basic acoustic data". *Interspeech-2005*, 2921–4. ISCA.

—. 2006a. "Fonologická vyjímečnost české znělé labiodentály". *Kapitoly z fonetiky a fonologie slovanských jazyků* (eds. Zdena Palková – Jana Janoušková), 251–64. Univerzita Karlova v Praze.

—. 2006b. "K nevyhraněnosti vlastností české labiodentální frikativy". *Tzv. základní výzkum v lingvistice – desideratum, nebo realis? Sborník příspěvků z 5. mezinárodní konference Setkání mladých lingvistů, konané na Filozofické fakultě Univerzity Palackého ve dnech 17.–19. května 2004* (eds. Petr Pořízka – Vladimír P. Polách), 308–14. Univerzita Palackého.

VSČ = Hála, Bohuslav et al. 1967₂. *Výslovnost spisovné češtiny I*. Academia.

Zec, Draga. 2007. "The syllable". *The Cambridge Handbook of Phonology* (ed. Paul de Lacy), 161–94. Cambridge University Press.

Zeman, Jiří. 2008. *Základy české ortoepie*. Gaudeamus.

Ziková, Markéta. 2008. *Alternace vokálů s nulou v současné češtině – laterální autosegmentální analýza*. Masaryk university. Unpublished PhD. thesis, available at <https://is.muni.cz/th/9336/ff_d/Disertace_definitivni_verze.pdf>.

INDEX OF SUBJECTS

The index of subjects is necessarily selective, but all major areas should be covered. The bold face marks the page where a key term is defined or particularly discussed.

Index of Languages

Index of Names